WORD HACKS™

Other Microsoft Windows resources from O'Reilly

Related titles	Word Pocket Guide Excel Pocket Guide Windows XP Hacks™ Excel Personal Trainer Excel Hacks™ Excel: The Missing Manual
Hacks Series Home	*hacks.oreilly.com* is a community site for developers and power users of all stripes. Readers learn from each other as they share their favorite tips and tools for Mac OS X, Linux, Google, Windows XP, and more.
Windows Books Resource Center	*windows.oreilly.com* is a complete catalog of O'Reilly's Windows and Office books, including sample chapters and code examples.
O'REILLY NETWORK	*oreillynet.com* is the essential portal for developers interested in open and emerging technologies, including new platforms, programming languages, and operating systems.
Conferences	O'Reilly brings diverse innovators together to nurture the ideas that spark revolutionary industries. We specialize in documenting the latest tools and systems, translating the innovator's knowledge into useful skills for those in the trenches. Visit *conferences.oreilly.com* for our upcoming events.
O'REILLY NETWORK Safari Bookshelf	Safari Bookshelf (*safari.oreilly.com*) is the premier online reference library for programmers and IT professionals. Conduct searches across more than 1,000 books. Subscribers can zero in on answers to time-critical questions in a matter of seconds. Read the books on your Bookshelf from cover to cover or simply flip to the page you need. Try it today with a free trial.

WORD HACKS™

Andrew Savikas

O'REILLY®

Beijing · Cambridge · Farnham · Köln · Paris · Sebastopol · Taipei · Tokyo

Word Hacks™

by Andrew Savikas

Copyright © 2005 O'Reilly Media, Inc. All rights reserved.
Printed in the United States of America.

Published by O'Reilly Media, Inc., 1005 Gravenstein Highway North,
Sebastopol, CA 95472.

O'Reilly books may be purchased for educational, business, or sales promotional use. Online
editions are also available for most titles (*safari.oreilly.com*). For more information, contact our
corporate/institutional sales department: (800) 998-9938 or *corporate@oreilly.com*.

Editor:	Brett Johnson	**Production Editor:**	Mary Anne Weeks Mayo
Series Editor:	Rael Dornfest	**Cover Designer:**	Hanna Dyer
Executive Editor:	Dale Dougherty	**Interior Designer:**	David Futato

Printing History:

November 2004:   First Edition.

 This book uses RepKover™, a durable and flexible lay-flat binding.

ISBN: 0-596-00493-1
[C]

For Stan

Contents

Credits

About the Author

Andrew Savikas works in the O'Reilly Tools Group, where he helps the Production department turn manuscripts into O'Reilly books. He developed and maintains the custom Word template and VBA macros used by all the O'Reilly authors who don't insist on writing in POD. Except for the ones who insist on writing in XML. Or *troff*.

Andrew also works with FrameMaker, FrameScript, InDesign, DocBook XML, Perl, Python, Ruby, and whatever else he finds lying around the office. He has a degree in Communications from the University of Illinois at Urbana-Champaign and lives in Boston with his wife Audrey, who loves to see her name in print.

Contributors

The following people contributed their hacks, writing, and inspiration to this book:

- Andrew Bruno (*http://qnot.org*) received his B.S. degree in Computer Science from the University of Buffalo. After enduring many long winters in Western New York, he now resides in Northern California, where the sun shines for more than two months out of the year. He currently works as a Software Engineer for O'Reilly Media, Inc., hacking on various internal software projects. He also enjoys programming in Perl, Java, and C++.
- Sean M. Burke is the author of O'Reilly's *RTF Pocket Guide*, *Perl and LWP*, and many of the articles in the *Best of the Perl Journal* volumes. An active member in the Perl open source community, he is one of *CPAN*'s most prolific module authors and is an authority on markup languages. Trained as a linguist, he also develops tools for software

internationalization and native-language preservation. He lives in Ketchikan, Alaska, with his feline overlord, Fang Dynasty.

- Ian Burrel
- Greg Chapman is a former mechanic who, after years of study from afar, discovered that he has exactly one trait in common with a good programmer: he's lazy enough to work hard at not repeating the same task over and over again. A former Microsoft MVP with more interests than time, he looks at Microsoft Word as a good place to learn development and manage systems so that he can spend more time flying and less time working. These activities keep him engaged in Chicago, Illinois, and it's easy to keep track of him through Dian Chapman's eZine, *TechTrax*, at its web site, *http://www.mousetrax.com*.
- Paul Edstein has been using personal computers since the late 1980s, mostly with a variety of word processors and spreadsheets. Along the way, he dabbled with PC-based assembly language programming and Windows-based VB and VBA coding. He has also designed some highly specialized mainframe and midrange applications. Drawing on his experience with Microsoft Office applications, Paul began contributing to various newsgroups in 2002. In the course of solving problems, he "taught" Word how to calculate logarithms and trigonometry values; add or subtract a number of days, weeks, months or years to/from a date; and perform various other document automation functions using field codes instead of macros.
- Mark Hammond is an independent Microsoft Windows consultant working out of Melbourne, Australia. He studied computer science at the South Australian Institute of Technology (now the University of South Australia) and then worked with several large financial institutions. He started his consulting operation in 1995. Mark has produced many of the Windows extensions for Python, including PythonWin, Active Scripting, and Active Debugging support, and coauthored the COM framework and extensions. He is also a leading authority on Active Scripting and related technologies and has spoken at Microsoft's three most recent Professional Developers conferences. Apart from being a father to his teenage daughter, having an interest in live music, and providing way too many free Python extensions, Mark has no life!
- Guy Hart-Davis has been working with Microsoft Word since before it learned to run on Windows. He writes macros and computer books for fun and (occasionally) profit. Guy's most recent books include *Windows XP and Office 2003 Keyboard Shortcuts*, *Mac OS X and Office v.X Keyboard Shortcuts*, and *Adobe Creative Suite Keyboard Shortcuts*.

- Evan Lenz is an application developer whose primary expertise is in XSLT. As a member of the W3C XSL Working Group, he has been contributing to the development of XPath 2.0, XSLT 2.0, and XQuery 1.0. He has spoken at various XML conferences and helped author Wrox's *Professional XML,* Second Edition, and *Early Adopter XQuery* (foreword). Evan holds a Bachelor of Music degree from Wheaton College, with majors in Piano Performance and Philosophy. He currently lives in Seattle, Washington, with his wife Lisa and son Samuel. Web site: *http://www.xmlportfolio.com.*

- Jack M. Lyon is a book editor who got tired of working the hard way and started creating programs to automate editing tasks in Microsoft Word. In 1996, he founded the Editorium (*www.editorium.com*) to make these programs available to other publishing professionals. Jack also publishes Editorium Update, a free newsletter about editing in Microsoft Word. The managing editor of a publishing house in Salt Lake City, he is the coauthor of *Managing the Obvious.*

- Dan Mueller is a software developer. Although he earned a computer engineering degree from the University of Illinois, he would have preferred to major in simple algebra (if there were such a major). Dan is the owner of several O'Reilly books and is ecstatic to have the opportunity to contribute to one.

- Gus Perez (*http://gusperez.com* and *http://blogs.msdn.com/gusperez*) is the QA Lead for the C# Compiler team at Microsoft, where he has worked for almost six years. He started with the Visual J++ and the Visual C++ teams before joining the Visual C# group, which he has been with since its inception. In his spare time, Gus hacks away on side programming projects; plays guitar in a small, local rock band (*http://opus80.com*); and plays golf whenever the rain isn't too bad in Seattle.

- Shyam Pillai (*http://www.mvps.org/skp/*)

- Phil Rabichow is a retired prosecutor who started tinkering with computers and Microsoft Word about 10 years ago. He was part of the old WOPR Lounge, and became a WMVP (Woody Most Valuable Professional) in January 2001. He spends his spare time coaching his daughter's soccer team, shooting pool, playing tennis, and climbing.

- Christopher Rath has been a computing enthusiast since first purchasing a programmable calculator in 1977. His first serious computer hobbying was focused on the HP-41c calculator, and he landed his first job in the industry because of his experience programming CPU microcode on the HP-41c processor. Besides VBacs, his other notable contribution to the Net community is his Songbook LaTeX style, which—along with other tools, tips, and opinion—is available from his vanity web site (*http://rath.ca*). Christopher works as a business consultant, leveraging his 20+ years of Information Technology experience to improve the value businesses gain from their IT investments.

- Omar Shahine (*http://www.shahine.com/omar*) is a Lead Program Manager at Microsoft Corporation working on the Hotmail "Front Door" team. Before that, Omar spent five years working on various products in the Macintosh Business Unit at Microsoft, where he helped ship numerous versions of Outlook Express, Entourage, and Virtual PC.

Preface

Few software applications are as ubiquitous as Microsoft Word, which has been around for more than 20 years—practically an eternity in computer time. Even as competitors, such as OpenOffice.org, emerge from the open source community, their success relies heavily on how much they look and act like Word. When most people think of word processing, they think of Microsoft Word.

Word is a powerful word processor, but it offers a lot more. It is almost infinitely customizable, which means you *don't* have to settle for the features and interface that come "out of the box." But more importantly, it is also almost infinitely programmable. Using Visual Basic for Applications (VBA), you can do from a program almost anything you can do from the Word interface, and you can usually do it much, much faster.

People often refer to programs written to control Word using VBA as *macros*. The term "macro," short for "macro command," typically means a sequence of commands (usually keystrokes) recorded from within an application and played back as a single command. While you can indeed record macros like that in Word using VBA, VBA is much more than a macro language: it's a powerful, full-featured programming language. But old habits die hard, so this book will often refer to VBA programs as macros.

Why Word Hacks?

Hacking has a bad reputation in the press. They use the term *hackers* to refer to people who break into systems or wreak havoc with computers as their weapons. Among people who write code, though, the term *hack* refers to a "quick-and-dirty" solution to a problem, or a clever way to get something done. And the term *hacker* is meant very much as a compliment, referring to someone as being *creative*, or having the technical chops to get things done. The Hacks series is an attempt to reclaim the word, document the good ways people are hacking, and pass the hacker ethic of creative participation on to the uninitiated. Seeing how others approach systems and problems is often the quickest way to learn about a new technology.

Word Hacks is about solving problems. That may mean automating repetitive tasks, adding sorely needed features, rearranging menus and toolbars, and even controlling Word from another program. Word is used by millions of people every day, and 100 hacks can't possibly cover all the problems those users will face. So this book is also about giving you the tools and the inspiration to hack solutions for your own unique Word problems. While you'll find beginning, intermediate, and advanced hacks between the covers, this book is not an exhaustive treatment of *everything* you can do with Microsoft Word.

You can use most of the hacks in this book even if you know nothing about VBA. But truly hacking Word means using VBA, and the dozens of macros in this book, ranging from simple to very complex, may even help you learn a bit of VBA.

When creating VBA macros for this book, I chose to use readable rather than more robust code. If you plan to use these macros in a business or production environment, you should include sufficient error handling and data validation. In many cases, I also sacrificed performance for readability. For most Word users, and most Word documents, the difference is negligible. However, if you work with long documents, you might find more efficient—but more complex—ways to perform many of these hacks. For tips on improving the performance of your VBA code, see "Optimize Your VBA Code" [Hack #64] in Chapter 7.

How to Use This Book

You can read this book from cover to cover if you like, but each hack stands on its own, so feel free to browse and jump to the different sections that interest you most. If there's a prerequisite you need to know about, a cross-reference will guide you to the right hack.

The hacks in this book are meant for a broad audience, from those who've just started to grasp the customization potential of Word to macro mavens looking for new perspectives on thorny problems. There's even a chapter on what is potentially the most significant addition to Word in years: support for XML (Extensible Markup Language), a data format that promises to make your documents compatible with the non-Word world.

A Note About Word Versions

There are substantial differences among the versions of Word still commonly used, which include Word 2000, Word 2002 (also known as Word XP), and Word 2003. Though most of the hacks in this book will work with any of these versions, there are some that use features not available in Word 2000 or Word 2002. This is noted in the text. And even though some folks are still banging away at Word 97, and many of these hacks will work with Word 97, this book explicitly covers only Word 2000, 2002, and 2003.

Chapter 10 is applicable only to Word 2003, and there are even some differences among versions of that version, which are noted in the text. However, in deference to the large group of users still hacking away with Word 2000, several of the hacks in this book show how to replicate some of the best features found in later versions, which just might save you the upgrade fee this time around.

Unfortunately, Word for Macintosh is, from a hacker's perspective, a completely different program than Word for Windows, as anyone who's tried to write macros on a Mac can attest. Though many of the hacks in this book could be adapted for use on a Macintosh, this book covers only Word for Windows.

Where to Learn More

Many of the hacks in this book, particularly the advanced ones, assume that you're familiar with certain Word features. If you're looking for more of a tutorial or reference on Word or Word macros, check out the following books also published by O'Reilly Media:

- *Word Pocket Guide*
- *Writing Word Macros*
- *VB and VBA in a Nutshell*

There are also a number of web sites devoted to Microsoft Word, along with a large online community of folks who've come together to help each other manage Microsoft Word. The following sites are particularly helpful:

- Microsoft's official Office Site (*http://office.microsoft.com/*)
  Official news and articles, plus tips and tricks.
- Office Update (*http://office.microsoft.com/officeupdate/*)
  Microsoft's update site for Office, which includes service packs, security patches, program updates, and new add-ins.

- Microsoft Help and Support (*http://support.microsoft.com/*)

  Valuable technical resources for all of Microsoft's products, including a searchable Knowledge Base with thousands of how-to and tech support articles on Word.

- Woody's Watch (*http://www.woodyswatch.com/*)

  Woody Leonhard's advice, news, and newsletters on all Microsoft Office products, including Word.

- Word's Most Valued Professional (MVP) Site (*http://word.mvps.org/*)

  Home to the members of Microsoft's Most Valuable Professional (MVP) group for Word, this site contains FAQs, tutorials, downloads, and other useful information.

- Word newsgroups

  Microsoft runs a news server that hosts a number of Word-related newsgroups. You can read the newsgroups using Outlook Express, or Internet Explorer 5.0 or later. The news server is *news://msnews.microsoft.com* (or just *msnews.microsoft.com* if you are configuring it in your newsreader); the Word newsgroups all start with *microsoft.public.word*.

- Microsoft Template Gallery (*http://office.microsoft.com/templates/*)

  Microsoft offers templates for all of the Office products, including Word.

How This Book Is Organized

The book is divided into several chapters, organized by subject:

Chapter 1, *Word Under the Hood*

> This chapter offers a couple of introductory hacks to bring you up to speed on several of the topics and techniques used throughout the rest of the book, such as modifying menus and toolbars and creating and editing VBA macros.

Chapter 2, *The Word Workspace*

> This chapter includes hacks for improving the way you interact with Word. Among other things, it shows you how to gain more control over view and options settings, as well as how to add custom images to toolbar buttons.

Chapter 3, *Formatting, Printing, and Table Hacks*

> This chapter explores Word's formatting features, including hacks on creating better image borders and custom watermarks. It also shows you how to create footnotes for tables.

Chapter 4, *Editing Power Tools*

From advanced wildcard searching to automatic cross-referencing, the hacks in this chapter are all about editing efficiently. Several hacks in this chapter show you how to add features not built into Word, such as the ability to remove all hyperlinks or bookmarks in a document at once.

Chapter 5, *Templates and Outlines*

This chapter includes hacks that show you how to take advantage of two of Word's most powerful features, and even how to use Word outlines to automatically generate attractive organizational charts.

Chapter 6, *Housekeeping*

This chapter tackles some of Word's most aggravating annoyances, such as document bloat and corrupt registry data, and also shows you a few ways to hack your way around some of Word's built-in limitations.

Chapter 7, *Macro Hacks*

The hacks in this chapter offer some intermediate and advanced techniques for improving macro performance. In addition, there are hacks on moving beyond VBA basics and on doing things such as adding a progress bar to a macro and creating macros that automatically respond to application events.

Chapter 8, *Forms and Fields*

The hacks in this chapter show you how to take full advantage of Word's fields, which can be intimidating but offer powerful control over document content. Among other things, this chapter shows you how to easily add an interactive calendar to a form, perform advanced date calculations automatically, and sequentially number documents.

Chapter 9, *Advanced Word Hacks*

In true hacking spirit, this chapter explores how to cajole and contort Word into doing things no word processor was meant to do, such as performing full system backups (with reporting) and emulating the popular Unix text editor Emacs. In addition, there are hacks on controlling Word from other Office applications and from three of the most popular scripting languages (Perl, Python, and Ruby), along with a hack on how to use VBScript's powerful regular expression functions from within Word.

Chapter 10, *Word 2003 XML Hacks*

This chapter shows you how important XML support is to Word 2003. There are several hacks on using *XSLT* (Extensible Stylesheet Language Transformations) to create, process, and edit Word documents, and even a hack on how to add a Google search feature to the Word 2003 Task Pane.

Conventions Used in This Book

The following is a list of the typographical conventions used in this book:

Italics

Used for emphasis, new terms where they are defined, and URLs.

`Constant width`

Used to show code examples, the contents of files, console output, and the names of variables, commands, and other code excerpts. Also used for VBA macro and module names.

`Constant width bold`

Used to highlight portions of code (typically new additions to old code) and to indicate text that should be typed literally by the user.

`Constant width italic`

Used in code examples and tables to show sample text that should be replaced with user-supplied values.

Color

Used to indicate a cross reference within the text.

_　Underscores are the *line-continuation character*s in the VBA language. An underscore at the end of a line of VBA code indicates that the statement continues to the next line. These line breaks have been added to fit the text to the width of a page, as well as to aid in readability. They are optional, but if used, must be the final character on a line and must be preceded by a space. Word treats two (or more) lines of code separated by such an underscore as a single line of code.

↵　Used to indicate an optional line break inserted within a field code. To insert a line break within Word, type Shift-Enter. The character doesn't display on screen unless you've checked the box marked Paragraph Marks under Tools → Options → View.

You should pay special attention to notes set apart from the text with the following icons:

This is a tip, suggestion, or general note. It contains useful supplementary information about the topic at hand.

This is a warning or note of caution, often indicating that your money or your privacy might be at risk.

The thermometer icons, found next to each hack, indicate the relative complexity of the hack:

 beginner   moderate   expert

Using Code Examples

This book will help you get your job done. In general, you may use the code in this book in your programs and documentation. You do not need to contact us for permission unless you're reproducing a significant portion of the code. For example, writing a program that uses several chunks of code from this book does not require permission. Selling or distributing a CD-ROM of examples from O'Reilly books *does* require permission. Answering a question by citing this book and quoting example code does not require permission. Incorporating a significant amount of example code from this book into your product's documentation *does* require permission.

We appreciate, but do not require, attribution. An attribution usually includes the title, author, publisher, and ISBN. For example: "*Word Hacks* by Andrew Savikas. Copyright 2004 O'Reilly Media, Inc., 0-596-00493-1."

If you feel your use of code examples falls outside fair use or the permission given above, feel free to contact us at *permissions@oreilly.com*.

How to Contact Us

We have tested and verified the information in this book to the best of our ability, but you may find that features have changed (or even that we have made mistakes!). As a reader of this book, you can help us to improve future editions by sending us your feedback. Please let us know about any errors, inaccuracies, bugs, misleading or confusing statements, and typos that you find anywhere in this book.

Please also let us know what we can do to make this book more useful to you. We take your comments seriously and will try to incorporate reasonable suggestions into future editions. You can write to us at:

O'Reilly Media, Inc.
1005 Gravenstein Highway North
Sebastopol, CA 95472
(800) 998-9938 (in the United States or Canada)
(707) 829-0515 (international/local)
(707) 829-0104 (fax)

To ask technical questions or to comment on the book, send email to:

bookquestions@oreilly.com

The web site for *Word Hacks* lists examples, errata, and plans for future editions. You can find this page at:

http://www.oreilly.com/catalog/wordhks

For more information about this book and others, see the O'Reilly web site:

http://www.oreilly.com

Got a Hack?

To explore Hacks books online or to contribute a hack for future titles, visit:

http://hacks.oreilly.com

Acknowledgments

Thanks first to all of my colleagues at O'Reilly, who have provided the most enriching and exciting workplace anyone could ask for. Thanks especially to Rael Dornfest, Simon St. Laurent, and Robert Luhn, for giving me the amazing opportunity to write this book. Thanks also to Brett Johnson, a capable and cordial editor, for steering me through my first book, and to Steve Saunders for a thorough technical review and more than a few helpful comments and suggestions. Thanks to Rachel Wheeler, for a copyediting job very well done, and to Mary Anne Weeks Mayo. Thanks also to Claire Cloutier, for giving me the freedom and encouragement to experiment with many of the things that later became hacks in this book.

I'd also like to thank all of the contributors—Andrew Bruno, Sean M. Burke, Ian Burrell, Greg Chapman, Paul Edstein, Guy Hart-Davis, Evan Lenz, Jack M. Lyon, Gus Perez, Shyam Pillai, Phil Rabichow, Christopher Rath, Omar Shahine, Mark Hammond, and Dan Mueller—for their clever and creative solutions, and especially for their willingness to share their work with the rest of the Word world, in true hacker's spirit. Thanks also to the denizens of the WOPR Lounge (*http://www.wopr.com*), an extraordinary community of folks who truly enjoy helping others understand Word. I'd especially like to thank Jefferson Scher, for helping pin down a particularly perplexing line of code, and Gary Frieder, for invaluable feedback and helpful suggestions.

Thanks also to my friends and family, who didn't forget about me despite several months spent hiding away in front of a computer, writing this book. Finally, I'd like to thank my wife, Audrey, for her patience, support, and love, and for believing I could do this when even I wasn't so sure.

Word Under the Hood

Hacks 1–2

Few consumer software packages are as malleable as Microsoft Word—it has to be malleable, to meet the unique needs of millions of users around the globe. However, many (perhaps most) Word users spend months, or even years, using Word "out of the box," without taking advantage of a single one of its limitless customization tools.

There's a palpable reluctance among long-time Word users to peek behind the curtain. They may curse the wretched Bullets and Numbering buttons 20 times a day or take 2 hours to manually change the font size of every heading in a lengthy report, but they will still not tear off the cover and start tinkering. For too long, they've been seduced by Word's supposed simplicity ("There must be a menu to fix this somewhere…").

If you're one of those users, this chapter will help you find your inner hacker. It asks you to choose the Red Pill and take a trip into Word's inner workings. You will also learn the very basics needed to start *really* hacking. For everyone else, consider it calisthenics for the rest of the book.

> For a more detailed view of Word, check out *Word Pocket Guide* (O'Reilly). It is an essential reference guide for any Word hacker.

HACK #1 Tweak the Interface

Take charge of toolbars, menus, and screen real estate with a few trips to the Tools menu.

Simple adjustments to the Word environment can save you lots of time. The gateway to tweaking your toolbars and menus is the Tools → Customize command, which brings up the dialog shown in Figure 1-1. Whenever this dialog is active, your menus and toolbars no longer perform their regular duties—they become adjustable elements of the interface that can be moved, modified, renamed, or even deleted.

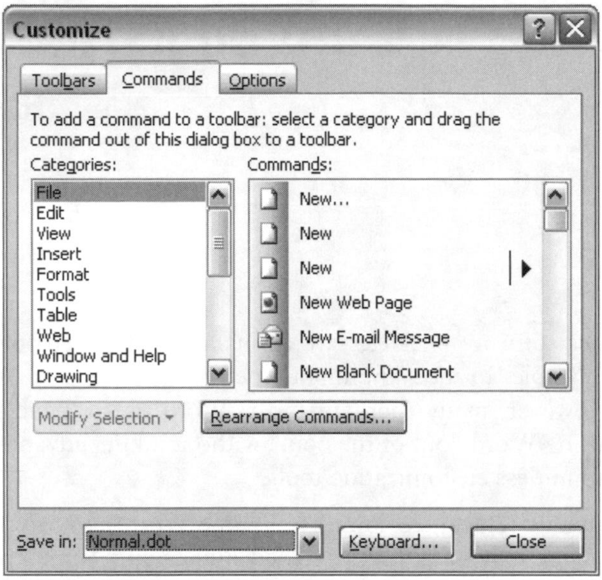

Figure 1-1. The Customize dialog lets you quickly customize your workspace

The big kahuna of the Customize dialog is the Commands tab, which we'll explore in the following two sections. But the other two tabs, Options and Toolbars, are also important for understanding—and hacking—Word.

Some of Word's more elusive options live on the Options tab, shown in Figure 1-2. For example, you can uncheck the "Always show full menus" box to turn off that unholy "Adaptive Menus" feature that displays only some commands on each menu. You can also tell Word to stop displaying font names in the fonts themselves, which can speed up the display on a slow machine. And the "Show shortcut keys in ScreenTips" setting can help you learn the shortcuts for toolbar buttons you use regularly.

Use the Toolbars tab to manage your toolbars, reset their default arrangements, or delete custom arrangements you've created but no longer need. You can also create new toolbars and make the Shortcut Menu toolbar [Hack #3] visible for modifying.

Use the Keyboard button (available on all three tabs in the Customize dialog) to add, remove, or modify keyboard assignments.

Figure 1-2. *The Options tab of the Customize dialog*

To print a list of active keyboard assignments in the current template, select File → Print and choose "Key assignments" from the "Print what" drop-down list.

Now, here are a few simple hacks to get your feet wet.

Replacing a Toolbar Button

The Standard toolbar includes a button for creating multiple text columns, which is illogically located next to the buttons for inserting tables and Excel worksheets. A more sensible neighbor for those buttons would be the Sort command, which usually requires a trip to the Table menu.

The Sort command also works on text not included in a table, such as a list of names you want to alphabetize.

Here's how to replace the Columns button with a Sort button.

First, select Tools → Customize. With the Customize dialog open, drag the Columns button off the Standard toolbar. (Don't worry; you can always restore it in a snap.)

Next, click the Commands tab in the Customize dialog and choose *Normal.dot* from the "Save in" drop-down list at the bottom of the dialog. If you select this setting, any customizations you make will affect all of your documents (whenever you're working in Word, even if you're working on a document based on another template, the Normal template is still present).

> To save changes you make to the Normal template, you must close Word.

In the Categories column (on the left), select All Commands. In the Commands column (on the right), scroll down and select TableSort, as shown in Figure 1-3. Drag it to the Standard toolbar, next to the Insert Excel Worksheet button.

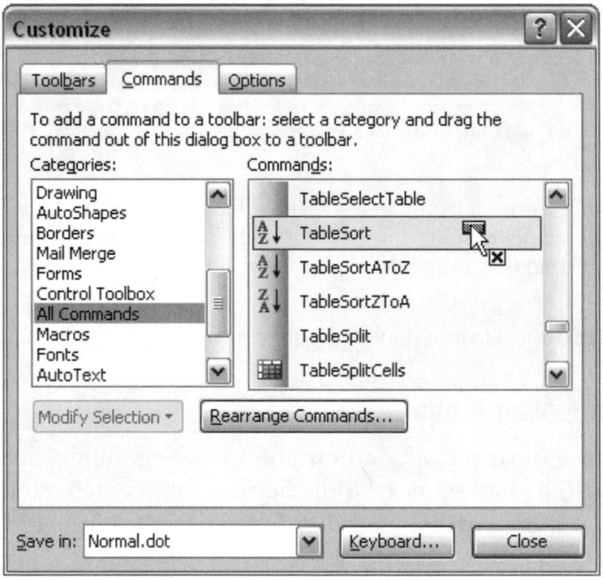

Figure 1-3. Find the TableSort command

By default, a command you drag to a toolbar appears with its name, not its icon, displayed. To change this, with the Customize dialog still open, right-click your new Table Sort button and select Default Style, as shown in Figure 1-4. The new button will be active after you close the Customize dialog.

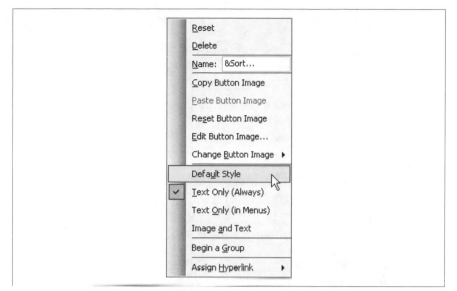

Figure 1-4. Change the Table Sort button to display an icon without text

Modifying a Menu Item

Many Word users frequently insert footnotes. But as of Word 2002, the Footnote command was moved to a new submenu on the Insert menu, called Reference (see Figure 1-5).

Here's how to move the Footnote command to the top of the Insert menu and make it more accessible.

First, select Tools ▸ Customize, click the Commands tab, and make sure you save the changes in *Normal.dot* (see the previous section "Replacing a Toolbar Button").

Next, select Insert from the Categories list and then select the Footnote command from the list on the right (Word 2002 and 2003 users will find it on a submenu). Drag it to the top of the Insert menu, as shown in Figure 1-6.

The Footnote command will work from its new home as soon as you close the Customize dialog.

Activating Important Viewing Options

To reliably control (or even understand) Word's features and formatting, you need to set a few important options.

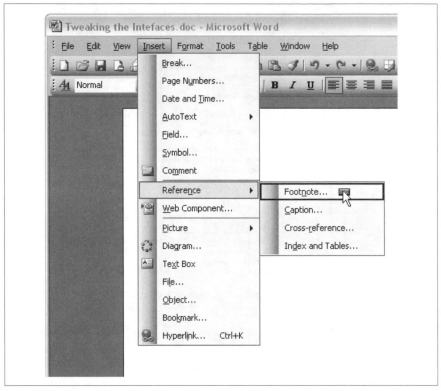

Figure 1-5. Finding the Footnote command on the Insert menu

A Word document offers more than just words (even if it lacks fancy pictures or tables). For example, a multitude of special nonprinting characters control how the words in a document are formatted.

To view some of these characters, select Tools → Options, click the View tab, and check the following items:

- Paragraph marks
- Tab characters
- Bookmarks

Also, set field shading to "Always."

None of the characters that you can now see will print, and you can always select File → Print Preview to view your document without them.

The value of these characters will become more apparent as you work with the other hacks in this book, but here's one quick example.

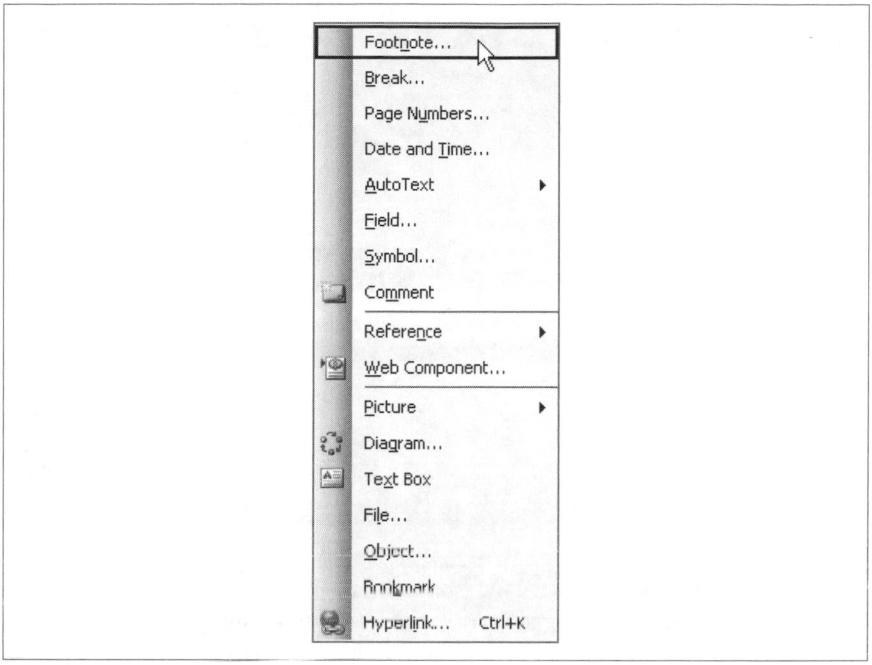

Figure 1-6. Relocating a menu item

Say your boss asks you to add some project background to her report and to format it with centered headings. The document contains only plain text, as shown in Figure 1-7.

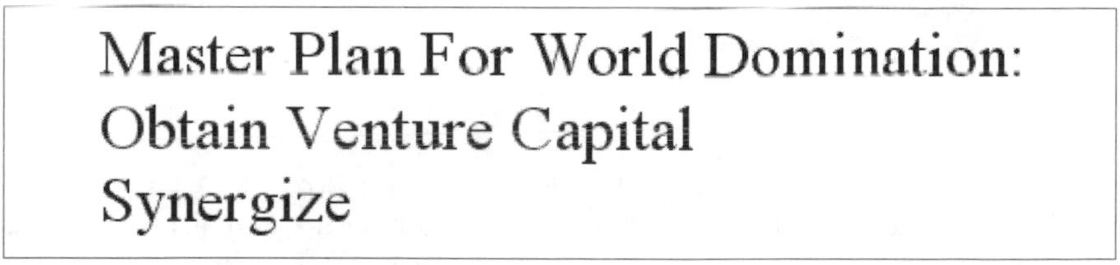

Master Plan For World Domination:
Obtain Venture Capital
Synergize

Figure 1-7. Some standard text in need of formatting

You want to center the first line as a heading, then add bullets to the next two items. With the heading selected, you press the Center button on the Formatting toolbar—but the paragraph below the heading moves too, as shown in Figure 1-8.

Yikes! After you press the Undo button, you decide to switch tactics. You select the second and third paragraphs and press the Bullets button on the Formatting toolbar. You start to sweat profusely when Word applies the

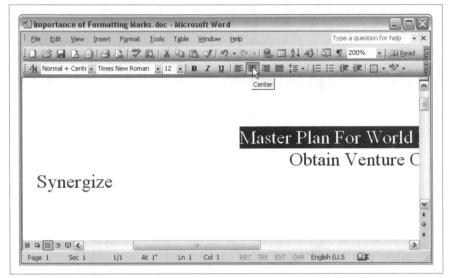

Figure 1-8. Unexpected formatting can be an unwelcome surprise

Bullets style to the heading and not the second paragraph, as shown in Figure 1-9.

Figure 1-9. Bizarre bullet results

What's going on here? With paragraph marks showing, as in Figure 1-10, the problem becomes clear. The first and second lines are actually part of the same paragraph. Your boss inserted a "soft" return after the heading (by pressing Shift-Enter) to force a line break without starting a new paragraph. So even though they appear as two separate paragraphs, they act as one. You can avoid similar headaches if you get into the habit of working with formatting marks showing.

> # Master Plan For World Domination:↵
> # Obtain Venture Capital¶
> # Synergize¶

Figure 1-10. With paragraph marks visible, you can quickly identify the problem

HACK #2 Macros 101: A Crash Course

This hack offers a whirlwind tour of macros, which can help you automate tedious and time-consuming tasks.

Word 6 or later lets you write, record, and play *macros*, or short programs that automate tasks in Word. The term macro comes from *macrocommand*, which originally referred to a bunch of commands strung together and executed all at once. Typically, you would record a sequence of commands, give the sequence a name, and then play it back as needed. You can certainly use Word macros for this purpose, but it represents only the tip of the iceberg.

You create Word macros using *Visual Basic for Applications*, usually abbreviated as *VBA*. Even recorded macros get translated into VBA, which you can then examine or edit.

VBA belongs to the BASIC family of computer languages. Compared to other computer languages, such as C or Java, you may find it easier to master. But like any language, you'll need to use it in order to learn it.

A true VBA tutorial falls outside the scope of this book. This hack simply shows you how to create and run a macro like the ones used in this book.

> For a thorough guide to Word macros, check out *Writing Word Macros* (O'Reilly).

Nuts and Bolts

Most of the macros in this book, as well as any you record within Word, use the *subroutine* (Sub) procedure. Each one begins with the following line:

```
Sub MacroName
```

where *MacroName* is the name of the macro. Each ends with this line:

```
End Sub
```

The instructions you give Word fit between these two lines. Cooking offers a useful analogy. In fact, you can think of a macro as a recipe. You begin with the list of ingredients at the top and then add a sequence of actions to transform those ingredients into something edible. You can even split some recipes into several shorter recipes—i.e., one for the sauce, one for the meat—to make them easier to follow. The same goes for macros. In the example below, note the list of "ingredients" at the top, followed by the rest of the code to work those ingredients into the main course:

```
Sub CountCommentsByBob( )
Dim oComment As Comment
Dim iCommentCount As Integer
Dim doc As Document

iCommentCount = 0
Set doc = ActiveDocument

For Each oComment In doc.Comments
    If oComment.Author = "Bob" Then
        iCommentCount = iCommentCount + 1
    End If
Next oComment

MsgBox "Bob made: " & iCommentCount & " comments"
End Sub
```

The next section shows you how to put macros to work in your documents.

Hello, World

A tradition in computer books is to present the first example as a simple program that announces its existence to the world. In Word VBA, that would go something like this:

```
Sub HelloWorld
MsgBox "Hello, World"
End Sub
```

To create this macro, select Tools → Macro → Macros to display the Macros dialog. A listbox at the bottom, labeled "Macros in," lists all the open templates and documents where you can store your macro, as shown in Figure 1-11. For example, choose the "All active templates and documents" option to create your macro in the *Normal.dot* template.

Next, type HelloWorld in the "Macro name" field and press the Create button, as shown in Figure 1-12.

When you press this button, Word does three things:

1. Within your Normal template, Word creates a new *module* to hold your macro code, named NewMacros.

2. Word launches the Visual Basic Editor.

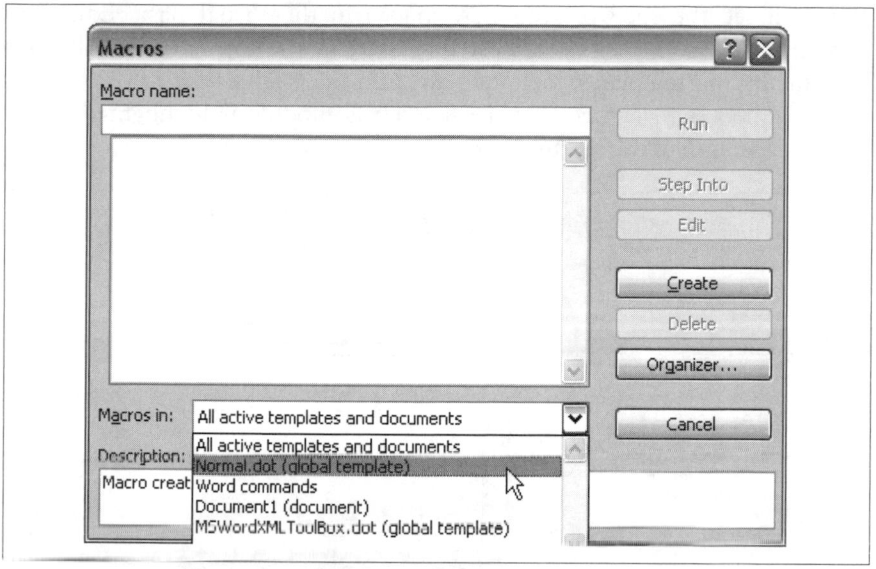

Figure 1-11. Choosing where to store a macro

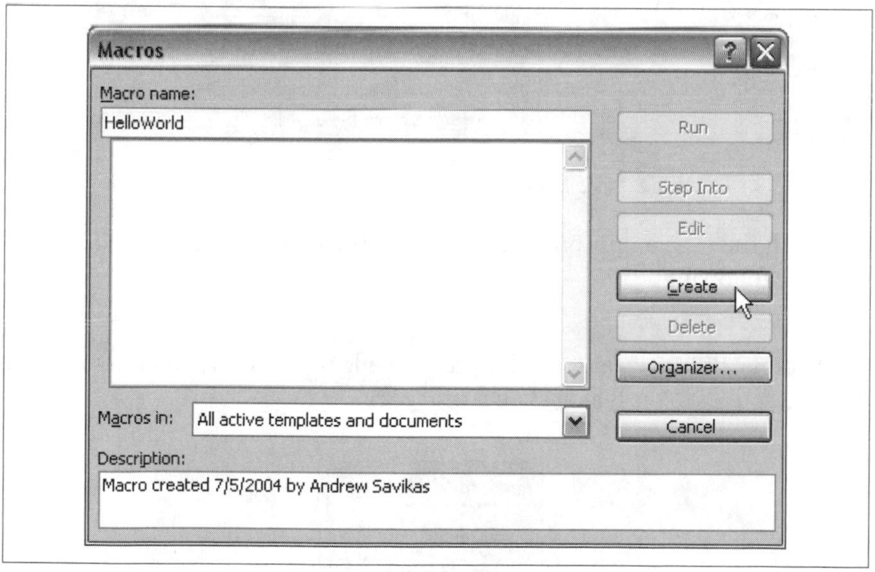

Figure 1-12. Creating a new macro from the Macros dialog box

3. Word fills in the first and last lines of the macro for you and inserts some comments about the macro. (The comments help the people who read the programs. In VBA, comments always start with a single quotation mark or apostrophe.)

You will see the shell of your new macro in the Visual Basic Editor, as shown in Figure 1-13. The Project Explorer, in the top left, lists all open documents and templates, including any add-ins (such as the MSWordXML ToolBox [Hack #92]). Notice that the NewMacros module is highlighted in the Modules section of the Normal template.

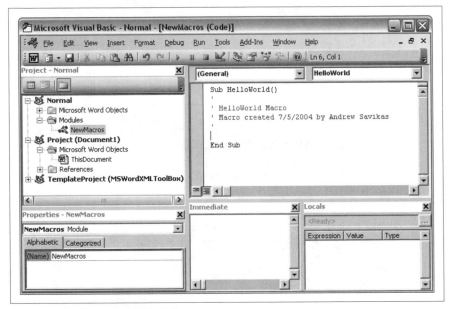

Figure 1-13. The Visual Basic Editor

To finish the macro, just put your cursor in the blank line above End Sub and type the following:

```
MsgBox "Hello, World!"
```

Now press the Play button (the green wedge) on the toolbar to run the macro. You'll see the dialog shown in Figure 1-14.

Figure 1-14. Greetings from your first macro

To create another macro in the same module within the Normal template, just start a new line after End Sub and type in the first line for another macro.

You can also paste code from other macros directly into the Visual Basic Editor.

Organizing and Debugging Your Macros

If you want to create a new module to help organize your macros, select the template or document where the new module will go from within the Project Explorer, then select Insert → Module. New modules created like this are always named Module1, Module2, and so on, as shown in Figure 1-15. In the Properties window, located just under the Project Explorer (see Figure 1-13), you can rename the modules.

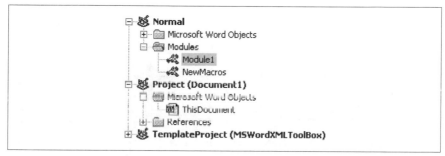

Figure 1-15. A new module inserted into the Normal template

To help you cut down (or at least easily pinpoint) the number-one source of program bugs—typing errors—you should always include the following as the very first line of code in any module:

```
Option Explicit
```

This tells Word to make sure you've *declared* every variable you use in the macro. To continue with the cooking analogy, it's like checking the recipe to make sure you listed every ingredient at the top. If you try to run a macro with a misspelled variable name, Word will warn you and highlight the undeclared variable, as shown in Figure 1-16.

Once you finish editing your macro, select File → Close and Return to Microsoft Word.

Running Macros

To run a macro from within Word, select Tools → Macro → Macros, select it from the list, and press the Run button, as shown in Figure 1-17.

If you frequently use the same macro, you can assign it a toolbar button or keyboard shortcut. Select Tools → Customize, click the Commands tab, and select Macros from the Categories column, as shown in Figure 1-18. In the

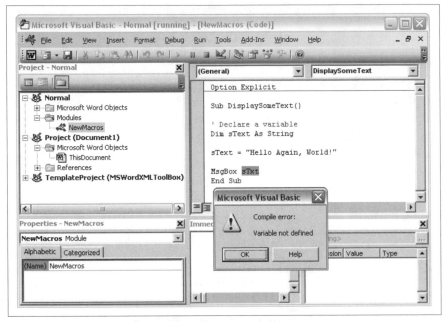

Figure 1-16. Word can help find mistakes in your macros

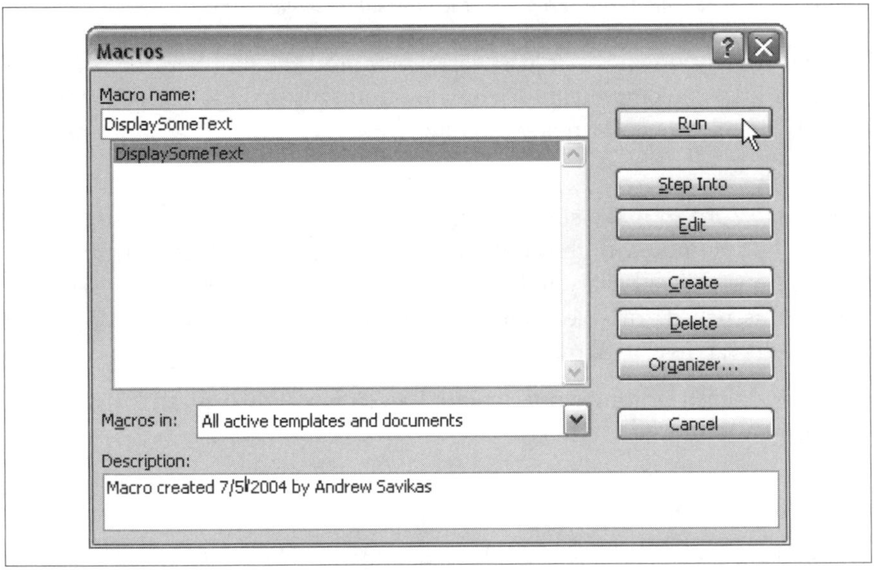

Figure 1-17. Running a Macro from within Word

Commands column, find the macro and drag it to a toolbar or menu. After you place the macro, you can right-click it to change its name or add an image to its button, as shown in Figure 1-19.

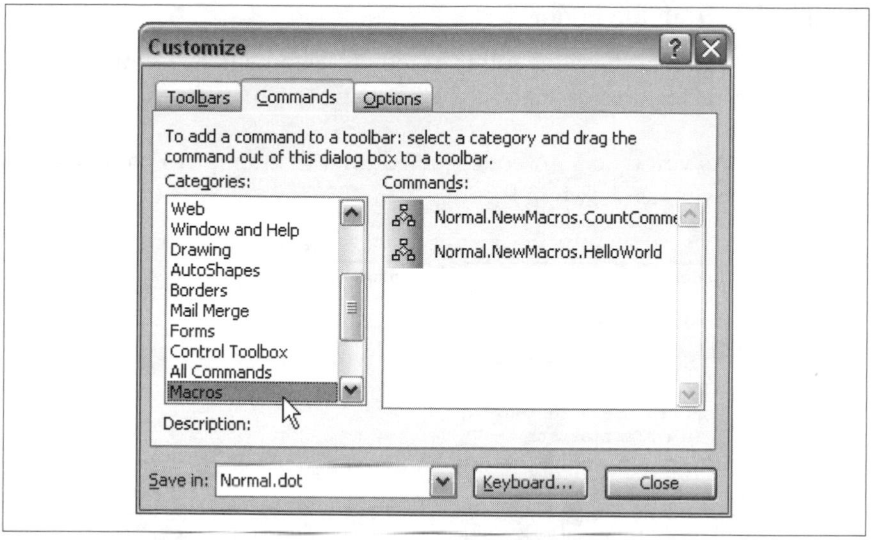

Figure 1-18. Selecting the Macros category from the Customize dialog

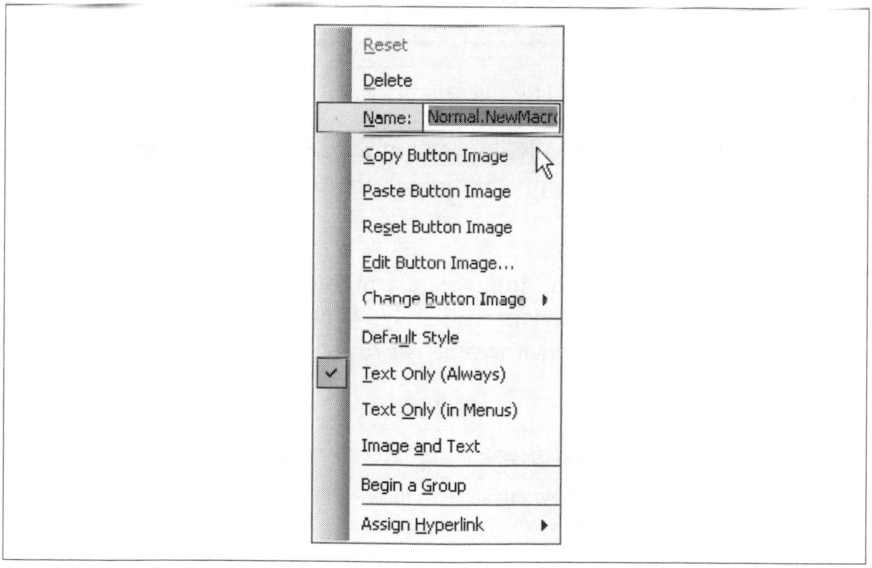

Figure 1-19. Changing the name of the button used to activate a macro placed on a toolbar or menu

If you use or create a set of macros that become an integral part of your workflow, consider separating those into a separate Macros template [Hack #50] that will load automatically whenever Word starts.

Getting Help from the Editor

The Visual Basic Editor is a full-featured development environment that includes several features designed to help you write VBA code.

IntelliSense. As you type VBA code, the editor will attempt to complete the statement for you, as shown in Figure 1-20.

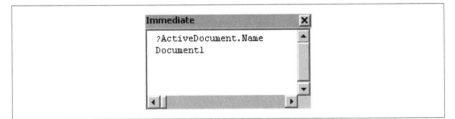

```
(General)                    DisplaySomeText

   Option Explicit

   Sub DisplaySomeText()

   ' Declare a variable
   Dim sText as str
                      String
   End Sub            Style
                      Styles
                      StyleSheet
                      StyleSheets
                      Subdocument
                      Subdocuments
```

Figure 1-20. The Visual Basic Editor can help you write code faster

Though the lists will generally appear automatically as you type, you can explicitly request a list of items that match the text you've already typed by pressing Ctrl-spacebar.

The Immediate window. In the Immediate window, you can enter individual statements that are executed immediately. When a statement is prefaced with a question mark, the return value is printed to the Immediate window, as shown in Figure 1-21.

```
Immediate                        ✕

   ?ActiveDocument.Name
   Document1
```

Figure 1-21. Using the Immediate window

The Immediate window is a helpful tool for testing out a macro. Type the following line of code in a macro:

```
Debug.Print StringToPrint
```

Replace *StringToPrint* with a text string or a string variable you want to keep an eye on, which will be printed to the Immediate window. This technique is shown in Figure 1-22.

Stepping through code. As you test out a macro, it can help to "step" through it as it runs. Word will execute one line of the macro, then wait for you to tell it to run the next line. In this way, you can slow down a macro and better understand it. If you hover your mouse over a variable while stepping through the code, Word displays the current contents of the variable as a ToolTip.

To step through a macro, put your cursor anywhere inside it and press F8. Each time you press F8, you execute another line of code. The line that will be executed the next time you press F8 will be highlighted in yellow, and an arrow will appear at the left, as shown in Figure 1-22.

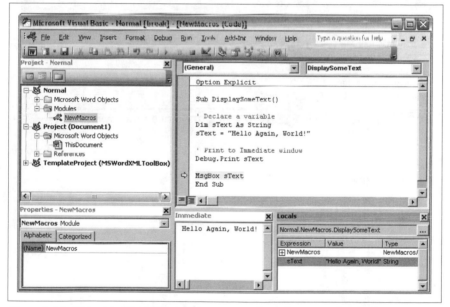

Figure 1-22. Using the Visual Basic Editor to step through a macro line by line

Exploring the Word Object Model

In Word VBA, all of Word's parts are represented as *objects*. A document is an object, a paragraph is an object, and even a font name is an object. All of these objects are interrelated, and evaluating and manipulating them is the basis of programming Word with VBA.

To browse the Word object model, select View → Object Browser from within the Visual Basic Editor. Using the Object Browser can be an overwhelming experience for beginners, but it can be a great help in figuring out how to automate a particular component or task within Word. The Object Browser is shown in Figure 1-23.

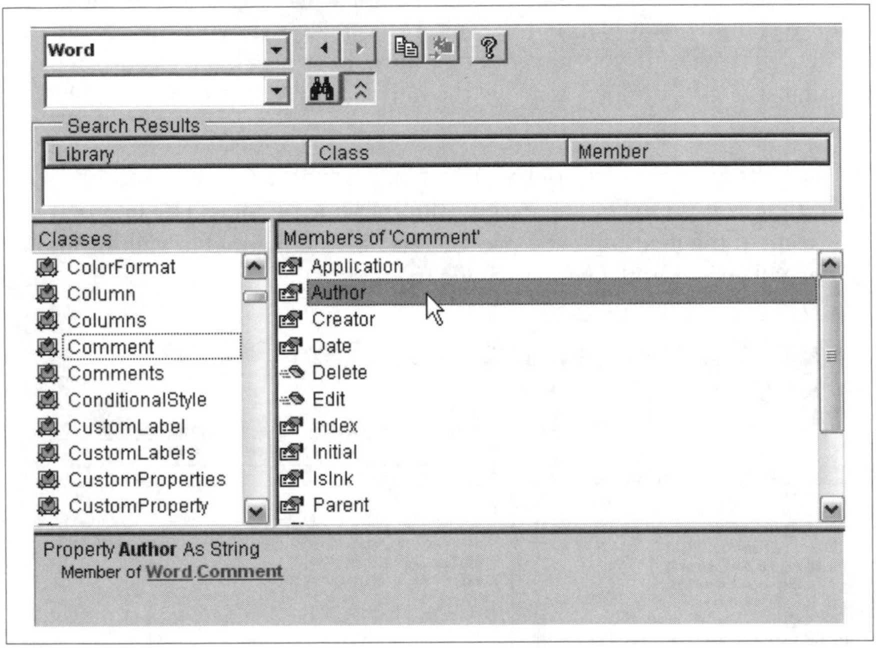

Figure 1-23. Using the VBA Object Browser

CHAPTER TWO

The Word Workspace
Hacks 3–13

Word offers an exceptionally hackable environment. Most any menu, tool-bar, or viewing option is adjustable. The hacks in this chapter show a few ways to fine-tune your workspace to help you work smarter. In addition, you'll learn a few ways to manage your documents better and how to finally and firmly take control of the much maligned Office Assistant.

HACK #3 Hack Your Shortcut Menus

To find relevant commands quickly, most Word users head straight for the shortcut menus. But like any Word menu, a shortcut menu is yours for the hacking.

In most applications, you're stuck with whatever the software company decides to put on its *shortcut menus* (the set of context-sensitive commands that appear when you right-click your mouse). For example, Microsoft must consider hyperlinks [Hack #28] *extremely* relevant; in Word 2003, you can insert a hyperlink from 26 of the 62 shortcut menus!

The shortcut menu you'll probably use most is the Text shortcut menu, which appears when you right-click within the text of a document. This menu is shown in its native form in Figure 2-1.

Fortunately, you can rearrange any of the 62 shortcut menus in Word according to *your* priorities. For example, if you insert a lot of comments, the mouse mileage needed to repeatedly select the text and then go up and choose Insert → Comment can really add up. This hack will show you how to give your wrist a rest by moving the Insert Comment command closer to where you're working—onto the shortcut menu.

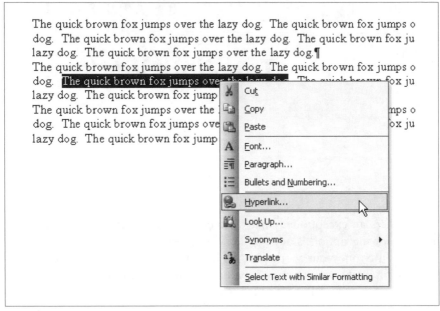

Figure 2-1. The default Text shortcut menu

Accessing the Shortcut Menu Toolbar

All of the menus in Word reside on toolbars. Even the main menu bar (with File, Edit, View, etc.) is actually a toolbar—appropriately named Menu Bar. Shortcut menus are no different, but the toolbar they live on is a bit harder to find. In fact, except for when you're customizing it, you'll never get to see the Shortcut Menu toolbar; notice it's not one of the choices offered when you select View → Toolbars.

To see the elusive Shortcut Menu toolbar, select Tools → Customize to display the Customize dialog. You can also right-click on the title bar of any toolbar or an unoccupied area of the main menu bar and choose Customize.

Select the Commands tab. If you want the shortcut menu changes to be available in every document you use, choose *Normal.dot* from the "Save in" drop-down list in the Customize dialog, as shown in Figure 2-2.

Next, click the Toolbars tab and check the "Shortcut Menus" box, as shown in Figure 2-3.

As soon as you check the box, a toolbar like the one in Figure 2-4 will appear on your screen, probably near the top left. *Don't* press the Close button on the Customize dialog. You can access the Shortcut Menu toolbar only with the Customize dialog open.

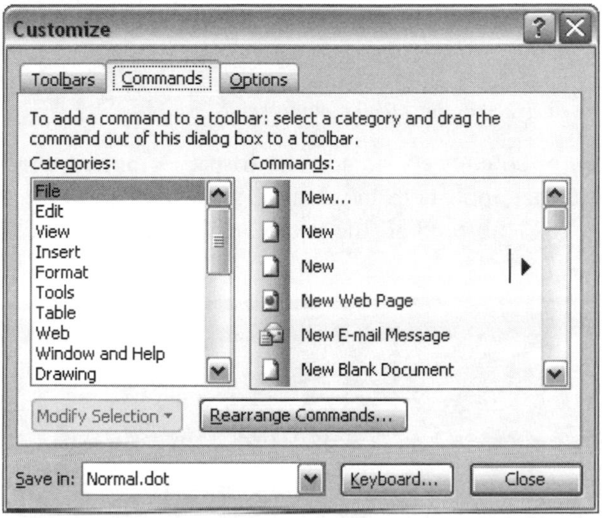

Figure 2-2. The Customize dialog

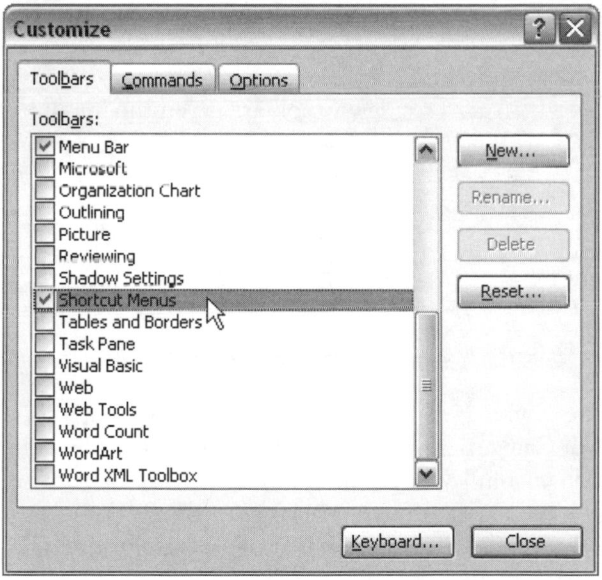

Figure 2-3. Getting to the shortcut menus

Modifying a Shortcut Menu

Word divides shortcut menus into three categories: Text, Table, and Draw. This can help you narrow your search for a particular shortcut menu among

Figure 2-4. The elusive Shortcut Menu toolbar

the five dozen or so choices. To add the Insert Comment command to the shortcut menu that appears from within regular text, choose the Text menu on the Shortcut Menu toolbar, then scroll down and select Text, as shown in Figure 2-5.

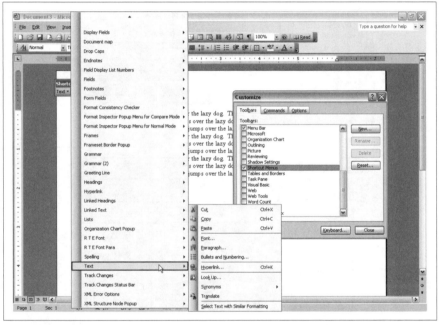

Figure 2-5. Accessing the Text shortcut menu for customization

Now click the Commands tab in the Customize dialog and choose Insert from the list of Categories on the left. Then, in the list of Commands on the right, scroll down until you get to Comment. Drag it from the Customize dialog to the Text shortcut menu. Once you release the mouse button, the Comment command will appear on the shortcut menu, as shown in Figure 2-6.

After you press Close on the Customize dialog, you'll be able to insert comments via the Text shortcut menu, without moving your mouse from the page.

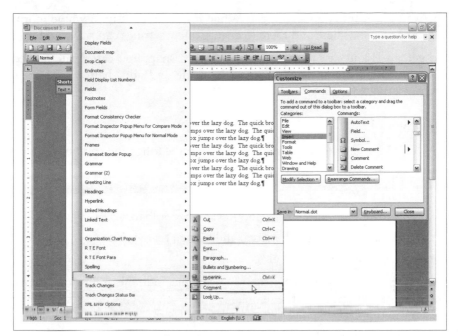

Figure 2-6. Adding a command to a shortcut menu

To save your changes to *Normal.dot*, you must exit Word.

Create Custom Views

You can easily get a bit disoriented as you change views, toolbars, and zoom levels within Word. This hack shows how to create predefined views and return to them instantly.

Word offers a multitude of viewing options. With the addition of Reading Layout view in Word 2003, you can now choose from six different views: Normal, Web Layout, Print Layout, Reading Layout, Outline, and Print Preview. Plus, you can turn on and off features such as paragraph marks, tabs, hidden text, field codes, and bookmarks, just to name a few. And as Word has more toolbars than you can fit on most screens, depending on the work you're doing you may want to change your view a few dozen times each day.

Even if you only occasionally zoom in or out, or use Reading Layout or an extra toolbar here and there, you've probably found that there are a handful of viewing combinations that you prefer. Unfortunately, reorienting Word the way you want is no small feat. While it may not eat up a whole morning, a few seconds here and there to change a few settings can really add up.

To get the layout just the way you like it in a snap, you can create named sets of viewing options using some VBA code and add them to the View menu for quick toggling.

The Code

Say you like to do your editing in Word under the following conditions:

- Normal view
- Zoom to 120%
- Only Standard, Formatting, and Reviewing toolbars visible
- Field shading, paragraph marks, and hidden text visible
- Revision tracking turned on

To make this configuration instantly available, put the following macro, named SetEditingView, in the template of your choice **[Hack #50]**. It sets all the viewing options listed above.

```
Sub SetEditingView( )
On Error Resume Next
Dim win As Window
Dim cbar As CommandBar
Dim sToolbarsToShow As String

' List toolbars to display
' All others will be hidden
sToolbarsToShow = "/Menu Bar/Standard/Formatting/Reviewing/"

' Hide any toolbars that aren't in the list
For Each cbar In Application.CommandBars
    If InStr(sToolbarsToShow, "/" & cbar.Name & "/") Then
        cbar.visible = True
    Else
        cbar.visible = False
    End If
Next cbar

' Change the View settings
Set win = Application.ActiveWindow
With win
    .View.Type = wdNormalView
    .View.Zoom = 120
    .View.FieldShading = wdFieldShadingAlways
    .View.ShowParagraphs = True
    .View.ShowHiddenText = False
End With
```

```
' Turn on revision tracking
ActiveDocument.TrackRevisions = True
End Sub
```

Putting the New View on the View Menu

Now you can create a new submenu on the View menu and add the new Editing view to it.

Select Tools → Customize and click the Commands tab. In the Categories column, scroll down to New Menu and then select New Menu again from the Commands column, as shown in Figure 2-7.

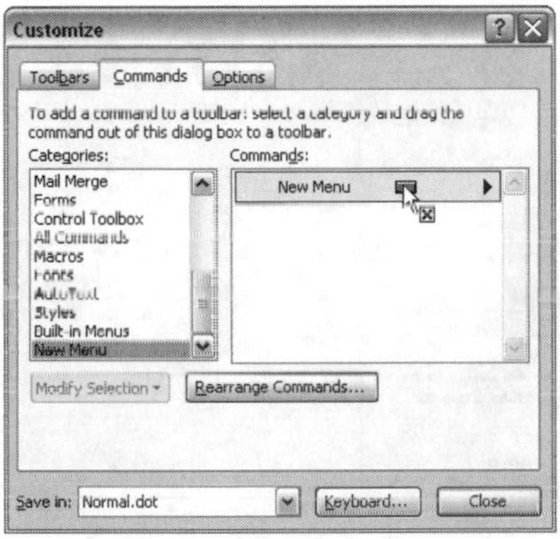

Figure 2-7. Selecting a new menu to drag to the View menu

Next, drag the New Menu item to the View menu (when you drag the item over View on the main menu bar, the View menu will open) and drop it just under Outline view, as shown in Figure 2-8.

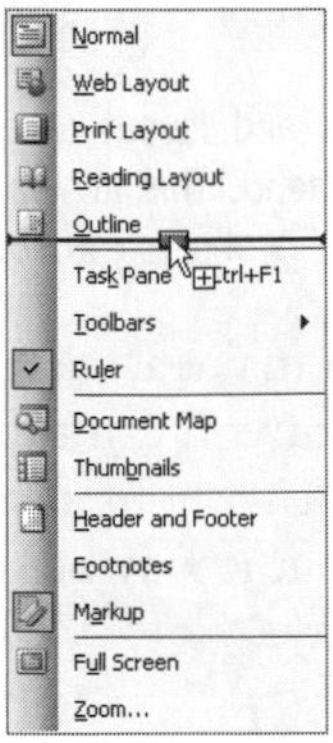

Figure 2-8. Placing the new menu on the View menu

After you place the new menu, right-click it, rename it "My Views," and select the option "Begin a new group."

Go back to the Customize dialog, click the Commands tab, and select Macros from the Categories column. From the Commands column, drag the SetEditingView macro to the new My Views menu. Then right-click it and rename it "Editing." Close the Customize dialog.

To run the macro, which will set the desired view options, just select it from the new My Views menu, as shown in Figure 2-9.

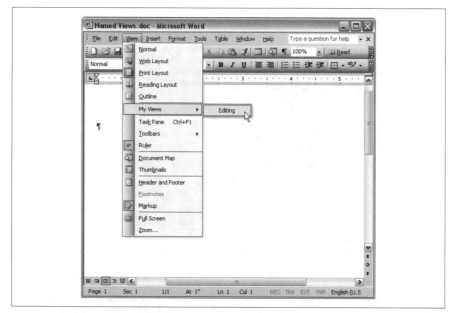

Figure 2-9. Selecting from the new My Views menu

Revert to Saved

Most other word processors and layout programs put a Revert to Saved command right on the File menu. This allows for a quick return to the last saved version of a file. This hack shows you how to add this feature in Word.

While editing a document, you make a mistake. A big mistake. You try the Undo command a few times, but you can't quite retrace your steps. In frustration, you close the document without saving your changes, then reopen it. This is a minor annoyance, but it may be something you have to do a lot. Fortunately, there's an easier way.

The Code

To put a Revert to Saved option on your File menu, add this macro to *Normal.dot*:

```
Sub FileRevertToSaved( )
Dim sDocPath As String
Dim sDocFullName As String

sDocFullName = ActiveDocument.FullName
sDocPath = ActiveDocument.Path

If Len(sDocPath) = 0 Then
    MsgBox "Can't revert a document that's never been saved."
    Exit Sub
End If

If MsgBox("Really revert to last saved version? " & _
        "(Can't be undone)", _
        vbYesNo) = vbNo Then
    Exit Sub
End If

Documents.Open FileName:=sDocFullName, Revert:=True
End Sub
```

Putting the Macro in Your File Menu

Select Tools → Customize and click the Commands tab. Choose *Normal.dot* from the "Save in" drop-down list. In the Categories list, select Macros, and in the Commands list, select the new FileRevertToSaved macro, as shown in Figure 2-10.

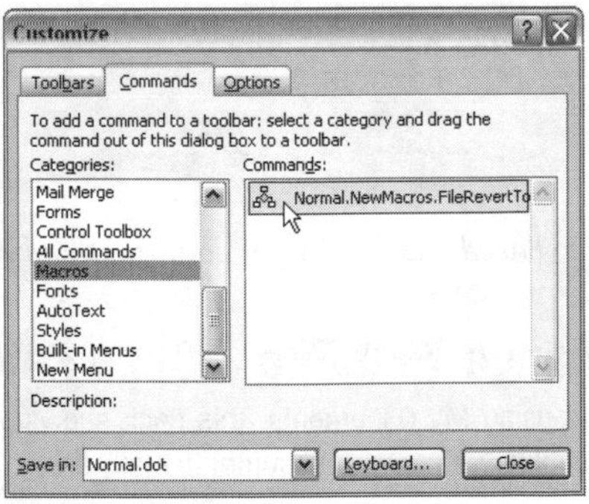

Figure 2-10. Selecting a macro from the Customize dialog

Next, drag the macro to the File menu, as shown in Figure 2-11. After you place it in the menu, you can right-click it and shorten its name to "Revert to

Saved." Since you stored this customization in *Normal.dot*, close and restart Word to prevent losing the change in case of a crash.

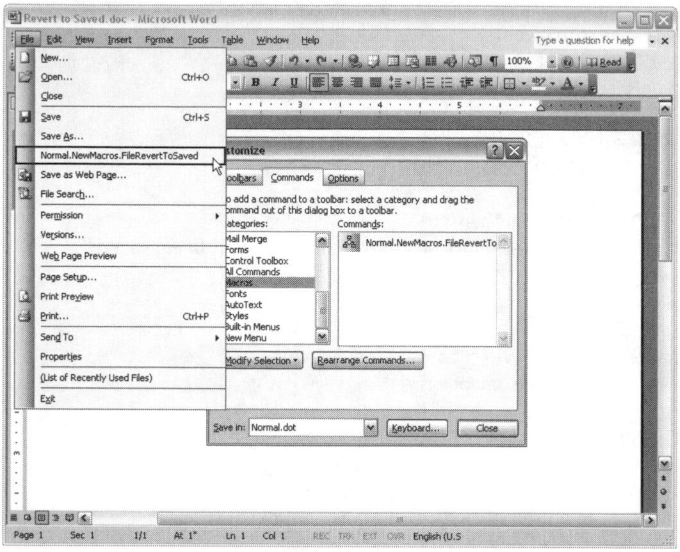

Figure 2-11. Adding the Revert to Saved macro to the File menu

The macro will notify you if you try to revert a document that hasn't yet been saved (and, of course, won't revert anything). It also asks for confirmation before reverting, as shown in Figure 2-12.

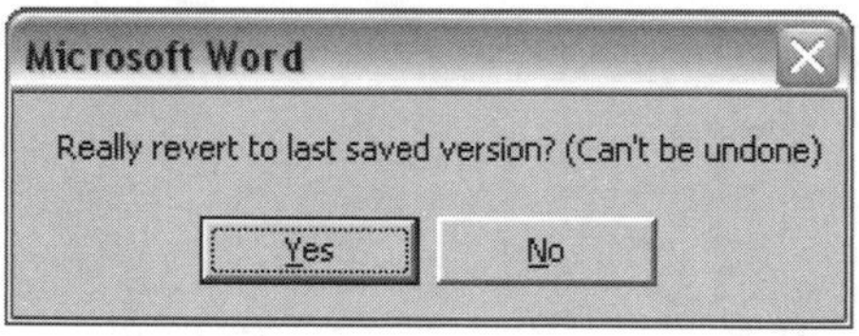

Figure 2-12. The Revert to Saved macro asks for confirmation before running

Quickly Change Your File → Open Path

HACK #6

Instead of always using My Documents, this hack shows you how to make Word open to the folder where your documents really are.

Few Word workers keep all their files in the *My Documents* folder. Much of the time they're on your desktop or in a different project folder deep on your hard drive. Sometimes they're not even "your" documents; they may live on a server across the office, or across the country. But when you want to get to one of those files, choosing File → Open always sends you to the same place: the *My Documents* folder.

Though you can change this default setting—Word will open to the folder of your choosing—it involves a long trip through Tools → Options → File Locations → Modify. You must then do some more mouse work as you browse for the folder you want to use. Many users give up and resign themselves to starting each workday with a trip through *My Documents*, but a short macro provides an easier way.

The Code

This macro provides an interactive way to change the File → Open folder to the folder in which the current document resides. Create the following macro, named ReAssignFileOpen, in the template of your choice **[Hack #50]**:

```
Sub ReAssignFileOpen( )
Dim sNewPath As String
Dim sCurrentPath As String
Dim sDefaultPath As String
Dim lResponse As Long

sNewPath = ActiveDocument.Path

' Current document must have been saved
' at least once to be in a folder
If Len(sNewPath) = 0 Then
    MsgBox "Please save this document first.", vbExclamation
    Exit Sub
End If

' Capture the default path by temporarily resetting the current one
sCurrentPath = Options.DefaultFilePath(wdDocumentsPath)
Options.DefaultFilePath(wdDocumentsPath) = ""
sDefaultPath = Options.DefaultFilePath(wdDocumentsPath)

' Restore to the current path
Options.DefaultFilePath(wdDocumentsPath) = sCurrentPath

' Prompt user to confirm change to current document's folder
lResponse = MsgBox("Really Change File...Open path to:" & _
            vbCr & vbCr & _
            sNewPath & "?" & _
            vbCr & vbCr & _
            "Press Cancel to reset to Default (" & sDefaultPath & ").", _
            vbYesNoCancel)

' Process response
Select Case lResponse
    Case Is = vbYes
        Options.DefaultFilePath(wdDocumentsPath) = sNewPath
```

```
            Case Is = vbNo
                Exit Sub
            Case Is = vbCancel
                Options.DefaultFilePath(wdDocumentsPath) = sDefaultPath
    End Select

    End Sub
```

Running the Hack

When you run this macro, you'll be prompted with the dialog shown in Figure 2-13, asking you to confirm the change. If you select Yes, the next time you choose File → Open, Word will place you in the chosen folder.

 If you point this setting to a folder on a network drive and select File → Open while no longer connected to the network, Word will return to its default File → Open folder (usually *My Documents*).

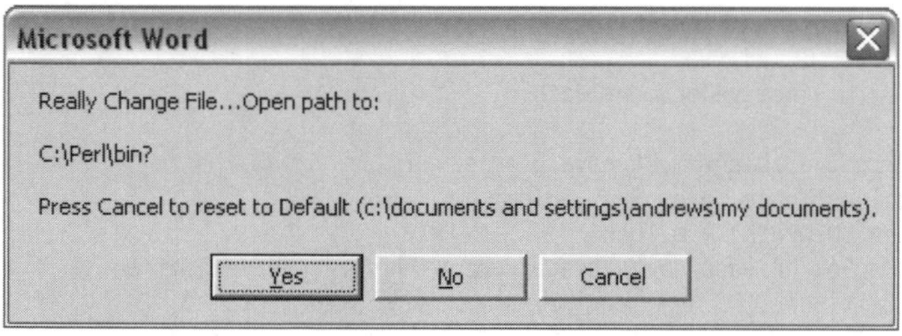

Microsoft Word   ⊠

Really Change File...Open path to:

C:\Perl\bin?

Press Cancel to reset to Default (c:\documents and settings\andrews\my documents).

        [_Yes_]   [_No_]   [Cancel]

Figure 2-13. Changing File → Open to default to the current document's folder

For quick access to this timesaver, put a button for it on the Standard toolbar **[Hack #1]** or add it to the File menu **[Hack #3]**.

See Also

- "Get Simple User Input for a Macro" **[Hack #57]**

HACK
#7
Report and Review Your Options

A freeware template from MouseTrax displays all of your Word Options settings in a convenient report format.

There are more than 200 settings that qualify as Options in Word 2003 (slightly fewer in earlier versions), and they're often the key to understanding Word's behavior. Sure, you can check most of them by scrounging around the Options dialog (Tools → Options), but having them all presented for you in a report makes a lot more sense.

A freeware template available from MouseTrax (*http://www.MouseTrax. com*) generates an easy-to-read Word document listing your current Options settings. Part of the first page of a sample report is shown in Figure 2-14.

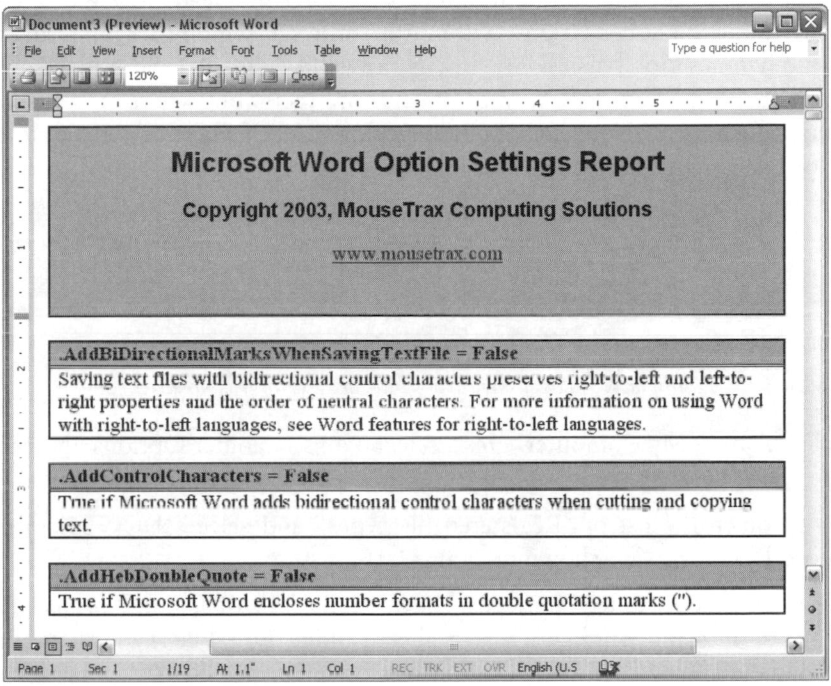

Figure 2-14. Review your Options settings in report form

After you download the template for your version of Word, just double-click it to create the report.

> If you've set your Macro Security Settings (Tools → Macro → Security) to High, you'll need to download the template into your templates folder before it will run.

Included with each setting and its current value is a brief description, which can acquaint you with some of Word's more esoteric options (e.g., AllowAccentedUppercase, which has to do with how Word treats accents over capital letters in French).

—*Greg Chapman*

H A C K
#8
Force Internet Explorer to Hand Off Word Documents

Trying to edit a Word document from a browser window is like typing with mittens on. This hack shows you how to stop Word documents from opening in Internet Explorer.

When you follow a hyperlink in Internet Explorer that leads to a Word document, the file opens right within the browser window. The resulting combination of toolbars and menus, as shown in Figure 2-15, can make editing a challenge. Some of the Word menus are there, but where are the toolbars? A better way is to leave Internet Explorer out of the equation and force Word documents to open in...well, Word.

Figure 2-15. Editing a Word document from Internet Explorer is no easy feat

Select Start → My Computer. Next, select Tools → Folder Options and click the File Types tab.

Scroll down the list of "Registered file types" and select "DOC Microsoft Word Document," as shown in Figure 2-16.

Now click the Advanced button at the bottom of the dialog and *uncheck* the "Browse in same window" box in the resulting Edit File Type dialog, as shown in Figure 2-17.

Click the OK button to accept the new setting and close the Folder Options dialog. Now whenever you click on a link that leads to a Word document, the document will open in Word—a simple solution obfuscated by a hard-to-find setting.

> You can apply this same technique to other Office files, such as PowerPoint (PPT) or Excel (XLS) documents.

Hacking the Hack

If you need to apply this fix to multiple computers, you can set up a *.reg* file to automate the change. A *.reg* file is a text file executed by Windows to modify the registry; you can use it to make multiple changes to the Windows registry without going into the registry itself. The following example

Figure 2-16. Find the DOC file extension in your list of known file types

code also makes the change for Excel and PowerPoint files, but you can leave out those files if you prefer.

> The registry stores vital system information. You should set a system restore point before you make any changes to the registry. To do so, select Start → Control Panel → Performance and Maintenance → System Restore (the location of System Restore may vary, depending on how you've configured Windows).

Enter the following code into a text editor (such as Notepad):

```
Windows Registry Editor Version 5.00
[HKEY_LOCAL_MACHINE\SOFTWARE\Classes\Word.Document.8]
@="Microsoft Word Document"
"EditFlags"=dword:00010000
"BrowserFlags"=dword:00000008

[HKEY_LOCAL_MACHINE\SOFTWARE\Classes\Excel.Sheet.8]
```

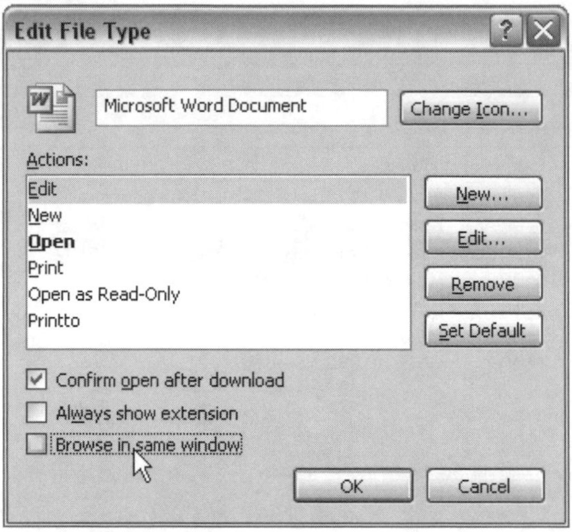

Figure 2-17. *With this setting turned off, Word files opened from Internet Explorer will open in Word*

```
@="Microsoft Excel Worksheet"
"EditFlags"=dword:00010000
"BrowserFlags"=dword:00000008

[HKEY_LOCAL_MACHINE\SOFTWARE\Classes\PowerPoint.Show.8]
@="Microsoft PowerPoint Presentation"
"EditFlags"=dword:00010000
"BrowserFlags"=dword:00000008
```

Save the file with a descriptive name, like *OpenOfficeDocsInOffice.reg*, and close the text editor. To run the *.reg* file, just double-click it.

—Gus Perez and Omar Shahine

HACK #9 Tweak the New Document Task Pane

The jury's still out on the Task Pane introduced in Word 2002, and poor documentation along with bad behavior has only hurt its case. This hack offers some tips on taming the worst offender: the New Document pane.

Many users find the New Document pane a welcome relief from the clutter of the Templates dialog, which is packed with obscure tabs (as shown in Figure 2-18). Others—particularly those who use many different templates—abhor the extra step needed to get to the Templates dialog, now that the Task Pane comes first. But like it or not, you expect the Task Pane to behave as advertised. Yeah, right.

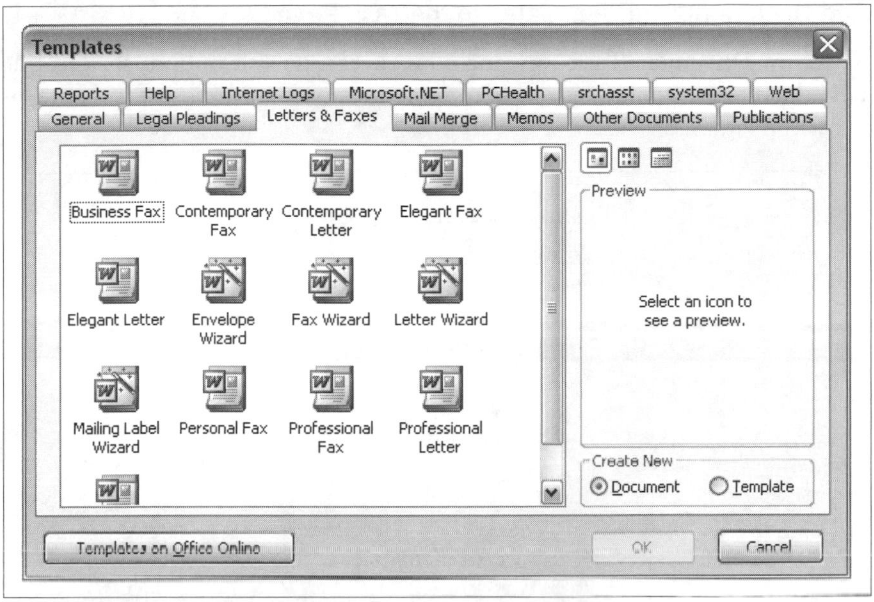

Figure 2-18. *The Templates dialog grows more crowded with each release*

Disabling the Task Pane When Word Starts

In a perfect world, you could select Tools → Options, click the View tab, and uncheck the "Startup Task Pane" box to disable the Task Pane. But for many Word users, this setting has absolutely no effect.

The fix is a registry hack that will put the Task Pane back in its place.

> Make sure you set a system restore point before you make any changes to the registry: select Start → Control Panel → Performance and Maintenance → System Restore (the location of System Restore may vary, depending on how you've configured Windows).

Close Word, select Start → Run, and enter regedit to open the registry editor. Navigate to the following key:

    HKEY_CURRENT_USER\Software\Microsoft\Office\11.0\Common\General\

Locate the subkey named DoNotDismissFileNewTaskPane and either delete it or set its value to 0.

Close the registry editor and restart Word. The Task Pane will now dutifully obey the checkbox on the View tab.

Add Documents and Templates to the Task Pane

The New Document Task Pane includes several default options for creating new documents, including access to templates on the Microsoft web site, as shown in Figure 2-19.

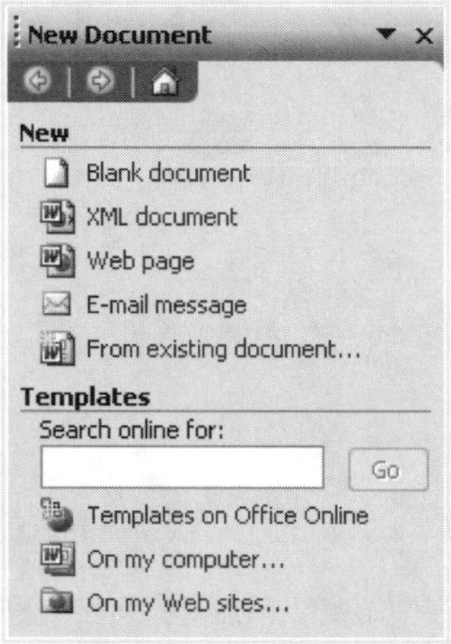

Figure 2-19. The New Document Task Pane

In addition to the two sections shown in Figure 2-19, there are two additional sections that will become visible only after you've done certain things in Word (such as creating a document based on a template other than *Normal.dot*). The four sections are the following:

- New
- Templates
- Recently used templates
- Other files

In addition to templates, the "Recently used templates" section contains any documents on which you've recently based a new document.

In VBA, you can add items to and remove items from each of the four sections using the NewDocument property. In Figure 2-20, new documents (with rather silly names) have been added to each section.

The Code

The NewDocument property has two methods: Add and Remove. The syntax for the two methods is identical. The syntax for Add follows:

Figure 2-20. The four sections of the New Document Task Pane

```
Application.NewDocument.Add(FileName, [Section], _
                    [DisplayName], [Action]) as Boolean
```

The brackets imply that you need only the *FileName* argument, but if you omit the *DisplayName* argument, you will not actually add anything to the Task Pane. You will, however, gunk up your registry with a useless entry.

You can use the arguments for Add to specify the following information:

FileName
> The actual name of the file, including the path, or a URL.

Section
> The section of the New Document Task Pane where the link will appear. You can use the following four Office VBA constants (their actual values are shown in parentheses):

msoNew(1)
> The "New" section

msoNewfromExistingFile(2)
> The "Recently used templates" section

msoNewfromTemplate(3)

The "Templates" section

msoBottomSection(4)

The "Other files" section (default)

DisplayName

The name of the file or URL as it will appear on the Task Pane.

Action

What happens when you follow the link to the file. You can use the following three Office VBA constants (their actual values are shown in parentheses):

msoEditFile(0)

Opens the file or template for editing (default).

msoCreateNewFile(1)

Creates a new document based on the document or template.

msoOpenFile(2)

Opens the file as if it were an external hyperlink (you'll get the File Download dialog box, even for files on your hard drive). Use this option when creating hyperlinks on the Task Pane.

The following macro adds the template *MyTemplate.dot* to the "Templates" section:

```
Sub AddTemplateToTaskBar( )
    Application.NewDocument.Add "c:\MyTemplate.dot", _
      msoNewfromTemplate, "My Template", msoCreateNewFile
End Sub
```

Because the syntax for the Remove method is identical to the syntax for Add, the following macro removes the same *MyTemplate.dot* file from the Task Pane:

```
Sub RemoveTemplateFromTaskBar( )
    Application.NewDocument.Remove "c:\MyTemplate.dot", _
      msoNewfromTemplate, "My Template", msoCreateNewFile

End Sub
```

Again, note that you must include the *DisplayName* argument to actually remove the file from the Task Pane.

Hacking the Hack

If you hack with the above functions for any amount of time, you'll likely end up with a few items on your Task Pane that you just can't shake. And there's no way, using VBA, to get a list of the items currently placed there.

To do some housecleaning, you'll need to hack the registry. Choose Start →
Run and enter regedit. Navigate to the following key, which lists any entries
you've added to the New Document pane:

```
HKEY_CURRENT_USER\Software\Microsoft\Office\11.0\Word\New Document
```

Regardless of the *FileName* or *DisplayName* used in VBA to create the Task
Pane entries, in the registry, the entries are always named Custom1, Custom2,
and so on. After you delete them from the registry, they won't reappear the
next time you open the New Document pane. To delete one of the entries,
select it (as shown in Figure 2-21) and choose Edit → Delete.

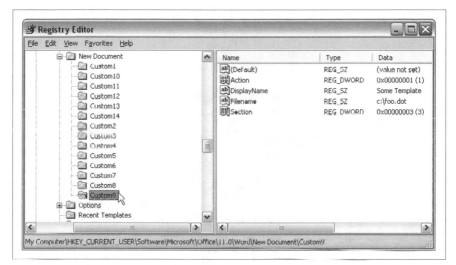

Figure 2-21. Cleaning out items from the New Documents Task Pane

> If you want to clean out the list of recently used templates as
> well, just clear the entries from the following key:
>
> ```
> HKEY_CURRENT_USER\Software\Microsoft\Office\11.0\
> Word\Recent Templates
> ```

Because the registry stores Task Pane entries, you can add new ones using a
.reg file. The following *.reg* file creates a new entry in the "Other files" section of the New Document Task Pane with a link to the O'Reilly web site,
as shown in Figure 2-22:

```
Windows Registry Editor Version 5.00

[HKEY_CURRENT_USER\Software\Microsoft\Office\11.0\Word\New Document\Custom9]
"Action"=dword:00000002
"DisplayName"="Visit oreilly.com"
"Filename"="http://www.oreilly.com"
"Section"=dword:00000004
```

Notice that the values for Action and Section correspond to the values described earlier in the syntax for the Add method (well, except for all the leading zeros).

Because you can easily distribute registry files across an office, this way you can add an intranet link or other useful shortcut to a user's Word workspace.

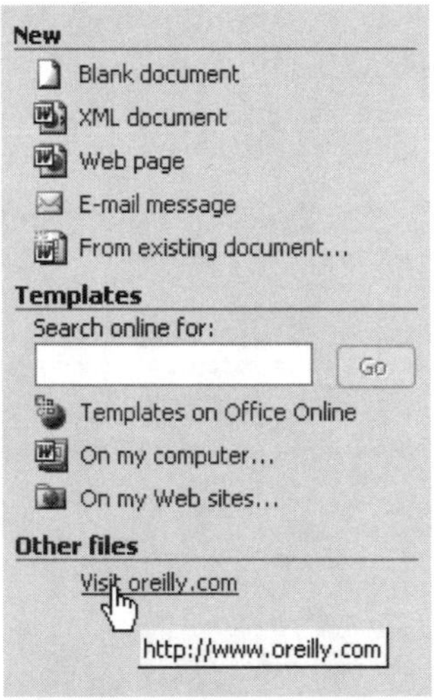

Figure 2-22. Putting an Internet hyperlink on the Task Pane

To run the *.reg* file, just double-click its icon.

Browse All Button Images

HACK #10

When you start adding buttons or menus to a document or template, it would be nice to have more than a few button images to choose from. This hack shows you how to browse all the button images available on your system.

Customized toolbars and menus can be easier to work with when they're labeled with meaningful images. You can modify most toolbar buttons (both custom and built-in) when you open the Customize dialog (select Tools → Customize). But when you right-click a button and choose Change Button Image, you're presented with a pretty limited selection, as shown in Figure 2-23.

In addition to this modest assortment, Microsoft Office includes more than 4,000 button images, or *faces*, that you can use or adapt as needed. Unfortunately, these poorly documented buttons can be difficult to access without

Figure 2-23. The selection of available button images seems quite limited

using VBA code (and even then, it helps if you know the *face ID number* of
the image).

If you want access to all the options, you can download a freeware add-in
from *http://www.mvps.org/skp/fidcode.htm* that lets you browse all the Office
faces, 100 at a time. The FaceID browser, shown in Figure 2-24, displays as
a separate toolbar. When you hover your mouse over one of the buttons, the
program displays its face ID number as a ToolTip.

Figure 2-24. Browsing available button images with the FaceID browser

Once you find an image you like, you can transfer it from the FaceID
browser to a button on your toolbar. For example, let's say you want to put
a button for the macro to unlink every hyperlink in a document [Hack #28]
right next to the Hyperlink button on the Standard toolbar.

First, put a button for the macro on your toolbar [Hack #1]. Next, select an appropriate image from the FaceID browser, such as the one selected in Figure 2-24. Open the Customize dialog (select Tools → Customize), right-click the button with the image you want to copy, and choose Copy Button Image, as shown in Figure 2-25.

Figure 2-25. Copying the image from one button to another

Next, with the Customize dialog still open, right-click the macro button you placed on the Standard toolbar and choose Paste Button Image, as shown in Figure 2-26. Select Default Style so that only the image appears on your button, as shown in Figure 2-27.

Hacking the Hack

When you create a toolbar or menu item from VBA code, you can specify which image to include by referencing its face ID. The face ID numbers have little organization, but they do tend to group together some related items. For example, the following macro creates an attractive (but nonfunctional) toolbar using the standard four card suits, as shown in Figure 2-28.

In addition to setting the image, you can also specify what text will appear when the mouse hovers over the button, using the TooltipText property:

```
Sub MakeNewToolbar( )
Dim cbar As CommandBar
Dim cbarctrl As CommandBarControl
Set cbar = CommandBars.Add(Name:="Pick a Card", Position:=msoBarFloating)
```

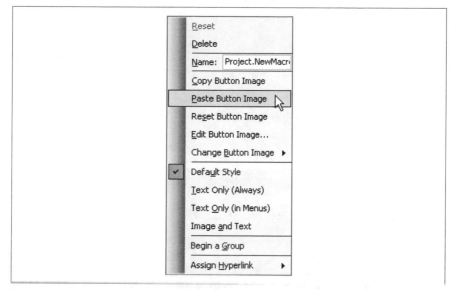

Figure 2-26. Pasting a button image onto a toolbar control

Figure 2-27. The new Unlink Hyperlinks button on the Standard toolbar

Figure 2-28. A new (nonfunctional) toolbar

```
Set cbarctrl = cbar.Controls.Add(Type:=msoControlButton)
cbarctrl.FaceId = 481
cbarctrl.TooltipText = "Hearts"

Set cbarctrl = cbar.Controls.Add(Type:=msoControlButton)
cbarctrl.FaceId = 482
cbarctrl.TooltipText = "Diamonds"

Set cbarctrl = cbar.Controls.Add(Type:=msoControlButton)
cbarctrl.FaceId = 483
cbarctrl.TooltipText = "Spades"

Set cbarctrl = cbar.Controls.Add(Type:=msoControlButton)
cbarctrl.FaceId = 484
cbarctrl.TooltipText = "Clubs"
```

```
cbar.Visible = True

End Sub
```

—Shyam Pillai

Create a Custom Button Image

HACK #11

Customize your controls with any image you can bitmap—even a favorite photo.

Putting a company logo or even a picture onto a toolbar button can give your Word workspace a truly custom look. Turning any graphic into a toolbar button is easier than it sounds.

The image must be a *.bmp*, *.jpg*, or *.gif* file. The optimal dimensions follow:

- 16×16 pixels
- 24-bit color depth

Word will scale oversized or not perfectly square images, but you'll be more satisfied with the results if you scale and crop the image yourself.

If you want your image to appear cut out, like most of the Word button images, you'll also need a *mask* for your image. The mask is a second image that defines the boundaries of the first. To create the mask, blacken the area of the 16×16 square occupied by your image and leave the rest white. The white area of your mask will be filled in by the toolbar color. You can use an image-processing program such as PhotoShop to do this, but many other programs, including SnagIt from TechSmith (*http://www.techsmith.com*), offer inexpensive image-editing tools.

For example, to create a button image using the animal shown in Figure 2-29, first scale it down to 16×16 pixels and then create a mask, as shown (and magnified considerably) in Figure 2-30.

The Code

The following macro creates a new floating toolbar with just one button, containing our sample image. From there, you can use the Copy Button Image and Paste Button Image commands to place the image as needed.

```
Sub DisplayNewImage()
Dim cbar As CommandBar
Dim cbarctrl As CommandBarControl
Dim pImage As IPictureDisp
Dim pMask As IPictureDisp
Dim sImageFile as String
Dim sMaskFile as String
```

Figure 2-29. The base image for a new toolbar button

Figure 2-30. The "mask" image for a toolbar button

```
sImageFile = "C:\Documents and Settings\My Documents\tarsier.bmp"
sMaskFile = "C:\Documents and Settings\My Documents\mask.bmp"

Set cbar = CommandBars.Add(Name:="My Picture", Position:=msoBarFloating)

Set cbarctrl = cbar.Controls.Add(Type:=msoControlButton)
Set pImage = stdole.StdFunctions.LoadPicture(sImageFile)
Set pMask = stdole.StdFunctions.LoadPicture(sMaskFile)

cbarctrl.Picture = pImage
cbarctrl.Mask = pMask

cbar.visible = True

End Sub
```

Running the macro produces the toolbar shown in Figure 2-31.

Hacking the Hack

If you'd rather hack on the existing buttons, you can capture and save the button images to file.

Figure 2-31. A button image created from a bitmapped image

The following macro goes through every button on all the toolbars and saves the images and their masks to a folder called *C:\Buttons*, which you should create before running the macro. Each file is named using the control's ID and saved as a *.bmp* file.

```
Sub GetButtonImageAndMask( )

Dim cbar As CommandBar
Dim cbarctrl As CommandBarControl

For Each cbar In Application.CommandBars
    For Each cbarctrl In cbar.Controls
        If cbarctrl.Type = msoControlButton Then
            stdole.SavePicture cbarctrl.Picture, _
                "c:\buttons\" & cbarctrl.ID & "_img.bmp"
            stdole.SavePicture cbarctrl.Mask, _
                "c:\buttons\" & cbarctrl.ID & "_mask.bmp"
        End If
    Next cbarctrl
Next cbar
End Sub
```

Once you've got the bitmap files, you can open and edit them as shown in Figure 2-32 (a screen shot from the SnagIt program mentioned earlier).

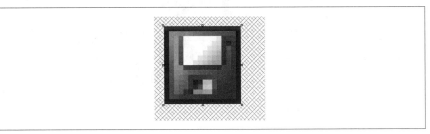

Figure 2-32. After saving the button images as files, you can edit them with an image-editing software program

Hack the Office Assistant

#12   Keep Clippit—Microsoft's annoying computer help character—on a short leash with the techniques shown in this hack.

Ironically, the Office Assistant can be one of the more difficult features to manage in Word. But the Assistant can also be a powerful way to deliver a message to the user of a macro. The following examples take sort of an aikido approach: turning the power of its irritation to a positive end.

Banishing the Assistant

Among the more common reactions to the Assistant are requests to get rid of the wretched thing, immediately and permanently. So for many users, including the following line of code in an AutoExec macro [Hack #60] is the quickest way to a Clippit-free life:

```
Assistant.On = False
```

Finding a Sympathetic Character

You can switch from one Office Assistant character to another even more easily via VBA than via the Office Assistant's interface. To change characters, use the Filename property of the Assistant object:

```
Assistant.Filename = "OffCat.acs"
```

The quickest way to run this one-liner is from the Immediate window of the Visual Basic Editor [Hack #2], as shown in Figure 2-33.

Figure 2-33. Changing the Assistant character from the Immediate window

The available Office Assistant characters depend on your version of Office and the characters installed. Check the *C:\Program Files\Microsoft Office\ <Version>* folder for *.acs* files (Microsoft Agent Character files). The name of the last folder, *<Version>*, depends on the version of Office involved—for example, OFFICE11 is typical for Office 2003.

Your selection may vary, but a list of the usual suspects for a typical installation follows:

- *F1.acs*
- *CLIPPIT.acs*
- *DOT.acs*

- *ROCKY.acs*
- *OFFCAT.acs*
- *MNATURE.acs*
- *LOGO.acs*

Invoking Invisibility

The Office Assistant just lurks in the background until you make a mistake that triggers its appearance. You can toggle the Office Assistant's visibility by setting its `Visible` property to `True` or `False`:

```
Assistant.Visible = True
```

You'll need to make sure the Assistant is turned on (`Assistant.On = True`) before you make it visible. Making the Assistant visible doesn't automatically turn it on. Again, you can quickly make this change from the Immediate window, as described above.

Getting the User's Attention

The Office Assistant usually appears (if currently hidden) or plays an animation (if displayed, but ignored) to get your attention. To play an animation, use `Assistant.Animation`. You can select animations—`msoAnimationAppear`, `msoAnimationEmptyTrash`, `msoAnimationRestPose`, and `msoAnimationSearching`—from the auto-complete list provided by the Visual Basic Editor.

The following code summons the Assistant for delivering an urgent message:

```
Assistant.Animation = msoAnimationGetAttentionMajor
```

Displaying Information and Presenting Choices

To display information and present choices to the user, you use a balloon from the Office Assistant.

The following code displays the Assistant as shown in Figure 2-34. By checking the state of the Assistant before displaying the message, the macro can decide whether or not to turn off the Assistant after it finishes.

```
Sub OA_CheckForMktngTemplate( )
Dim sMarketingTemplate As String
Dim blnAssistantWasOn As Boolean

sMarketingTemplate = "Marketing.dot"
If ActiveDocument.AttachedTemplate = sMarketingTemplate Then Exit Sub
With Assistant
    blnAssistantWasOn = .On
    .On = True
    .Visible = True
```

Figure 2-34. Use the Office Assistant to present information and straightforward choices from within a macro

```
        .Animation = msoAnimationGetAttentionMajor
    With .NewBalloon
        .Heading = "Attach Correct Template"
        .Text = "This document doesn't use the new Marketing template."
        .BalloonType = msoBalloonTypeBullets
        .Labels(1).Text = "You must use the Marketing template"
        .Labels(2).Text = "Press OK to attach now"
        .Icon = msoIconAlertQuery
        .Button = msoButtonSetOkCancel
        If .Show = msoBalloonButtonOK Then
            ActiveDocument.AttachedTemplate = sMarketingTemplate
        End If
    End With
    .On = blnAssistantWasOn
End With
End Sub
```

You can display your message using a variety of balloons, icons, and buttons, as detailed in the following tables.

Table 2-1 lists the types of balloons you can display.

Table 2-1. The three types of Assistant balloons

Balloon type	Constant	Value
Balloon with buttons (default)	msoBalloonTypeButtons	0
Balloon with bullets	msoBalloonTypeBullets	1
Balloon with numbered list	msoBalloonTypeNumbers	2

To control the text that appears in the balloon, use the following properties:

Heading

Displays a heading at the top of the balloon. You can use only one heading.

Text

Displays a single paragraph of text.

Labels(n).Text

Displays a bulleted or numbered paragraph, depending on the balloon type.

Table 2-2 lists the six icons you can display with the balloon (you can also display no icon).

Table 2-2. The icon choices for the Assistant dialogs

Icon	Constant	Value
No icon (default)	msoIconNone	0
Alert	msoIconAlert	2
Tip	msoIconTip	3
Information	msoIconAlertInfo	4
Warning	msoIconAlertWarning	5
Question mark	msoIconAlertQuery	6
Critical problem	msoIconAlertCritical	7

Table 2-3 lists the various button options for dismissing the dialog.

Table 2-3. The button options for the Assistant dialogs

Buttons	Constant	Value
No buttons	msoButtonSetNone	0
OK	msoButtonSetOK	1
Cancel	msoButtonSetCancel	2
OK, Cancel	msoButtonSetOkCancel	3
Yes, No, Cancel	msoButtonSetYesNoCancel	4
Yes, No	msoButtonSetYesNo	5

Table 2-3. *The button options for the Assistant dialogs (continued)*

Buttons	Constant	Value
Back, Close	msoButtonSetBackClose	6
Next, Close	msoButtonSetNextClose	7
Back, Next, Close	msoButtonSetBackNextClose	8
Retry, Cancel	msoButtonSetRetryCancel	9
Abort, Retry, Ignore	msoButtonSetAbortRetryIgnore	10
Search, Close	msoButtonSetSearchClose	11
Back, Next, Snooze	msoButtonSetBackNextSnooze	12

—*Guy Hart-Davis*

HACK #13   Build a Better MRU

Summon more than your nine most recently used files at the touch of a button with this hack.

When you work in Word, you often need to access files you were using earlier. To help you, Word provides a list of the most recently used files: the MRU, which appears by default at the bottom of the File menu.

How Word's MRU Works

Barring any action on your part, Word automatically adds files to the MRU when you do the following:

- Open an existing document.
- Save a file for the first name.
- Use the Save As command to save a file under a different name.

> When you open a file from a macro, you can use the
> AddToRecentFiles property to prevent Word from adding it
> to the MRU:
>
> ```
> Documents.Open FileName:="Foo.doc",_
>     AddToRecentFiles:=False
> ```

Generally, the MRU works well for light users of Word. To change the number of entries on the MRU, select Tools → Options, click the General tab, and adjust the "Recently used file list" setting, as shown in Figure 2-35. Word can remember up to nine of your most recently used files, or you can choose zero to disable the MRU.

If you want to wipe the MRU clean, clear the checkbox, close the Options dialog box, reopen it, and specify how many entries you want for your fresh

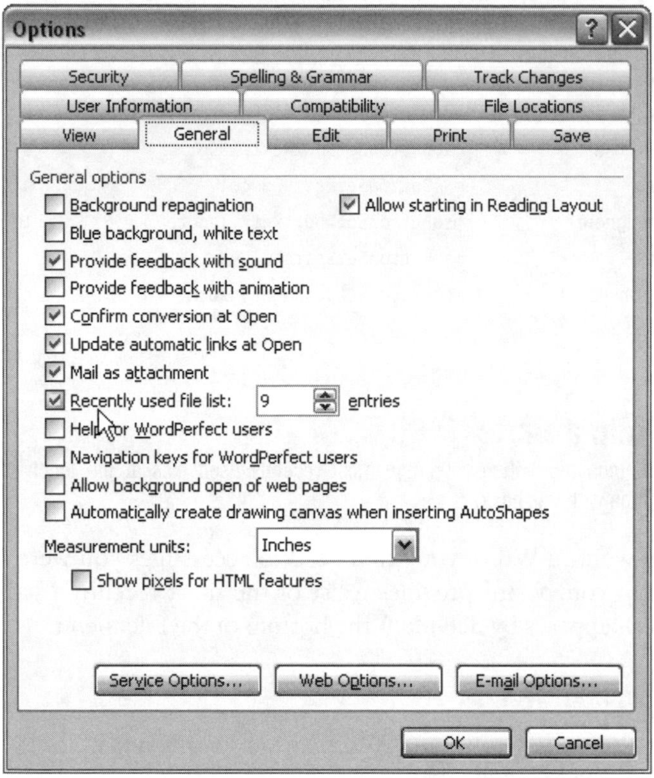

Figure 2-35. Changing your MRU settings

start. (Remember that other lists, such as the My Recent Documents list in Windows XP and Windows 2000, can still betray your indiscretions.)

> You'll confuse the MRU if you delete, move, or rename any of the files it currently lists. Word will suggest you check the file's permissions, make sure you have enough free memory and disk space to open the document, or open the file with the Text Recovery converter. But it will not remove the file from the MRU, as you probably expect (and want).

The MRU is handy, but for a power user it doesn't go nearly far enough. If you open 90 documents each day, a list of 9 is a waste of time. Here's how to pump up the MRU to power-user proportions, creating a MegaMRU.

Getting Started

You will implement this MegaMRU as a user form (see Figure 2-36) that displays the names of the last 25 documents you used in Word. To open a document, select it from the list and click the Open button.

```
Most Recently Used Word Documents                                    [X]

Most Recently Used Documents

D:\Documents and Settings\All Users\Documents\Examples\Industrial Decline and Fail.doc
D:\Documents and Settings\All Users\Documents\Examples\Document with pictures and links.doc
D:\Documents and Settings\All Users\Documents\Examples\The Institute of Mental Health.doc
D:\Documents and Settings\All Users\Documents\PC\Incorp\587205ta.doc
D:\Documents and Settings\All Users\Documents\Examples\Yet Another Test Document.doc
Z:\Public\Document\Budget\Memos\Description of the 2005 Budget Process for All Departments.do
Z:\Public\Document\Budget\Memos\Description of the 2005 Budget Process for All Departments - St
Z:\Public\Document\Budget\Memos\Description of the 2005 Budget Process for All Departments (or
C:\Private\Ballad of the Black Helicopters.doc
Z:\Public\Document\Budget\Memos\Description of the 2005 Budget Process for All Departments [Ja
D:\Documents and Settings\All Users\Documents\PC\Edit\Ch01.doc
D:\Documents and Settings\All Users\Documents\PC\Edit\Ch08.doc
D:\Documents and Settings\All Users\Documents\PC\Edit\Ch07.doc
D:\Documents and Settings\All Users\Documents\PC\Edit\Ch06.doc
D:\Documents and Settings\All Users\Documents\PC\Edit\Ch05.doc
D:\Documents and Settings\All Users\Documents\PC\Backup\Back02.doc
D:\Documents and Settings\All Users\Documents\PC\Backup\Back04.doc
D:\Documents and Settings\All Users\Documents\PC\Backup\Back11.doc
C:\Private\email0503.doc
D:\Documents and Settings\All Users\Documents\PC\Backup\Back09.doc
c:\Ref\Photo Guidelines.doc
c:\Ref\Naming Conventions.doc
c:\Ref\AutoCorrect Entries.doc
c:\Private\Clean Break in the FEMA.doc
c:\temp\scratch44.doc

                    [ Open ]        [ Cancel ]
```

Figure 2-36. A custom MRU lets you access far more of your recent documents

The key to this hack is the `PrivateProfileString` command **[Hack #67]**, which lets you store data in a plain-text *.ini* settings file on your system. For this hack, create the following *.ini* file:

```
[MRU_Files]
MRU01=C:\Dox\Doc 1.doc
MRU02=C:\Dox\Doc 2.doc
```

The Code

The MegaMRU uses an event handler **[Hack #69]** with the `DocumentBeforeClose` event to get its information:

1. Open the Visual Basic Editor and make sure you display the Project Explorer and the Properties window.

2. In the Project Explorer, right-click Normal and select Insert → Class to create a new class in *Normal.dot*. Press F4, type the name for the class (MRUClass), and press Enter.

3. Press F7 to activate the Code window for the class module and insert the following code, which will ignore unsaved documents. It will, however, alert you to save previously saved documents.

```
Public WithEvents MyMRU As Word.Application

Private Sub MyMRU_DocumentBeforeClose(ByVal Doc As Document, _
    Cancel As Boolean)
With ActiveDocument
    If .Path <> "" Then
            Add_to_MRU
        Else
            If .Saved = False Then
                Select Case MsgBox("Do you want to save the changes " & _
                                    "to " & .Name & "?", _
                    vbYesNoCancel + vbExclamation, _
                    "Microsoft Office Word")
                Case vbYes
                    Dialogs(wdDialogFileSaveAs).Show
                    If .Saved = True Then Add_to_MRU
                Case vbNo
                    .Close SaveChanges:=wdDoNotSaveChanges
                Case vbCancel
                    End
                End Select
            End If
        End If
    End With
End Sub
```

4. Click the Close button to close the MRUClass window.

Creating the MRU module. Next, create a code module in *Normal.dot* with the macro for initializing the class module, the macro for displaying the user form, and the macro for adding items to the MRU. To create a new module, select Normal in the Project Explorer and choose Insert → Module. Select the module and change its name in the Properties window to MegaMRU. You should place the rest of the code in this section in the MegaMRU module.

Initializing the class module. The code for initializing the class module consists of a declaration of MyMRU as a new member of the MRU class and a short macro that assigns the Word.Application object to the MyMRU property of the MyMRU object:

```
Dim MyMRU As New MRUClass

Sub Initialize_MyMRU( )
    Set MyMRU.MyMRU = Word.Application
End Sub
```

Each time you start Word, you must run the `Initialize_MyMRU` macro to start your event handler. Usually, you put a call to the macro in your `AutoExec` macro **[Hack #60]**. If you don't have an `AutoExec` macro already, you can simply name the `Initialize_MyMRU` macro above `AutoExec` instead.

Displaying the user form. To display the user form, use its `Show` method:

```
Sub Open_MyMRU( )
    frmMRU.Show
End Sub
```

Because you'll use this macro to open one of the documents on your MRU, create a menu item, a toolbar button, or a keyboard shortcut **[Hack #1]** for the macro—or even all three.

Adding a document's information to the MRU. The macro for adding a document's information to the MRU moves all the existing entries in the MRU list (except the last entry) one place down the list: item 25 drops off the list, item 24 moves to item 25, item 23 moves to item 24, and so forth. (You use a `For... Next` loop with a negative increment to make this change, because working positively propagates the same item through the list: item 1 becomes 2 becomes 3 becomes 4, and so on.) The new document then enters at the top of the chart.

```
Sub Add_to_MRU( )
    Dim i As Integer
    For i = 24 To 1 Step -1
    System.PrivateProfileString(FileName:="c:\windows\mru.ini", _
        Section:="MRU_Files", Key:="MRU" & Format(i + 1, "00")) = _
        System.PrivateProfileString(FileName:="c:\windows\mru.ini", _
        Section:="MRU_Files", Key:="MRU" & Format(i, "00"))
    Next i
    System.PrivateProfileString(FileName:="c:\windows\mru.ini", _
        Section:="MRU_Files", Key:="MRU01") = ActiveDocument.FullName
End Sub
```

Creating the User Form

Here's how to create the user form used to display the MegaMRU, as shown in Figure 2-36:

1. Right-click Normal in the Project Explorer and select Insert → UserForm.

2. Press F4 to activate the Properties window, type frmMRU as the name, and press Enter.

3. Use the down arrow key to move to the Caption property, type **Most Recently Used Word Documents** as its value, and press Enter.

4. Increase the user form's height to about 350 pixels and its width to about 400 pixels. (Either drag the sizing handle or type the measurements in the Properties window.)

5. Add a label with the caption **Most Recently Used Documents**, with AutoSize set to True and WordWrap set to False. Position the label at the upper-left corner of the user form.

6. Add a listbox, name it lstMRU, and make it about 250 pixels high and 360 pixels wide. To make sure the user can select only one item in the list at a time, set the MultiSelect property to 0 - fmMultiSelectSingle. Center the listbox horizontally in the user form (Select Format → Center In Form → Horizontally).

7. Create a command button named cmdOpen, set Accelerator to 0, set Caption to Open, set Default to True, and set Enabled to False. You may want to reduce the button's height and width a little from the (rather big) default measurements.

8. Create a second command button. Name this one cmdCancel, set its Accelerator to C, set Cancel to True, set Caption to Cancel, set Default to False, and make sure Enabled is True. If you changed the height or width of cmdOpen, make this button the same size.

9. Select and group the buttons (Format → Group), position the group at the bottom of the user form, and center it horizontally.

Adding the Code to the User Form

After laying out the user form, select the user form and press F7 to display its code sheet in a window. Then create the following four macros.

Creating the UserForm_Initialize macro. The UserForm_Initialize macro adds the items in the MRU file to the listbox in the user form. This macro runs when you call the user form.

```
Private Sub UserForm_Initialize( )
Dim i As Integer
For i = 1 To 25
    lstMRU.AddItem System.PrivateProfileString( ,_
        FileName:="d:\windows\mru.ini", _
        Section:="MRU_Files", Key:="MRU" & Format(i, "00"))
    Next i
End Sub
```

Creating the lstMRU_Click macro. The `lstMRU_Click` macro enables the cmdOpen button on the user form as soon as the user clicks an entry. This macro prevents the user from clicking the Open button with no entry selected.

```
Private Sub lstMRU_Click( )
    cmdOpen.Enabled = True
End Sub
```

Creating the cmdCancel_Click macro. The `cmdCancel_Click` macro hides the user form and then unloads it from memory after the user clicks the Cancel button:

```
Private Sub cmdCancel_Click( )
    frmMRU.Hide
    Unload frmMRU
End Sub
```

Creating the cmdOpen_Click macro. The `cmdOpen_Click` macro hides the user form, opens the document corresponding to the item chosen in the listbox, and then unloads the user form from memory. This macro also contains a short error handler, but it reports an error only if Word can't find the file.

```
Private Sub cmdOpen_Click( )
    On Error GoTo Trap
    frmMRU.Hide
    Documents.Open lstMRU.Value
    Unload frmMRU
    End
Trap:
    If Err.Number = 5174 Then MsgBox "Word cannot find the file " _
        & lstMRU.Value & "." _
        & vbCr & vbCr &_
            "The file may have been renamed, moved, or deleted.", vbOKOnly ˃
    vbCritical, "MRU - File Not Found"
End Sub
```

After you make your changes, click the Save Normal button in the Visual Basic Editor to save *Normal.dot*.

Using the MRU

With all these items in place, you're ready to use the user form. Run the `Initialize_MyMRU` macro to initialize your event handler, which will start monitoring Word's document closures. Each document you close will be added in turn to your MRU. To open a document on your MRU, use the menu, toolbar, or keyboard customization you created to display the user form. Next, click the document in the listbox and click the Open button.

Hacking the Hack

You can modify the MegaMRU in several ways:

- Increase the number of documents involved. You can track as many documents as you want, but you will likely reach the point of diminishing returns somewhere between 100 and 200 documents. If you add too many entries to the list, rewriting the *.ini* file can slow down an aging PC, but today's brawny processors sneer at such trivial tasks. To increase the number of files to, for example, 100, change the 25 in the UserForm_Initialize procedure to 100 and the 24 in the Add_to_MRU procedure to 99.

- To present the documents on the MRU list by date, file size, or another useful attribute, create a separate section for each document within the *.ini* file: MRUFile01 for the first document, MRUFile02 for the second document, and so on. You can then use the keys to create further subdivisions of data:

```
[MRUFile01]
Name=c:\dox\Example 1.doc
Size=144048
Creator=Adam Schmidt
[MRUFile02]
Name=Z:\Public\Memo 1443.doc
Size=256074
Creator=Stelios Jones
```

- To exclude certain documents, folders, or templates from the MRU, add one line to the MyMRU_DocumentBeforeClose procedure. For example, to exclude documents based on a template named *Secret.dot*, make the following the first line of the Add_to_MRU macro:

```
If ActiveDocument.AttachedTemplate = "Secret.dot" Then Exit Sub
```

—Guy Hart-Davis

CHAPTER THREE

Formatting, Printing, and Table Hacks

Hacks 14–26

Word is increasingly being pressed into service as a desktop publishing program, for everything from simple forms and newsletters to custom pieces destined for a professional printing shop. The hacks in this chapter show how to go beyond the basics of several formatting features to make Word a more useful tool for creating high-quality documents.

HACK #14 Insert Placeholder Text

When designing a template or experimenting with formatting, sometimes you just need text—any text—to play around with.

To quickly and easily fill a paragraph, a page, or an entire document with text, just type the following on a blank line in any open document and press Enter:

```
=rand( )
```

By default, you get three paragraphs with four sentences each, as shown in Figure 3-1. The sentence used depends on the language of your version of Word. The English version uses "The quick brown fox jumps over the lazy dog," which happens to use every letter in the alphabet.

If you need more or less than the default amount of text, provide numerical values to the rand( ) function:

```
=rand(paragraphs, sentences)
```

Both arguments are optional, but if you want to specify the number of *sentences*, you must also specify the number of *paragraphs*.

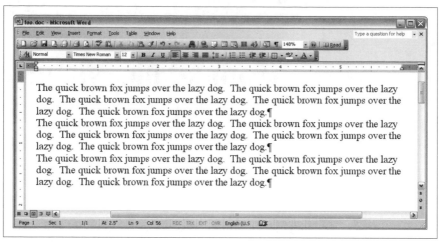

Figure 3-1. Word's placeholder text

> This little trick works only if you select Tools → AutoCorrect Options, click the AutoCorrect tab, and check the "Replace text as you type" box.

Make Your Own Placeholder Text with AutoCorrect

If foxes and dogs aren't for you, you can create your own placeholder text as an AutoText entry.

> The template on which you based the current document stores all new AutoText entries. If you did not explicitly choose a template, the Normal template will store the new entry, and it will then be available in all your documents.

Type your placeholder text, select it, and choose Insert → AutoText → New. Choose a name for the placeholder text, as shown in Figure 3-2. You should choose a name that you won't likely type for any other reason.

Now whenever you type the name of the AutoText entry, Word will offer to insert your placeholder text, as shown in Figure 3-3.

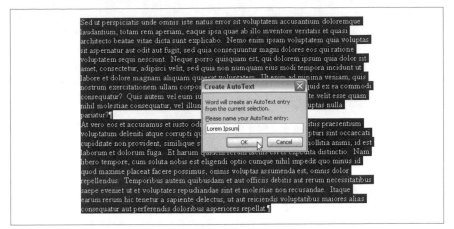

Figure 3-2. *Choose a name for your placeholder AutoText entry that won't likely come up elsewhere in a document*

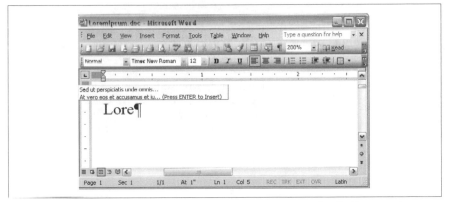

Figure 3-3. *As you type the name of your AutoText entry, Word will offer to replace it with the predefined text*

Sample Your System Fonts

Your system probably offers more than 100 fonts. How do you choose the right one? If you rely on simple trial and error, you'll quickly find yourself frustrated. Instead, use this hack to get a sample of every available font.

They say there's no accounting for taste, and that's certainly true about fonts. With hundreds of fonts coming preinstalled on most computers, and thousands more available for purchase online, there's something for everybody.

The tried-and-true method of choosing a font in Word is to select some text and then scroll through the Font pull-down menu on the Formatting toolbar until something strikes your fancy. But when you can see only about a dozen fonts at a time, as in Figure 3-4, it's hard to compare all your options.

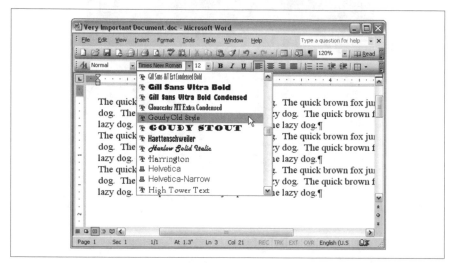

Figure 3-4. It's difficult to compare over 100 fonts when you can see only 12 at a time

> You can stop Word from displaying your most recently used fonts at the top of the font list. Open up the Windows registry and find the following registry key:
>
> HKEY_CURRENT_USER\Software\Microsoft\Office*Version*\ Word\Options
>
> Add a new String value (Edit → New) named NoFontMRUList and give it a value of 1.

Word includes a built-in Font menu, but it's not part of the main menu bar by default. To view it, select Tools → Customize, click the Commands tab, and select "Built-in Menus" from the Categories list. In the Commands section, select the Font menu and drag it to your main menu bar.

You can scroll through the font menu as described above, but a more efficient, more organized, and more fruitful method of comparing your fonts would be to generate a table of some sample text, formatted in each of the available fonts on your system.

This hack creates a new document containing a two-column table with a row for each available font. The first column lists the font's name, and the second column provides some sample formatted text. The macro sorts the font names alphabetically. A portion of the results is shown in Figure 3-5.

Goudy Old Style	abcdefghijklmnopqrstuvwxyz ABCDEFGHIJKLMNOPQRSTUVWXYZ 0123456789 ,.:;!@#$%^&*()
Goudy Stout	**ABCDEFGHIJKLMN** **OPQRSTUVWXYZ** **ABCDEFGHIJKLMN** **OPQRSTUVWXYZ** **0123456789** **,.:;!@#$%^&*()**
Haettenschweiler	abcdefghijklmnopqrstuvwxyz ABCDEFGHIJKLMNOPQRSTUVWXYZ 0123456789 ,.:;!@#$%^&*()

Figure 3-5. Font sampler output

If you have a large number of fonts installed, this macro could take a few
moments to run.

The Code

The new document this macro creates will be based on the Normal template, and the font names will be displayed in Times, a standard font nearly
guaranteed to be on any computer.

Put the following code in the template of your choice [Hack #50]:

```
Sub FontSampleTable()
Dim vFontName As Variant
Dim iFontCount As Integer
Dim i As Integer
Dim tbl As Table
Dim sSampleText As String
Dim doc As Document
Dim rng As Range

sSampleText = "abcdefghijklmnopqrstuvwxyz"
sSampleText = sSampleText & Chr$(32) & UCase(sSampleText)
sSampleText = sSampleText & Chr$(32) & "0123456789"
sSampleText = sSampleText & Chr$(32) & ",.:;!@#$%^&*()"
Application.ScreenUpdating = False

Set doc = Documents.Add
iFontCount = Application.FontNames.Count

Set rng = doc.Range
rng.Font.Name = "Times"
rng.InsertAfter ("Font Name" & vbTab & "Sample" & vbCr)
i = 1
For Each vFontName In Application.FontNames
```

```
            StatusBar = "Preparing Sample " & i & " of " & _
                    iFontCount & " available fonts: " & vFontName
        rng.Collapse wdCollapseEnd
        rng.InsertAfter (vFontName & vbTab & sSampleText & vbCr)
        rng.Font.Name = vFontName
        i = i + 1
    Next vFontName

    StatusBar = "Formatting Sample Table ... Please Wait"

    doc.Content.ConvertToTable Format:=wdTableFormatWeb1
    Set tbl = doc.Tables(1)

    tbl.Rows.First.Range.Font.Bold = True
    tbl.Rows.First.HeadingFormat = True
    tbl.Columns.First.Select

    Selection.Font.Name = "Times"
    Selection.Rows.AllowBreakAcrossPages = False
    Selection.Collapse wdCollapseStart

    tbl.SortAscending

    StatusBar = "Done"
    Application.ScreenUpdating = True
    End Sub
```

To help speed things along, this macro takes advantage of Word's
ScreenUpdating property. If you set it to False at the start of the macro,
Word will not waste valuable CPU resources constantly redrawing the display. While screen updating will automatically resume once the macro finishes, it's considered good form to explicitly restore it at the end of your
code.

Because this macro may take a few minutes to run on a computer with a lot
of fonts installed, you can use the StatusBar property to report on the code's
progress [Hack #65]. The status bar provides meaningful user feedback, particularly if the macro takes time to run. Setting the ScreenUpdating property to
False will not affect the status bar.

Hacking the Hack

With a few modifications, the generated table can use selected text instead
of arbitrary sample characters. This trick is especially useful if your text contains symbols or special characters that may not be defined in certain type-
faces, as in the case of the Harrington font, shown in Figure 3-6.

The following code is a variation of the FontSampleTable macro shown
above. With this version, the macro uses the currently selected text as the

Harlow Solid Italic	™©§®½¼¾
Harrington	™ © § ® □□□
Helvetica	™©§®½¼¾
Helvetica-Narrow	™©§®½¼¾
High Tower Text	™©§®½¼¾
Impact	™©§®½¼¾
Imprint MT Shadow	™©§®½¼¾
Informal Roman	™©§®½¼¾

Figure 3-6. Seeing samples of special characters can help you narrow the choices among fonts on your system

sample text for each font. If you select more than one paragraph, it uses only the text in the first paragraph.

```
Sub FontSamplesUsingSelection()
Dim sel As Selection
Dim vFontName As Variant
Dim iFontCount As Integer
Dim i As Integer
Dim tbl As Table
Dim sSampleText As String
Dim doc As Document
Dim rng As Range

Set sel = Selection
If sel.Characters.Count >= sel.Paragraphs.First.Range.Characters.Count Then
    sSampleText = sel.Paragraphs.First.Range.Text
    ' Need to strip off the trailing Paragraph mark
    ' for the table to generate properly
    sSampleText = Left$(sSampleText, Len(sSampleText) - 1)
Else
    sSampleText = sel.Text
End If
Application.ScreenUpdating = False

Set doc = Documents.Add
iFontCount = Application.FontNames.Count

Set rng = doc.Range
rng.Font.Name = "Times"
rng.InsertAfter "Font Name" & vbTab & "Sample" & vbCr
i = 1
For Each vFontName In Application.FontNames
    StatusBar = "Preparing Sample " & i & " of " & iFontCount & _
```

```
                " available fonts: " & vFontName
                rng.Collapse wdCollapseEnd
                rng.InsertAfter vFontName & vbTab & sSampleText & vbCr
                rng.Font.Name = vFontName
                i = i + 1
        Next vFontName

        StatusBar = "Formatting Sample Table ... Please Wait"

        doc.Content.ConvertToTable Format:=wdTableFormatWeb1
        Set tbl = doc.Tables(1)

        tbl.Rows.First.Range.Font.Bold = True
        tbl.Rows.First.HeadingFormat = True
        tbl.Columns.First.Select

        Selection.Font.Name = "Times"
        Selection.Rows.AllowBreakAcrossPages = False
        Selection.Collapse wdCollapseStart

        tbl.SortAscending

        StatusBar = "Done"
        Application.ScreenUpdating = True
        End Sub
```

HACK #16 Tab Me to Your Leader

Tables have superseded tab stops, which have largely gone the way of the
IBM Selectric typewriter. However, tabs are still the best tool for the job when
working with leaders. This hack offers some tips for taming those tabs.

People often use tab leaders to fill the spaces between entry spots on forms
filled out by hand, such as job applications or fundraising pledge forms (see
Figure 3-7).

Name _____	Telephone_____	
Address _____ City_____ ZIP _____		

Figure 3-7. Underscore leaders used to underline fill-in spots

Many of these forms are created in what can only be called The Hard Way:
you type the first entry, then type a series of underscores to the next item,
and then fill the rest of the line with underscores. This method will cause
trouble for the person responsible for maintaining the form for two reasons:

- If any text changes, the underscores from one line will either spill over
  to the next or not match up at the end of the line.

- Unless you use a *constant-width* font such as Courier, in which every character is the same width, the ends of each line will rarely line up vertically or extend all the way to the right margin.

But with some planning and the use of one of Word's Drawing features, creating and maintaining forms like this is a breeze.

Because you want each line in the form to use different tab stops, create a separate paragraph in your document for each line. Next, select View → Toolbars → Drawing (the Drawing toolbar may first appear docked to the bottom of your Word window). On the Drawing toolbar, select Draw → Grid to display the dialog shown in Figure 3-8. Input **6 pt** for horizontal and vertical spacing and then check the "Display gridlines on screen" box.

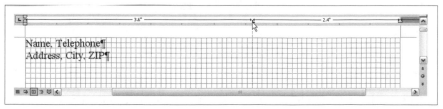

Figure 3-8. Turning on the drawing grid

The drawing grid can help you line up items in a lengthy form. The grid will appear on your screen as shown in Figure 3-9.

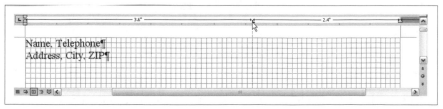

Figure 3-9. Using the grid when setting tab stops can help ensure correct and consistent alignment

Next, double-click the square box at the left edge of the ruler, shown in Figure 3-10, until you get a Left Tab (looks like a capital "L"). If you click your cursor in the ruler, you will insert the tab type (Right, Left, Centered, Decimal) selected in the box.

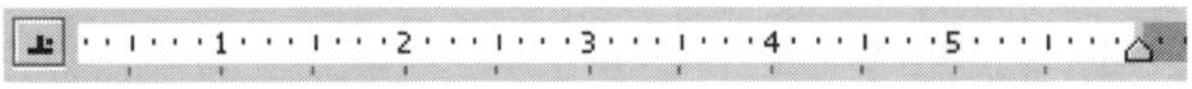

Figure 3-10. You can use the box at the far left of the ruler to choose a type of tab stop

Put your cursor in the first line of your form. Hold down the Alt key, click in the ruler, and drag the tab stop to the desired position, as shown in Figure 3-9. Holding down the Alt key displays the exact position of the cursor, measured from each margin. The location of the tab stop will be where the next word begins. After you've placed a tab stop for each entry in the first line of the form, put one more tab stop at the right edge of the ruler, at the location of the right margin.

Repeat this procedure for each line in the form, setting one tab stop for each entry, then a final tab stop at the right margin.

Next, put your cursor in the first line of the form to create the lines, or *leaders*, that will fill in the spaces between entries. Double-click any of the tabs in the ruler to display the Tabs dialog shown in Figure 3-11.

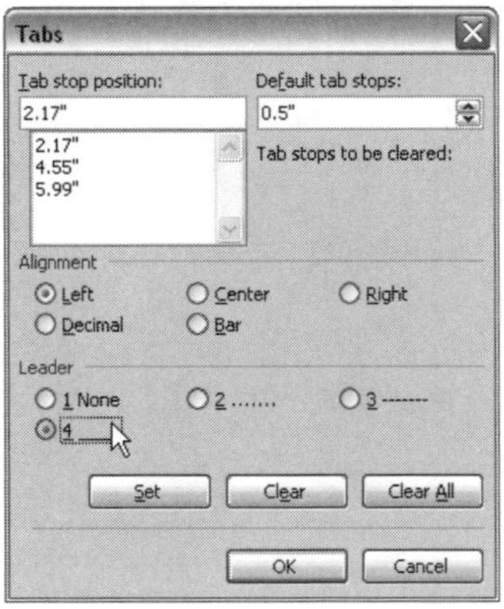

Figure 3-11. Adding the leader to the tab stops

Select the first tab stop listed, then select the radio button next to the underscore leader and click the Set button. Repeat these steps for each of the tab stops in the paragraph, then click the OK button. Follow this procedure for each line in the form.

Though it takes a bit more work up front to set tab stops and leaders, your effort will be repaid many times over.

Make Styles More Manageable with Aliases

Assigning short nicknames to styles can really speed up your formatting time.

To quickly apply a style to selected text, put your cursor in the Styles pull-down menu on the Formatting toolbar, type in the style name, and press Enter.

To instantly move your cursor into the Styles pull-down menu, press Ctrl-Shift-S.

In fact, Word will even attempt to complete the style name as you type, as shown in Figure 3-12. This feature helps if you're applying, say, the Heading 1 style, but it's not much of a shortcut for any of the other heading styles.

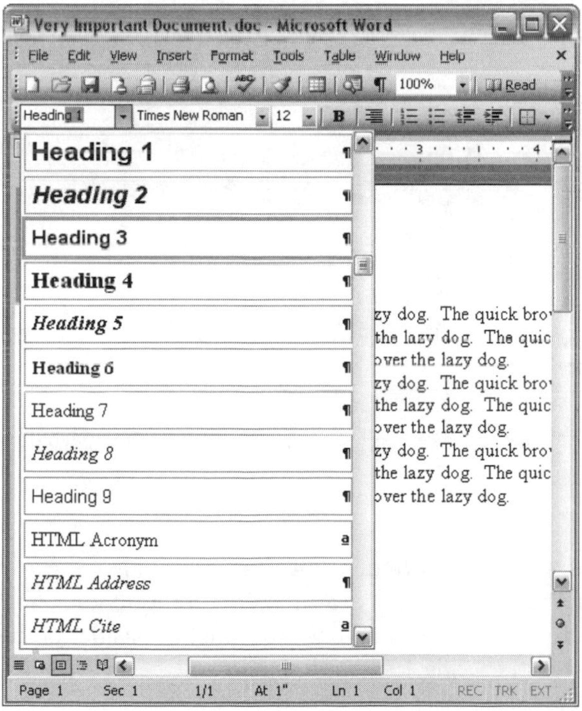

Figure 3-12. Word attempts to automatically complete the style's name as you type

You can't rename any of Word's built-in styles, but if you create an alias to a style (such as "h6" for the Heading 6 style), you can type the alias instead of the style's "real" name into the Styles pull-down menu.

To create an alias for a style, select Format → Styles and Formatting, click the desired style, and choose Modify. Put a comma at the end of the style's name, and then put the alias after the comma (don't include a space after the comma, or it will be interpreted as the first character of your alias's name). Figure 3-13 shows you how to create an alias for the Heading 6 style.

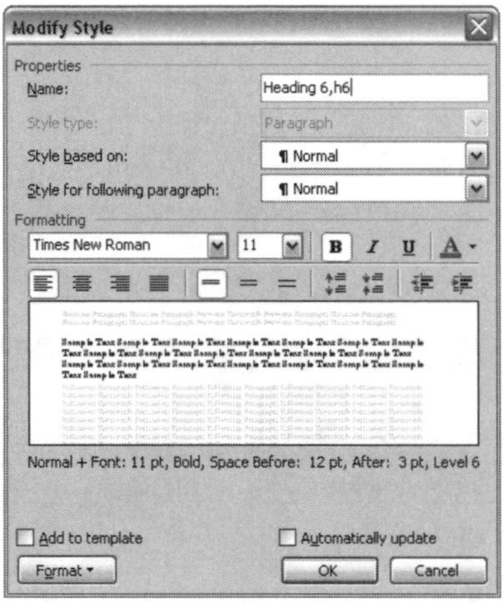

Figure 3-13. To create an alias for a style, just put the alias after a comma at the end of the style's name

Now, to apply the Heading 6 style, just enter "h6" in the Styles pull-down menu and press Enter.

> Styles can have multiple aliases, but no two styles can have the same alias.

In addition to creating shortcut names for styles, aliases can provide alternate descriptions of a style. For example, if you set up your document to use the Heading 1 style for chapter titles, you might consider adding an alias so the style's called "Heading 1,Chapter."

Strings of aliases after each style can look a bit strange in the Styles pull-down menu (see Figure 3-14). But if you use the aliases, you'll rarely see the menu anyway.

Figure 3-14. A list of styles with multiple aliases

Using Aliases in VBA

When you apply a style from a macro, you can use its "real" name, any of its aliases, or its full name, including all of its aliases. For example, if the Heading 6 style had an alias of "h6," as described above, any of the following would apply it to the paragraph referenced by the variable para:

```
para.Style = "Heading 6"
para.Style = "Heading 6,h6"
para.Style = "h6"
para.Style = "h" & CStr(6)
```

Because Heading 6 is one of Word's built-in styles, the following also works:

```
para.Style = wdStyleHeading6
```

You can quickly remove all aliases in a document with a simple macro if, for example, you added aliases to someone else's document while you edited it:

```
Sub RemoveAllStyleAliases
Dim sty As Style
For Each sty In ActiveDocument.Styles
    sty.NameLocal = Split(sty.NameLocal, ",")(0)
Next sty
End Sub
```

The Split function used in this manner just removes everything after, and including, the first comma in the style name. If the style doesn't have any aliases, it leaves the name as is.

Make a Simple Bar Graph

HACK
#18   Simple graphics can really spice up a document. This hack shows you how to create a bar graph by fiddling with some table formatting.

Word can't really match a true layout or graphics program like Quark or Freehand for complex layouts and graphics, but you can use more than text and clip art to create visually appealing documents in Word.

For example, say that each month you dutifully put together the company newsletter in Word. Last month, you asked everyone to cast their votes for the name of the company's new softball team (Lions, Tigers, or Bears). You want to publish the results in the newsletter using a simple bar graph like the one shown in Figure 3-15.

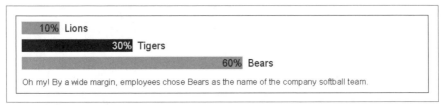

Figure 3-15. A simple bar graph, created with a Word table

To create a simple bar graph, you can just hack a well-planned table. Of course, you'll need to do your own math when measuring the individual bars.

To create the bar graph shown in Figure 3-15, first select Tools → Options, click the General tab, and change your default measurement unit to points. Next, select Table → Insert Table and insert a table with two columns and four rows.

With your cursor inside the table, right-click and choose Table Properties. On the Table tab, click the Options button, and change the cell margins to 0 points on all sides.

Now insert the text for the first three rows, putting the percentage in the first column and the team name in the second column. Select the entire last row, right-click, and choose Merge Cells, as shown in Figure 3-16.

To make the graph accurate, set the widths of each bar proportionate to the percentage of the total that each represents. If you look at the ruler at the top of the page, the right margin just passes the 432-point mark. You can round this number to 400 points and use it as your maximum. In this case, just multiply by four to translate the percentages into point widths. For 10, 30, and 60 percent, you get 40, 120, and 240 points, respectively.

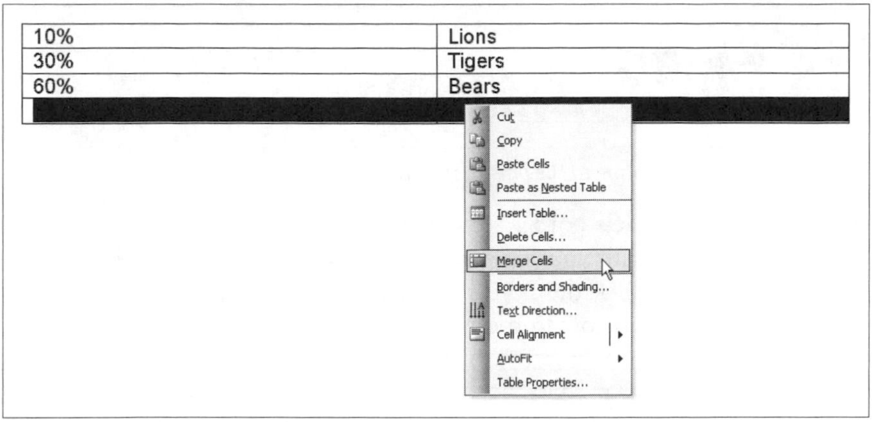

10%	Lions
30%	Tigers
60%	Bears

Figure 3-16. Merging the cells in the last row

Next, select the first cell of the first column in the table. Hold down the Alt key and select the divider between the first and second columns. As you move the divider to the left, notice that the ruler displays the exact width of the cell, as shown in Figure 3-17.

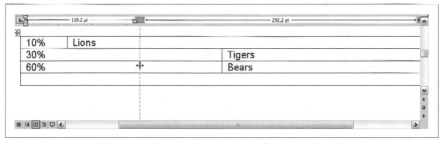

Figure 3-17. With the Alt key depressed, moving a cell divider displays exact measurements in the ruler

You won't likely get an exact match, so set the cell width for just under 40 points. Repeat the steps for the other two percentage cells. Now select the first cell in the table again, right-click, and choose Table Properties. Click the Cell tab and enter **40 pt** in the "Preferred width" box. Repeat this step for the other two percentage cells, specifying the exact size in points.

Next, type the text for the graph's caption in the fourth row of the table.

Now select all three percentages and click the Right Align button on the For-matting toolbar. With your cursor in the first cell, right-click and choose Borders and Shading. Go to the Shading tab and select 30% gray shading. Repeat this for the third row, but apply black to the second, as shown in Figure 3-18.

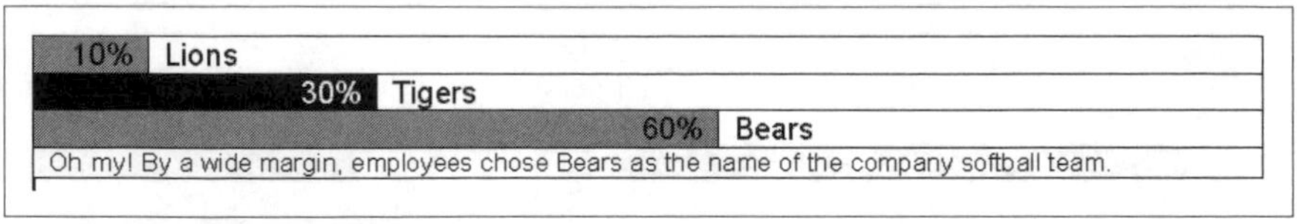

10%	Lions		
	30%	Tigers	
		60%	Bears
Oh my! By a wide margin, employees chose Bears as the name of the company softball team.			

Figure 3-18. Apply shading to the bars in the graph

Now change the table's border setting so that only the outermost edges are set with a border. With your cursor in the table, right-click and choose Borders and Shading. Click the Borders tab, choose the Box setting, and select Table from the "Apply to" drop-down list, as shown in Figure 3-19.

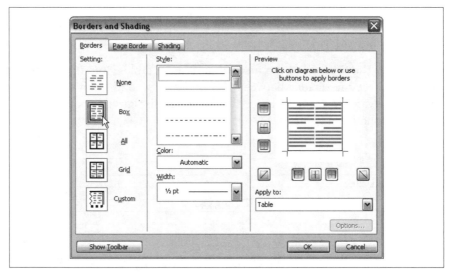

Figure 3-19. Applying the table border

Finally, right-click from within the table and choose Table Properties. Click the Table tab, click the Options button, check the "Allow spacing between cells" box, and put **6 pt** as the spacing, as shown in Figure 3-20.

Your bar graph should now look like the one shown in Figure 3-15.

To use the bar graph again, store it as an AutoText entry. Select the entire table and press Alt-F3. Word will prompt you to name the entry; you should select something you won't likely type otherwise, such as "_bargraph4x3." Whenever you want to insert a similar bar graph, just type the AutoText entry's name.

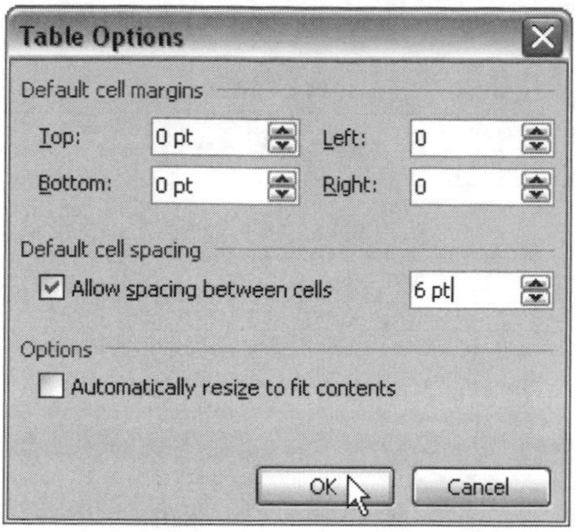

Table Options

Default cell margins

Top: `0 pt`   Left: `0`

Bottom: `0 pt`   Right: `0`

Default cell spacing

☑ Allow spacing between cells   `6 pt`

Options

☐ Automatically resize to fit contents

OK   Cancel

Figure 3-20. Setting the spacing between the cells

Put Footnotes in Tables
#19

This hack shows you how to implement this sorely needed feature in a table.

There's no simple way to create a separate set of footnotes just for a table, but with a few well-placed section breaks, it's at least possible.

Here's how to create a footnote that appears right below the table, as shown in Figure 3-21.

Language	Creator
Perl	Larry Wall[A]
Python	Guido van Rossum
Ruby	Yukihiro Matsumoto

[A] **This is a table footnote**

Figure 3-21. A table with a dedicated footnote

First, while in Normal view (View → Normal), select Insert → Break and insert continuous section breaks directly above and below the table, as shown in Figure 3-22.

Next, put your cursor where the first footnote reference should appear and select Insert → Reference → Footnote to display the Footnote and Endnote dialog, shown in Figure 3-23. Select the Endnotes radio button and choose "End of section" for the location. Choose "A, B, C, ..." as the number

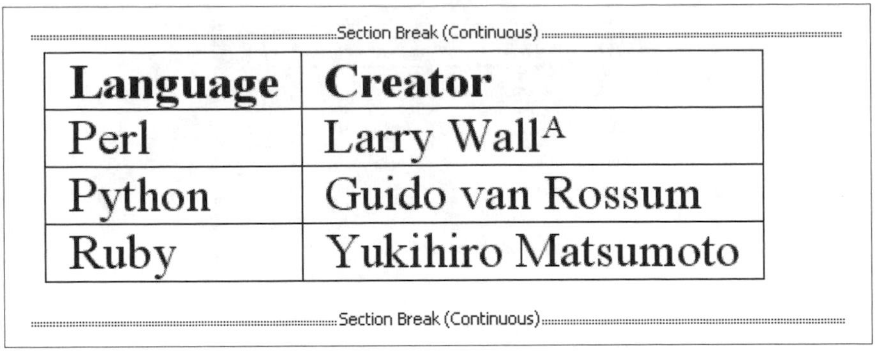

Language	Creator
Perl	Larry Wall[A]
Python	Guido van Rossum
Ruby	Yukihiro Matsumoto

Figure 3-22. The table in Normal view, showing the section breaks

format, select "Restart each section" from the Numbering drop-down list, and click the Apply button.

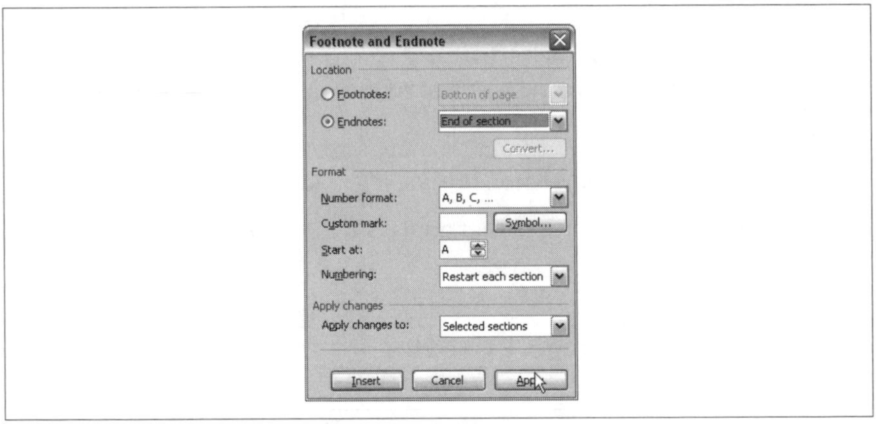

Figure 3-23. Inserting a table footnote as a section endnote

By default, Word includes a horizontal ruler as a separator between the text and the footnotes. To remove this unattractive separator from within Normal view, select View → Footnotes and choose Endnote Separator from the pull-down menu at the top of the Footnotes pane, as shown in Figure 3-24. Just delete the endnote separator and click the OK button to close the Footnotes pane.

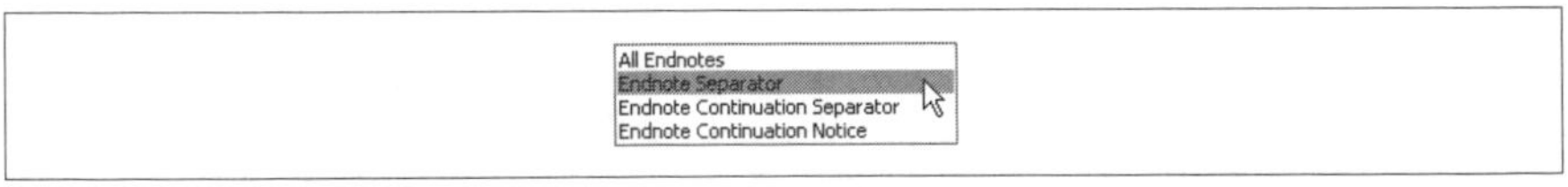

Figure 3-24. Removing the endnote separator

Repeat a Section Heading Across Pages

HACK
#20

Instructions or examples in a document can span multiple pages. This hack
shows you how to help your readers follow along by repeating the heading on
each page.

If you've got a lengthy example, such as a procedure or a sample computer
program, you may want the title of the example to repeat on each page. If
you were absolutely, positively sure your page breaks wouldn't change, you
could duplicate the heading with a REF field at the top of each page.

But what if your page breaks change? Here's a way to get your heading to
repeat on multiple pages.

First, select all of the text in the section, including the heading (you can
always add or remove text later).

Next, select Table → Convert → Text to Table and press the OK button, as
shown in Figure 3-25.

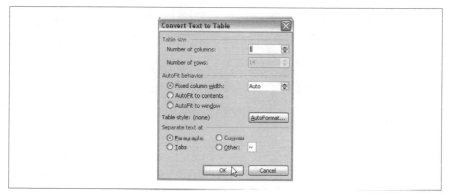

*Figure 3-25. To get your section heading to repeat if the section spans pages, turn it into
a table*

Next, select Table → Table Properties and choose "None" for the border.
Now select just the section heading and again select Table → Table
Properties. Click the Row tab and check the "Repeat as header row at the
top of each page" box, as shown in Figure 3-26.

Now if your section spans multiple pages, the heading will repeat at the top
of each page, as shown in Figure 3-27.

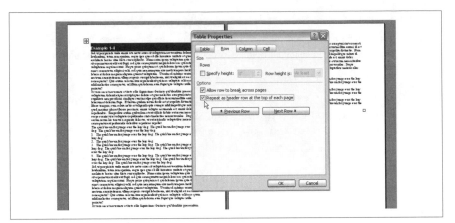

Figure 3-26. Tell Word to repeat the heading on each page

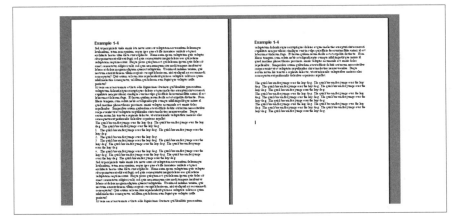

Figure 3-27. Repeating heading rows in action

Simplify Borders Around Imported Images

For a clean, professional look, the borders around imported images in a document should be attractive and consistent. If you create a paragraph style especially for "holding" your images, your image borders will look better and be easier to adjust if needed.

With a "figure holder" paragraph style, you can create consistency for your imported graphics. You can also change the width and spacing of the borders around all your figures at once.

First, open the New Style dialog. In Word 2002 and 2003, you get there from the Styles and Formatting Task Pane, as shown in Figure 3-28. For users with earlier versions of Word, select Format → Styles and click the New Style button.

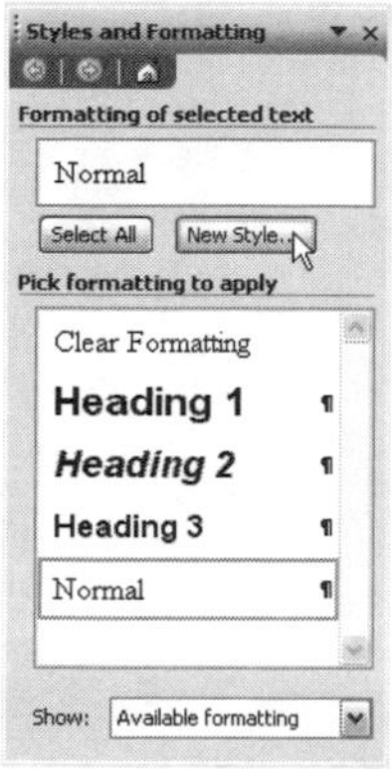

Figure 3-28. Creating a new style

In the New Style dialog, create a paragraph style named "FigureHolder." If you plan to use captions with your figures, you might want to change the "Style for following paragraph" setting to Caption (or whatever style you use for your captions), as shown in Figure 3-29.

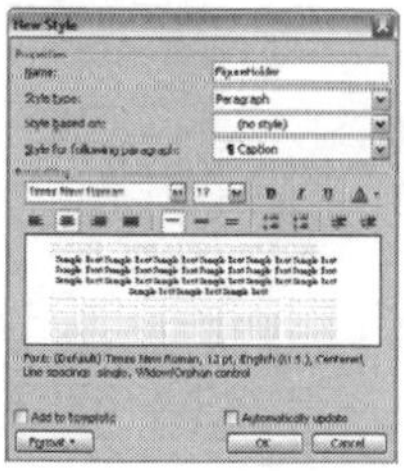

Figure 3-29. Setting the properties for a FigureHolder style

Next, select Format → Borders and choose the Box setting, as shown in Figure 3-30. Click the Options button, change the spacing to six points on all sides, and click the OK button, as shown in Figure 3-31.

Click the OK button again to return to the New Style dialog. Now select Format → Paragraph, click the Indents and Spacing tab, and change the alignment to Centered, the left and right indentation to 0.1 inches, and the spacing before and after to six points, as shown in Figure 3-32. You may also want to click the Line and Page Breaks tab and check the "Keep with next" box to prevent page breaks between figures and captions.

Click the OK button to return to the New Paragraph dialog. Next, select Format → Font and change the font color to red (or another bright color).

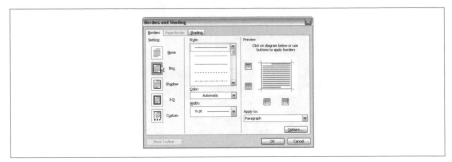

Figure 3-30. Adding the border for your figures

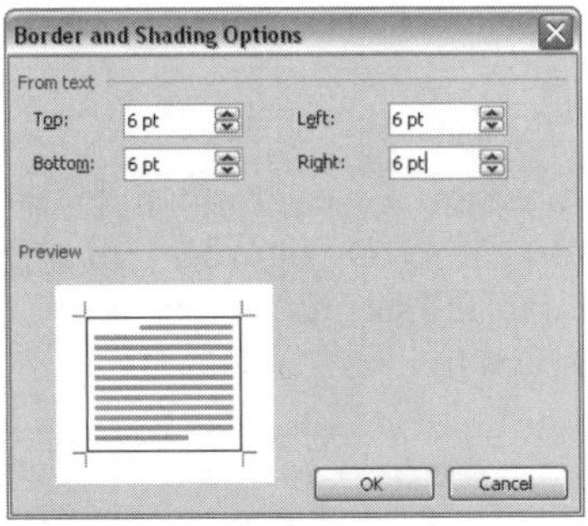

Figure 3-31. This setting adjusts how much space there will be between the border and the graphic

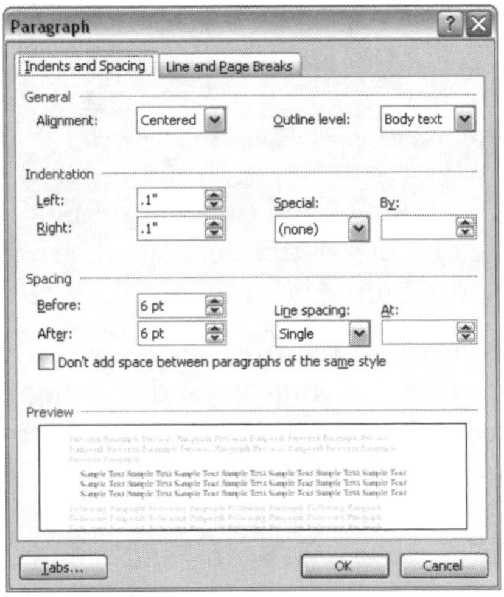

Figure 3-32. Setting the right spacing for the FigureHolder style

The red will serve as a visual warning in case you accidentally place text inside one of your figure boxes. Click the OK button to return to the Modify Paragraph dialog, and click the OK button.

To insert a figure in line with your text, create a blank paragraph where you want the figure inserted and apply the new FigureHolder style. All the images in your document will have the same style border, as shown in Figure 3-33. With a figure holder paragraph style, you can even leave the figures out while you work, since the empty boxes will serve as placeholders.

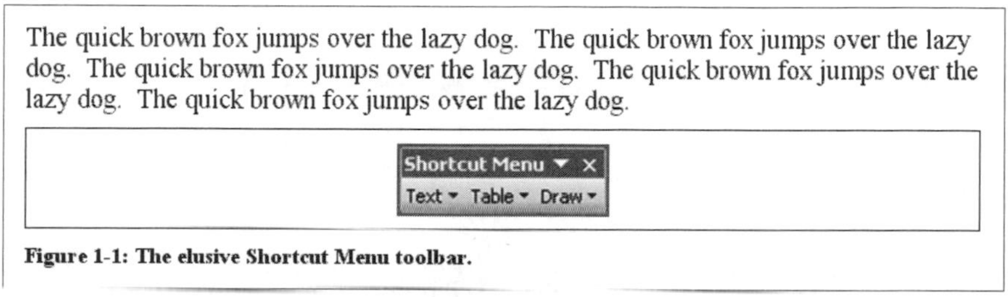

> The quick brown fox jumps over the lazy dog. The quick brown fox jumps over the lazy dog. The quick brown fox jumps over the lazy dog. The quick brown fox jumps over the lazy dog. The quick brown fox jumps over the lazy dog.
>
> Shortcut Menu ▼ ×
> Text ▼ Table ▼ Draw ▼
>
> **Figure 1-1: The elusive Shortcut Menu toolbar.**

Figure 3-33. The FigureHolder style in action

If you want to change the width or spacing of the borders on all figures in your document, you can now just modify the FigureHolder paragraph style.

Hacking the Hack

When you apply a border to a paragraph style, as with the FigureHolder style described above, the border extends to each margin. If you want the border just around the image itself, you can use the same technique we used for the FigureHolder paragraph style, but this time with a character style.

Because the FigureHolder paragraph style helps maintain consistent spacing before and after figures, you should continue to use it, but remove the border. Right-click it on the Styles and Formatting Task Pane (Word 2002/2003) and choose Modify Style. In the Modify Style dialog, go to Format → Border and select None.

Next, you'll create a new character style named FigureBorder. Follow the steps described above for creating a new style, except this time choose Character as the style type, as shown in Figure 3-34.

Choose Format → Border and select the Box setting, as shown in Figure 3-35.

After you import a figure into a paragraph styled as FigureHolder, you can select the figure and apply the FigureBorder character style. If you ever want to change the width of the borders on all the figures in your document, you can just change the width of the border in the FigureBorder character style.

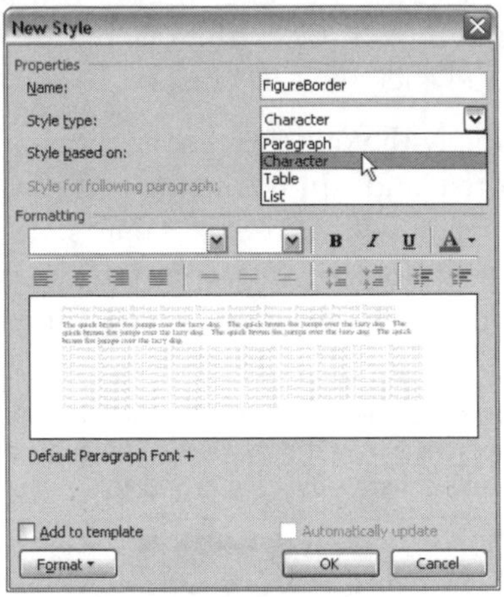

Figure 3-34. This time, create a character style

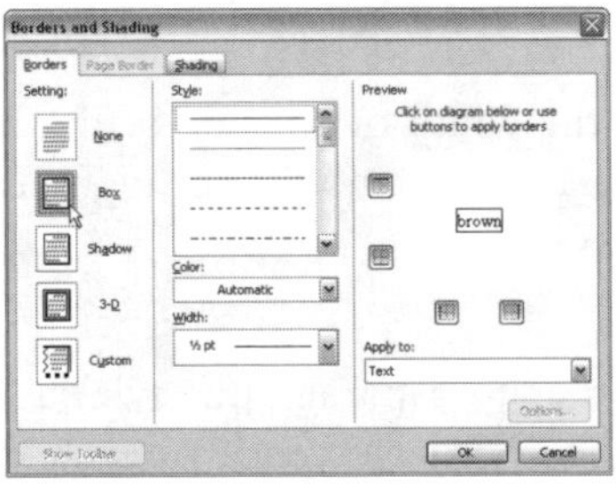

Figure 3-35. The border will appear only around the image, instead of extending to the margins

Make More Flexible Captions

HACK
#22

Word offers a built-in captions feature, but it allows you to use a heading style only for the chapter number. This hack shows you how to expand your options.

If you ask Word to include the chapter number in a caption, you must specify the heading level. But what if you use a style other than one of the built-in heading styles to number your chapters? By using two kinds of fields, you can have your captions use any style you like as the base for the chapter number. The following example shows you how to create a figure caption that gets its chapter number from a custom paragraph style named "ChapterLabel."

Put your cursor where you want to place the caption. Next, type the word "Figure," followed by a space. Select Insert → Field and insert a STYLEREF field pointing to the ChapterLabel paragraph style, as shown in Figure 3-36.

> The ChapterLabel paragraph style (or any other style you specify) must exist within the document for this hack to work, and it must also actually be in use within the document.

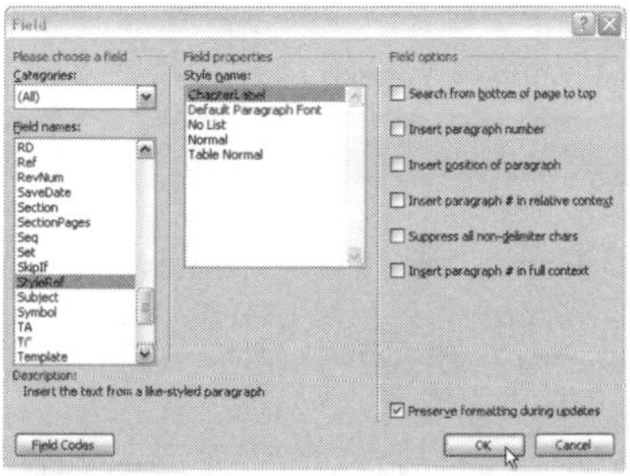

Figure 3-36. Creating a caption using a STYLEREF field

Click the OK button to insert the field in your document. If you've turned on the option to make field codes always visible (Tools → Options → View), the field will look like Figure 3-37. If you don't see the field code, select the text you just inserted, then right-click and choose Toggle Field Codes.

{ STYLEREF ChapterLabel * MERGEFORMAT }

Figure 3-37. A STYLEREF field, one of the building blocks for a caption

Immediately after the field, put in a hyphen. Then select Insert → Field and insert a SEQ field. Use "Figure" as the identifier, as shown in Figure 3-38.

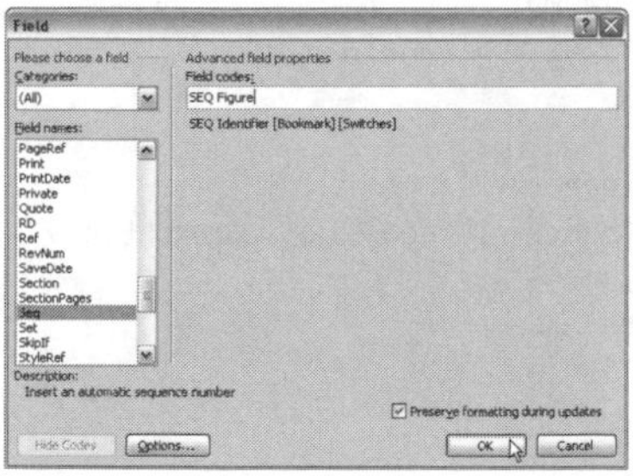

Figure 3-38. Adding a SEQ field to a caption to increment the numbering

With these fields in the document, your caption should now look like Figure 3-39. The figure shows two captions: the first shows the field results and the second shows the field codes.

Figure **1-1**¶

Figure { STYLEREF ChapterLabel * MERGEFORMAT }-{ SEQ Figure * MERGEFORMAT }¶

Figure 3-39. The field results (top) and the field codes used to produce the results (bottom)

Finish the caption label with a period, and you can now type the caption text.

> In the next section, you will learn how to create captions like this with a macro, but in a pinch you can always copy and paste to create additional captions.

Though the syntax used is slightly different, Word's built-in captions feature also uses a combination of STYLEREF and SEQ fields, as shown in Figure 3-40. In this case, the captions are set to get the chapter number from the Heading 1 style.

Figure { STYLEREF 1 \s }-{ SEQ Figure * ARABIC \s 1 }

Figure 3-40. Word's caption feature also uses a combination of STYLEREF and SEQ fields

Automating the Captions

Obviously, a macro would help you insert captions much faster. The following example comes from the macros used to insert the captions for this book:

```
Sub InsertFigureCaption( )
Dim bIsParagraphEmpty As Boolean

With Selection
    .Expand wdParagraph
    If .Characters.Count = 1 Then bIsParagraphEmpty = True
    .Collapse wdCollapseStart
    .Style = "Caption"
    .InsertBefore "Figure "
    .Collapse wdCollapseEnd
    .Fields.Add _
        Range:=Selection.Range, _
        Type:=wdFieldStyleRef, _
```

```
        Text:="ChapterLabel", _
        PreserveFormatting:=True
    .Collapse wdCollapseEnd
    .InsertAfter "-"
    .Collapse wdCollapseEnd
    .Fields.Add _
        Range:=Selection.Range, _
        Type:=wdFieldSequence, _
        Text:="Figure", _
        PreserveFormatting:=True
    .InsertAfter ". "
    .Collapse wdCollapseEnd
    If hIsParagraphEmpty = True Then
        .InsertAfter "Caption Text Goes Here"
    Else
        .Expand wdParagraph
    End If
End With
End Sub
```

If the paragraph already contains text when you run this macro, it prefaces the text with a caption label. If no text exists, it inserts some dummy text for you to replace later.

Make PDFs Without Acrobat

HACK #23

PDF has become a nearly universal file format for displaying documents. But while you can download Adobe Reader for free, you must shell out nearly $300 for the full version if you want to create PDFs. Fortunately, you can use the free Ghostscript and GhostWord programs to create PDFs instead.

By taking advantage of some free utilities, you can easily create full-featured PDFs from Word files without purchasing the full version of Adobe Acrobat. The *Ghostscript* utility, a freeware program available for any platform, can create PDFs from PostScript files. PostScript is a page-description language understood by most printers, and it is usually the format your files are converted to behind the scenes when you send them to your printer.

From Word, you can print your document to a file instead of to a printer; the file that's created will likely be a PostScript file if the printer driver you use is for a PostScript-compatible printer. That means you can use Ghostscript to create a PDF from the file.

To see whether your printer is a PostScript printer, print a small document to file (select File → Print and check the "Print to file" box), then open the file in a text editor such as Notepad. Though Word will give the file a *.prn* extension, the file will still likely be a PostScript file. PostScript files will have a line beginning with the text %!PS near the top of the file, as shown in Figure 3-41.

```
 1  %-12345X@PJL JOB
 2 @PJL SET RESOLUTION = 600
 3 @PJL SET BITSPERPIXEL = 2
 4 @PJL SET ECONOMODE = OFF
 5 @PJL SET HOLDKEY = "0000"
 6 @PJL ENTER LANGUAGE = POSTSCRIPT
 7 %!PS-Adobe-3.0
 8 %%Title: Microsoft Word - PDFs without Acrobat.doc
 9 %%Creator: Windows NT 4.0
10 %%CreationDate: 18:39 7/4/2004
11 %%Pages: (atend)
12 %%BoundingBox: 13 13 599 779
13 %%LanguageLevel: 2
14 %%DocumentNeededFonts: (atend)
15 %%DocumentSuppliedFonts: (atend)
16 %%EndComments
17 %%BeginProlog
18
19 %%BeginResource: procset NTPSOct95
20 /NTPSOct95 100 dict dup begin/bd{bind def}bind def/ld{load def}bd/ed{exch def}
21 bd/a{currentpoint}bd/c/curveto ld/d/dup ld/e/eofill ld/f/fill ld/tr/translate
22 ld/gr/grestore ld/gs/gsave ld/j/setlinejoin ld/L/lineto ld/M/moveto ld/n
23 /newpath ld/cp/closepath ld/rm/rmoveto ld/sl/setlinewidth ld/sd/setdash ld/g
24 /setgray ld/r/setrgbcolor ld/s/stroke ld/t/show ld/aw/awidthshow ld/im
25 /imagemask ld/MS{moveto show}bd/SF{findfont exch scalefont setfont}bd/SM{cmtx
26 setmatrix}bd/MF{findfont exch makefont setfont}bd/CM{/cmtx matrix currentmatrix
27 def}bd/B{M exch dup 0 rlt exch 0 exch rlt neg 0 rlt}bd/CB{B cp eoclip}bd/EA{1
28 index 0/G0 put 4 string 1 1 4 -1 roll{3 copy neg exch cvs dup 0 71 put cvn 3 -1
29 roll exch put}for pop}bd/rlt/rlineto ld/L2?/languagelevel where{pop
30 languagelevel 2 ge}{false}ifelse def end def
31 %%EndResource
```

Figure 3-41. A PostScript file viewed in a text editor

If you don't have a PostScript printer, don't worry; printer drivers are available from many printer manufacturers. For example, one such printer driver is available from Hewlett-Packard at *ftp://ftp.hp.com/pub/printers/software/lj485en.exe*.

Since you're using the driver only to print to files, you don't need the actual printer.

Once you've located or installed a PostScript printer or printer driver, you can use Ghostscript, Ghostview, and GhostWord together to create PDFs from Word files.

> For more information on using PDFs, both with Word and in general, check out *PDF Hacks* (O'Reilly).

Getting Ghostscript and GSview

You can download Ghostscript free from the University of Wisconsin's web site (*http://www.cs.wisc.edu/~ghost/*). Ghostscript itself is a complicated command-line program that can be hard for novices to use. Fortunately, the site also has information on where to obtain a viewer to accompany Ghostscript, such as the free *GSview* viewer, available from *http://www.cs.wisc.edu/~ghost/gsview/index.htm*.

GSview provides a graphical interface to Ghostscript and can be used to view PostScript, PDF, and other file types. GSview is free to use, but you're asked to register the software for $25. If you choose not to register, you'll have to dismiss a reminder dialog each time you launch the program.

You won't need GSview to run this hack, but it's a handy tool to have for viewing PostScript files.

Getting GhostWord

GhostWord is a Ghostscript interface that integrates with Word. It adds a toolbar button to Word that launches the GhostWord GUI, shown in Figure 3-42. Use the GUI to convert the currently active Word document to a full-featured PDF. You can also run the GUI from outside of Word. Ghost-Word even has a command-line interface.

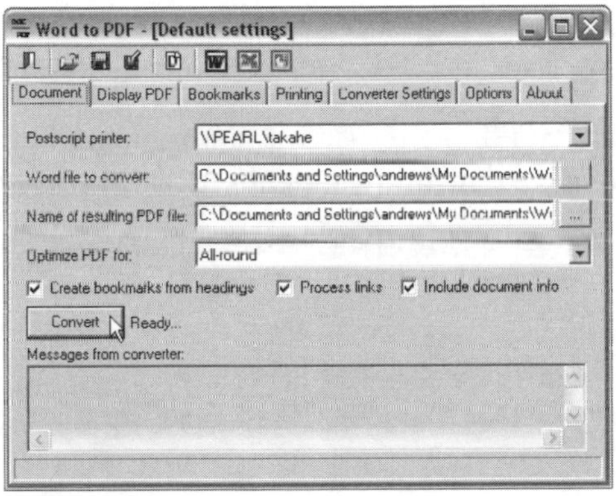

Figure 3-42. The GhostWord interface

GhostWord can add bookmarks, links, metadata, and display settings to a PDF. It also manages your Ghostscript settings. Select a hardcoded Ghost-script profile from the "Optimize PDF for" drop-down box or tweak Ghost-script settings individually under the Converter Settings tab. You can save these settings to a configuration file **[Hack #67]** for later retrieval.

GhostWord is distributed free of charge from *http://www.et.dtu.dk/software/ghostword.*

HACK #24 Create a Custom Text Watermark

Instead of using Word's predefined options, you can create your own watermark text with a few lines of PostScript slipped inside your document.

Word includes a neat feature for inserting a watermark behind a document. You can either choose a picture to use as the watermark, or choose from among a list of text options.

To see the available options for text watermarks, select Format → Background → Printed Watermark to display the dialog shown in Figure 3-43.

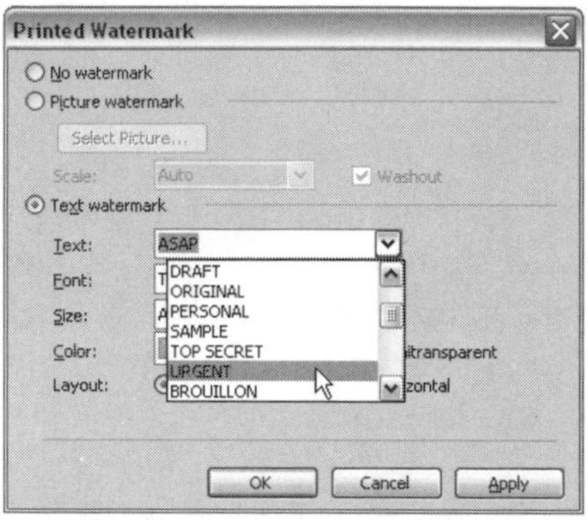

Printed Watermark

- ○ No watermark
- ○ Picture watermark
  - Select Picture...
  - Scale: Auto ☑ Washout
- ⊙ Text watermark
  - Text: ASAP
    - DRAFT
    - ORIGINAL
    - PERSONAL
    - SAMPLE
    - TOP SECRET
    - URGENT
    - BROUILLON
  - Font:
  - Size:
  - Color: transparent
  - Layout: zontal

OK   Cancel   Apply

Figure 3-43. You must choose from a predefined list of text watermarks

But what if the text you'd like to use for a watermark isn't on that list? Or how about including the date or document author as part of the watermark?

Fortunately, you can use a PRINT field and a few lines of PostScript to create your own custom watermark.

> You can also use the PRINT field to put crop marks on a document **[Hack #26]**.

The PRINT field embeds *PostScript* instructions within a document. PostScript is a computer language that tells a printer how to draw a page. Most modern printers have a built-in PostScript interpreter that can translate PostScript instructions into a printed page.

If you go to File → Print and choose "Print to file" instead of sending the file to a printer, the file may have a *.prn* extension, but it's really a PostScript file.

> A PRINT field works only if you print to a PostScript-compatible printer. See "Make PDFs Without Acrobat" **[Hack #23]** for one method of determining if your printer is a PostScript printer.

To print crop marks, you need to include the PostScript instructions for drawing the marks on a page within the PRINT field.

There are some important things to note about PostScript before diving in:

- The comment character in PostScipt is %. The interpreter ignores any line that begins with a %.
- PostScript uses standard (X,Y) coordinates to refer to each page, with 0,0 at the bottom left and 612,792 at the top right on a standard letter page. The numbers represent points measuring 1/72 of an inch.
- Unlike most computer languages, the arguments to a PostScript function come before the function itself. For example, to move to the point 10,10 on a page, you would type 10 10 moveto, not moveto 10 10.

> For a detailed reference on PostScript, see the *PostScript Language Tutorial & Cookbook* located at *http://www-cdf.fnal.gov/offline/PostScript/BLUEBOOK.PDF*.

The Field Code

To insert a watermark with the text "Super Secret," press Ctrl F9 to create a new, blank field in your document and enter the following text between the field braces, as shown in Figure 3-44:

```
PRINT \p page "% Watermark
/Helvetica findfont
54 scalefont
setfont
200 350 moveto
45 rotate
.75 setgray
(SUPER  SECRET) show
"
```

The field produces the watermark shown in Figure 3-45.

To create a watermark that appears on every page in a document, place the PRINT field within the document's header.

To include dynamic content in the watermark, you can nest another field, such as a DATE field, within the PRINT field, as shown in Figure 3-46.

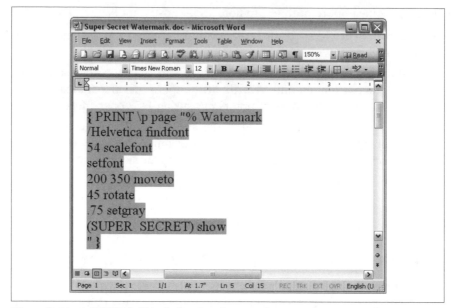

Figure 3-44. A PRINT field including PostScript code to create a watermark

Figure 3-45. A watermark created with a PRINT field

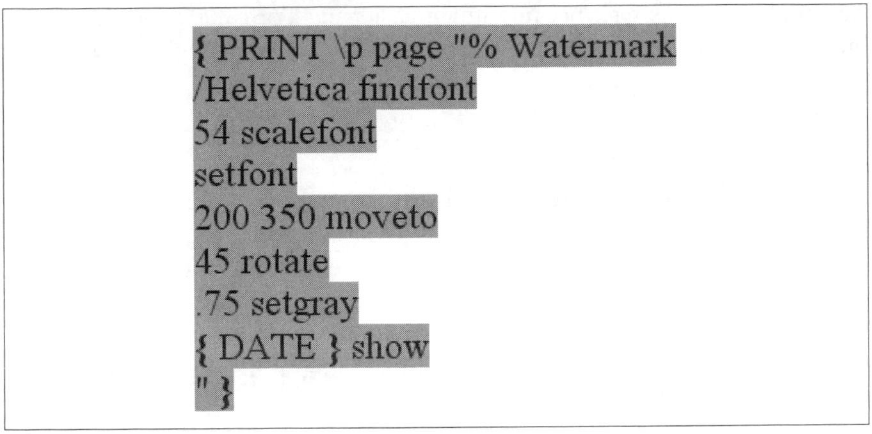

```
{ PRINT \p page "% Watermark
/Helvetica findfont
54 scalefont
setfont
200 350 moveto
45 rotate
.75 setgray
{ DATE } show
" }
```

Figure 3-46. Nesting fields inside the PRINT fields is a way to include dynamic content in a text watermark

Include Only Part of a Heading in a TOC

HACK #25

Give your headings more flexibility while keeping the table of contents (TOC) under control.

Tables of content can provide useful roadmaps for navigating long documents. Typically, a TOC displays a document's headings alongside the page numbers on which they appear. Sometimes, however, you may want only part of a heading to appear in the TOC.

For example, consider the document shown in Figure 3-47. The title is included on the same line as the chapter number, but in the TOC only the chapter number should appear, as shown in Figure 3-48.

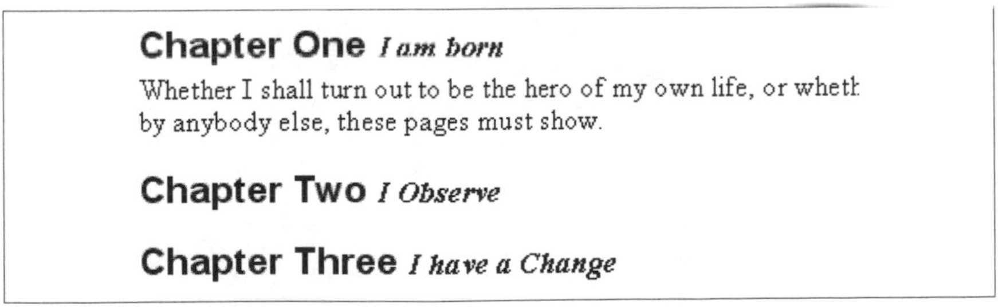

Chapter One *I am born*

Whether I shall turn out to be the hero of my own life, or wheth by anybody else, these pages must show.

Chapter Two *I Observe*

Chapter Three *I have a Change*

Figure 3-47. Chapter numbers and titles appear on the same line

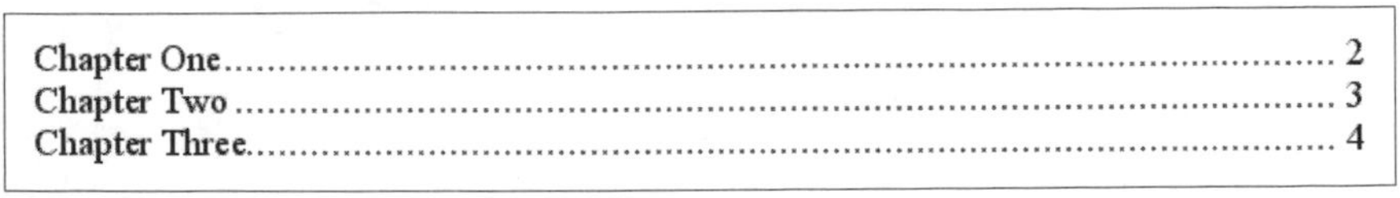

Chapter One.. 2
Chapter Two 3
Chapter Three... 4

Figure 3-48. Only the chapter number should be included in the TOC

Accomplishing this task became much easier in Word 2002, but it's still a bit tricky. How you implement these "run-in headings" depends on which version of Word you're using.

Word 2002 and Higher

Microsoft included a feature in Word 2002 to make it easier to include only part of a heading in the TOC. A new type of formatting mark, called a *StyleSeparator*, creates a hidden barricade between portions of text in a paragraph. As the name implies, this mark lets you use two different paragraph styles within the same paragraph (and you avoid the Char Char problem [Hack #55] typically encountered with multiple paragraph styles applied within the same paragraph).

Immediately following a heading, you can insert one of these new StyleSeparators to create, in effect, a new paragraph that starts on the same line as the heading, as shown in Figure 3-49. Thus, you can apply a paragraph style independent of the heading, which means it won't appear in the TOC.

By default, you can access the StyleSeparator only from the Commands tab of the Customize dialog. Select Tools → Customize, then select All Commands in the Categories column, as shown in Figure 3-49. Once you've located the *InsertStyleSeparator* command in the Commands list, you can place it on the menu or toolbar of your choice [Hack #1] while you've got the Customize dialog open.

Figure 3-49. Locating the InsertStyleSeparator command

To create a run-in heading (such as those shown in Figure 3-47) using a StyleSeparator, put your cursor anywhere in the heading paragraph, then select the *InsertStyleSeparator* command you just placed on a menu or toolbar. If you've got paragraph marks turned on **[Hack #1]**, you'll notice that the one at the end of the heading paragraph is no longer visible.

> Documents that include StyleSeparators will still open and function correctly if you send them to someone using Word 2000. Word 2000 interprets the separators as hidden paragraph marks. When you get the document back, however, Word leaves the StyleSeparators as hidden paragraph marks (which they suspiciously resemble anyway).

Word 2000

To get the run-in-heading effect in Word 2000, you need to do a bit more legwork.

First, select Tools → Options, click the View tab, and check the "Paragraph marks" box. Next, make sure you *uncheck* the "Hidden text" box, then click the OK button.

Select the trailing paragraph mark for the first heading you'd like to run in. Then select Format → Font, check the Hidden box, and press the OK button (or press Ctrl-Shift-H). Now you've got two paragraphs on the same line, as shown in Figure 3-47. You can style the second paragraph with its own paragraph style, independent of the heading, which means it won't appear in the TOC.

It would be tedious work to apply this hack to every heading in a document, but you can simplify it with a Find and Replace.

1. In the "Find what" box, put **^p**.
2. Click the More button if the Format button isn't visible.
3. With your cursor in the "Find what" box, click the Format button, select Style, and select Heading 1 (or the heading style that you'd like to run in).
4. In the "Replace with" box, put **^&**.
5. With your cursor in the "Replace with" box, click the Format button, choose Font, and check the Hidden box.
6. Click the Replace All button.

Put Crop Marks on a Page

#26
Commercial print shops usually require crop marks for custom-sized print pieces. This hack shows you how to include these important guides in a Word document.

With its improved graphics and typography features, many individuals and small businesses rely on Word as a standalone desktop publishing program, especially as the price of full-featured programs such as InDesign remains high.

Word does a fair job of handling layout tasks, but it still operates primarily as a word processor. It also lacks a few features essential for preparing printer-ready documents, such as the ability to insert *crop marks*.

Printers (the trade, not the device) use crop marks when trimming paper to a particular size. Figure 3-50 shows a document with crop marks. These are most often used when the final printed piece will have smaller dimensions than a standard paper size, such as letter. It's much easier and cheaper to print a document using a standard paper size and trim it afterward than to print directly on paper that's unusually sized.

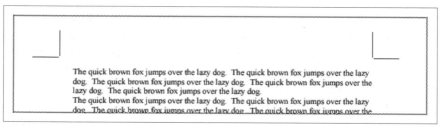

Figure 3-50. A PDF of a document that includes crop marks

To create crop marks in a Word document, you can use the seldom-used PRINT field, discussed in "Create a Custom Text Watermark" [Hack #24].

The Field Code

To see how a PRINT field can put crop marks on a page, open or create a single-page document. Next, put your cursor anywhere on the page and press Ctrl-F9 to insert an empty field at the insertion point.

With your cursor still between the field braces, type the following:

```
PRINT \p page "
% Crop Marks
.5 setlinewidth
% bottom left
72 88 moveto
```

```
72 52 lineto
70 90 moveto
34 90 lineto

% top left
70 720 moveto
34 720 lineto
72 722 moveto
72 758 lineto

% top right
522 722 moveto
522 758 lineto
524 720 moveto
560 720 lineto

% bottom right
522 88 moveto
522 52 lineto
524 90 moveto
560 90 lineto
stroke
"
```

The PostScript instructions are divided into four main parts, one for each of the four corners of the document where crop marks will be inserted. Each moveto, lineto pair corresponds to one of the eight lines needed for a full set of crop marks (two perpendicular lines in each corner of the document).

After you've created the PRINT field, print your document to file **[Hack #23]** to save it as a PostScript file. If you have a PostScript printer, when you print the document, it will have crop marks like the ones shown in Figure 3-50.

> If you print to a non-PostScript printer, the PostScript instructions will appear as text within the document.

These crop marks correspond to a 1-inch top and bottom margin and a 1.25-inch left and right margin. To accommodate different margins, adjust the PostScript instructions accordingly.

> To print crop marks on every page in a document, put the PRINT field in the document header.

Hacking the Hack

The PostScript code shown in the previous section works if you're working with Word's default margins, but if you want crop marks on a page with different margins, you need to work out the new coordinates. As much fun as a flashback to high-school geometry might be, it's better to work out the details once and then use a macro to adjust the coordinates for different margins.

The following code creates a PRINT field with the correct coordinates based on a document's margins. The field is placed in the header of the section where the cursor is currently located. In most cases, that puts crop marks on every page of the document, though if you've explicitly defined multiple sections with different headers, you may need to adjust the macro to get the desired results.

Place these five procedures in the template of your choice [Hack #50] and run the main PlaceCropmarks procedure from the Tools → Macro → Macros dialog or by putting a button for it on a menu or toolbar [Hack #1]:

```
Sub PlaceCropmarks( )
Dim sngLeft As Single
Dim sngRight As Single
Dim sngTop As Single
Dim sngBottom As Single
Dim sPrintField As String
Dim rng As Range
With ActiveDocument.PageSetup
    sngLeft = .LeftMargin
    sngRight = .RightMargin
    sngTop = .TopMargin
    sngBottom = .BottomMargin
End With

' Include initial field switches and PostScript instructions
sPrintField = " \p page " & Chr$(34) & " .5 setlinewidth "
' Get correct coordinates using the four functions
sPrintField = sPrintField & BottomLeft(sngLeft, sngBottom)
sPrintField = sPrintField & TopLeft(sngLeft, sngTop)
sPrintField = sPrintField & TopRight(sngRight, sngTop)
sPrintField = sPrintField & BottomRight(sngRight, sngBottom)

' Add final PostScript instruction and close the field instruction
sPrintField = sPrintField & "stroke" & Chr$(34)
Set rng = Selection.Sections.First.Headers(wdHeaderFooterPrimary).Range
rng.Collapse wdCollapseStart
rng.Fields.Add Range:=rng, _
    Type:=wdFieldPrint, _
    Text:=sPrintField, _
    PreserveFormatting:=False
End Sub
```

```
Function BottomLeft(sngLeft As Single, sngBottom As Single) As String
Dim sReturn As String
sReturn = sngLeft & " " & sngBottom - 2 & " moveto "
sReturn = sReturn & sngLeft & " " & (sngBottom - 2) - 36 & " lineto "
sReturn = sReturn & sngLeft - 2 & " " & sngBottom & " moveto "
sReturn = sReturn & (sngLeft - 2) - 36 & " " & sngBottom & " lineto "
BottomLeft = sReturn
End Function

Function TopLeft(sngLeft As Single, sngTop As Single) As String
Dim sReturn As String
sReturn = sngLeft & " " & (792 - sngTop) + 2 & " moveto "
sReturn = sReturn & sngLeft & " " & (792 - (sngTop + 2)) + 36 & " lineto "
sReturn = sReturn & sngLeft - 2 & " " & 792 - sngTop & " moveto "
sReturn = sReturn & (sngLeft - 2) - 36 & " " & 792 - sngTop & " lineto "
TopLeft = sReturn
End Function

Function TopRight(sngRight As Single, sngTop As Single) As String
Dim sReturn As String
sReturn = 612 - sngRight & " " & (792 - sngTop) + 2 & " moveto "
sReturn = sReturn & 612 - sngRight & " " & (792 - (sngTop + 2)) + 36 & "
lineto "
sReturn = sReturn & (612 - sngRight) + 2 & " " & 792 - sngTop & " moveto "
sReturn = sReturn & ((612 - sngRight) + 2) + 36 & " " & 792 - sngTop & "
lineto "
TopRight = sReturn
End Function

Function BottomRight(sngRight As Single, sngBottom As Single) As String
Dim sReturn As String
sReturn = 612 - sngRight & " " & sngBottom - 2 & " moveto "
sReturn = sReturn & 612 - sngRight & " " & (sngBottom - 2) - 36 & " lineto "
sReturn = sReturn & (612 - sngRight) + 2 & " " & sngBottom & " moveto "
sReturn = sReturn & ((612 - sngRight) + 2) + 36 & " " & sngBottom & " lineto
"
BottomRight = sReturn
End Function
```

PRINT fields aren't visible in a document unless you've chosen to view field codes. To quickly see all the field codes in a document, press Alt-F9.

—Dan Mueller and Andrew Savikas

CHAPTER FOUR

Editing Power Tools
Hacks 27–44

Word is probably used more for editing existing text than writing new documents. Revising, reviewing, and reformatting likely make up most of your work in Word. The hacks in this chapter show how to automate some of the more mundane editing chores and speed up some common formatting commands.

HACK #27 Crunch Numbers Quickly in Word

Sometimes a spreadsheet is overkill. For quick and dirty math, dust off one of Word's oldest commands: Calculate.

If you used Word when the first President Bush was in office, you might remember a handy feature from the Tools menu: the Calculate command. With the standard four functions, plus exponents and percentages, Calculate could handle a lot of the math needed for simple sales reports or budget proposals.

Though Microsoft removed the command from the Tools menu in Word 6.0, you can still find it if you know where to look.

> This hack shows you how to put the Calculate command back on the Tools menu, but you can also put it on any of the toolbars or shortcut menus [Hack #3].

Resurrecting Calculate

First, select Tools → Customize and click the Commands tab. In the Categories column, choose All Commands. Scroll down until you find ToolsCalculate, as shown in Figure 4-1.

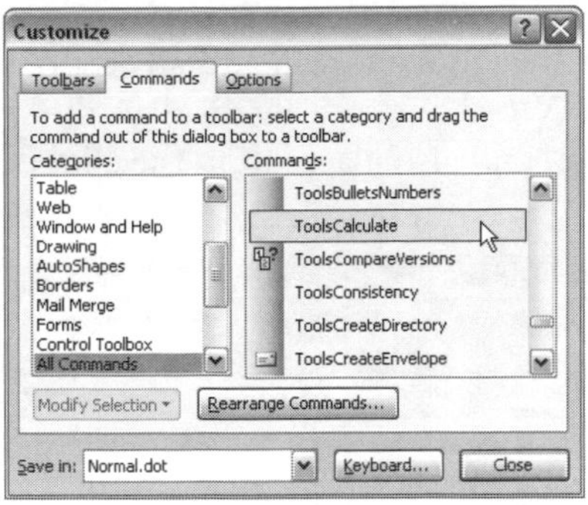

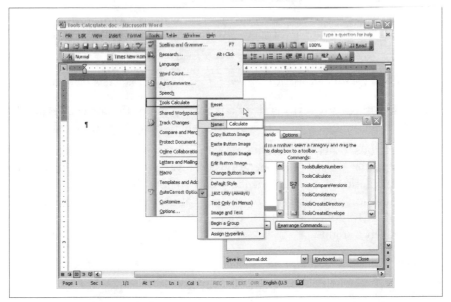

Figure 4-1. Locating the Calculate command buried deep in Word

Drag the command to the Tools menu and place it right under the Speech option (or anywhere else on the menu). Right-click the new menu item and rename it "Calculate," as shown in Figure 4-2.

Figure 4-2. Returning Calculate to the Tools menu

When you first place the command on a menu or toolbar, it may appear grayed-out. Calculate is available only when you've selected some text.

Using Calculate

By default, the Calculate command will add any set of selected numbers separated by whitespace. Word temporarily displays the result in the status bar, as shown in Figure 4-3, and also places it on the clipboard.

Figure 4-3. The sum of the selected numbers is temporarily displayed in the status bar

Calculate ignores any text that isn't a number, except for currency symbols, periods, and commas, which it recognizes when these are part of a number.

For operations other than addition, you must include the mathematical operator. Table 4-1 lists the operations in reverse order of precedence. To force a calculation out of precedence order, enclose the expression in parentheses. Addition and subtraction are of equal precedence and are evaluated left to right. Multiplication and division also are of equal precedence and are evaluated left to right.

Table 4-1. Syntax for the Calculate command, in reverse order of precedence

Operation	Operator	Example	Result
Addition	+ or space	220 + 419 982	1621
Subtraction	- or ()	1440 (312) - 96	1032
Multiplication	*	24 * $199	$4776.00
Division	/	$20,000/36	$555.56
Exponential (power or root)	^	(32^(1/5))^8	256
Percentage	%	$89 * 15%	$13.35

Though Calculate is most often used in tables, it works on any selected text. For example, you can use this command to quickly add all the numbers in a paragraph of text, as shown in Figure 4-4.

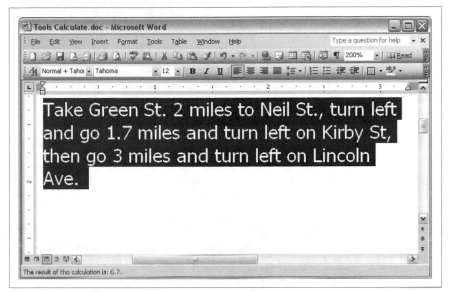

Figure 4-4. Calculate works with selected text and displays the results in the status bar

Hacking the Hack

The calculation results are displayed in the status bar for only a few seconds. After that, if you want to see the results, you must either paste them from the clipboard or redo the calculation, paying closer attention to the status bar. If you prefer to display the calculation results more directly, you can intercept the command [Hack #61] and have Word display the results in a message box.

Place the following macro in the template of your choice [Hack #50]. It will run in place of the Calculate command when you select Tools → Calculate.

```
Sub ToolsCalculate( )
MsgBox Selection.Range.Calculate
End Sub
```

However, when you intercept the command, Word neither displays the calculation results in the status bar nor copies them to the clipboard. To also put the results in the status bar, use the following code instead:

```
Sub ToolsCalculate( )
Dim sResult as String
sResult = Selection.Range.Calculate
```

```
StatusBar = "The result of the calculation is: " & sResult
Msgbox sResult
End Sub
```

It takes a bit more work to get the results copied to the clipboard. There's no direct way to access the clipboard from VBA, so you need to use Windows API calls. You can find sample code for accessing text on the clipboard at *http://support.microsoft.com/default.aspx?scid=kb;en-us;138909*.

With the code from that site included in the same module, use the site's example `Clipboard_SetData` subroutine to put the results on the clipboard:

```
Sub ToolsCalculate()
Dim sResult As String
sResult = Selection.Range.Calculate
StatusBar = "The result of the calculation is: " & sResult
MsgBox sResult
ClipBoard_SetData (sResult)
End Sub
```

Unlink Every Hyperlink

Sometimes uninvited, often distracting, and always hard to wrangle, hyperlinks tend to stick around your documents like unwelcome guests at a party. Here's how to show them the door.

Maybe it's because they're so difficult to edit; maybe it's the tacky combination of blue *and* underline; or maybe it's having to continually dismiss that web browser or email editor you didn't mean to open. Whatever the reason, many users have just one thing to say about hyperlinks in Word: "How do I get rid of them!?"

> To stop Word from creating hyperlinks, select Tools → AutoCorrect Options (Tools → AutoCorrect in Word 97 and 2000), click the "AutoFormat As You Type" tab, and uncheck the "Internet and network paths with hyperlinks" box.

To unlink a single hyperlink, select it, then right-click and choose Remove Hyperlink from the shortcut menu, as shown in Figure 4-5.

You can also unlink a hyperlink by selecting it and then pressing Ctrl-Shift-F9. However, this key command unlinks all the fields in the current selection. So selecting all the text in your document and then pressing Ctrl-Shift-F9 would remove all the hyperlinks and unlink *every other* field in your document, making it a poor choice for the task at hand.

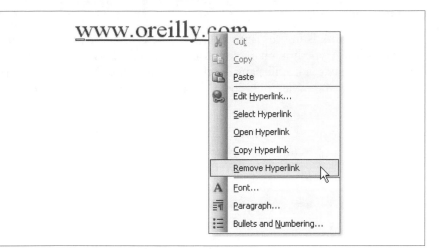

Figure 4-5. Removing a hyperlink with the Hyperlink shortcut menu

Word offers no built-in way to unlink just every hyperlink in a document all at once. However, you can use a macro to get the job done.

The Code

Place this macro in the template of your choice **[Hack #50]** and either run it from the Tools → Macro → Macros dialog or put a button for it on a menu or toolbar **[Hack #1]**.

Running the following macro achieves the same result as selecting each hyperlink and choosing Remove Hyperlink from the shortcut menu:

```
Sub RemoveAllHyperlinks()
Dim i As Integer
For i = ActiveDocument.Hyperlinks.Count To 1 Step -1
    ActiveDocument.Hyperlinks(i).Delete
Next i
End Sub
```

Notice that while the shortcut menu uses the term "remove," in this macro, each hyperlink is "deleted." Though the terminology is inconsistent, the result is the same: the text remains in your document, but it is no longer an active hyperlink and no longer appears as blue and underlined.

 You may want to add this macro to the Hyperlink shortcut menu **[Hack #3]**.

Hacking the Hack

When a hyperlink is inserted into your document (either manually or auto-matically), the Hyperlink character style is applied to its text. The Hyper-link character style is just like any other character style in Word. You can see it displayed in the Styles pull-down menu on the Formatting toolbar, as shown in Figure 4-6.

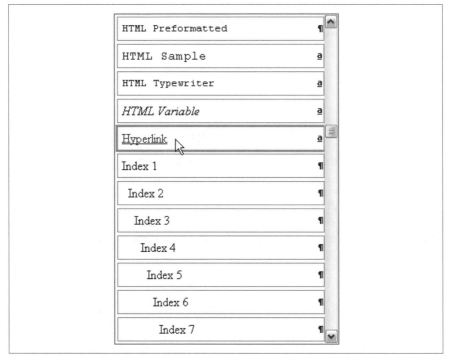

Figure 4-6. Hyperlink is just another built-in character style

If you like having the links but can't stand the blue underlining, you can change it. Select Format → Styles and Formatting (Format → Style in Word 2000), choose the Hyperlink style, and click the Modify button. Next, click the Format button and choose Font. The Font dialog, shown in Figure 4-7, lets you change the style to suit your tastes.

If you remove a hyperlink, the Hyperlink character style goes with it. The reverse, however, is not true—that is, if you select a hyperlink and alter its styling (e.g., remove the underlining), you will still be left with a fully "click-able" hyperlink.

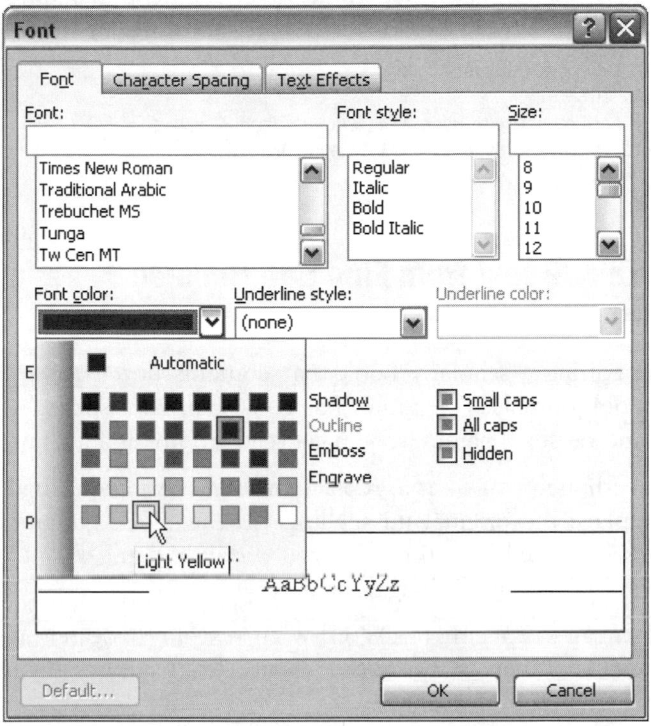

Figure 4-7. Choosing a more mellow format for Word hyperlinks

You can apply any style or formatting you like to a hyperlink, and it will remain active. But if you apply the Hyperlink style to regular text, it won't create a hyperlink (though its appearance will certainly confuse you).

If you want to remove all the hyperlinks in a document but keep the Hyperlink character style applied to the text, modify the macro as follows:

```
Sub RemoveHyperlinksKeepStyle( )
Dim oHyperlink As Hyperlink
Dim i As Integer
Dim rng As Range
For i = ActiveDocument.Hyperlinks.Count To 1 Step -1
    Set oHyperlink = ActiveDocument.Hyperlinks(i)
    Set rng = oHyperlink.Range
    oHyperlink.Delete
    rng.Style = wdStyleHyperlink
Next i
End Sub
```

To completely remove all the hyperlinks in a document, including their text, change the RemoveAllHyperlinks macro to the following:

```
Sub ReallyRemoveAllHyperlinks( )
Dim i As Integer
For i = ActiveDocument.Hyperlinks.Count To 1 Step -1
    ActiveDocument.Hyperlinks(i).Range.Delete
Next i
End Sub
```

HACK #29 Exclude Text from Find and Replace

This hack turns "Find what" into "Find not what."

Say you're editing a scholarly book that contains dozens of block quotations from old journals. The author has consistently misspelled several geographical and personal names, so you get ready to fire up Find and Replace.

But wait—although you want to replace the *author's* misspellings, you *don't* want to replace the original misspellings in the block quotations. Those should be reproduced verbatim. And you certainly don't want to OK every replacement by hand in this long, long book.

Though you can't explicitly tell Word what text *not* to search in, this hack takes advantage of the fact that Word automatically ignores any hidden text in its searches.

Let's say all of your block quotations use Word's built-in Block Text style. If you set the text in that style as hidden, Word will skip over it during your Find/Replace.

Select Format → Styles and Formatting (Format → Styles in Word 2000). Choose the Block Text style and click the Modify button.

In the next dialog, click the Format button and choose Font to display the dialog shown in Figure 4-8.

Check the Hidden box, click the OK button, and then click the OK button again to exit the Modify Style dialog. Finally, click the Close button on the Styles dialog to return to your document.

All of the block quotations will have disappeared—as long as you're not displaying hidden text. If you still see the block quotes, select Tools → Options, click the View tab, and check the "Hidden text" box.

Now, with your block quotations hidden, you can find and replace the misspellings in the rest of your text.

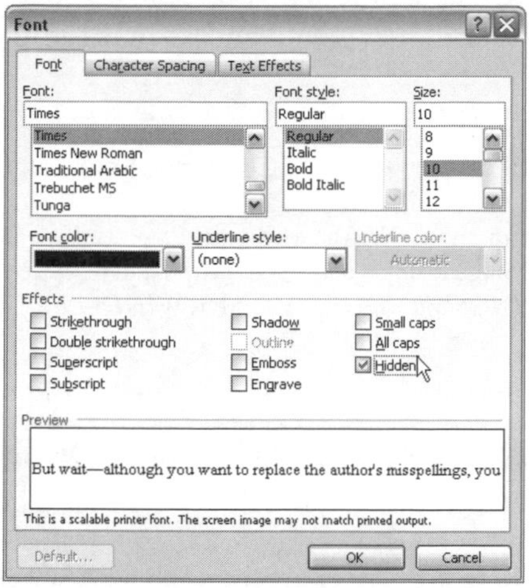

Figure 4-8. Find and Replace will skip over any hidden text

Once you finish, just repeat the above procedure (this time *unchecking* the Hidden box) to make your block quotations visible again. All of your block quotations will reappear, with their misspellings intact.

—*Jack Lyon*

HACK #30 Use Character Codes to Find or Insert Special Characters

It's easy to find common characters on the keyboard. But when you need to find or create an uncommon character, using character codes can make things much easier.

Word uses *Unicode* characters to internally store all the text you type, including special characters and symbols. Unicode is, to paraphrase the official Unicode web site (*http://www.unicode.org*), a universal character-encoding standard, designed to ensure that any text can be represented on any platform, and in any language.

Prior to the introduction of the Unicode standard, many software programs used (and many still do use) other character encodings, such as the original *ASCII* character set, or similar encodings that include the ASCII characters and some additional ones. ASCII and other older character-encoding standards do not have the capacity to represent all the characters possible in multiple languages, and they often create problems when transferring text among applications used in different countries or regions.

Though Word uses Unicode internally, its ASCII roots poke through when you insert characters into documents and search for characters using Find and Replace.

> In this hack, the term "ASCII" refers to the characters represented in Word by the codes 0–255. ASCII is a bit less of a mouthful than "Windows Code Page 1052," the real name of the encoding set—see *http://www.unicode.org/Public/ MAPPINGS/VENDORS/MICSFT/WINDOWS/CP1252.TXT*.

Inserting Special Characters

You can use both ASCII character codes and Unicode character codes to insert special characters into text in Word.

Using ASCII codes. There are 256 characters in the ASCII set, numbered from 0 to 255. Not all of the codes represent printable characters, and not all are used in Windows, but if you're familiar with the code for a particular symbol, entering it from the keypad can be quicker than going through Insert → Symbol.

For example, the ASCII code for a micro sign (µ) is 181. To insert a micro sign at the insertion point, do the following:

1. Turn on Num Lock for the numeric keypad.
2. Hold down the Alt key.
3. On the numeric keypad, type **0181**.
4. Release the Alt key.

The micro symbol will be inserted into your document.

Using Unicode codes. Unicode supports many more than 256 characters. It has enough "space" to represent every character in every language, with plenty to spare. Unicode codes are usually represented as *hexadecimal* values, so they're a mix of digits and the letters A–F.

Not all fonts support Unicode, but many of the common ones, such as Times and Arial, do.

The Unicode code for a musical eighth-note character is 266A. To insert one at the insertion point, do the following:

1. Type **266A**.
2. Press Alt-X.

The code you typed will be converted to the eighth-note symbol.

Though you can search for characters by their Unicode numbers in Word 2000 (as described in the next section), you can't insert them directly using this method in Word 2000.

You may find that it's easier to search for codes using the links available at the Unicode web site (*http://www.unicode.org*) and insert characters using this method than it is to search among the thousands of characters in the Insert → Symbol dialog.

Searching for Special Characters

You can use these same character codes when searching for special characters in text. The ASCII codes are particularly useful when you're performing a wildcard search.

Searching with ASCII codes. Independent of the ASCII and Unicode codes, Word includes several special character codes that you've likely seen before, such as ^p to search for a paragraph mark or ^t to search for a tab. The Word help files cover these codes extensively, but three deserve special attention because they can match more than one character:

- ^# matches any digit.
- ^$ matches any letter.
- ^w matches any whitespace.

The special character codes will help you with simple searches, but if you check the "Use wildcards" box in the Find and Replace dialog, you'll get the error message shown in Figure 4-9.

> **Microsoft Office Word**   ☒
>
> ⚠ ^p is not a valid special character for the Find What box or is not supported when the Use Wildcards check box is
>   selected.
>
>   [OK]

Figure 4-9. Some of Word's special codes can't be used with wildcard searching active

So how do you match a paragraph mark when wildcard searching is active? By using the ASCII code. To search for a character by its ASCII code, type ^0 in the "Find what" box, followed by the character code.

The ASCII code for a paragraph mark (technically, it's a *carriage return*) is 13. So, to search for paragraph marks while wildcard searching is activated, you'd type ^013 in the "Find what" box.

Be aware that some fonts assign different characters to the
ASCII codes.

With wildcard searching active, you can also search for ranges of characters. For example, type [^0100-^0104] in the "Find what" box to search for
characters between *d* and *f*.

Searching with Unicode codes. You can also search for a character using its
Unicode code by prefacing it with ^u. However, you can't directly search
using the hexadecimal code; you must enter its decimal equivalent.

For example, the decimal equivalent of 266A, the musical eighth-note character, is 9834. So, to search for that character, enter **^u9834** in the "Find
what" box.

Unlike ASCII codes, Unicode codes won't work with wildcard searching active.

So how do you convert a hexadecimal number to a decimal number? Fortunately, VBA includes a function that will do it for you. To convert a "hex"
number to its decimal equivalent, select Tools → Macro → Visual Basic Editor to display the Visual Basic Editor in a separate window.

In the small window titled "Immediate" near the bottom of the screen, type
the following and press Enter:

```
?CDec(&Hcode)
```

code is the Unicode code, as shown in Figure 4-10.

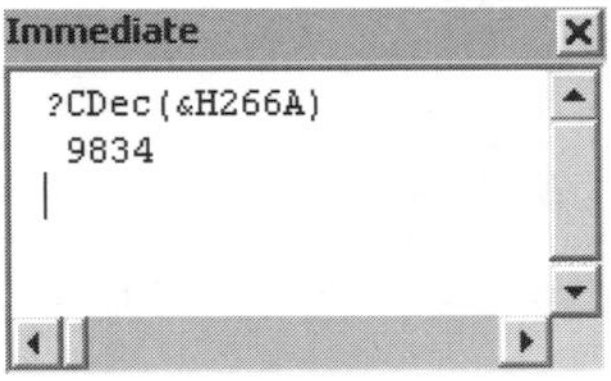

```
Immediate
?CDec(&H266A)
 9834
```

Figure 4-10. Converting a hexadecimal value to its decimal equivalent

What's That Character?

What if you need to replace some obscure character in an unusual font? For
example, say you open a giant document from a client and find the same

odd character at the beginning of every paragraph. If Word won't let you paste the character into its Find and Replace dialog, it seems you're stuck repairing it by hand.

If you knew the character's numeric code, you could search for it, but this character falls way off the usual list. How can you find its numeric code? Put the following macro in the template of your choice **[Hack #50]**, select Tools → Macro → Macros, choose WhatCharacterCode from the list, and click the Run button:

```
Sub WhatCharacterCode( )
MsgBox Asc(Selection.Text)
End Sub
```

This macro will display the ASCII character code for the first character in the current selection; you can then search for it using the ^0 syntax.

If the macro reports a value of 63 and fails to match the character, you may be facing a Unicode character. The following macro will report the Unicode code of a character, which you can search for using the ^u syntax:

```
Sub WhatUnicodeCharacterCode( )
MsgBox AscW(Selection.Text)
End Sub
```

> The result displayed will be the decimal version of the Unicode character code, not the hexadecimal version used when inserting Unicode characters.

—Jack Lyon and Andrew Savikas

HACK #31 Find/Replace in Multiple Files

Make the same substitution on several files at once using the code in this hack.

Find and Replace is a real time-saver, but when you have to perform the same substitution on multiple files, it can seem like more of a hindrance than a help.

If you regularly perform the same types of substitutions on multiple documents, developing a set of macros to do the work for you can represent a real improvement in efficiency.

The Code

For example, say your law firm, Dewey & Cheatham, just added a partner, and now you're Dewey, Cheatham & Howe. The following macro searches all the Word documents in the folder *C:\My Documents* and replaces the old name with the new name wherever it occurs:

```
Sub FindReplaceAllDocsInFolder()
Dim i As Integer
Dim doc As Document
Dim rng As Range

With Application.FileSearch
    .NewSearch
    .LookIn = "C:\My Documents"
    .SearchSubFolders = False
    .FileType = msoFileTypeWordDocuments
    If Not .Execute() = 0 Then
        For i = 1 To .FoundFiles.Count
            Set doc = Documents.Open(.FoundFiles(i))
            Set rng = doc.Range
            With rng.Find
                .ClearFormatting
                .Replacement.ClearFormatting
                .Text = "Dewey & Cheatem"
                .Replacement.Text = "Dewey, Cheatham & Howe"
                .Forward = True
                .Wrap = wdFindContinue
                .Format = False
                .MatchCase = False
                .MatchWholeWord = False
                .MatchWildcards = False
                .MatchSoundsLike = False
                .MatchAllWordForms = False
                .Execute Replace:=wdReplaceAll
            End With

            doc.Save
            doc.Close

            Set rng = Nothing
            Set doc = Nothing
        Next i
    Else
        MsgBox "No files matched " & .FileName
    End If
End With
End Sub
```

The macro uses the `FileSearch` object to examine each file in the folder. If it finds a Word document, it opens the file, changes the name wherever it occurs, and then saves and closes the file. If the macro finds no Word files in the folder, it displays a message on the screen.

Place this macro in the template of your choice [Hack #50] and either run it from the Tools → Macro → Macros dialog or assign it a button on a menu or toolbar [Hack #1].

Hacking the Hack

The code in the first section has a subtle problem related to the Find object. When you perform a substitution from VBA, it includes only the main part of the document in the substitution. It leaves the headers, footers, comments, footnotes, text boxes, and so forth out of the search.

To modify the macro above to search every nook and cranny in a document, wrap the replacement inside a For Each loop [Hack #66] that cycles through each part of the document. The modified sections are highlighted in bold:

```
Sub FindReplaceAllDocsInFolder( )
Dim i As Integer
Dim doc As Document
Dim rng As Range

With Application.FileSearch
    .NewSearch
    .LookIn = "C:\My Documents"
    .SearchSubFolders = False
    .FileType = msoFileTypeWordDocuments
    If Not .Execute() = 0 Then
        For i = 1 To .FoundFiles.Count
            Set doc = Documents.Open(.FoundFiles(i))
                For Each rng In doc.StoryRanges
                With rng.Find
                    .ClearFormatting
                    .Replacement.ClearFormatting
                    .Text = "Dewey & Cheatem"
                    .Replacement.Text = "Dewey, Cheatem & Howe"
                    .Forward = True
                    .Wrap = wdFindContinue
                    .Format = False
                    .MatchCase = False
                    .MatchWholeWord = False
                    .MatchWildcards = False
                    .MatchSoundsLike = False
                    .MatchAllWordForms = False
                    .Execute Replace:=wdReplaceAll
                End With
                Next rng
        doc.Save
        doc.Close

        Set rng = Nothing
        Set doc = Nothing
```

```
        Next i
    Else
        MsgBox "No files matched " & .FileName
    End If
End With
End Sub
```

Find and Replace Without Find and Replace

HACK #32

This brute-force hack lets you power through simple substitutions without complicated code.

VBA newbies (and even veterans) find it frustrating to use the Find and Replace command from within a macro.

Why the difficulty? Most people think of Find and Replace as an action, which would translate to a *procedure* in VBA. Word, however, uses a Find *object* to handle searching and replacing.

Scripting languages such as Python and Ruby implement their substitution capabilities as objects, too. If you implement Find as an object, you can assign and retain properties in memory for the next time you use the object. The same phenomenon occurs when you do a search and the text you last searched for remains in the "Find what" box.

While the Find object is a powerful tool for working with Word from VBA, its complexity can really bog you down when all you need is a quick fix. Find has more than two dozen properties, and while it does execute very quickly, you will probably spend any time you save using the Find object figuring out *how* to use it. This hack shows you how to replace it (pun intended) with a simple For Each loop [Hack #66].

For example, say your document uses four different highlighting colors in each paragraph: red, blue, yellow, and green. Just as you finally finish applying the highlighting, your boss decides she prefers teal instead of blue and asks you to make the change. The clock reads 10 minutes to noon, and you want this project wrapped up before your lunch date.

First, you try Edit → Replace, but you quickly discover that although you can search for highlighting, you cannot specify a color.

You decide to try a macro instead, but 30 minutes later you still need to figure out how to coerce the Find object into doing your bidding. Hungry and frustrated, you finally give up and start making the change by hand. There must be a better way!

The Code

It would probably take you five minutes to write these five lines of code with the help of VBA's IntelliSense **[Hack #1]**, and maybe another five minutes to test and debug it on a snippet of your document. And five lines of brute-force VBA is all it takes:

```
Sub FixHighlightColor( )
Dim char As Range
For Each char In ActiveDocument.Characters
    If char.HighlightColorIndex = wdBlue Then
        char.HighlightColorIndex = wdTeal
    End If
Next char
End Sub
```

Notice that the macro iterates through *each character* in the active document (including spaces).

Running the Hack

Place this macro in the template of your choice **[Hack #50]** and either run it from the Tools → Macro → Macros dialog or put a button for it on a menu or toolbar **[Hack #1]**.

Obviously, it takes some time to run such a resource-intensive procedure. But on a sample 27-page document, with 83,000 characters (including spaces), this macro took a grand total of four minutes. You might have made that lunch date after all.

Of course, if your document is hundreds of pages long, or if you have dozens of documents to fix, it might make sense to develop more efficient code. But even if your document was 10 times longer than our sample (or you had nine more of them), this macro would have solved your problem before you even finished lunch.

Hacking the Hack

Although "each character in the active document" sounds all-encompassing, it leaves out a few important things. Each document is actually made of several *story ranges*: one for the main text, another for the footnotes, another for the headers and footers, and so on. The macro, however, searches only the main text story range, so if a header contained highlighting, the FixHighlightColor macro would fail to catch it.

To solve this problem, nest your code inside another For Each loop:

```
Sub FixHighlightColorInAllStories( )
Dim char As Range
```

```
Dim stry as Range
For Each stry In ActiveDocument.StoryRanges
    For Each char In stry.Characters
        If char.HighlightColorIndex = wdBlue Then
            char.HighlightColorIndex = wdTeal
        End If
    Next char
Next stry
End Sub
```

To see how much simpler a For Each loop can be, take a look at the following macro, which performs the same substitution as the five-line FixHighlightColor macro shown above.

The Find object works a lot faster (about 70% faster on that same test document), but it's a lot trickier to code:

```
Sub FixHighlightUsingFind( )
Dim rngToSearch As Range
Dim rngResult As Range

Set rngToSearch = ActiveDocument.Range
Set rngResult = rngToSearch.Duplicate

Do
    With rngResult.Find
        .ClearFormatting
        .Text = ""
        .Forward = True
        .Wrap = wdFindStop
        .Highlight = True
        .Execute
    End With

    If rngResult.Find.Found = False Then
        Exit Do
    End If

    If rngResult.HighlightColorIndex = wdBlue Then
        rngResult.HighlightColorIndex = wdTeal
    End If
    rngResult.MoveStart wdWord
    rngResult.End = rngToSearch.End
Loop Until rngResult.Find.Found = False

End Sub
```

As the bolded lines show, the part of the macro that does the actual substitution is nearly identical to the FixHighlightColor macro above. Everything else is excess baggage.

Just like the For Each loop in the FixHighlightColor macro, the Find object in this macro misses items not in a document's main story range. To find everything, including headers, footers, footnotes, and text boxes, you need to wrap the Find and Replace inside of a For Each loop, as the following code shows:

```
Sub FindInEveryStory( )
Dim rngStory As Range
Dim rngToSearch As Range
Dim rngResult As Range
For Each rngStory In ActiveDocument.StoryRanges
    Set rngToSearch = rngStory
    Set rngResult = rngToSearch.Duplicate

    Do
        With rngResult.Find
            .ClearFormatting
            .Text = ""
            .Forward = True
            .Wrap = wdFindStop
            .Highlight = True
            .Execute
        End With

        If rngResult.Find.Found = False Then
            Exit Do
        End If

        If rngResult.HighlightColorIndex = wdBlue Then
            rngResult.HighlightColorIndex = wdTeal
        End If
        rngResult.MoveStart wdWord
        rngResult.End = rngToSearch.End
    Loop Until rngResult.Find.Found = False
Next rngStory
End Sub
```

If you do a Find and Replace from the Word interface, it *will* catch text in the headers, footers, footnotes, and so on, as long as you search All rather than Up or Down. If, however, you play back a recorded macro of the same Find and Replace, it will leave those items untouched.

Quickly Create a Custom Dictionary

HACK
#33

Adding items to a custom dictionary one by one is a tedious exercise. Here's how to add an entire list of words to your existing custom dictionary, or as a separate, new custom dictionary.

When Word performs a Spelling and Grammar check on your document, it uses whichever dictionary is available for your language. You can select Tools → Language → Set Language to change the dictionary, as shown in

Figure 4-11. Any language listed with a checkmark next to it has a dictionary installed on your computer.

Figure 4-11. Word uses the dictionary for the language specified here

For example, if you're working on a document for a client from the United Kingdom, and you change the language to "English (U.K.)," Word marks words such as "color" as misspellings and prompts you to change them to their English counterparts, as shown in Figure 4-12.

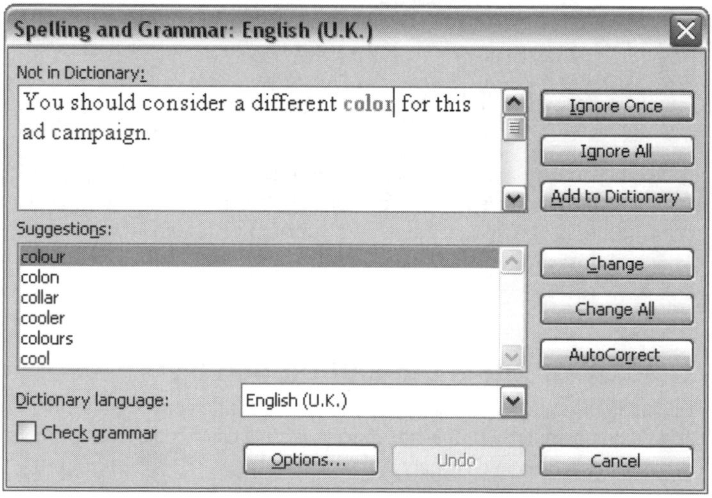

Figure 4-12. When using the U.K. English dictionary, "color" is a misspelling

But often a document or set of documents uses a very specialized set of terms not included in any of the installed dictionaries. Although you can add words to the dictionary—or, rather, to the default *custom dictionary file* (in most cases, *CUSTOM.DIC*)—if the project exists for only a short time, you may not want those new entries for future documents. Rather than temporarily adding the terms to your standard custom dictionary, which you may prefer to reserve for items you use all the time, you're better off adding a new custom dictionary for your project or client, which you can later remove when the project's finished.

The method for creating and populating a custom dictionary from within Word involves the use of a lot of dialogs, and it can become a real pain if you want to enter a long list of words at once.

Fortunately, there's an easier way. A custom dictionary is nothing more than a text file with a *.dic* extension, saved in a special folder. In Word 2000, 2002, and 2003, the folder is typically *C:\Documents and Settings\<username>\Application Data\Microsoft\Proof*.

Creating the Custom Dictionary

To create your new custom dictionary, create a list of the words you want to add using your favorite text editor, such as Notepad, and save the file with a *.dic* extension in the Proof folder.

> Though you can create plain-text files using Word, you can avoid the possibility of extraneous formatting characters being included by using a standard text editor, such as Notepad.

As an example, let's say that while writing a book about Word macros, you want the Spelling and Grammar check to ignore certain terms, such as "AutoExec" and "DocumentBeforeClose." After you enter the list of terms in a text editor, save the file in the Proof directory described above, as shown in Figure 4-13.

Activating the Custom Dictionary

To tell Word to start checking your new custom dictionary during the Spelling and Grammar check, you must first activate it.

Select Tools → Options and click the Spelling and Grammar tab. Click the Custom Dictionaries button to display the Custom Dictionaries dialog shown in Figure 4-14.

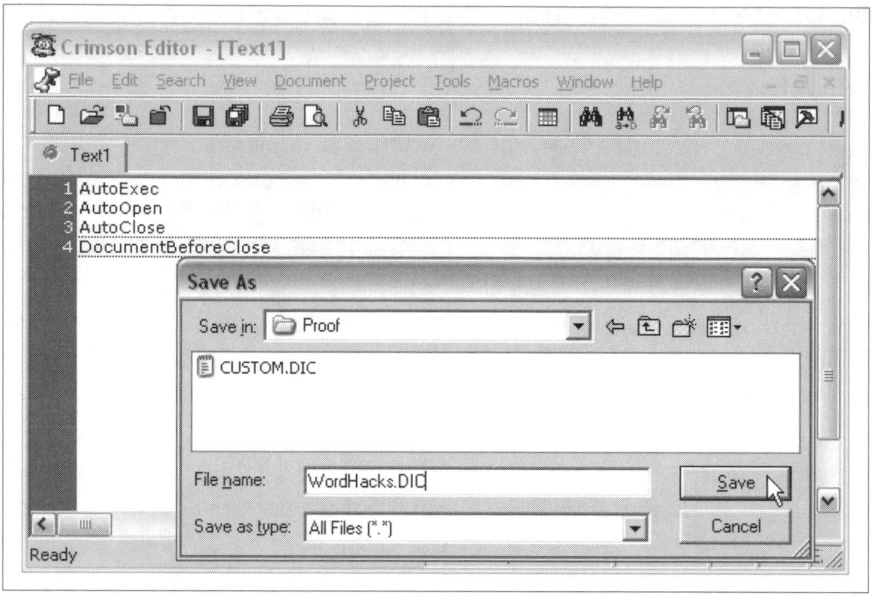

Figure 4-13. Saving a list of words as a custom dictionary file

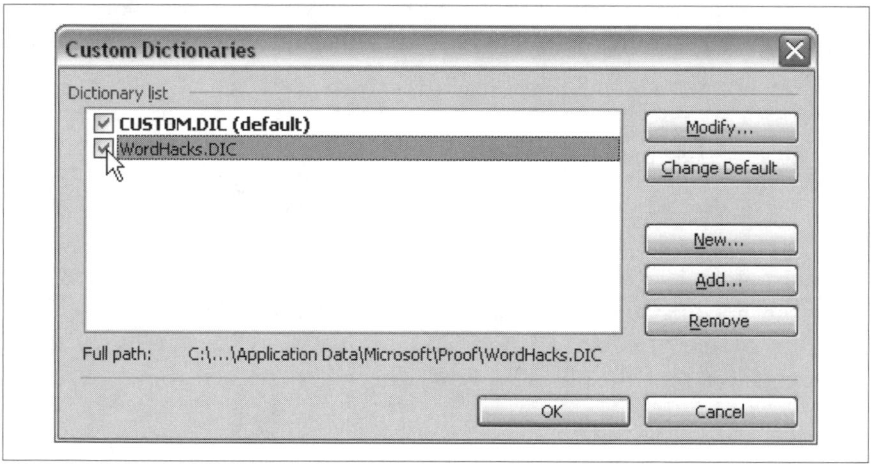

Figure 4-14. Loading a new custom dictionary

Any *.dic* files in the Proof directory will be included in the dictionary list. To activate your new custom dictionary, just check the box next to its name and click the OK button. When you're finished with the project, use the same dialog to deactivate the custom dictionary.

Create a Dictionary Exclusion List
You can't remove words from any of Word's built-in dictionaries, but you can create a list of words that the Spelling and Grammar check will always flag.

An *exclusion list* contains words you want the Spelling and Grammar check to find, regardless of their spelling or usage, as if they'd been excluded from the Dictionary. For example, say you decide to write a book on Microsoft Word and add "word" to your exclusion list. After you complete each chapter, you can then run the Spelling and Grammar check to make sure you didn't mix up "Word" and "word" somewhere along the way.

To create an exclusion list, make a list of words to exclude (in the sense that they will be flagged, rather than passed over as correct) using a standard text editor such as Notepad and save the file in your Proof directory (*C:\Documents and Settings\<username>\Application Data\Microsoft\Proof*). The exclusion list must use the same name as the dictionary you use. For example, Word uses the dictionary named *Mssp3en.lex* for U.S. English. If you're using this dictionary, you *must* name the exclusion list *Mssp3en.exc*. (Note that the file uses the *.exc* extension.) The list will take effect the next time you start Word.

To add an exclusion list for a different dictionary, you need to know its name. Windows-based systems store the dictionaries in *C:\Program Files\ Common Files\Microsoft Shared\Proof*, as shown in Figure 4-15.

1033	MSHY2_EN.LEX	MSSP3ES.DLL	MSTH3ES.LEX
1036	MSHY3ES.DLL	MSSP3ES.LEX	MSTH3FR.DLL
3082	MSHY3ES.LEX	MSSP3FR.DLL	MSTH3FR.LEX
CHAPI3T1.DLL	MSHY3FR.DLL	MSSP3FR.LEX	MSTH3ES.DLL
CSAPI3T1.DLL	MSHY3FR.LEX	MSSP3PFR.LEX	MSWDS_EN.LEX
CTAPI3T2.DLL	MSHYPH2.DLL	MSSPELL3.DLL	MSWDS_ES.LEX
MSGR3EN.LEX	MSLID.DLL	MSTH3AM.LEX	MSWDS_FR.LEX
MSGR3ES.LEX	MSSP3EN.LEX	MSTH3BR.LEX	
MSGR3FR.LEX	MSSP3ENA.LEX	MSTH3ES.DLL	

Figure 4-15. Create an exclusion list for any installed dictionary (files ending in .lex)

As the name of the folder implies, the Office programs share all the dictionaries. If you create an exclusion list in Word, you will also exclude those words from the Spelling and Grammar checks of all the other Office applications.

Disable Overtype Permanently

Inspiration strikes, and you begin a flurry of typing with nary a glance at the screen. A few minutes later, you look up and discover with horror that you've accidentally entered Overtype mode, that zero-sum game of editing by attrition. This hack shows you how to disable Overtype mode once and for all.

Do you know *anyone* who uses Overtype mode? Didn't think so. In fact, many people simply reassign the Insert key to some other function—typically Paste, though any command will do. Word even includes an option to use the Insert key for pasting: simply select Tools → Options, click the Edit tab, and check the "Use the INS key for paste" box.

But if you've been burned before, even this may not be enough to assuage your fears. With this hack, Overtype can never hurt you again. It also offers a great example of intercepting built-in commands **[Hack #61]**, one of the most powerful customization features available in Word.

Select Tools → Macro → Macros, choose Word Commands from the "Macros in" drop-down list, and select Overtype from the "Macro name" list, as shown in Figure 4-16.

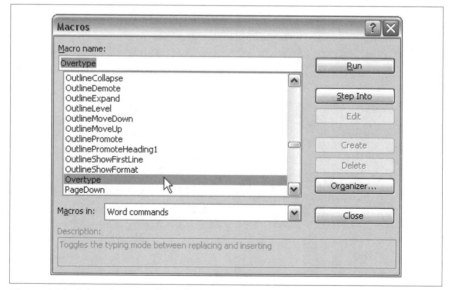

Figure 4-16. Select Overtype from the list of Word macros

Next, choose *Normal.dot* (or the template of your choice **[Hack #50]**) from the "Macros in" drop-down list and click the Create button, as shown in Figure 4-17.

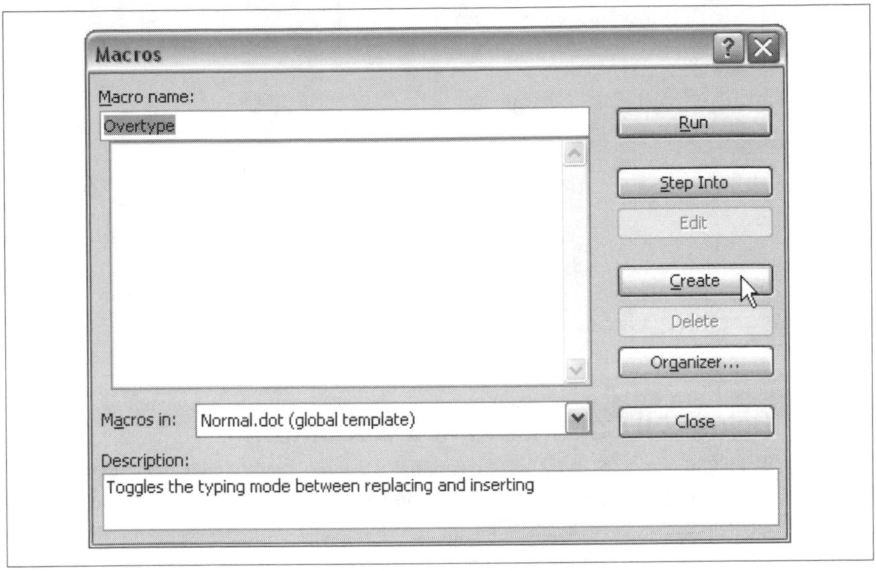

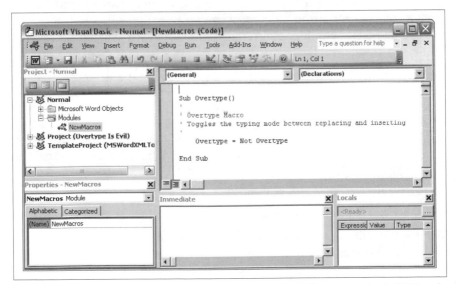

Figure 4-17. Preparing to create a new Overtype macro in Normal.dot

The Visual Basic Editor will open, and you'll see a brand new macro named Overtype, already filled in with the VBA code equivalent to toggling the Insert button, as shown in Figure 4-18.

Figure 4-18. When you create a macro based on one of Word's commands, the VBA code to perform the command is inserted automatically

Select the line of code that says:

```
Overtype = Not Overtype
```

and replace it with the following:

```
Selection.Paste
```

Now select File → Save, and then go to File → Close and Return to Microsoft Word.

> If you prefer to *completely* disable Overtype, just delete the following line of code:
> ```
> Overtype = Not Overtype
> ```

HACK #36   Delete All Comments in a Document

Word 2002 and 2003 include a command on the Reviewing toolbar that deletes all the comments in a document. For users of earlier versions of Word, this hack does the same thing.

Comments let one or more reviewers comment on the text of a document without interfering with the content of the document. But once you finish editing or reviewing a document, getting rid of those comments can be a hassle.

To quickly delete a single comment, right-click its reference and choose Delete Comment from the shortcut menu **[Hack #3]**. But if you're facing dozens or hundreds of comments, deleting each one in turn will take you quite a while.

Another method for deleting comments is to use Find and Replace. Select Edit → Replace and do the following:

1. Leave the Find What box empty.
2. Click the Format button, choose Style, and select the Comment Reference style. (Don't see the Format button? Click the More button to make it visible.)
3. Leave the Replace With box empty.
4. Click the Replace All button.

But occasionally some comments just won't go quietly, so a VBA macro is your best bet for quickly getting rid of them.

The Code

Place this macro in the template of your choice [Hack #50] and either run it from the Tools → Macro → Macros dialog or put a button for it on a menu or toolbar [Hack #1]:

```
Sub DeleteAllComments
Dim i As Integer
For i = ActiveDocument.Comments.Count To 1 Step -1
    ActiveDocument.Comments(i).Delete
Next i
End Sub
```

If you're concerned about running the macro unintentionally, perhaps because you've placed it on a toolbar near another command you use frequently, the following version includes a prompt asking you to confirm that you do indeed want all the comments deleted, as shown in Figure 4-19. It also pops up a message when it finishes, notifying you how many comments were removed.

```
Sub DeleteAllCommentsAndConfirm( )
Dim i As Integer
Dim iNumberOfComments As Integer
If MsgBox( _
    "Are you sure you want to delete All comments in this document?", _
        vbYesNo) = vbYes Then
    iNumberOfComments = ActiveDocument.Comments.Count
    For i = iNumberOfComments To 1 Step -1
        ActiveDocument.Comments(i).Delete
    Next i
MsgBox iNumberOfComments & " Comment(s) Deleted", vbInformation
End If
End Sub
```

Figure 4-19. Confirming that you want to delete all comments in a document

HACK #37 Delete All Bookmarks in a Document

Word offers no built-in way to delete all of a document's bookmarks at once. This hack shows you how to do it with some VBA.

Bookmarks let you quickly navigate through a document. But if you will eventually import your document into another program, such as Quark or

FrameMaker, those bookmarks can cause trouble—for example, FrameMaker attempts to convert some bookmarks into its own similar "marker" feature, but it often creates unresolved cross-references that you must delete. Conversely, when exporting to Word format from another program, the program may create bookmarks of questionable value in the Word document.

You can select Insert → Bookmark and delete bookmarks one at a time, but if a document has dozens or more, you'll be clicking for a while. The macro in this hack will delete them all at once.

The Code

Place this macro in the template of your choice [Hack #50] and either run it from the Tools → Macro → Macros dialog or put a button for it on a menu or toolbar [Hack #1].

The following macro deletes every bookmark in a document:

```
Sub DeleteAllBookmarks()
Dim i As Integer
For i = ActiveDocument.Bookmarks.Count To 1 Step -1
    ActiveDocument.Bookmarks(i).Delete
Next i

End Sub
```

Hacking the Hack

Word hides some of the bookmarks it creates, such as the ones for cross-references, by default. A hidden bookmark isn't included when iterating through each bookmark in a document, unless the "Hidden bookmarks" box in the Insert → Bookmark dialog is checked. To be sure you get all of them, this version of the macro turns on that setting before running:

```
Sub DeleteAllBookmarksIncludingHidden()
Dim i As Integer
Activedocument.Bookmarks.ShowHidden = True
For i = ActiveDocument.Bookmarks.Count To 1 Step -1
    ActiveDocument.Bookmarks(i).Delete
Next i

End Sub
```

Turn Comments into Regular Text

#38 This hack shows you how to replace a comment's reference with its text and author.

Comments let reviewers annotate the text without interfering with the text. But if you later import the document into another program, such as Quark or FrameMaker, those comments can cause trouble. Also, when you save a file as a plain-text (*.txt*) file, you lose any comment references, and the comments end up tacked on at the end, out of context.

In many cases, you can just delete all the comments [Hack #36], but if those comments contain important instructions for a compositor, or other useful information, you may prefer to incorporate the comments into the text and set them off with a bit of markup. A macro can quickly convert those comments into regular text, while retaining their positions in the document.

Select Tools → Options and click the User Information tab to view the author name assigned to comments you create.

The Code

This macro replaces each comment reference in a document with the text of the comment itself and adds the name of the comment's author at the end. The entire entry is surrounded in brackets and styled with the built-in Emphasis character style, as shown in Figure 4-20.

> The quick brown fox jumps over the lazy dog. The quick brown fox jumps over the lazy dog. The quick brown fox *[I think you're spending too much time talking about foxes and dogs here. -- Andrew Savikas]* jumps over the lazy dog. The quick brown fox jumps over the lazy dog. The quick brown fox jumps over the lazy dog.

Figure 4-20. A Word comment converted to text

Place this macro in the template of your choice [Hack #50] and either run it from the Tools → Macro → Macros dialog or put a button for it on a menu or toolbar [Hack #1]. Be sure your cursor is currently in the main text of the document when you run this macro.

```
Sub ConvertCommentsToInlineText( )
Dim c As Comment
Dim i As Integer
For i = ActiveDocument.Comments.Count To 1 Step -1
    Set c = ActiveDocument.Comments(i)
    c.Reference.Style = wdStyleEmphasis
    c.Reference.Text = " [" & c.Range.Text & " -- " & c.Author & "] "
```

```
Next i
End Sub
```

Though the code never explicitly deletes the comments, Word removes them when the macro replaces their references with text.

Hacking the Hack

Rather than retaining the comments within the text, you can create a separate document containing just the comments.

The following macro creates a table listing each comment in a document, along with the comment's author. The table is created in a new, blank document.

```
Sub CreateTableOfComments
Dim c As Comment
Dim i As Integer
Dim docForComments As Document
Dim docActive As Document

Set docActive = ActiveDocument
Set docForComments = Documents.Add
docForComments.Range.InsertAfter _
    "Comment" & vbTab & "Author" & vbCr

For Each c In docActive.Comments
docForComments.Range.InsertAfter _
    c.Author & vbTab & c.Range.text & vbCr
Next c
docForComments.Range.ConvertToTable _
    Separator:=vbTab, _
    Format:=wdTableFormatList1
End Sub
```

See Also

- "Batch-Process Word Documents with XSLT" [Hack #95]

HACK #39   Apply Context-Sensitive Formatting

Which character style you apply to a selection of text may depend on its context. This hack makes it easy to apply the correct one of several similar styles by using a macro to examine the selection's surroundings.

A complex document template may have several similar character styles, each fulfilling a different semantic purpose in the document's structure. The template used for this manuscript, for example, has two styles used to emphasize portions of text: one called *emphasis* (used to emphasize normal body text) and the other *replaceable* (used to emphasize text presented in a constant-width font). Which style is used depends on the context of the text to be emphasized.

One way to ensure the correct application of several different, but similar, character styles is to provide users with a detailed set of instructions about which style to use in any particular situation (and when *not* to use a particular style, such as in a heading). But many people will simply do what they've always done in Word to emphasize text: press the I button on the Formatting toolbar.

Unfortunately, this action only applies direct formatting on top of the paragraph style already in use. You can try just telling people not to reach for the I button, or you can opt to intercept the Italic command **[Hack #61]** and apply the correct character style based on the current paragraph style.

For example, assume that there are two character styles, *emphasis* and *replaceable*, governed by the following four rules:

- Do not apply character styles with multiple paragraphs selected.
- Do not use character styles in headings.
- If the paragraph style's name includes the word "Code," use the *replaceable* character style.
- In all other situations, use the *emphasis* character style.

The Code

The following macro examines the context of the selected text when you press the I button and then, based on the rules described above, performs one of three possible actions:

- Ignores the command
- Warns the user that the attempted action is not permitted
- Applies one of the two character styles

After you place this macro in the template of your choice **[Hack #50]**, it will run whenever you press the I button on the toolbar or the key command associated with italic (typically Ctrl-I):

```
Sub Italic( )
Dim sel As Selection
Dim sParagraphStyleName As String

Set sel = Selection

' Quietly exit if selection spans multiple paragraphs
If sel.Range.Paragraphs.Count <> 1 Then Exit Sub
```

```
' Warn then exit if selection is in a heading
sParagraphStyleName = sel.Range.Paragraphs.First.Style
If InStr(sParagraphStyleName, "Heading") Then
    MsgBox "Sorry, Character Styles aren't allowed in headings"
    Exit Sub
End If

' Apply appropriate character style
If InStr(sParagraphStyleName, "Code") Then
    sel.Style = "replaceable"
Else
    sel.Style = "emphasis"
End If

End Sub
```

For another example of intercepting toolbar buttons, check out "Corral Basic Bullets and Numbering" **[Hack #42]**.

HACK #40 Send a Document as a Plain-Text Outlook Email

Use a macro to turn the text of a Word document into the body of an Outlook email.

Sometimes sending a document as an email attachment is overkill, especially if you just want the recipient to review the text of a simple document. And if the recipient is under a particularly restrictive mail server, he may not be able to receive Word document attachments, for fear of a virus.

Now, you can always try to cut and paste the text into the body of an email, but that rarely produces anything better than a giant block of continuous text that can be difficult to read from an email window.

Another option is to save the document as a plain-text *.txt* file, open up that file in a text editor such as Notepad, add some extra line breaks for readability, then cut and paste *that* into an email. Yuck.

Here's an easier option: after changing a few settings from within the Visual Basic Editor, you can write macros that directly access Outlook from within Word, let you get the text-only contents of a document, add some extra line breaks for readability, quickly create a new email message, and insert the text as the message body.

Setting the Reference to Outlook

First, make sure you can access the Outlook object model from within Word. Select Tools → Macro → Visual Basic Editor, then choose Tools → References. Scroll down and check the "Microsoft Outlook 11.0 Object Library" box, as shown in Figure 4-21.

> If you're using an earlier version of Outlook, select the reference to that version. The code in this hack will still work.

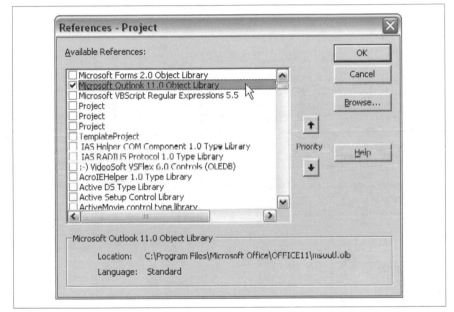

Figure 4-21. Setting a reference to the Outlook object model

Once you've established that reference, you can access the Outlook object model from your Word macros.

The Code

Place this macro in the template of your choice [Hack #50] and either run it from the Tools → Macro → Macros dialog or put a button for it on a menu or toolbar [Hack #1].

Since there's a good chance Outlook may already be open when running a macro that accesses it, the code first tries to reference the currently open

instance of Outlook. If it can't find one, the code creates and uses a new
instance of Outlook.

```
Sub doc2outlookemail( )
Dim sDocText As String
Dim oOutlook As Outlook.Application
Dim oMailItem  As Outlook.MailItem

' Get currently running Outlook, or create new instance
On Error Resume Next
Set oOutlook = GetObject(Class:="Outlook.Application")
If Err.Number = 429 Then
    Set oOutlook = CreateObject(Class:="Outlook.Application")
ElseIf Err.Number <> 0 Then
    MsgBox "Error: " & Err.Number & vbCr & Err.Description
    Exit Sub
End If

sDocText = ActiveDocument.Content.Text
' Replace each paragraph break with two paragraph breaks
sDocText = Replace(sDocText, Chr(13), String(2, Chr(13)))
Set oMailItem = oOutlook.CreateItem(olMailItem)

oMailItem.Body = sDocText
oMailItem.Display

' Clean up references to Outlook objects
Set oMailItem = Nothing
Set oOutlook = Nothing
End Sub
```

The code leaves the email open and unaddressed. Just fill in the recipient's
address and click the Send button.

Hacking the Hack

Rather than sending the entire contents of a Word document, you may want
to send just the outline as a plain-text email. To do so, first switch to Outline view in your document and select the outline level you want included in
the email. Only the text visible from Outline view will be included in the
email.

Now make a minor adjustment to the earlier macro, as shown in bold:

```
Sub SendOutlineOnly( )
Dim sDocText As String
Dim oOutlook As Outlook.Application
Dim oMailItem  As Outlook.MailItem

' Get currently running Outlook, or create new instance
On Error Resume Next
Set oOutlook = GetObject(Class:="Outlook.Application")
```

```
If Err.Number = 429 Then
    Set oOutlook = CreateObject(Class:="Outlook.Application")
ElseIf Err.Number <> 0 Then
    MsgBox "Error: " & Err.Number & vbCr & Err.Description
    Exit Sub
End If
' Just want the outline
ActiveDocument.Content.TextRetrievalMode.ViewType = wdOutlineView
sDocText = ActiveDocument.Content.Text
' Replace each paragraph break with two paragraph breaks
sDocText = Replace(sDocText, Chr(13), String(2, Chr(13)))
Set oMailItem = oOutlook.CreateItem(olMailItem)

oMailItem.Body = sDocText
oMailItem.Display

' Clean up references to Outlook objects
Set oMailItem = Nothing
Set oOutlook = Nothing
End Sub
```

HACK #41 Swap Revision Authors

This hack shows you how to edit the information Word stores when you edit a document using the Track Changes feature.

In addition to marking revisions in a document, Word's Track Changes feature remembers who made the revisions. It lets you view up to eight different revision authors in a single document, each of whose changes are displayed in a different color.

Select Tools ▸ Options and click the Track Changes tab to modify how Word displays revisions.

But what if you want to modify the name of the author of a particular set of revisions? For example, say you took some work home for the weekend and accidentally did your editing while logged into your computer as one of your kids. Now all your revisions appear as though your teenage son made the changes. Many coworkers would be forgiving, but a client would hardly look kindly on this error.

Unfortunately, you can't modify a revision author from VBA. It does have a Revision object with an Author property, but the property is read-only, meaning you can't give it a different value.

To make the change, you'll need to get the document into a format that takes it out of Word's control, such as *RTF* (Rich Text Format). When you save a document as an RTF file, you retain the revision information. You can then edit the RTF file with any standard text editor, such as Notepad.

Here's how to change the author of a set of revisions in a Word file.

First, select File → Save As and choose Rich Text Format in the "Save as type" field to save the file as an .rtf file. Next, open the file with a text editor such as Notepad.

> You can find many free text editors available on the Internet with a lot more to offer than Notepad. Check out http:// www.crimsoneditor.com for one such free editor.

To locate the part of the file that contains the names of the revision authors, do a search in the file for the following:

```
{\*\revtbl
```

You will see a list of revision authors following the string characters, as shown in Figure 4-22. The first entry in the list is always *Unknown*, which you should leave as is. If you edit any of the other names in the list, all revisions attributed to that name will show the change when you open the document in Word.

```
145 360 }}\ls8}{\listoverride\listid815411582\listoverridecount0\ls9}{\listoverr
146 \listoverride\listid501703208\listoverridecount0\ls13}{\listoverride\listid645
147 39\listoverridecount0\ls17}{\listoverride\listid1593276091\listoverridecount
148 {\*\revtbl {Unknown;}{Andrew Savikas;}{Brett Johnson;}{Rael Dornfest;}-
149 \sb0\sa0}}{\*\generator Microsoft Word 11.0.6113;}{\info{\title WordHack
150 {\nofwords13294}{\nofchars75777}{\*\company O'Reilly and Associates, In
151 enddoc\revisions\noxlattoyen\expshrtn\noultrlspc\dntblnsbdb\nospaceforul\l
```

Figure 4-22. The list of revision authors inside an RTF file

After you make the change to the RTF file, save it, and then open it in Word. You can now select File → Save As and return it to the native .doc format.

> Be careful when you edit the RTF file. Word (and any other program that reads RTF files) is very sensitive to the correct positioning of those braces. Make sure you don't accidentally delete one of the braces when you edit the name. If you do, Word may not be able to open the file.

Hacking the Hack

Editing RTF files by hand is tricky business. If you regularly swap revision authors in a document, a Perl script can take over the dirty work.

You can download Perl for a Windows machine for free from
http://www.activestate.com.

The following script requires the RTF::Tokenizer module. If you use the
ActiveState distribution of Perl, you can use the Perl Package Manager, available from the ActivePerl entry on your Start menu, to install RTF::Tokenizer.

```perl
#!/usr/bin/perl

use strict;
use Getopt::Long;
use RTF::Tokenizer;

my %opts = ();
GetOptions (\%opts, 'from=s', 'to=s');

my $filename = shift;

die "Please provide an rtf file to parse.\n" unless $filename;

my $tokenizer = RTF::Tokenizer >new( file => $filename);

while( my ( $type, $arg, $param ) = $tokenizer->get_token( ) ){
    last if $type eq 'eof';

    if($type eq 'control' and $arg eq 'revtbl') {
        my $match = 0;
        put($type, $arg, $param) if $opts{from} and $opts{to};

        my $brace = 1;

        while($brace > 0){
            my @attr = $tokenizer->get_token( );

            $brace++ if $attr[0] eq 'group' and $attr[1] == 1;
            $brace-- if $attr[0] eq 'group' and $attr[1] == 0;

            if( $attr[0] eq 'text') {
                $attr[1] =~ s/;$//;

                if( $opts{from} and $opts{to} ){
                    if( $opts{from} eq $attr[1] ) {
                        $attr[1] = $opts{to};
                        $match = 1;
                    }

                    $attr[1] .= ';';
                    put( @attr);
```

```
                        } else {
                            print $attr[1], "\n" unless $attr[1] eq 'Unknown';
                        }
                    } else {
                        put(@attr) if $opts{from} and $opts{to};
                    }
                }

                if($opts{from} and $opts{to} and !$match) {
                    print STDERR "The author $opts{from} was not found
                                    in the document!\n";
                }
            } else {
                put($type, $arg, $param) if $opts{from} and $opts{to};
            }
        }

        sub put {
            my ($type, $arg, $param) = @_;

            if( $type eq 'group' ) {
                print $arg == 1 ? '{' : '}';
            } elsif( $type eq 'control' ) {
                print "\\$arg$param";
            } elsif( $type eq 'text' ) {
                print "\n$arg";
            }
        }
```

Save the script as "authorswap.pl" and put it in the same folder as the RTF file. Run it at a DOS prompt without any arguments to get a list of the revision authors in the document, as shown below:

```
> perl authorswap.pl MyDoc.rtf
> Brett Johnson
  Rael Dornfest
```

To replace one revision author with another, use the to and from options, as shown below. Place the names inside quotation marks.

```
> perl authorswap.pl -from "Brett Johnson" -to "Bob Smith" MyDoc.rtf >
NewFile.rtf
```

The file *NewFile.rtf* will reflect the changes.

—Andrew Savikas and Andy Bruno

Corral Basic Bullets and Numbering

HACK #42

Word offers 10 reliable, customizable, and, best of all, predictable built-in styles for making bulleted and numbered lists. So how come they've got nothing to do with those decidedly *unpredictable* list buttons on the toolbar? Here's how to hack some more helpful buttons.

Admit it: the first time you ever clicked one of those little list buttons, you were impressed. Bullets! Numbers! Indented and aligned! How do they *do* that? Not very well, as it turns out.

What happens when you press one of those buttons depends not on the document you're using, nor on the template on which the document is based. It doesn't even necessarily depend on what happened the *last* time you clicked the button. It depends on which one of the seven different available list formats you last chose from the Format → Bullets and Numbering dialog, as shown in Figure 4-23.

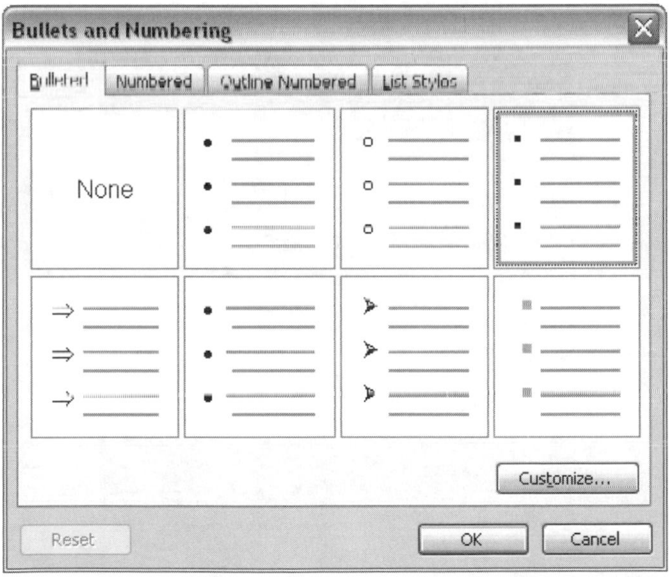

Figure 4-23. When you click the Bullets button on the Formatting toolbar, it will apply the formatting selected here

And those seven formats? They aren't necessarily the *same* seven each time. Which of the seven you last chose is stored in the Windows registry, a massive internal database Windows uses to store information. If you click the same button, in the same document, on two different computers, it can yield different results. Still impressed? It gets worse. Once you've gone through the trouble of populating a long document with lists by using the Bullets or Numbering toolbar buttons, there's no easy way to globally change how those lists are formatted.

Most Word pros avoid these two buttons like the Plague. They prefer to use a paragraph style to include lists in a document. If you use paragraph styles, you can modify every paragraph that uses a particular style at the same time. For the same reason, many power users eschew the Bold and Italic buttons in favor of the Strong and Emphasis character styles (see "Apply Context-Sensitive Formatting" [Hack #39]).

Word provides a boatload of built-in list styles for you. In addition to the 10 bullet and numbering styles, Word has 10 more for nonnumbered lists and list-continuation paragraphs. The list styles all come factory-set with some basic formatting (the "List Bullet 2" style is indented more than the "List Bullet" style, for example). You can see a few of these styles in Figure 4-24. The five List Bullet styles, as they're formatted by default, are shown in Figure 4-25.

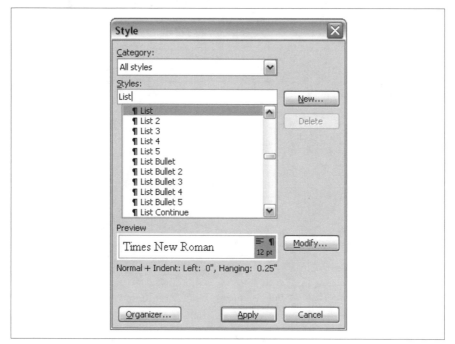

Figure 4-24. Word includes several dozen built-in list styles

But even users who know all about built-in list styles rarely go so far as to actually *remove* the list buttons from the Formatting toolbar. So the buttons

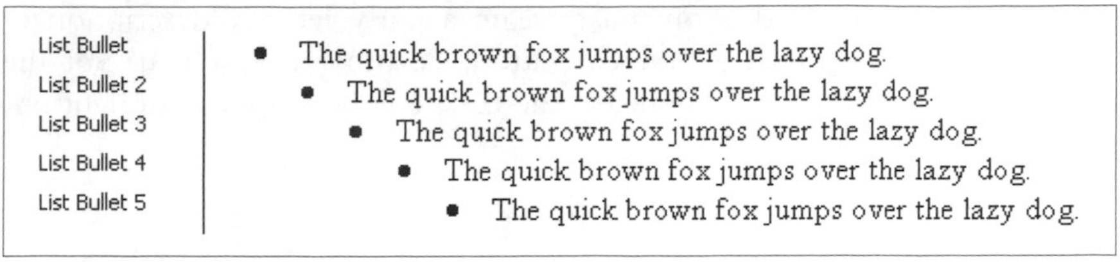

List Bullet	• The quick brown fox jumps over the lazy dog.
List Bullet 2	• The quick brown fox jumps over the lazy dog.
List Bullet 3	• The quick brown fox jumps over the lazy dog.
List Bullet 4	• The quick brown fox jumps over the lazy dog.
List Bullet 5	• The quick brown fox jumps over the lazy dog.

Figure 4-25. The built-in list styles are already indented proportionally

get used anyway, especially for short documents and, unfortunately, for long documents you thought were going to be short.

By intercepting some built-in commands **[Hack #61]**, you can reeducate those buttons (along with the Increase Indent and Decrease Indent buttons) to apply Word's predictable and reliable built-in list styles, which you can easily modify as needed in your documents or templates.

Mapping the Styles to the Buttons

In addition to the Bullets and Numbering buttons, this hack also intercepts the Decrease Indent and Increase Indent buttons. These four buttons, shown in Figure 4-26, sit adjacent to each other on the formatting toolbar.

Figure 4-26. The Four Buttons of the Apocalypse

This hack will use those four buttons to selectively apply the 10 built-in bullet and numbering list styles (List Bullet, List Bullet 2, List Bullet 3, List Bullet 4, List Bullet 5, List Number, List Number 2, List Number 3, List Number 4, and List Number 5).

When you implement this hack, the action taken when you click each of the four buttons will depend on the style currently applied to the selected text. For example, if you select text styled as "List Bullet 2," the following will happen when you click each of the four buttons:

Bullets
   Change back to Normal

Numbering
   Change to "List Number"

Increase Indent
   Change to "List Bullet 3"

Decrease Indent
   Change to "List Bullet"

To implement this hack, you must create a fairly lengthy description of which style gets applied for which button. Fortunately (for you, not the author), that's already been done, so the code below will work straight out of the box, so to speak.

The Code

This hack is a combination of five separate macros: one that makes the decisions and applies the formatting, and four others that intercept the commands used by the four toolbar buttons. Each of the macros used to intercept the buttons "calls" the fifth macro, the one that does the formatting, and "tells" it which button was clicked.

The selected text will always be in one of 11 possible states: either one of the 10 list styles, or some *other* style altogether. For each scenario, you can take four possible actions—one for each button.

These are the four macros that intercept the buttons. Put these, along with the BetterBulletsAndNumbering macro that follows, in the template of your choice [Hack #50].

```
Sub FormatBulletDefault( )
Call BetterBulletsAndNumbering(Selection, "Bullets")
End Sub

Sub FormatNumberDefault( )
Call BetterBulletsAndNumbering(Selection, "Numbering")
End Sub

Sub IncreaseIndent( )
Call BetterBulletsAndNumbering(Selection, "IncreaseIndent")
End Sub

Sub DecreaseIndent( )
Call BetterBulletsAndNumbering(Selection, "DecreaseIndent")
End Sub
```

These four macros must be named *exactly* as shown, or Word won't use them in place of the commands they're named after.

The next macro does the real work of deciding which style to use and applying it to the selected text. To efficiently handle such a large number of options, this code uses VBA's Select Case statements, a much neater alternative to a massive set of complex If... Then... Else statements.

```
Function BetterBulletsAndNumbering(ByRef sel As Selection, _
                                   ByVal sButton As String)
```

```
' We'll convert the passed sButton string
' to a constant for more efficient code
Const cBULLETS = 1
Const cNUMBERING = 2
Const cINCREASE_INDENT = 3
Const cDECREASE_INDENT = 4

Dim DocStyles As Styles
Dim styBullet1 As Style
Dim styBullet2 As Style
Dim styBullet3 As Style
Dim styBullet4 As Style
Dim styBullet5 As Style
Dim styNumber1 As Style
Dim styNumber2 As Style
Dim styNumber3 As Style
Dim styNumber4 As Style
Dim styNumber5 As Style
Dim styBodyText As Style

Dim iButtonPressed As Integer
' A variable for looping through
' each paragraph in the selection
Dim para As Paragraph

Set DocStyles = sel.Document.Styles
Set styBullet1 = DocStyles(wdStyleListBullet)
Set styBullet2 = DocStyles(wdStyleListBullet2)
Set styBullet3 = DocStyles(wdStyleListBullet3)
Set styBullet4 = DocStyles(wdStyleListBullet4)
Set styBullet5 = DocStyles(wdStyleListBullet5)

Set styNumber1 = DocStyles(wdStyleListNumber)
Set styNumber2 = DocStyles(wdStyleListNumber2)
Set styNumber3 = DocStyles(wdStyleListNumber3)
Set styNumber4 = DocStyles(wdStyleListNumber4)
Set styNumber5 = DocStyles(wdStyleListNumber5)

' Assumes you want the "default" body text to be
' Normal style.
Set styBodyText = DocStyles(wdStyleNormal)

Select Case sButton
    Case Is = "Bullets"
        iButtonPressed = cBULLETS
    Case Is = "Numbering"
        iButtonPressed = cNUMBERING
    Case Is = "IncreaseIndent"
        iButtonPressed = cINCREASE_INDENT
    Case Is = "DecreaseIndent"
        iButtonPressed = cDECREASE_INDENT
End Select
```

```
For Each para In sel.Paragraphs

    Select Case para.Style

        ' Paragraph is  List Bullet
        Case Is = styBullet1
            Select Case iButtonPressed
                Case Is = cBULLETS
                    para.Style = styBodyText
                Case Is = cNUMBERING
                    para.Style = styNumber1
                Case Is = cINCREASE_INDENT
                    para.Style = styBullet2
                Case Is = cDECREASE_INDENT
                    para.Style = styBodyText
            End Select

        ' Paragraph is List Bullet 2
        Case Is = styBullet2
            Select Case iButtonPressed
                Case Is = cBULLETS
                    para.Style = styBodyText
                Case Is = cNUMBERING
                    para.Style = styNumber2
                Case Is = cINCREASE_INDENT
                    para.Style = styBullet3
                Case Is = cDECREASE_INDENT
                    para.Style = styBullet1
            End Select

        ' Paragraph is List Bullet 3
        Case Is = styBullet3
            Select Case iButtonPressed
                Case Is = cBULLETS
                    para.Style = styBodyText
                Case Is = cNUMBERING
                    para.Style = styNumber3
                Case Is = cINCREASE_INDENT
                    para.Style = styBullet4
                Case Is = cDECREASE_INDENT
                    para.Style = styBullet2
            End Select

        ' Paragraph is List Bullet 4
        Case Is = styBullet4
            Select Case iButtonPressed
                Case Is = cBULLETS
                    para.Style = styBodyText
                Case Is = cNUMBERING
                    para.Style = styNumber4
                Case Is = cINCREASE_INDENT
                    para.Style = styBullet5
                Case Is = cDECREASE_INDENT
```

```
                        para.Style = styBullet3
        End Select

' Paragraph is List Bullet 5
Case Is = styBullet5
        Select Case iButtonPressed
            Case Is = cBULLETS
                para.Style = styBodyText
            Case Is = cNUMBERING
                para.Style = styNumber5
            Case Is = cINCREASE_INDENT
                ' Do Nothing
            Case Is = cDECREASE_INDENT
                para.Style = styBullet4
        End Select

' Paragraph is List Number
Case Is = styNumber1
        Select Case iButtonPressed
            Case Is = cBULLETS
                para.Style = styBullet1
            Case Is = cNUMBERING
                para.Style - styBodyText
            Case Is = cINCREASE_INDENT
                para.Style = styNumber2
            Case Is = cDECREASE_INDENT
                para.Style = styBodyText
        End Select

' Paragraph is List Number 2
Case Is = styNumber2
        Select Case iButtonPressed
            Case Is = cBULLETS
                para.Style = styBullet2
            Case Is = cNUMBERING
                para.Style - styBodyText
            Case Is = cINCREASE_INDENT
                para.Style = styNumber3
            Case Is = cDECREASE_INDENT
                para.Style = styNumber1
        End Select

' Paragraph is List Number 3
Case Is = styNumber3
        Select Case iButtonPressed
            Case Is = cBULLETS
                para.Style = styBullet3
            Case Is = cNUMBERING
                para.Style = styBodyText
            Case Is = cINCREASE_INDENT
                para.Style = styNumber4
            Case Is = cDECREASE_INDENT
```

```
                                para.Style = styNumber2
                        End Select

                    ' Paragraph is List Number 4
                    Case Is = styNumber4
                        Select Case iButtonPressed
                            Case Is = cBULLETS
                                para.Style = styBullet4
                            Case Is = cNUMBERING
                                para.Style = styBodyText
                            Case Is = cINCREASE_INDENT
                                para.Style = styNumber5
                            Case Is = cDECREASE_INDENT
                                para.Style = styNumber3
                        End Select

                    ' Paragraph is List Number 5
                    Case Is = styNumber5
                        Select Case iButtonPressed
                            Case Is = cBULLETS
                                para.Style = styBullet5
                            Case Is = cNUMBERING
                                para.Style = styBodyText
                            Case Is = cINCREASE_INDENT
                                ' Do Nothing
                            Case Is = cDECREASE_INDENT
                                para.Style = styNumber4
                        End Select

                    Case Else
                        Select Case iButtonPressed
                            Case Is = cBULLETS
                                para.Style = styBullet1
                            Case Is = cNUMBERING
                                para.Style = styNumber1
                            Case Is = cINCREASE_INDENT
                                WordBasic.IncreaseIndent
                            Case Is = cDECREASE_INDENT
                                WordBasic.DecreaseIndent
                        End Select

            End Select

        Next para

    End Function
```

This code has two important features:

- Sometimes you might click one of the indent buttons when you've
  selected text that isn't part of a list. In that case, the macro just "passes"
  the command on to Word, which will indent as it would if the button
  had never been intercepted.

- If you select multiple paragraphs with different styles applied, the code loops through and formats each paragraph in the selection separately, using a For Each loop [Hack #66].

Running the Hack

Once you've placed these macros in an active template, they'll spring into action when you click any of the four toolbar buttons shown in Figure 4-26.

If you want to change the formatting of the bullets or numbering, modify the corresponding built-in list style.

HACK #43 Cross-Reference Automatically

Using the Cross-reference dialog to insert references, particularly in a lengthy document, can be frustrating because it shows you only a few headings at a time. This hack shows you how to create references automatically, without a visit to the dialog.

Whoever decided that the Cross-reference dialog in Word (Insert → Reference → Cross-reference or Insert ▸ Cross-reference, depending on your version of Word) should display only nine items at a time clearly didn't have your best interests in mind. Most lengthy documents include more than nine headings, captions, or other items to reference.

In many cases, creating a cross-reference means converting static text into a dynamic reference by selecting it, then replacing it with the corresponding item from the Cross-reference dialog (as shown in Figure 4-27). But since there's that nine-item limit, you're in for some serious scrolling if you need to make many references. In a Sisyphean spiral, the longer your document is, the more references you likely need, and the longer it will take to find each item in that teeny, tiny list.

This hack shows you two ways to use VBA to automatically create cross-references to headings. In each case, the selected text is compared to the headings in a document, trying to find a match and create a cross-reference.

Referencing the Way Word Does

The procedure shown in this section uses Word VBA's GetCrossReferenceItems method, which returns a list of potential reference targets in a document. Because Word continually updates and indexes this list, accessing it is very fast. This code runs significantly faster than the code in the next section, but that speed comes at a price: you're limited to creating cross-references to items that

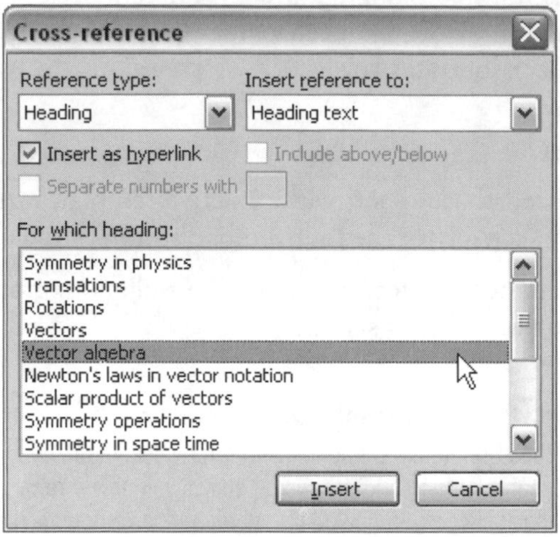

Figure 4-27. Only nine items at a time are visible in the Cross-reference dialog

Word considers potential targets, such as headings that use one of the built-in heading styles. If you've also got a different kind of heading style in your document, such as SidebarTitle, those headings don't "count" as possible reference targets.

Place this macro in the template of your choice [Hack #50] and either run it from the Tools → Macro → Macros dialog or put a button for it on a menu or toolbar [Hack #1].

If your current selection includes more than one paragraph, the macro exits without taking any action.

```
Sub InsertAutoXRef( )

Dim sel As Selection
Dim doc As Document
Dim vHeadings As Variant
Dim v As Variant
Dim i As Integer

Set sel = Selection
Set doc = Selection.Document

' Exit if selection includes multiple paragraphs
If sel.Range.Paragraphs.Count <> 1 Then Exit Sub

' Collapse selection if there are spaces or paragraph
' marks on either end
sel.MoveStartWhile cset:=(Chr$(32) & Chr$(13)), Count:=sel.Characters.Count
sel.MoveEndWhile cset:=(Chr$(32) & Chr$(13)), Count:=-sel.Characters.Count
```

```
vHeadings = doc.GetCrossReferenceItems(wdRefTypeHeading)

i = 1
For Each v In vHeadings
    If Trim (sel.Range.Text) = Trim (v) Then
        sel.InsertCrossReference _
            referencetype:=wdRefTypeHeading, _
            referencekind:=wdContentText, _
            referenceitem:=i
        Exit Sub
    End If
    i = i + 1
Next v

MsgBox "Couldn't match: " & sel.Range.Text
End Sub
```

There are two important limitations to note about this code. First, if multiple headings match the selected text, the code creates a reference to the first match and ignores subsequent matches. This limitation is a problem if you have multiple headings with the same text, such as "The Code," used throughout this book.

Second, the code offers no protection against creating a self-reference. If the match found by the code is the text you've selected, the reference that's created will replace the text it's supposed to reference, resulting in a broken reference, as shown in Figure 4-28.

Error! Reference source not found.

Figure 4-28. Self-referencing creates a broken reference

This kind of inadvertent text deletion is also possible when creating references from the Word Cross-reference dialog. When you create a self-reference, Word displays a message telling you the reference is empty—but only after the text has been deleted.

A Better Way to Reference

This method won't match the speed offered by the code shown above, but its flexibility makes it a better starting point for hacking your own solutions.

Rather than looking only at paragraphs that use one of Word's built-in heading styles, this code examines every paragraph in the document, looking for a match to the selected text. That means you can easily create a reference to a heading that uses a custom paragraph style, such as SidebarTitle.

Unlike the code in the previous section, this procedure also checks to be sure the match it's found isn't the selected text, avoiding the possibility of a self-reference.

This code is divided into five separate procedures: the MakeAutoXRef procedure and four supporting procedures, each of which performs an operation needed to create the reference. Place all five procedures in the template of your choice [Hack #50] and run the one named MakeAutoXRef to create a reference in place of the selected text.

The first procedure, named MakeAutoXRef, is shown first. In conjunction with the supporting procedures shown afterward, it examines each paragraph in the document. If it finds one that matches the selected text, it creates a bookmark around the match and then replaces the selected text with a reference pointing to the bookmark. If the matched paragraph has already been referenced elsewhere, the existing bookmark is used.

```
Sub MakeAutoXRef( )
Dim sel As Selection
Dim rng As Range
Dim para As Paragraph
Dim doc As Document
Dim sBookmarkName As String
Dim sSelectionText As String
Dim lSelectedParaIndex As Long

Set sel = Selection
Set doc = sel.Document

If sel.Range.Paragraphs.Count <> 1 Then Exit Sub

lSelectedParaIndex = GetParaIndex(sel.Range.Paragraphs.First)

sel.MoveStartWhile cset:=(Chr$(32) & Chr$(13)), Count:=sel.Characters.Count
sel.MoveEndWhile cset:=(Chr$(32) & Chr$(13)), Count:=-sel.Characters.Count

sSelectionText = sel.Text

For Each para In doc.Paragraphs
    Set rng = para.Range
    rng.MoveStartWhile cset:=(Chr$(32) & Chr$(13)), _
        Count:=rng.Characters.Count
    rng.MoveEndWhile cset:=(Chr$(32) & Chr$(13)), _
        Count:=-rng.Characters.Count
    If rng.Text = sSelectionText Then
        If Not GetParaIndex(para) = lSelectedParaIndex Then
            sBookmarkName = GetOrSetXRefBookmark(para)
            If Len(sBookmarkName) = 0 Then
                MsgBox "Couldn't get or set bookmark"
                Exit Sub
            End If
        End If
```

```
        sel.InsertCrossReference _
            referencekind:=wdContentText, _
            referenceitem:=doc.Bookmarks(sBookmarkName), _
            referencetype:=wdRefTypeBookmark, _
            insertashyperlink:=True
            Exit Sub
    Else
        MsgBox "Can't self reference!"
    End If
End If

    Next para

    End Sub
```

The code shown in bold is the part of the procedure that actually creates the reference. Note that it's very similar to part of the code shown in the previous section.

The supporting procedures. The following function removes from a string characters that Word won't allow in bookmark names (except for spaces, which are replaced by underscores in a different procedure):

```
Function RemoveInvalidBookmarkCharsFromString(ByVal str As String) As String
Dim i As Integer
For i - 33 To 255
    Select Case i
        Case 33 To 47, 58 To 64, 91 To 96, 123 To 255
            str = Replace(str, Chr (i), vbNullString)
    End Select
Next i
RemoveInvalidBookmarkCharsFromString = str
End Function
```

The next function takes a string and turns it into a valid bookmark name, including prefacing it with "XREF" for easier identification and adding in a five-digit random number [Hack #68] to ensure that it's unique.

In addition, the function replaces underscores with spaces. So, for example, the heading "Foo the bar" would be converted into something like "XREF56774_ Foo_the_bar"—a bit easier to work with than the "_Ref45762234"-style names that Word assigns to its own cross-reference bookmarks.

```
Function ConvertStringRefBookmarkName(ByVal str As String) As String
str = RemoveInvalidBookmarkCharsFromString(str)
str = Replace(str, Chr$(32), "_")
str = "_" & str
str = "XREF" & CStr(Int(90000 * Rnd + 10000)) & str
ConvertStringRefBookmarkName = str
End Function
```

This next function just determines a paragraph's index in the document (e.g., the second paragraph in the document has an index of 2):

```
Function GetParagraphIndex(para As Paragraph) As Long
GetParagraphIndex = _
    para.Range.Document.Range(0, para.Range.End).Paragraphs.Count
End Function
```

The final function creates cross-reference bookmarks in paragraphs that do not contain bookmarks and returns the bookmark name for use in the cross-reference. If the paragraph already has a cross-reference bookmark, it simply returns the existing bookmark name for use in the cross-reference.

```
Function GetOrSetXRefBookmark(para As Paragraph) As String
Dim i As Integer
Dim rng As Range
Dim sBookmarkName As String

If para.Range.Bookmarks.Count <> 0 Then
    For i = 1 To para.Range.Bookmarks.Count
        If InStr(1, para.Range.Bookmarks(i).Name, "XREF") Then
            GetOrSetXRefBookmark = para.Range.Bookmarks(i).Name
            Exit Function
        End If
    Next i
End If

Set rng = para.Range
rng.MoveEnd unit:=wdCharacter, Count:=-1
sBookmarkName = ConvertStringRefBookmarkName(rng.Text)
para.Range.Document.Bookmarks.Add _
    Name:=sBookmarkName, _
    Range:=rng
GetOrSetXRefBookmark = sBookmarkName
End Function
```

Running the hack. This hack wouldn't be much of a time-saver if you had to go through a menu to run it. This code is most helpful when assigned to a keyboard shortcut.

To assign a macro to a keyboard shortcut, select Tools → Customize and click the Keyboard button. Save your changes in the same template in which you installed the code. In the Categories column, select Macros, and in the Commands column, select MakeAutoXRef. Choose and assign a keyboard shortcut using the dialog.

Hack More Flexible Cross-Referencing

Word's cross-referencing feature locks you into a box of predetermined possibilities. This hack shows you how to build a better box.

Word's Cross-referencing dialog offers only a few choices for the types of items you can create cross-references to, as shown in Figure 4-29.

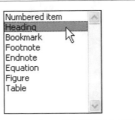

Figure 4-29. Choosing one of Word's predefined cross-reference types

But what if the items you want to reference aren't in that list? If you're working in a template that has several different types of headings, including some that aren't styled using one of Word's built-in styles, creating cross-references to those headings is no simple task.

This hack shows you how to build your own cross-reference dialog, like the one shown in Figure 4-30. The left column lists every paragraph style in the document, and the right column lists each paragraph that uses the selected style.

In addition to offering more choices of items to cross-reference, the dialog lists many more at once than does Word's dialog, which means less scrolling to find what you're looking for.

> If you want to create cross-references from one Word document to another, be sure to check out "Cross-Reference Among Documents" [Hack #78].

Making the Dialog

Here's how to create the user form shown in Figure 4-30. To keep this example simple, extras such as titles for the listboxes have been left off. Feel free to modify the dialog's design to suit your needs.

First, select Tools → Macro → Visual Basic Editor. Then, with the template of your choice [Hack #50] selected in the Project Explorer, choose Insert → UserForm.

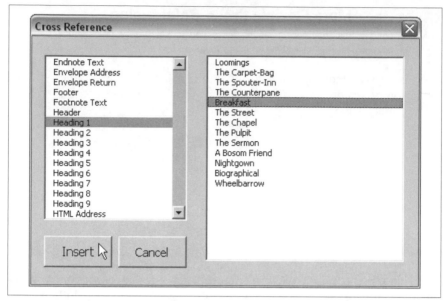

Figure 4-30. A better cross-reference dialog

In the Properties window, change the user form's name to "ufXRefs" and change its caption to "Cross Reference."

Resize the user form to about 380 pixels wide by 260 pixels deep by grabbing and dragging the resizing handle in the form's bottom-right corner.

Next, from the Toolbox, insert two listboxes, as shown in Figure 4-31. From the Properties window, name the one on the left "lbStyles" and the one on the right "lbParas."

Now insert two CommandButtons underneath the first listbox. Name them "cmbInsert" and "cmbCancel," and change their captions accordingly.

The Code

The code for this hack relies on a few utility functions introduced in "Cross-Reference Automatically" **[Hack #43]**:

- GetOrSetXRefBookmark
- ConvertStringToXRefBookmarkName
- GetParagraphIndex

Be sure these three procedures are located in the same template as the user form before trying out this hack.

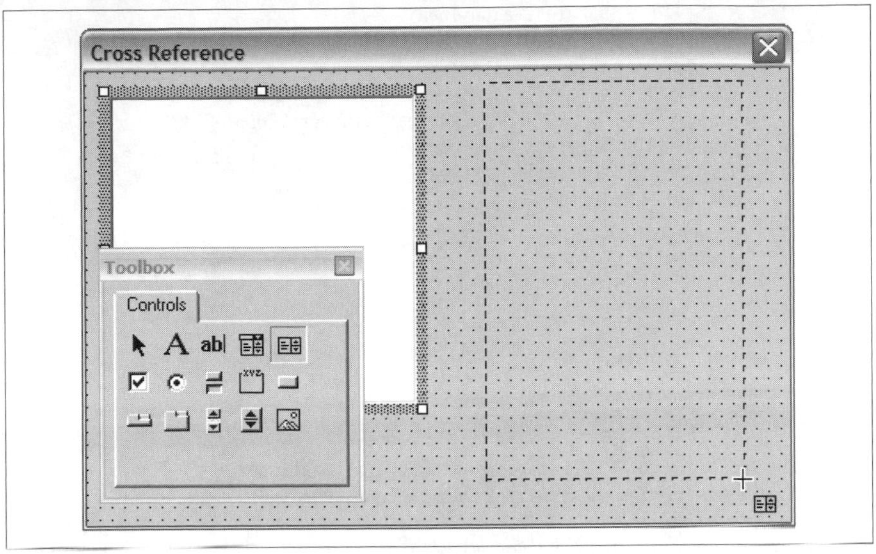

Figure 4-31. Drawing the listboxes in the ufXRefs user form

With the user form still open, select View ▸ Code to access the form's code module and insert the following code:

```
Option Explicit
Private colParagraphData As Collection

Private Sub cmbCancel_Click()
    Unload Me
End Sub

Private Sub UserForm_Initialize()
Dim v As Variant
Dim sty As Style
For Each sty In ActiveDocument.Styles
    If sty.Type = wdStyleTypeParagraph Then
        lbStyles.AddItem sty.NameLocal
    End If
Next sty
lbStyles.Selected(0) = True
End Sub

Private Sub lbStyles_Change()
Dim col As Collection
Dim para As Paragraph
Dim k As Integer
Set colParagraphData = New Collection
lbParas.Clear

k = 1
For Each para In ActiveDocument.Paragraphs
```

```
        If para.Style = lbStyles.Value Then
            Set col = New Collection
            col.Add Key:="Index", Item:=k
            col.Add Key:="Text", Item:=Left(para.Range.Text, _
                            para.Range.Characters.Count - 1)
            colParagraphData.Add Item:=col
            lbParas.AddItem (col("Text"))
            Set col = Nothing
        End If
    k = k + 1
    Next para
    End Sub

    Private Sub cmbInsert_Click()
    Dim lSelectedParaIndex As Long
    Dim sBookmarkName As String
    Dim para As Paragraph
    lSelectedParaIndex = colParagraphData(lbParas.ListIndex + 1)("Index")
    Set para = ActiveDocument.Paragraphs(lSelectedParaIndex)

    sBookmarkName = GetOrSetXRefBookmark(para)
        If Len(sBookmarkName) = 0 Then
            MsgBox "Couldn't get or set bookmark"
            Unload Me
        End If
    Selection.InsertCrossReference _
        referencekind:=wdContentText, _
        referenceitem:=ActiveDocument.Bookmarks(sBookmarkName), _
        referencetype:=wdRefTypeBookmark, _
        insertashyperlink:=True

    Unload Me
    End Sub
```

Each time a different style is selected in the lbStyles listbox, the
colParagraphData collection is reset and then populated with information
about all the paragraphs in the document that have the selected style
applied. In this example, that information is each paragraph's position in the
document (its index) and its text.

Running the Hack

In the same template that contains the user form, insert the following into
one of the code modules:

```
Sub ShowBetterCrossReferenceDialog
    ufXRefs.Show
End Sub
```

To display the dialog, run the ShowBetterCrossReferenceDialog macro, either
from Tools → Macro → Macros or by assigning it to a menu or toolbar [Hack #1].

When you select a paragraph and click Insert, it creates a bookmark around the target paragraph and replaces the current selection with a cross-reference pointing to that bookmark. The bookmark and the reference are shown in Figure 4-32. The reference field codes are also shown at the bottom of the figure.

Figure 4-32. A bookmark and cross-reference created with the code in this hack

If the paragraph you want to reference has been referenced before, the existing bookmark is used, and no new bookmark is created.

CHAPTER FIVE

Templates and Outlines
Hacks 45–50

Outlines are an excellent way to organize and edit complex documents, and templates offer the best way to ensure standardized documents and to store customizations. The hacks in this chapter show a few ways to maximize your use of these two key Word features.

HACK #45 Create an Outline-Only Copy of a Document

This hack shows you how to quickly extract just the outline from a document.

While working on a long document, you may want to pass along a copy to someone else to review. But what if you just want a copy of the document's outline? With the macro in this hack, you'll be able to create a copy of a document that includes only the text at or above the specified outline level.

There are nine outline levels, corresponding to each of Word's nine built-in heading styles. The lower the number, the higher the outline level: Level 1 is the highest, Level 9 the lowest. The rest of the text in a document has no outline level; Word calls it "body text."

> While in Outline view, you can select File → Print to print just the outline of a document. The Print Preview feature, however, will not correctly display the document.

The Code

Place this macro in the template of your choice [Hack #50] and either run it from the Tools → Macro → Macros dialog or put a button for it on a menu or toolbar [Hack #1].

Running this macro brings up the dialog shown in Figure 5-1. The macro first asks the user what the lowest outline level to include should be (1 being the highest). Once the user has chosen a valid outline level, the macro creates a new, blank document. It then copies every paragraph in your document at or above the specified outline level into the new document.

Figure 5-1. Select which outline levels to include from your document

The default outline level is the initial value assigned to lngMaxLevel, which in this case is 4.

```
Sub MakeOutlineOnlyCopyOfCurrentDoc()
Dim docFull As Document
Dim docOutline As Document
Dim lngMaxLevel As Integer
Dim strUserInput As String
Dim para As Paragraph

lngMaxLevel = 4
Set docFull = ActiveDocument
Application.ScreenUpdating = False

Do
    strUserInput = _
        InputBox("Create an outline-only copy of this document " & _
                        "to what level (1-9)?", _
                    "Outline Maker", _
                    lngMaxLevel)
    If Len(strUserInput) = 0 Then Exit Sub

    If Not strUserInput Like "[1-9]" Then
    MsgBox Chr(34) & strUserInput & Chr(34) & _
        " is not a valid Outline Level.", _
            vbInformation
    End If
Loop Until strUserInput Like "[1-9]"

lngMaxLevel = CLng(strUserInput)

Set docOutline = Documents.Add
StatusBar = "Collecting outline information. Please wait ..."

For Each para In docFull.Paragraphs
    If para.OutlineLevel <= lngMaxLevel Then
```

```
            para.Range.Copy
            docOutline.Range(docOutline.Range.End - 1).Paste
      End If
   Next para

   StatusBar = ""
   docOutline.Activate
   Application.ScreenUpdating = True
   End Sub
```

Most of the code here deals with the user interface. The actual copying is done by a simple For Each loop [Hack #66], which checks each paragraph in the document and decides whether or not to copy it into the new document.

HACK #46   Build a Better Outline

Many Word users are at least aware of Outline view, and many use it to help structure lengthy documents. But when the outline *is* the document, few take advantage of the features Outline view has to offer.

Outlining is a common Word task. In its simplest form, you use Word's built-in heading styles to sketch out a document's structure, promoting, demoting, and rearranging headings as you work.

Though you can create an actual outline, complete with numbering and indenting, using Word's Outline Numbering feature (go to Format → Bullets and Numbering and choose the Outline Numbered tab), why bother duplicating the effort when Word's heading styles are already set up for it?

There is a bit of work involved in setting up your outline template, but the time you'll save in the long run makes it well worth the effort.

First, select File → New and create a new template. Save your new template as *Outline.dot*.

Next, select Format → Styles and Formatting (Format → Style in Word 2000), choose the Heading 1 style, and click the Modify button to display the Modify Style dialog shown in Figure 5-2. Choose "(no style)" from the "Style based on" drop-down list, and choose "Heading 2" from the "Style for following paragraph" drop-down list. For the formatting, choose Times New Roman, 12 points, with no Bold applied.

Click the Format button and choose Paragraph, and change the Space Before and After settings to 6 and 3 points, respectively, as shown in Figure 5-3.

Next, modify the Heading 2 style. Make the same changes as for Heading 1, except instead of "(no style)," choose "Heading 1."

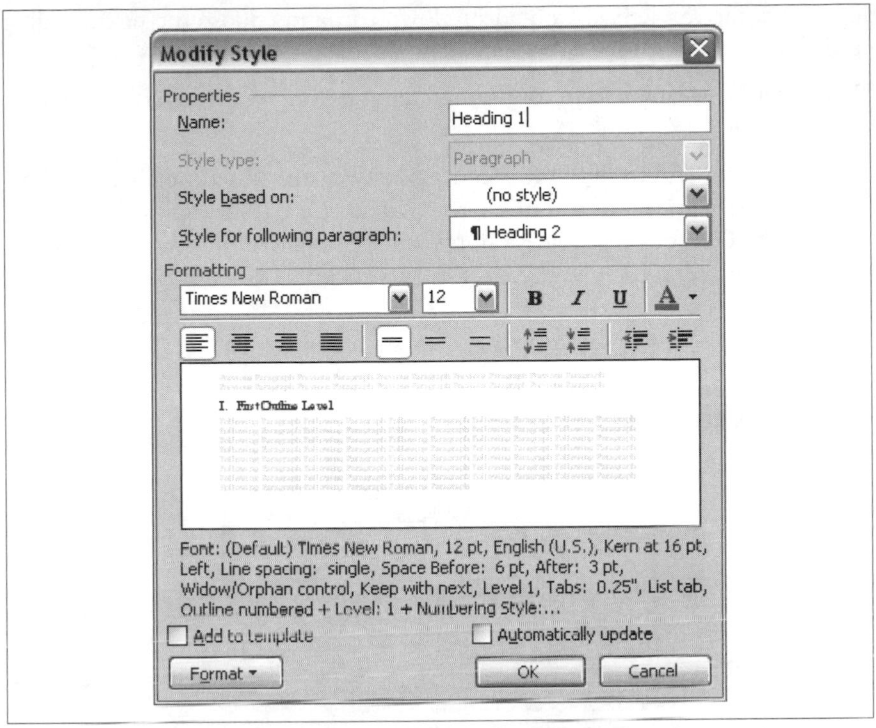

Figure 5-2. Modifying the heading styles for the Outline template

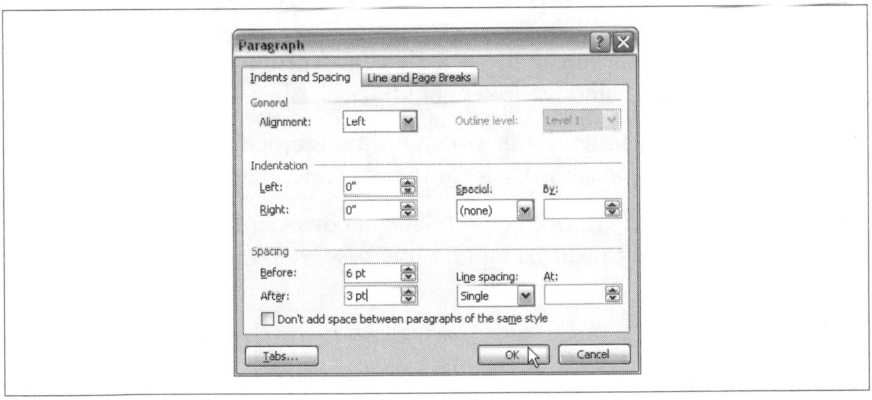

Figure 5-3. Changing the Space Before and After settings makes text look better on the page

Repeat these steps for each of the remaining seven headings. Change the font to Times New Roman, change the point size to 12, turn off Bold and Italic, and change the Space Before and After settings. Select the previous heading level from the "Style based on" drop-down list, and choose the next heading level from the "Style for following paragraph" drop-down list.

When you're finished, save your template (you don't want to have to do *that* all over again).

Now, go back and modify the Heading 1 style, but this time click the Format button and choose Numbering to display the dialog shown in Figure 5-4. One of the choices should look like an outline with a heading style name listed at each level. Select it, and click the Reset button.

Figure 5-4. Choose the one that looks like an outline, with the heading style names included

Click the OK button, and then click the OK button again in the Modify Style dialog. Save and close your new Outline template.

To create a new document with your Outline template, select File → New and choose *Outline.dot* as the basis for the new document.

Outlines created with *Outline.dot* will have a consistent appearance, behave reliably, and be easy to edit using Outline view. A sample outline is shown in Figure 5-5.

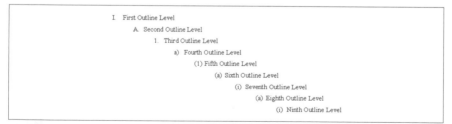

Figure 5-5. The Outline.dot template in action

To promote or demote a paragraph, use the Promote and Demote keyboard shortcuts: Shift-Alt-Left Arrow and Shift-Alt-Right Arrow.

Use an Outline to Build an Org Chart

#47 Word's outlining feature excels at managing hierarchical information. This hack shows you how to use an outline to create an organizational chart on the fly.

Maintaining a company's organizational charts can be a time-consuming task. Word does include a Diagram feature that makes it easy to create an organizational chart (select Insert → Diagram), but editing charts can be a real challenge, particularly after any substantial reorganization.

Unfortunately, the macro recorder ignores diagrams, which removes a valuable tool for deciphering unfamiliar Word objects. But you can still automate diagrams—you just need to decipher the Diagram object on your own. The code in this hack should give you a good starting point.

Rather than manipulating an existing diagram, you can store the organizational information in an outline and create the diagram from scratch after any changes. With your organizational information stored in an outline, like the one shown in Figure 5-6, you can quickly add, remove, or rearrange entries.

Once you complete your outline, the code will use it to produce a diagram like the one shown in Figure 5-7.

The next time you need to change the chart, just edit the outline and make a new one.

The Code

Place this macro in the template of your choice [Hack #50] and either run it from the Tools → Macro → Macros dialog or put a button for it on a menu or toolbar [Hack #1].

The text for the top-level entry (or *root node*) is culled from the CompanyName property in the outline document. To enter a company name, select File → Properties and go to the Summary tab. If you don't fill in the property, Word inserts some dummy text.

Though your chart could go 10 levels deep (9 for each of Word's outline levels, plus one more for the body-text level), this code goes only 4 levels deep. Adding more levels would require substantially more code, most of which would be nearly identical to that for the first four levels. You'll need to add your own additional code to handle an outline more than four levels deep.

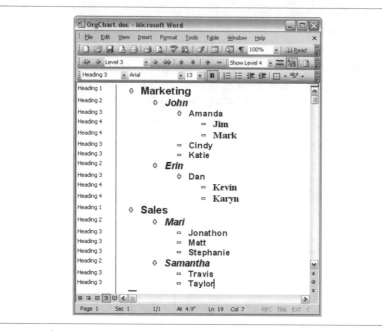

Figure 5-6. Edit your organization information in Outline view

```
Sub MakeOrgChartFromOutline( )
Dim doc As Document
Dim para As Paragraph
Dim sCompanyName As String
Dim sParaText As String
Dim nodeRoot As DiagramNode
Dim shShape As Shape
Dim node1 As DiagramNode
Dim node2 As DiagramNode
Dim node3 As DiagramNode
Dim node4 As DiagramNode

Set doc = ActiveDocument

sCompanyName = doc.BuiltInDocumentProperties("Company")
If Len(sCompanyName) <= 1 Then
    sCompanyName = "Type Company Name Here"
End If

Set shShape = _
    Documents.Add.Shapes.AddDiagram(msoDiagramOrgChart, 0, 0, 500, 500)
Set nodeRoot = shShape.DiagramNode.Children.AddNode
nodeRoot.TextShape.TextFrame.TextRange.text = sCompanyName

For Each para In doc.Paragraphs
    Select Case para.OutlineLevel
```

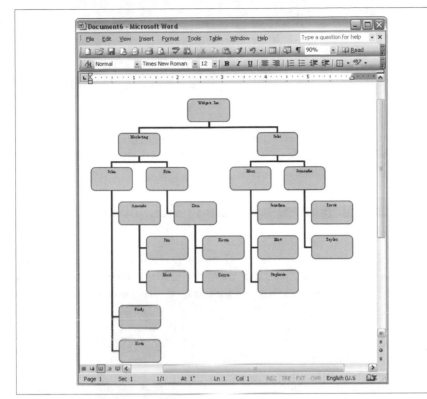

Figure 5-7. An organizational chart created from an outline

```
Case wdOutlineLevel1
    sParaText = Left(para.Range.text, _
        para.Range.Characters.Count - 1)
    Set node1 = nodeRoot.Children.AddNode
    node1.TextShape.TextFrame.TextRange.text = sParaText
    Set node2 = Nothing
    Set node3 = Nothing
    Set node4 = Nothing
Case wdOutlineLevel2
    sParaText = Left(para.Range.text, _
        para.Range.Characters.Count - 1)
    Set node2 = node1.Children.AddNode
    node2.TextShape.TextFrame.TextRange.text = sParaText
    Set node3 = Nothing
    Set node4 = Nothing
Case wdOutlineLevel3
    sParaText = Left(para.Range.text, _
        para.Range.Characters.Count - 1)
    Set node3 = node2.Children.AddNode
    node3.TextShape.TextFrame.TextRange.text = sParaText
    Set node4 = Nothing
```

```
        Case wdOutlineLevel4
            sParaText = Left(para.Range.text, _
                para.Range.Characters.Count - 1)
            Set node4 = node3.Children.AddNode
            node4.TextShape.TextFrame.TextRange.text = sParaText
    End Select
Next para

End Sub
```

Rather than attempting to position elements in the diagram, the macro just relies on Word's default automatic behavior to align and position the entries.

HACK #48   Attach the Same Template to Multiple Files

Use a macro to update or change the template for all the files in a folder.

When documents are passed around among reviewers or contributors, you'll often want to reattach the correct template when you get the files back. Doing that for more than a few files can be a real chore, though. This hack shows how to attach the template used by the current document to all the documents in the same folder as the current document.

The Code

Place this macro in the template of your choice **[Hack #50]** and either run it from the Tools → Macro → Macros dialog or put a button for it on a menu or toolbar **[Hack #1]**:

```
Sub DocTemplateToAllFilesInFolder( )
Dim i As Integer
Dim doc As Document
Dim sFolder As String
Dim oTemplate As Template
Dim sFileFullName As String
Dim sFileName As String

sFolder = ActiveDocument.Path
If Len(sFolder) = 0 Then
    MsgBox "Please save this document first"
    Exit Sub
End If
Set oTemplate = ActiveDocument.AttachedTemplate
With Application.FileSearch
    .NewSearch
    .LookIn = sFolder
    .SearchSubFolders = False
    .FileType = msoFileTypeWordDocuments
    If Not .Execute( ) = 0 Then
```

```
            For i = 1 To .FoundFiles.Count
                sFileFullName = .FoundFiles(i)
                sFileName = Right(sFileFullName, _
                        (Len(sFileFullName) - _
                        (InStrRev(sFileFullName, "\"))))
                If sFileName Like "[!~]*" Then
                    If Not sFileName = ActiveDocument.Name Then
                        Set doc = Documents.Open(sFileFullName)
                        doc.AttachedTemplate = oTemplate
                        doc.UpdateStyles
                        doc.Save
                        doc.Close
                        Set doc = Nothing
                    End If
                End If
            Next i
        Else
            MsgBox "No files found"
        End If
    End With
End Sub
```

This macro is just a modified version of the code demonstrated in "Do Something to Every File In a Directory" [Hack #59].

Hacking the Hack

Another common scenario is needing to attach the same template to several open files, which may not be in the same folder. The following macro attaches the template used by the current document to all the other open documents.

Place this macro in the template of your choice [Hack #50] and either run it from the Tools → Macro → Macros dialog or put a button for it on a menu or toolbar [Hack #1]:

```
Sub ThisTemplateToAllOpenDocs( )
Dim i As Integer
Dim oTemplate As Template
Set oTemplate = ActiveDocument.AttachedTemplate
For i = 1 To Documents.Count
    If Not Documents(i).FullName = ActiveDocument.FullName Then
        Documents(i).AttachedTemplate = oTemplate
        Documents(i).UpdateStyles
    End If
Next i
End Sub
```

Quickly Attach a Workgroup Template

#49 It's a rare corporate Word user who knows offhand the location of her Workgroup templates on the network. Word knows where they are, but try attaching one to an existing document, and you get a pop quiz on the subject! Reeducate Word with this hack.

In addition to templates stored locally, Word allows you to specify a location for document templates on a network, called the *Workgroup templates folder*. This feature is especially useful in a corporate environment, where multiple users may share the same set of templates.

When you specify a Workgroup templates location (select Tools → Options and click the File Locations tab), Word kindly adds any appropriate tabs to the Templates dialog the next time you choose File → New. But Workgroup templates aren't as easily integrated into your routine when it comes to attaching them to existing documents.

The Templates and Add-Ins dialog (Tools → Templates and Add-Ins), shown in Figure 5-8, defaults to your *local* templates folder when you click the Attach button (actually, it goes to the folder you specified for User templates under Tools → Options → File Locations). So if you regularly attach both local and Workgroup templates, you're in for a lot of folder browsing.

Figure 5-8. If you click the Attach button, Word takes you to the User templates folder

The Code

Word's `Options` object has a `DefaultFilePath` property that represents the value assigned to the User templates folder. If you temporarily set this to the Workgroup templates folder, you also change where you end up when you click the Attach button in the Templates and Add-Ins dialog.

This hack uses the techniques described in "Use Word Dialogs in a Macro" **[Hack #63]**.

```
Sub AttachWorkGroupTemplate( )
Dim sWorkgroupTemplateFolder As String
Dim sUserTemplatesFolder As String
Dim dial As Dialog

Set dial = Dialogs(wdDialogToolsTemplates)
sUserTemplatesFolder = Options.DefaultFilePath(wdUserTemplatesPath)
sWorkgroupTemplateFolder = Options.DefaultFilePath(wdWorkgroupTemplatesPath)

If Len(sWorkgroupTemplateFolder) = 0 Then
    MsgBox "No workgroup templates location has been specified." & vbCr & _
           "To specify one, go to Tools -> Options -> File Locations.", _
           vbExclamation
    Exit Sub
End If

Options.DefaultFilePath(wdUserTemplatesPath) = sWorkgroupTemplateFolder
    If dial.Display = -1 Then
        dial.Linkstyles = True
        dial.Execute
    End If

Options.DefaultFilePath(wdUserTemplatesPath) = sUserTemplatesFolder
End Sub
```

The macro ignores the "Automatically update document styles" box in the Templates and Add-ins dialog and updates the styles regardless of the value set in the box. Most corporate users are instructed to update their documents to reflect any changes to the template, but if you'd rather decide manually, remove or comment out the following line:

```
dial.Linkstyles = True
```

> When you run this macro, clicking the OK button on *any* of the tabs in the Templates and Add-Ins dialog is the same as clicking the OK button on the Templates tab. For more information, see "Use Word Dialogs in a Macro" **[Hack #63]**.

Running the Hack

Put this macro into the template of your choice [Hack #50] and put a button for it on the Tools menu, right below the Templates and Add-Ins button. Rename the button "Attach Workgroup Templates," or something similarly descriptive.

HACK #50 Manage Macros with Templates

By default, Word stores macros in the ubiquitous Normal template. This works fine in the short term, but macros you plan to keep and reuse should go in a separate template.

When you first start working with macros, those macros will be stored (with many of your other customizations) as part of Word's default template, *Normal.dot*. *Normal.dot* is such an integral part of Word that if you delete or rename it, Word will create a new version of the template using default settings stored in the program itself.

Whenever you're working in Word, you're working with *Normal.dot*. Even if a particular document is based on another template, *Normal.dot* is still there, including any macros stored in it.

Normal.dot's secret is that it's a chameleon of a template. When you create a new, blank document, *Normal.dot* functions as that document's template, like any other *document template*. But *Normal.dot* also behaves like a *global template*, also referred to as an *add-in*. A document can be associated with only one document template, but many global templates may be open and running at any given time.

Global templates are primarily used to store macros and toolbar customizations. For example, GhostWord [Hack #23] is a global template that adds a toolbar and provides certain macro features used to interact with Ghostscript from within Word. Many third-party applications are supplied as add-ins, allowing them to add features and customizations to Word.

But why bother keeping macros anywhere except *Normal.dot*? In its dual role as document template and global template, as well as general repository for myriad customizations, *Normal.dot* can log a lot of miles in a short amount of time. The more macros that are stored in it, the larger and slower to load it can become, which can potentially contribute to corruption over time.

If you suspect a corrupt Normal template, try the techniques in "Troubleshoot Common Word Problems" [Hack #51].

Many regular macro users prefer to keep their macros in their own global template. This template can be set to load automatically, just like third-party add-ins such as GhostWord.

Creating the Global Template

There are just two simple steps to creating a global template that will load whenever Word starts up [Hack #52]:

1. Create a new, blank document.
2. Select File → Save As and choose "Document template" in the "Save as type" field to save the document as a template. When you choose to save as a template, Word automatically places you in the templates folder, which is usually *C:\Documents and Settings\<username>\Application Data\Microsoft\Templates*.

   Navigate up one directory, then back down to *C:\Documents and Settings\<username>\Application Data\Microsoft\Word\STARTUP*. Save your template in that folder, naming it *MacrosTemplate.dot* or something similarly descriptive.

The next time you start Word, the template you just created will be listed as a loaded add-in from the Templates and Add-ins dialog (select Tools → Templates and Add-ins), as shown in Figure 5-9. Any other add-ins you've installed, such as the FaceID browser [Hack #10]], will also be listed.

Even though it's not listed, *Normal.dot* also acts like a global template whenever you work in Word. If you work on a document based on *Normal.dot*, then it also acts like a document template.

Adding Macros to the Global Template

When a global template is loaded, you can't edit it. To make changes to a global template, such as adding macros or creating a toolbar, you must first unload it (using the Templates and Add-ins dialog shown in Figure 5-9) and then select File → Open and choose the template file.

Because it takes a bit of work to open the global template for editing, you may find it easier to create your macros in *Normal.dot* and then periodically move any new macros you plan to keep over to the global template. This is a great habit to get into, because it also gives you an opportunity to delete any old, unused macros.

There are two ways to transfer macros from one template to another. First, you can select Tools → Macro → Macros, click the Organizer button, and

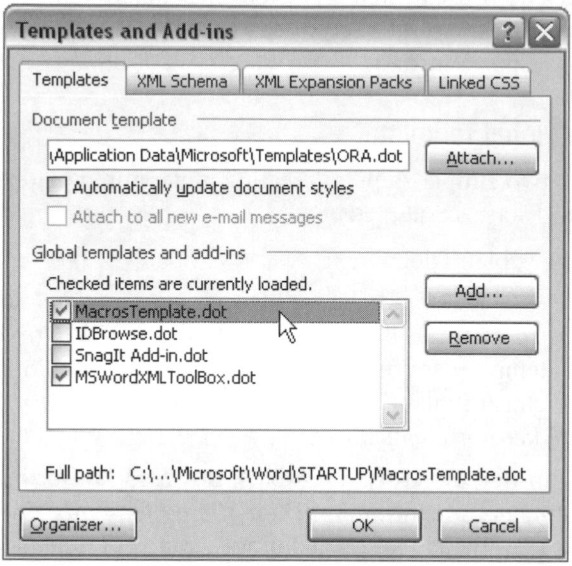

![Templates and Add-ins dialog]

Figure 5-9. Viewing currently loaded global templates

copy the macros (along with styles, custom toolbars, and AutoText entries) from one template to another.

The second way is to copy the macros directly from within the Visual Basic Editor [Hack #2]. Since you'll be regularly moving your macros from Normal to your MacrosTemplate global template, the only *module* in *Normal.dot* should be the NewMacros module Word inserts when you create a macro from the Word interface. After deleting any macros you don't want to keep (just select the code and delete it), you can drag and drop a copy of the NewMacros module into the MacrosTemplate template, as shown in Figure 5-10.

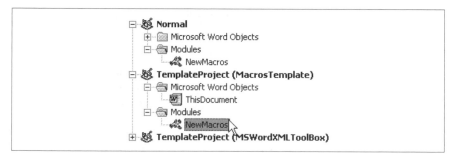

Figure 5-10. Copying a code module from one template to another by dragging it in the Visual Basic Editor

After copying the module, rename it using the Properties window just below the Project Explorer. Then either delete the NewMacros module from *Normal.dot* (right-click it and choose Remove) or clear out its contents from within the Code window.

Save and close the global template, and the next time you start Word, your macros will be waiting.

CHAPTER SIX

Housekeeping
Hacks 51–56

Word is a big, complicated piece of software that tends to produce (with some help from us, of course) some big, complicated files. That's a recipe for trouble, and if you've worked with Word for any length of time, you know the heartache of a corrupt document or a sudden crash that can wipe out a lot of work.

The hacks in this chapter show a few ways to tackle the most common Word problems, as well as how to hack some of the parts of a Word document that are next to impossible to get at from Word itself.

HACK #51 Troubleshoot Common Word Problems
This hack offers a systematic approach to fixing common frustrations.

You can solve a number of common Word problems using the same systematic approach. Typical symptoms include:

- Missing toolbars
- Word crashes repeatedly
- Word freezes right after opening
- Any strange Word behavior unrelated to a particular document

There are three likely culprits: your Normal template, an add-in, or a corrupt data key in your registry. Additionally, extraneous temporary files can contribute to the problems.

If you run Word 2002 or 2003, Microsoft offers trouble-shooting templates for automating most of this process. You can find these templates at:

• *http://support.microsoft.com/default.aspx?scid=kb;en-us;319299&Product=wd2002*

• *http://support.microsoft.com/default.aspx?scid=kb;en-us;319299&Product=wd2003*

Delete Any Temporary Files

Whenever you open a document, Word creates a temporary file to store various information about the file. Word usually deletes these temporary files when you close the document, but they can overstay their welcome and occasionally cause real trouble when Word or Windows crashes.

The easiest way to delete your temporary files is from Windows Explorer:

1. Close any open Windows applications.
2. Click an empty spot on the taskbar and press F3 to open the Search feature in Windows Explorer.
3. Make sure you look in your primary hard drive and check "include subfolders."
4. Type the following in the "named" box, as shown in Figure 6-1:

    `*.tmp;~*.do?;~*.wbk`

5. Click the Search button.
6. Delete the files listed in the search results.

Sometimes people (or programs) include a tilde (~) in filenames, usually to force a file to the top of the folder list. Before you delete all of the files returned by the search, first make sure they're really temporary files.

If the problem persists, you need to check the templates Word loads when it starts.

Start Word with a Clean Slate

Every time you start Word, your Normal template loads, along with any add-ins in your Startup folder. You can also tell Word to start up without loading any templates [Hack #52]:

1. Start Word from the Start → Run menu by typing:

    `winword.exe /a`

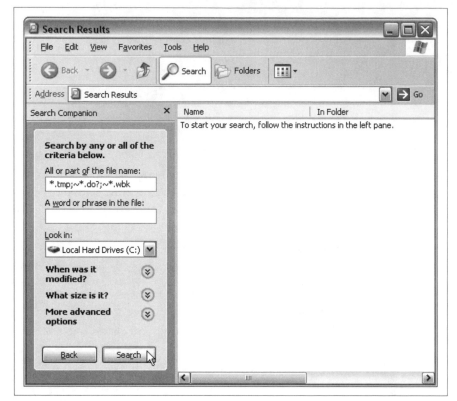

Figure 6-1. Searching for obsolete temporary files

Now press Enter. Note the space before the /a. This starts Word without any add-ins, global templates, or *Normal.dot*. If that fixed the problem, continue to Step 2. Otherwise, you can skip ahead to the next section.

2. Close Word.

3. Use the Windows Find feature to locate *Normal.dot*:

   a. Click an empty spot on the taskbar and press F3 to display the Search window again.

   b. Make sure you're searching your primary hard drive and check "include subfolders."

   c. Type **Normal.dot** in the "named" box and click the Search button.

 Depending on your version of Windows, *Normal.dot* may be a hidden system folder. In Windows Explorer, select Tools → Folder options, click the View tab, and check the "Show hidden files and folders" box.

4. Right-click *Normal.dot* in the search results and rename it *Normal.old*.

5. Restart Word.

When you delete or rename your *Normal.dot* file, Word creates a new one based on default settings. If the problem goes away, you had a corrupt Normal template. If not, check any other templates loaded when you start Word.

Disable Other Global Templates and COM Add-ins

If your Normal template wasn't at fault, try your other global templates and add-ins next:

1. Find out what, if any, global templates and add-ins Word loads when it starts. To do so, locate your *STARTUP* folder (usually *C:\Documents and Settings\<username>\Application Data\Microsoft\Word\STARTUP*).

2. Move each of these out of the *STARTUP* folder.

3. Close Word and drag each add-in back into the *STARTUP* folder, one at a time. Open, test, and then close Word after each one. When and if the problem reappears, you will have located the add-in causing the problem.

If the problem persists, you may have a corrupt data key in your registry.

Delete the Word Data Key

When you delete the data key, Word rebuilds it using default settings. The data key stores many of the customizations you've made to Word, so to avoid losing those, first make a quick backup:

1. Go to Tools → Macro → Record New Macro (or double-click REC in the status bar) to begin recording a new macro. Name the macro RestoreOptions and save it in *Normal.dot*.

2. Go to Tools → Options. Visit each tab in the Options dialog, and then press OK.

3. Stop recording.

The macro you've just recorded includes the current settings for many of the items stored in the data key and most of the items in the Options dialog. After you've recorded this macro, you're ready to delete the data key:

1. Back up the registry.

   In Windows XP, create a system restore point by going to your Start menu and choosing Accessories → System Tools → System Restore. To restore the registry later, go to the same place and follow the instructions under "Restore my computer to an earlier time."

In earlier versions of Windows, select Start → Run and type **scanregw**. (Windows also automatically makes backups of the registry every time you boot up your PC; it keeps the last five backups and overwrites previous copies.) When you back up using scanregw, the file will be replaced in five days. As an alternative, you can use the "Export Registry File" option in the registry editor.

If you need to restore your registry later, follow these steps:

  a. Select Start → Shut Down and click "Restart in MS-DOS mode." When in DOS, type **scanreg** and hit Enter. Windows will probably tell you there is nothing wrong and you don't need to restore, but you can override that.

  b. Click View Backups and highlight the backup you wish to restore (by the time/date stamp). Then click the Restore button.

  c. After restoring your registry, Windows will reboot into MS-DOS mode again. This time, type **exit** and hit Enter to return to the normal Windows mode.

2. Close Word. Select Start → Run and type **regedit** to launch the registry editor. Navigate to the following key:

    `HKEY_CURRENT_USER\Software\Microsoft\Office\`*version*`\Word\Data`

Use the following list to find your *version*, and then either rename or delete the Data key:

  • Word 97: 8.0
  • Word 2000: 9.0
  • Word 2002: 10.0
  • Word 2003: 11.0

3. Restart Word to rebuild the key using the default settings.

After you've rebuilt the data key. Restore your default options by running the RestoreOptions macro you created. Five other changes that may require your attention will also take place when you delete the data key:

1. Your Standard and Formatting toolbars will share one line. To correct this, select Tools → Customize and check the "Show Standard and Formatting toolbars on two rows" box. (In Word 2000, uncheck the "Standard and Formatting toolbars share one row" box.)

2. The dreaded Office Assistant may reappear. To banish the Office Assistant [Hack #12], right-click it, choose Options, and uncheck the "Use the Office Assistant" box.

3. You will lose the list of your most recently used files on the File menu.

4. You will lose all the files on the Work menu.

5. You will need to reattach any global templates or add-ins not in your *STARTUP* folder.

Once you restore Word to its former state, you may want to export the data key from the registry (it shouldn't be corrupt again just yet) to a safe location on your hard drive. Then if you need to delete the data key again, you can restore it from this backup and save yourself the trouble of those last five steps.

—Phil Rabichow

Control Word Startup

This hack lets you start Word with your favorite template or macro. It also shows you how to open Word with a recent or specific document, suppress the Word splash screen, and do away with the wretched default blank document.

Every day, in hundreds of millions of homes and offices around the world, Word starts the same way: a tired click of the Word item on the Start menu, the brief irritation of the well-worn Word splash screen (see Figure 6-2), and then the new blank document based on *Normal.dot* that almost everyone closes immediately because they need to either create a document based on another template or work with an existing document.

Figure 6-2. "Will no one rid me of this turbulent splash screen?" Startup switch /q to the rescue!

Standardization can be wonderful, but even Microsoft realizes it's not always efficient (let alone entertaining). To make things better, you can control the Word startup via startup switches. You can also augment this control over startup by using AutoMacros **[Hack #60]**.

Startup Switches

Startup switches are special commands you can provide when you launch a program. For example, select Start → Run and enter the following to start Word normally:

```
winword
```

Word opens as if you launched it the usual way. But if you enter some extra commands on the line, you can tell Word to start differently. For example, select Start → Run and enter the following:

```
winword /n
```

Word launches, but this time without the familiar blank document. Some switches include additional information. If you enter the following, Word will launch and create a new document based on the "Contemporary Memo" template:

```
winword /t"Contemporary Memo"
```

Note that if the template or filename used with a switch contains spaces, you need to enclose it in quotes.

Table 6-1 lists the startup switches you can use with Word, in alphabetical order.

Table 6-1. Word startup switches

Startup switch	What it does	What to use it for
/a	Prevents the loading of all global templates (including *Normal.dot*) and any add-ins. Prevents Word from writing data to or reading data from the registry.	Troubleshooting problems with Word startup or instability; running Word consistently in a student or lab environment.
/laddinpath	Loads the specified add-in or global template.	Loading an add-in or global template needed for a particular task but not for normal running of Word.
/c	Launches a new Word session and then starts NetMeeting.	Seldom if ever useful.
/m	Prevents the AutoExec macro (if one exists) from running.	Suppressing the running of your standard AutoExec macro.
/mmacro	Runs the specified macro instead of running the AutoExec macro (if one exists).	Setting up a Word session in a different way than usual (for example, to perform a specific task) or running a VBA application hosted on Word.
/mfilen	Opens the file specified by the number on the most recently used list.	Opening the last document or documents saved in the previous session; occasionally useful.

Table 6-1. Word startup switches (continued)

Startup switch	What it does	What to use it for
/n	Launches a new Word session but does not create a new document based on *Normal.dot*.	Suppressing the creation of a useless document; launching a second or subsequent Word session.
pathname\ filename	Opens the specified file or files after launching Word.	Consistently opening one or more files to work with.
/q	Suppresses the Word splash screen. Works only in some versions of Word, including Word 2000 SR-1 and Word 2003.	Preventing the splash screen from appearing, which can be good for VBA applications hosted on Word and for removing a widespread irritant.
/r	Starts Word in the background, reregisters its registry settings, and then closes Word.	Fixing registry problems. Be warned that although Word stays in the background, the Windows installer appears in the foreground for most versions of Word. Warn users before you use this switch.
/safe	Like /a, prevents the loading of all global templates (including *Normal.dot*) and any add-Ins, and prevents Word from writing data to or reading data from the registry. In addition, does not create a new document; suppresses the recovery of damaged documents and prevents the loading of smart tags, toolbar customizations, and the AutoCorrect list. Works interactively in Word XP and Word 2003.	Troubleshooting problems with Word startup or instability, especially those caused by attempting to recover damaged documents.
/t*template*	Creates a document from the specified template instead of creating a document based on *Normal.dot*.	Starting Word and creating the type of document you need to use.
/w	Launches a new Word session and creates a new document based on *Normal.dot*.	Creating multiple sessions of Word.
/x	Launches a new Word session from the operating shell, limited to responding to one DDE request.	Seldom, if ever, useful. Use /w instead when you need a new Word session.

You can use any of the startup switches from the Start → Run dialog. However, if you want to include a switch every time Word starts, create a desktop shortcut. Every time you double-click the shortcut, Word launches with the startup switch.

To create the new shortcut, right-click your desktop and choose New → Shortcut to launch the Shortcut Wizard. Click the Browse button, navigate to *WINWORD.EXE* (for Office 2003, that's in *C:\Program Files\Microsoft Office\OFFICE11*), and click the OK button. The Shortcut Wizard fills in the full path. At the end of the path, include the switch /n, as shown in Figure 6-3, and then click the Next button.

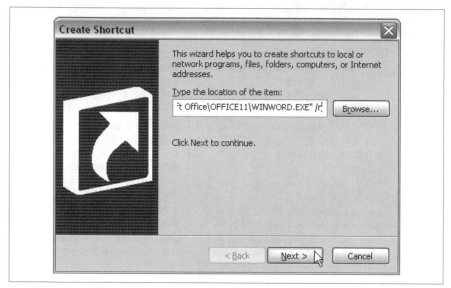

Figure 6-3. Creating a customized Word startup shortcut

The wizard asks you to name your new shortcut. Name it "Word No Blank," or something similar. The shortcut is placed on your desktop. Now whenever you want to launch Word without creating a blank document, just double-click this shortcut. You can create additional shortcuts using other switches, making it easy to launch Word in a variety of ways, depending on the task at hand.

From the descriptions in Table 6-1, you can see that there are three main themes to startup switches: troubleshooting startup problems, launching further Word sessions, and opening the files you need. Let's take a closer look at how to use the more useful switches.

Troubleshooting problems. If you have Word 2002 or Word 2003, use the /safe switch to recover from Word crashing on startup. If Word still will not run with several of the leading potential sources of instability **[Hack #51]** eliminated, use the /r switch to register Word. If even this does no good, you may need to reinstall Word.

Running further sessions of Word. One Word session at a time is enough for most mortals. After all, you can open dozens of documents, each in its own window, in one session. But sometimes you need another Word session for testing or for performing special tasks.

The switches /n and /w will start a new instance of Word, but remember that *Normal.dot* acts as a choke point for saving any modifications you might make in a second or subsequent session of Word. If you save changes to *Normal.dot* in one session, it will overwrite any changes saved to *Normal.dot* from previous sessions.

Usually, this problem emerges when you exit each session in turn, and the second or subsequent session warns you that *Normal.dot* already exists and asks if you want to replace it (see Figure 6-4). Click the Yes button to replace *Normal.dot*, click the Cancel button to return to the Word session, or click the No button to save this version of *Normal.dot* under a different name or in a different folder (you can then manually integrate the changes to this version of *Normal.dot* with the changes to the other versions later—if you can remember the changes you made).

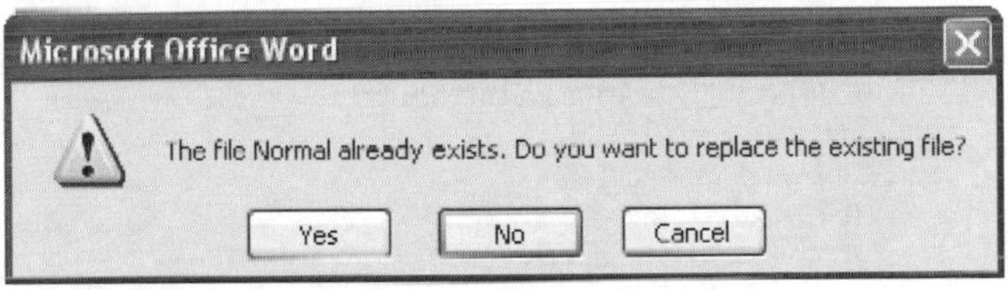

Figure 6-4. When you run multiple Word sessions, you may get into situations where you've changed two or more copies of Normal.dot and cannot easily save changes without overwriting the current Normal.dot

Opening one or more files. Perhaps the most popular use of startup switches is to quickly open the documents you need. You can use the /mfile*n* switch to open one of the files on the most recently used (MRU) list **[Hack #13]**. The *pathname\filename* switch is even more useful because it lets you specify any files you want. To open multiple files, put a space between the names:

```
winword "z:\public\Strategic Plan.doc" c:\private\my_subversive_novel.doc
```

Again, note that if the filename or pathname includes a space, you'll need to put quotes around the entire name.

Hacking the Hack

You can use the startup switch /m to run a macro and gain full control over a Word session you launch. You can use this switch to do anything from running a custom application (for example, one that gathers user input through user forms, executes a task, and then quits) to simply setting up the Word window for quick work.

> In theory, you can use the /t switch together with the /m switch to run a macro in a new document based on a specific template. However, it works much better if you store the macro in *Normal.dot* and then use the /m switch to run the macro on startup.

The following short macro automatically opens a document in two windows: one window for editing in full-screen Print Preview, and the other window showing an outline at Level 3. It also minimizes the second window to keep it out of the way until you need it.

```
Sub Set_Up_Word_Window( )

    ' Opens another window, applies Outline view, and minimizes it
    ' Applies Print Preview and editing view to the main window

        With ActiveWindow
            .NewWindow
            Windows(1).Activate
            .WindowState = wdWindowStateNormal
            .Left = 0
            .View = wdOutlineView
            .View.ShowHeading 3
            .Caption = "Outline View"
            Windows(2).Activate
            Windows(1).WindowState = wdWindowStateMinimize
        End With

        ActiveDocument.PrintPreview
        CommandBars("Print Preview").Visible = False
        With ActiveWindow
            .View.Magnifier = False
            .DisplayHorizontalScrollBar = False
            .WindowState = wdWindowStateMaximize
            .Caption = "Editing View"
        End With

    End Sub
```

To run the macro, specify the document to open and then use the /m switch with the macro name:

```
winword "D:\Projects\Pergelisol Tragedy.doc" /mSet_Up_Word_Window
```

This method has one big advantage: it lets you run the macro selectively. If you used an AutoMacro [Hack #60] instead, the macro would run every time you started Word.

—Guy Hart-Davis

HACK #53 Sidestep Formatting Restrictions

Formatting protection can help keep documents rigidly consistent, but sometimes you gotta break the rules.

Word 2003 introduced *formatting restrictions* as a way to restrict the kinds of formatting users can apply to a document. To activate formatting protection, select Tools → Protect Document. In the Protect Document Task Pane, shown in Figure 6-5, you can specify which types of editing and formatting restrictions to enforce.

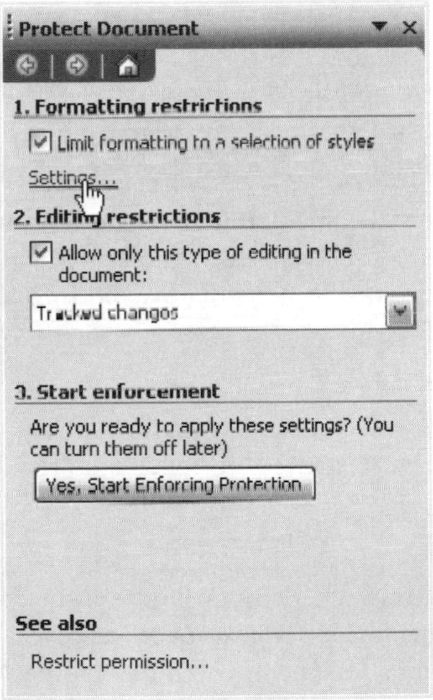

> **Protect Document** ▼ ✕
>
> ⊖ | ⊕ | ⌂
>
> **1. Formatting restrictions**
>
> ☑ Limit formatting to a selection of styles
>
> Settings...
>
> **2. Editing restrictions**
>
> ☑ Allow only this type of editing in the document:
>
> Tracked changes ⌄
>
> **3. Start enforcement**
>
> Are you ready to apply these settings? (You can turn them off later)
>
> Yes, Start Enforcing Protection
>
> **See also**
>
> Restrict permission...

Figure 6-5. Setting editing and formatting restrictions in a document

When you click the "Yes, Start Enforcing Protection" button, you can optionally supply a password. As you're about to see, including a password is fairly useless, but it may keep some users from futzing with the formatting.

In general, consider the formatting restrictions about as
secure as a lock on your backyard fence—you might keep
out those looking for a convenient shortcut, but anyone who
really wants in can just climb over.

When the formatting restrictions are in effect, none of the direct formatting
commands, such as the Bold and Italic buttons on the toolbar, can be used.
If you try, you get the message shown in Figure 6-6.

> **Microsoft Office Word**
>
> (i) This command is unavailable because formatting in the current document is restricted. Apply the styles available in
> the Styles and Formatting task pane.
>
> [OK]

Figure 6-6. What you see when you try to format a protected document

However, you can get around this obstacle fairly easily. For example, create
a new, blank document and fill in some placeholder text **[Hack #14]**. From the
Protect Document Task Pane, turn on formatting protection. Many of the
buttons on the Formatting toolbar will appear grayed out.

Select some text in the document and click the Bold button. You'll get the
dialog shown in Figure 6-6. Now select Tools → Macro → Visual Basic Editor, enter the following in the Immediate window **[Hack #2]**, and then press
Enter:

```
Selection.Font.Bold = True
```

Go back to the document and view your formatting changes. From VBA,
you can apply any of the "restricted" formatting in the document.

Hacking the Hack

Applying some formatting with VBA is fine as a quick fix for an unexpectedly protected document, but if you want to remove all the formatting and
editing protection from a document, you'll need to hack the document as an
RTF file.

With your "protected" document open, go back to the Protect Document
Task Pane and set the Editing Protection to Read Only. Now select File →
Save and save the file as Rich Text Format.

Close the file from Word, and then open it in a standard text editor, such as
Notepad. Find the following two statements and remove them from the file.

```
\lsdlockeddef1{\lsdlockedexcept Normal;Default Paragraph Font;HTML Top of
Form;HTML Bottom of Form;Normal Table;No List;}
```

```
\annotprot
```

Save and close the RTF file, and then reopen it in Word. You'll see that the protection is no longer active. The moral of the story? Restriction settings can help you cut down on undesired formatting and editing, but don't rely on them for more than superficial protection.

Rename Built-in Styles

HACK #54

Word is often merely the input phase in a production line that ends with a more formidable layout package, such as Adobe InDesign or QuarkXPress. This hack shows you how to make Word documents more palatable to other programs.

When Word is part of a production workflow, to work with it optimally would impose some restrictions on other parts of the workflow. For example, your company's designers probably prefer their own styles to Word's. Those styles may have identical names to Word's built-in styles, but chances are they don't.

Many choose (or are forced) to create custom styles in Word that correspond to those used by the layout software. But that means missing out on some of the advantages of using Word's built-in styles, such as being able to use Outline view. The other (equally inconvenient) choice is to stick with Word's styles and then perform a bunch of Find and Replace operations on the files after you import them into the layout software. Either option is a drag on your workflow.

Let's look at an example. Say you turn over some Word files for layout to a design staff that uses InDesign. They've got an extensive set of templates, and in those templates the styles for the first four heading levels are named *HeadA*, *HeadB*, *HeadC*, and *HeadD*. Typically, they import Word files directly into InDesign, then take the time to replace Heading 1 with HeadA, Heading 2 with HeadB, and so forth. Then they delete the imported Word heading styles from the InDesign document. It would certainly be easier if you named your heading styles the same as theirs, but again, that means losing out on the benefits of using Word's built-in heading styles.

While you can't change Word's built-in style names, you can change anything you want about an RTF file, which, after all, is just plain text. And whatever layout program you use (Quark, InDesign, or FrameMaker) can definitely import an RTF file.

The trick is to save the files as RTF, then modify Word's style names to match those of the layout software. Then, when you open the documents in the other program, the text will assume the formatting defined by the styles with those names in that program.

> After you modify the RTF files, import them into the layout software—*don't* reopen them in Word. If you reopen them in Word, any built-in styles will be recreated, which may cause undesired results (at the very least, Word will recreate all the built-in styles you just renamed).

Continuing with the example above, to change the Heading 1 style to HeadA, the Heading 2 style to HeadB, and so on, you'll first need to get your file into RTF format by selecting File → Save As and choosing "Rich Text Format" from the "Save as type" field. Next, open the file in a standard text editor such as Notepad.

RTF stores information about each of the styles in a document in a place called the *style table*. Everything about a style is listed there, from its name to its indent amount. Each style is also assigned a number, such as \s2. Whenever text in the document uses a style, the number notes which style should be applied. That means you only need to change the style's name in the style table; everywhere else in the document, the style is referenced by number, not by name. A sample style table entry for the Heading 1 style in a Word document is shown in Figure 6-7.

```
8  \s1\ql \li0\ri0\sb240\sa60\keepn\widctlpar\aspalpha\aspnum\
   faauto\outlinelevel0\adjustright\rin0\lin0\itap0 \b\f1\fs32\
   lang1033\langfe1033\kerning32\cgrid\langnp1033\
   langfenp1033 \sbasedon0 \snext0 heading 1;}
```

Figure 6-7. The Heading 1 style defined in an RTF file

If you change "Heading 1" in the RTF file to "HeadA," when you open the file in InDesign, any text that used the Heading 1 style in Word will be formatted with the HeadA style defined in InDesign.

Hacking the Hack

While editing RTF files by hand can be quite educational, it's also a bit tedious. It's better to relegate the dirty work to a script, such as the following Perl script, which changes Word's built-in Heading 1, Heading 2, Heading 3, and Heading 4 styles to HeadA, HeadB, HeadC, and HeadD in an RTF file.

This section assumes that your have Perl installed on your system and that you can run Perl scripts from the DOS command line. To download a free version of Perl for Windows, go to the ActiveState web site at *ttp://www.activestate.com*.

This script uses the RTF::Parser module. If you're running the ActivePerl distribution for Windows, you can install RTF::Parser from the Perl Package Manager. You can also download RTF::Parser from *http://www.cpan. org*. Save this script in the same folder as the file you're modifying and name it *changestyles.pl*.

```perl
#!/usr/bin/perl

use RTF::Tokenizer;

my $filename = shift;

my $tokenizer = RTF::Tokenizer->new( file => $filename);

while( my ( $type, $arg, $param ) = $tokenizer->get_token() ){
    last if $type eq 'eof';

    if($type eq 'control' and $arg eq 'stylesheet') {
        put( $type, $arg, $param );

        while( my @args = $tokenizer->get_token() ) {
            for (@args) {
                $_ =~ s/Heading 1/HeadA/i;
                $_ =~ s/Heading 2/HeadB/i;
                $_ =~ s/Heading 3/HeadC/i;
                $_ =~ s/Heading 4/HeadD/i;
            }

            put( @args );

            last if $args[0] eq 'control' and $args[1] eq 'generator';
        }
    } else {
        put( $type, $arg, $param );
    }
}

sub put {
    my ($type, $arg, $param) = @_;

    if( $type eq 'group' ) {
        print $arg == 1 ? '{' : '}';
    } elsif( $type eq 'control' ) {
        print "\\$arg$param";
    } elsif( $type eq 'text' ) {
```

```
        print "\n$arg";
    }
}
```

On Windows, you'd run the script from a DOS prompt:

```
> perl changestyles.pl MyFile.rtf
```

For more on hacking Word from Perl, check out "Hack Word from Perl" **[Hack #86]**.

HACK **Clean Out Linked "Char" Styles**
#55 Documents created or edited in Word 2002 or 2003 have a nasty habit of sprouting hidden character styles that are hard to see, let alone eliminate. This hack shows you how to lead a "Char-free" life with Word.

In most programs that offer style-based formatting (such as InDesign, FrameMaker, or QuarkXPress), if you try to apply a paragraph style to just *part* of a paragraph, the *entire* paragraph is modified to reflect the new style. But in Word, things aren't so simple. In older versions of Word, when you apply a paragraph style to only part of a paragraph, the paragraph retains its original style, but the selected text takes on the character formatting of the paragraph style you tried to apply. That introduces a lot of *direct* formatting into documents, which can make them difficult to modify and maintain.

Apply paragraph styles only with all or none—never some—of the paragraph selected to avoid this "feature."

Starting in Word 2002, rather than just applying the character formatting of the paragraph style, Word creates a *new*, hidden character style based on the paragraph style and tacks the word "Char" on the end, such as "Heading 1 Char."

Ostensibly, this is an improvement of the behavior of earlier versions of Word. Rather than changing Word to behave like other programs (and thus encouraging the conscientious use of character styles), Microsoft changed Word to behave in a strange, new, and—surprise!—poorly documented way. Because the Char styles are *linked* to the paragraph styles on which they're based, if you later change the paragraph style, the character style also changes.

Spotting Char Styles

To see these bizarre styles in action (assuming you are using a newer version of Word), open a new document and drop in a few paragraphs of place-holder text [Hack #14].

Now select a word or two within one of the paragraphs and apply the "Heading 1" style to the selection. Check your styles, either using the Task Pane or the Styles pull-down menu on the Formatting toolbar. See anything amiss? Well, that's a trick question. There are two things amiss, but you won't see them right away on the Styles pull-down menu or the Task Pane:

- Word created a new character style based on the formatting properties of the "Heading 1" style.
- Word has not told you about this new style, which, as you've discovered, doesn't appear with the other styles in the usual places.

Now, hold down the Shift key and click on the Styles pull-down menu on the Formatting toolbar. Scroll down to the "H" section, as shown in Figure 6-8, and you'll see the new style. You can also view the linked style from the Reveal Formatting Task Pane.

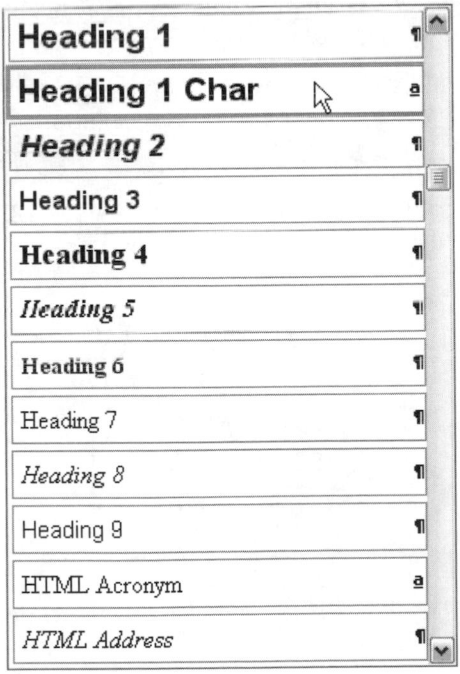

Figure 6-8. The elusive Char style

You can work in a document for weeks and never notice these styles. However, if you send your document to someone using an older version of Word that doesn't support these "linked styles," they'll appear right away in the Styles pull-down menu and the Styles and Formatting dialog.

Once you cut and paste the styles around your document, among different documents, and back and forth across different versions of Word, something even stranger happens. They evolve. Mutate. Fester. Until your document is rife with monstrosities like the following:

```
Body Text Char Char, Body Text Char1 Char Char, Body Text Char Char
```

Sometimes the "Char" extension even gets added to some of your paragraph styles. Does the fun ever stop?

Unfortunately, you can't prevent Word from creating these styles. And even if you still use Word 2000, these styles *will* show up in documents worked on by Word 2002 and 2003 users.

The situation gets even stranger when you try to delete these styles. In Word 2000, you at least stand a chance. Since 2000 doesn't have linked styles, you can rename or delete them as needed, just like any other style. But in Word 2002 and 2003—the source of these bizarre styles—you aren't so lucky. When you try to delete "Heading 1 Char," the silence is deafening. Nothing. Not even a dialog admonishing your efforts.

So maybe you should try a little VBA? Running the following code in the Immediate window [Hack #2] would seem to be a solution:

```
ActiveDocument.Styles("Heading 1 Char").Delete
```

When you run the code, the dialog shown in Figure 6-9 greets you. But take a look at your document again—the style's gone.

Figure 6-9. Deleting the linked style generates a runtime error

What's going on here? For a clue, try the following code in the Immediate window:

```
ActiveDocument.Styles("Heading 1").Delete
```

You get your old friend, Runtime Error 4198.

Remember, the styles are *linked*. If you change one, you change both—and that goes for deletion as well. However, you can't delete a built-in style, which is why you're greeted with Runtime Error 4198 (and why nothing happened when you tried to delete it from within Word).

So what if you repeat this with a Char style not based on one of Word's built-ins? Then there's nothing stopping Word from deleting *both* styles and *removing all of the formatting from any text that used them*. Yikes! Fortunately, there's a fix. With the code in this hack, you can quickly clear out any linked Char styles in your document, without losing any other styles.

The Code

This code will delete any character style with the word "Char" in it and remove the word "Char" from the name of any paragraph style. Since deleting a linked style also deletes any style it's linked to, the link must first be broken (which is accomplished by linking it to, ironically, the Normal style).

 This macro deletes character styles from your document. You will lose any formatting applied to text using the deleted character styles. If you want to keep the character formatting, see the upcoming section "Hacking the Hack."

Because Word 2000 (and Word 97) doesn't have a LinkStyle property for styles, if you're using that version of Word, this code will not run unless you comment out one line, as noted within the code. Note that there are two procedures here: the main DeleteCharCharStyles macro and a supporting function named SwapStyles. Both are needed for this hack to work.

```
Sub DeleteCharCharStyles()
Dim sty As Style
Dim i As Integer
Dim doc As Document
Dim sStyleName As String
Dim sStyleReName As String
Dim bCharCharFound As Boolean

Set doc = ActiveDocument
Do
    bCharCharFound = False
    For i = doc.Styles.Count To 1 Step -1
        Set sty = doc.Styles(i)
        sStyleName = sty.NameLocal
        If sStyleName Like "* Char*" Then
            bCharCharFound = True
            If sty.Type = wdStyleTypeCharacter Then
```

```
                    On Error Resume Next
                    '#############################################
                    ' COMMENT OUT THE NEXT LINE IN WORD 2000 OR 97
                    sty.LinkStyle = wdStyleNormal
                    sty.Delete
                    Err.Clear
                Else
                    sStyleReName = Replace(sStyleName, " Char", "")
                    On Error Resume Next
                    sty.NameLocal = sStyleReName
                    If Err.Number = 5173 Then
                        Call SwapStyles(sty, doc.Styles(sStyleReName), doc)
                        sty.Delete
                        Err.Clear
                    Else
                        On Error GoTo ERR_HANDLER
                    End If
                End If
                Exit For
            End If
            Set sty = Nothing
        Next i
    Loop While bCharCharFound = True
    Exit Sub
    ERR_HANDLER:
    MsgBox "An Error has occurred" & vbCr & _
            Err.Number & Chr(58) & Chr(32) & Err.Description, _
            vbExclamation
    End Sub

    Function SwapStyles(ByRef styFind As Style, _
                        ByRef styReplace As Style, _
                        ByRef doc As Document)
    With doc.Range.Find
        .ClearFormatting
        .Text = ""
        .Wrap = wdFindContinue
        .MatchCase = False
        .MatchWholeWord = False
        .MatchWildcards = False
        .MatchSoundsLike = False
        .MatchAllWordForms = False
        .Style = styFind
        .Replacement.ClearFormatting
        .Replacement.Style = styReplace
        .Replacement.Text = "^&"
        .Execute Replace:=wdReplaceAll
    End With
    End Function
```

The second procedure, SwapStyles, is there because of a scenario that often occurs when documents that have these linked styles go back and forth between different versions of Word. Often, what started as one paragraph style—for example, Sidebar—may have mutated into two paragraph styles, such as:

- Sidebar
- Sidebar Char Char

In that situation, if the code just tries to remove the "Char" strings from the second Sidebar style, an error will be raised because the name Sidebar is already taken. With the SwapStyles procedure, all the text formatted with the second style is modified and formatted with the first, and then the second style is simply deleted.

Running the Hack

After you put both procedures in the template of your choice [Hack #50], and either run it from the Tools → Macro → Macros dialog or put a button for it on a menu or toolbar [Hack #1].

This code affects only styles with the string " Char", including the leading space. If you plan to use this macro to clean your documents, you should avoid deliberately using the string " Char" in any of your styles. However, feel free to *begin* a style name with Char, as in "CharacterStyleNumberOne."

Hacking the Hack

If you want to delete the linked Char styles but retain the character formatting on the text, use this version of the code. It includes an additional procedure, StripStyleKeepFormatting, that removes the character style applied to the text but retains the formatting defined by that style. Again, if you use an earlier version of Word, you'll need to comment out the line that unlinks the character style, as noted in the code

```
Sub DeleteCharCharStylesKeepFormatting()
Dim sty As Style
Dim i As Integer
Dim doc As Document
Dim sStyleName As String
Dim sStyleReName As String
Dim bCharCharFound As Boolean

Set doc = ActiveDocument
Do
    bCharCharFound = False
    For i = doc.Styles.Count To 1 Step -1
        Set sty = doc.Styles(i)
        sStyleName = sty.NameLocal
        If sStyleName Like "* Char*" Then
```

```
                        bCharCharFound = True
                        If sty.Type = wdStyleTypeCharacter Then
                            Call StripStyleKeepFormatting(sty, doc)
                            On Error Resume Next
                            '############################################
                            ' COMMENT OUT THE NEXT LINE IN WORD 2000 OR 97
                            sty.LinkStyle = wdStyleNormal
                            sty.Delete
                            Err.Clear
                        Else
                            sStyleReName = Replace(sStyleName, " Char", "")
                            On Error Resume Next
                            sty.NameLocal = sStyleReName
                            If Err.Number = 5173 Then
                                Call SwapStyles(sty, doc.Styles(sStyleReName), doc)
                                sty.Delete
                                Err.Clear
                            Else
                                On Error GoTo ERR_HANDLER
                            End If
                        End If
                        Exit For
                End If
                Set sty = Nothing
            Next i
        Loop While bCharCharFound = True
        Exit Sub
ERR_HANDLER:
MsgBox "An Error has occurred" & vbCr & _
        Err.Number & Chr(58) & Chr(32) & Err.Description, _
        vbExclamation
End Sub


Function SwapStyles(ByRef styFind As Style, _
                    ByRef styReplace As Style, _
                    ByRef doc As Document)
With doc.Range.Find
    .ClearFormatting
    .Text = ""
    .Wrap = wdFindContinue
    .MatchCase = False
    .MatchWholeWord = False
    .MatchWildcards = False
    .MatchSoundsLike = False
    .MatchAllWordForms = False
    .Style = styFind
    .Replacement.ClearFormatting
    .Replacement.Style = styReplace
    .Replacement.Text = "^&"
    .Execute Replace:=wdReplaceAll
End With
End Function
```

```
Function StripStyleKeepFormatting(ByRef sty As Style, _
                                  ByRef doc As Document)
Dim rngToSearch As Range
Dim rngResult As Range
Dim f As Font

Set rngToSearch = doc.Range
Set rngResult = rngToSearch.Duplicate

Do
    With rngResult.Find
        .ClearFormatting
        .Style = sty
        .Text = ""
        .Forward = True
        .Wrap = wdFindStop
        .Execute
    End With

    If Not rngResult.Find.Found Then Exit Do

    Set f = rngResult.Font.Duplicate
    With rngResult
        .Font.Reset
        .Font = f
        .MoveStart wdWord
        .End = rngToSearch.End
    End With
    Set f = Nothing
Loop Until Not rngResult.Find.Found
End Function
```

For an alternative method, check out "Remove Linked "Char" Styles with XSLT" [Hack #98].

HACK #56 Reduce Document Bloat by Deleting Old List Templates

Long documents and documents that have been heavily edited can become needlessly bloated by the remnants of lists long since deleted from the text. This hack shows how to clean out this cruft.

Every list you create in Word is based on an internally defined *list template*. These templates function like paragraph styles, allowing the properties of a list to be defined once, then referenced many times later on.

But once it's been created, you can't remove a list template. Over time, a large document may accumulate hundreds, or even thousands, of these list templates. As you might imagine, that can have a negative impact on both the file's size and its stability.

With Word 2003, the situation is greatly improved: Word caps the number of inactive list templates in a document at 50, automatically removing any old, unused templates once that threshold is met. However, many individuals and offices still use older versions of Word, which makes their documents susceptible to serious bloating issues from extraneous list templates.

To see how quickly these list templates can accumulate, try the following:

1. Open a new, blank Word document.

2. With your cursor in the document, alternately click the Bullets button and the Numbering button a dozen or so times.

3. Select Tools → Macro → Visual Basic Editor (or press Alt-F11), type the following in the Immediate window [Hack #2], and press Enter:

   ```
   ?ActiveDocument.ListTemplates.Count
   ```

VBA will report the number of list templates you created (see Figure 6-10). Notice that the number matches the number of times you clicked the Bullets and Numbering buttons. That's a lot of list templates for a blank document!

Figure 6-10. Counting the number of list templates in a document

Remember, you can't delete list templates, and only Word 2003 removes old lists when the number gets above 50. If you use an older version of Word, however, you can create a hack to help you clean out your list templates.

As with "Swap Revision Authors" [Hack #41], you can convert your document into a format such as RTF and delete anything you please. The RTF files put all the list templates in one place, and then use numbers to reference them in the document text. You can remove any list templates not referenced in the document without affecting the existing text.

> The gory details of RTF are beyond the scope of this book. For an excellent introduction and reference to RTF, check out O'Reilly's *RTF Pocket Guide*.

The Code

The following Perl script will clean out unused list templates from an RTF
file. It uses the RTF::Parser module. If you're running the ActivePerl distribution for Windows, you can install RTF::Parser from the Perl Package
Manager. You can also download the RTF::Parser from *http://www.cpan.org*.

```perl
#!/usr/bin/perl

use strict;
use RTF::Parser;

my $file = shift;

die "Please provide an rtf file to parse.\n" unless $file;

open(RTFIN, "< $file") or die "Failed to open $file for reading: $!\n";

my $tokenizer = RTF::Tokenizer->new( file => \*RTFIN );

my @listoverride;
while(my ( $type, $arg, $param ) = $tokenizer->get_token()) {
    last if $type eq 'eof';

    if( $type eq 'control' and $arg eq 'listoverridetable' ) {
        my $brace = 1;

        while( $brace > 0 ) {
            my @attr = $tokenizer->get_token();

            $brace++ if $attr[0] eq 'group' and $attr[1] == 1;
            $brace-- if $attr[0] eq 'group' and $attr[1] == 0;

            if( $attr[0] eq 'control'
                    and ($attr[1] eq 'listid' or $attr[1] eq 'ls')) {
                push( @listoverride, $attr[2] );
            }
        }
    }
}

seek(RTFIN, 0, 0);
my %list_map = @listoverride;

for my $key (keys %list_map) {
    my $matches = 0;

    while(<RTFIN>) {
        my @ls = $_ =~ m/\\(ls$list_map{$key})(?:\s|\\|\n|\})/g;
```

```
            $matches += scalar(@ls);
    }
    seek(RTFIN, 0, 0);

    if ($matches > 1) {
        delete $list_map{$key};
    }
}


seek(RTFIN, 0, 0);
$tokenizer->read_file( \*RTFIN );

while(my ( $type, $arg, $param ) = $tokenizer->get_token( )) {
    last if $type eq 'eof';

    if( $type eq 'control'
          and ($arg eq 'listoverridetable' or $arg eq 'listtable') ) {
        put( $type, $arg, $param);
        my $brace = 1;

        my @listkeep;
        while( $brace > 0 ) {
            my @attr = $tokenizer->get_token( );

            $brace++ if $attr[0] eq 'group' and $attr[1] == 1;
            $brace-- if $attr[0] eq 'group' and $attr[1] == 0;

            my @listitem;
            my $delete = 0;
            push( @listitem, \@attr);

            while( $brace > 1 ) {
                my @attr = $tokenizer->get_token( );

                $brace++ if $attr[0] eq 'group' and $attr[1] == 1;
                $brace-- if $attr[0] eq 'group' and $attr[1] == 0;

                if( $attr[0] eq 'control' and $attr[1] eq 'listid') {
                    $delete = 1 if( exists $list_map{$attr[2]} );
                }

                push( @listitem, \@attr);
            }

            unless($delete) {
                push( @listkeep, \@listitem);
            }
        }

        for (@listkeep) {
            for (@$_) {
                put(@$_);
            }
```

```
    }
  } else {
      put( $type, $arg, $param );
  }
}

close(RTFIN);

sub put {
    my ($type, $arg, $param) = @_;

    if( $type eq 'group') {
        print $arg == 1 ? '{' : '}';
    } elsif( $type eq 'control' ) {
        print "\\$arg$param";
    } elsif( $type eq 'text') {
        print "\n$arg";
    }
}
```

Save the script as *cleanlists.pl*.

Running the Hack

As described earlier, create a new, blank document and alternately click the Bullets and Numbering buttons a few dozen times. Use VBA to make sure that you soiled the file with extra list templates, as shown in Figure 6-10. Now save the file as RTF and name it *DirtyFile.rtf*.

With the script in the same directory as the *DirtyFile.rtf* file, enter the following at a DOS command prompt:

```
> perl cleanlists.pl DirtyFile.rtf > CleanFile.rtf
```

Open the new file, *CleanFile.rtf*, from Word. Once you're satisfied the script hasn't altered any existing formatting, you can save it in *.doc* format.

> Parsing RTF is a complicated task, and RTF files (particularly those with embedded graphics) can be quite large, so this script may take a few minutes to run on a lengthy file.

—*Andy Bruno and Andrew Savikas*

Macro Hacks

Hacks 57–69

When it comes to hacking Word, VBA macros are often the answer. From automating routine tasks to redefining Word's behavior, macros are a potent weapon in your Word arsenal. The hacks in this chapter show several ways to move beyond basic automation, as well as how to make your macros faster, friendlier, and more flexible.

HACK #57 Get Simple User Input for a Macro

Macros that interact with the user can be very useful. This hack shows you how to get feedback from a user without the overhead or complexity of a VBA UserForm.

When you get input from a user (often yourself), you may want to present the person with several choices. You can use a UserForm with radio buttons or checkboxes, but it might add unnecessary overhead and complexity. Instead, use the dialogs already built into VBA, such as the MsgBox and InputBox.

For example, if you just need the user to select between two choices—say, "Red" or "Blue"—you could display a standard MsgBox with its included "Yes" and "No" buttons. The following macro displays the dialog shown in Figure 7-1:

```
Sub PickRedOrBluePlease( )
Dim lResponse As Long
lResponse = MsgBox(Prompt:="Press Yes for Red, Press No for Blue", _
                Buttons:=vbYesNo, _
                Title:="Pick a color")
If lResponse = vbYes Then
    MsgBox "You picked Red"
Else
    MsgBox "You picked Blue"
End If
End Sub
```

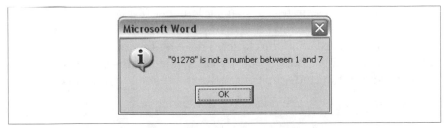

Figure 7-1. Hack VBA's built-in dialogs to get simple user input

Note the disabled Close button on the dialog's titlebar. To offer the choice of canceling the dialog, use the vbYesNoCancel value for the Buttons parameter.

But what if you need more than two or three choices? How about choosing a number between 1 and 7? Try an InputBox and validate the response:

```
Sub ChooseAmongSeven( )
Dim sResponse As String
sResponse = InputBox(prompt:="Please choose a number from 1 to 7", _
                    Title:="Pick a Number", _
                    Default:=CStr(5))

' Dialog was canceled
If Len(sResponse) - 0 Then Exit Sub

If Not sResponse Like "[1-7]" Then
    MsgBox Chr(34) & sResponse & Chr(34) & _
        " is not a number between 1 and 7", _
            vbInformation
Else
    MsgBox "You picked: " & sResponse
End If

End Sub
```

If the user fails to enter a whole number between 1 and 7, the macro displays the dialog in Figure 7-2.

Figure 7-2. Using VBA's built-in dialogs to provide interaction from a macro

Hacking the Hack

If the user does not enter a valid choice, you can continue to offer the dialog instead of exiting the macro. The following code uses a Do loop to repeatedly prompt the user for a valid choice:

```
Sub PromptUntilValid( )
Dim sResponse As String

Do
    sResponse = InputBox(prompt:="Please choose a number from 1 to 7", _
                    Title:="Pick a Number", _
                    Default:=CStr(5))

    If Len(sResponse) = 0 Then Exit Sub

    If Not sResponse Like "[1-7]" Then
       MsgBox Chr(34) & sResponse & Chr(34) & _
          " is not a number between 1 and 7", _
             vbInformation
    Else
       MsgBox "You picked: " & sResponse
    End If
Loop Until sResponse Like "[1-7]"

End Sub
```

Keep the Macros Dialog Box Tidy

Reduce clutter in your Macros dialog box by preventing it from displaying some of your macros.

When developing a macro, it's often best to split the macro into several small parts, each responsible for performing some part of the overall action. This makes the macro easier to write, easier to debug, and—best of all—easier to reuse.

The downside to this strategy is that the number of macros in the Macros dialog box (Tools → Macro → Macros) quickly balloons, making it hard to find the one you need amid the clutter. True, you can assign macros to toolbars or menu buttons [Hack #1], but if you use the macros only occasionally, you may not want to clutter up your toolbars or menus with them either.

Here are two things you can do to keep that dialog neat.

Name Macros Clearly and Consistently

If your Macros dialog box is full of macros with names like test, fixer, and mymacro, you'll have a much more difficult time finding what you need than if you use descriptive names like DeleteAllHyperlinks or SetLandscapeMargins.

Practically speaking, your macro names can be as long as you want, so use the space.

Plus, if you use the above naming convention (starting each word in the name with a capital letter) and assign the macro to a toolbar button, Word will separate the words in the ToolTip that appears when you hover the mouse over the button. For example, Figure 7-3 shows one of the macros used to write the manuscript for this book.

Figure 7-3. When you use capital letters to start new words in a macro name, Word automatically inserts spaces between them in the ToolTip text

Hide Macros from the Macros Dialog Box

If you write a procedure that either requires an input value to run or returns an output value when it finishes (or both), the procedure will not appear in the Macros dialog box. From the Word interface alone, there is no way for the macro to get the input it needs or handle the output it provides. For that, you need additional macro code.

For example, the following two procedures will not appear in the Macros dialog box:

```
Sub ComplimentMe(sName as String)
    MsgBox sName & " is a lovely name."
End Sub

Function OppositeDay(bInput as Boolean) As Boolean
    OppositeDay = Not bInput
End Function
```

Thus, to keep a macro out of the Macros dialog box, you can trick it into *thinking* it needs a value to run by using an `Optional` argument:

```
Sub SuperSecretMacro(Optional bFakeInput As Boolean)
    MsgBox "Curses, foiled again"
End Sub
```

Now the only way to run this macro is from another macro, as with the following code:

```
Sub ShowSecretMacro( )
    Call SuperSecretMacro
End Sub
```

Microsoft uses this particular technique extensively in the Office Wizards to keep the code from appearing in the Macros dialog.

HACK #59 Do Something to Every File in a Directory

Even the simplest Word task becomes arduous when it must be repeated more than a handful of times. Give your mouse a rest, and let Word do the work with this hack.

Opening a document, accepting all the revisions, then saving, printing, and closing it sounds simple enough. But what if you need to do that for each of the 50 Word files in a folder? Even if you put an "Accept All Revisions" button on your toolbar, you're still looking at about 250 different mouse clicks. And amid all that clicking, chances are you'll miss a step (or a document) somewhere.

The Code

Place this macro in the template of your choice [Hack #50] and either run it from the Tools → Macro → Macros dialog or put a button for it on a menu or toolbar [Hack #1].

You can adapt this macro to perform a variety of batch-processing tasks, but in this example, it accepts all revisions and then prints the document:

```
Sub RunOnAllFilesInFolder()
Dim i As Integer
Dim doc As Document

With Application.FileSearch
    .NewSearch
    .LookIn = "C:\My Documents"
    .SearchSubFolders = False
    .FileType = msoFileTypeWordDocuments
    If Not .Execute() = 0 Then
        For i = 1 To .FoundFiles.Count
            Set doc = Documents.Open(.FoundFiles(i))
            ' #### Do stuff to document here ####

            doc.AcceptAllRevisions
            doc.PrintOut
            doc.Save
            doc.Close

            ' ##################################
            Set doc = Nothing
        Next i
    Else
        MsgBox "No files matched " & .FileName
```

```
      End If
   End With
   End Sub
```

This macro uses the Visual Basic FileSearch object's FileType property to make sure it opens only Word documents, not other types of files that might be in the same folder. The FileType property can be set to any of the 24 constants listed in Table 7-1.

Table 7-1. Available values for the FileType property

msoFileTypeAllFiles	msoFileTypeBinders
msoFileTypeCalendarItem	msoFileTypeContactItem
msoFileTypeCustom	msoFileTypeDatabases
msoFileTypeDataConnectionFiles	msoFileTypeDesignerFiles
msoFileTypeDocumentImagingFiles	msoFileTypeExcelWorkbooks
msoFileTypeJournalItem	msoFileTypeMailItem
msoFileTypeNoteItem	msoFileTypeOfficeFiles
msoFileTypeOutlookItems	msoFileTypePhotoDrawFiles
msoFileTypePowerPointPresentations	msoFileTypeProjectFiles
msoFileTypePublisherFiles	msoFileTypeTaskItem
msoFileTypeTemplates	msoFileTypeVisioFiles
msoFileTypeWebPages	msoFileTypeWordDocuments

It also uses a .FileName property, which supports standard Windows file *globbing* (meaning you can use * and ? as wildcards, so .FileName="*.doc" will match any file ending with the *.doc* extension).

Hacking the Hack

When you open a document, Word creates one or more temporary files in the document's folder. If you're working on a document named *Foobar.doc*, you might see the following files in *Foobar.doc*'s folder when you look in Windows Explorer:

- ~$obar.doc
- ~WRL2402.tmp
- ~WRL1748.tmp

 If you don't see files like this in the folder of an open Word document, you need to tell Windows Explorer to show *hidden* files. Select Tools → Folder Options, click the View tab, and check the "Show hidden files and folders" box.

Here's where it gets interesting: the first file, despite its *.doc* extension, isn't a Word file at all. The other files *are* Word files, despite their *.tmp* extensions. A new *.tmp* file is created every time you save your document, and they're deleted when you close the document.

The *~$obar.doc* file is also normally deleted when you close the document, but if it's not properly disposed of (e.g., when Word or Windows crashes), the file can remain even if no documents are open. If it's left floating around in a folder, this file can cause problems when you try running a macro on all the Word files in that folder.

This version of the RunOnAllFilesInFolder macro tests all the files in a folder and ignores any whose names begin with a ~:

```
Sub RunOnAllRealFilesInFolder()
Dim i As Integer
Dim doc As Document
Dim sFileFullName As String
Dim sFileName As String
With Application.FileSearch
    .NewSearch
    .LookIn = "C:\My Documents"
    .SearchSubFolders = False
    .FileType = msoFileTypeWordDocuments
    If Not .Execute() = 0 Then
        For i = 1 To .FoundFiles.Count
            sFileFullName = .FoundFiles(i)
            sFileName = Right$(sFileFullName, _
                        (Len(sFileFullName) - _
                        (InStrRev(sFileFullName, "\"))))
            If sFileName Like "[!~]*" Then
                Set doc = Documents.Open(sFileFullName)
                ' #### Do stuff to document here ####
                doc.AcceptAllRevisions
                doc.PrintOut
                doc.Save
                ' #################################
                doc.Close
                Set doc = Nothing
            End If
        Next i
    Else
        MsgBox "No files matched " & .FileName
    End If
End With

End Sub
```

Run Macros Automatically

Macros are all about automation, but to run they typically require you to click a toolbar button or select a menu item. This hack shows you how to create macros with minds of their own that run whenever you create, open, or close certain templates or documents.

If you often do the same thing when you first open a document, such as checking one of the document properties or turning on field-code shading, why not have Word do it for you?

There are five special names you can give your macros that cause them to run when certain things happen in the Word world. These are known as *AutoMacros*, and how they behave depends both on their names and on where they're stored.

These are the five AutoMacros available in Word:

AutoOpen
> This macro runs (or "fires") when you open a file where the macro is stored. However, if you create a macro named AutoOpen in a template, the macro won't fire when you create a new document based on the template (for that you'd use an AutoNew macro, described below).

AutoNew
> This macro fires when you base a new document on the document or template where you stored the macro.

AutoClose
> This macro fires when you close the document or template where you stored the macro.

AutoExec
> This special AutoMacro runs only when stored in a global template. It fires when the global template is loaded. If you a put a macro named AutoExec in your Normal template, it will run every time you start Word.

AutoExit
> This special AutoMacro runs only when stored in a global template. It fires when you unload the global template. If you put a macro named AutoExit in your Normal template, it will run every time you exit Word.

You might find it easier to organize and keep track of your AutoMacros if you create separate code modules for them. For example, if you rename a code module in a template as AutoNew, whenever you create a document based on that template, Word will execute the macro named Main within that module.

To change the name of a code module, open the Visual Basic Editor [Hack #2], select the module, and then rename it using the Properties window.

Disabling AutoMacros

In addition to using the Word startup switches [Hack #52], you can open documents from within VBA to control which, if any, AutoMacros run.

The following macro opens a document named *foo.doc*, but first disables any AutoMacros:

```
Sub OpenFooDoc( )
WordBasic.DisableAutoMacros
Documents.Open("C:\foo.doc")
End Sub
```

The Word documentation mentions the DisableAutoMacros command but provides no information on the corresponding command to reenable the macros (it's *not* EnableAutoMacros, as you might expect). You just need to supply an optional argument to the DisableAutoMacros command:

```
Sub ReactivateAutoMacros( )
WordBasic.DisableAutoMacros False
End Sub
```

> For another way of making VBA code run when certain events occur in Word, check out "Hack with Application Events" [Hack #69].

HACK #61 Intercept Word Commands

This hack shows you how to change the way Word works with the ominous-sounding technique of command interception.

What happens when you choose Save from the File menu? Obviously, Word saves the current file. But that's not the whole story. You've executed the FileSave command, which tells Word to do the actual work of writing the file to disk on your computer. Likewise, when someone dials your phone number, a computer somewhere inside the phone company directs the call to the phone line in your house. If you move, you can just ask the phone company to send calls to your new house instead. You can even temporarily forward your calls just about anywhere, and the people dialing your number will be none the wiser.

Word lets you do the same sort of thing with its built-in commands (such as FileSave). The concept of *intercepting* commands has been around for a long time, but Word has made it very easy to do—and, perhaps more importantly, very easy to undo.

You can intercept only commands executed from the Word interface.

To run the sample macros in this section, place them in the template of your choice [Hack #50]. They will run when you execute the commands after which they're named.

To continue with the telephone analogy, this example shows you how to forward calls made to `FileSave`:

```
Sub FileSave( )
MsgBox "You have executed the FileSave command!"
End Sub
```

Go ahead, try and save the file. You'll get the dialog shown in Figure 7-4.

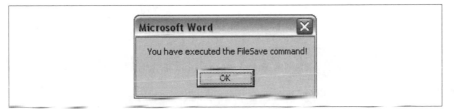

Figure 7-4. A simple example of an intercepted command

In this example, the intercepted command does not save the file, nor will it unless you include some additional code in your macro. To actually save the file, change the macro as follows:

```
Sub FileSave( )
ActiveDocument.Save
MsgBox "You've saved the file."
End Sub
```

This may seem like a trivial example, but it shows how easily you can change Word's behavior.

Finding the Command's Name

To intercept a command, you need to know its name. For some commands, like `Bold`, it's pretty easy. Others, like `MailMergeAskToConvertChevrons`, aren't so straightforward. Fortunately, you can figure out the exact name of a command in several ways.

If you have a general idea of the command name, or if you just want to browse the available commands, select Tools → Macro → Macros and choose Word Commands from the "Macros in" pull-down menu, as shown in Figure 7-5.

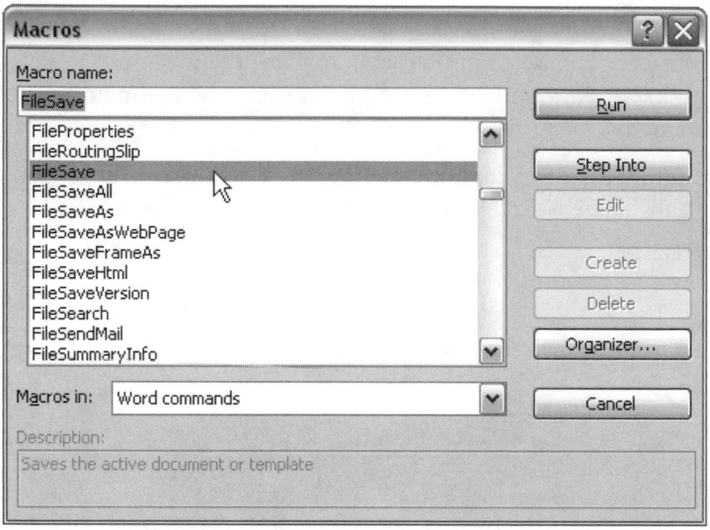

Figure 7-5. A description of each command is also provided (even if it is grayed out)

Select the command you want to intercept, choose the template or document where you want to create the macro from the "Macros in" drop-down menu, and click the Create button to display the Visual Basic equivalent of the command you selected, as shown in Figure 7-6. You can then replace the VBA code with your own code.

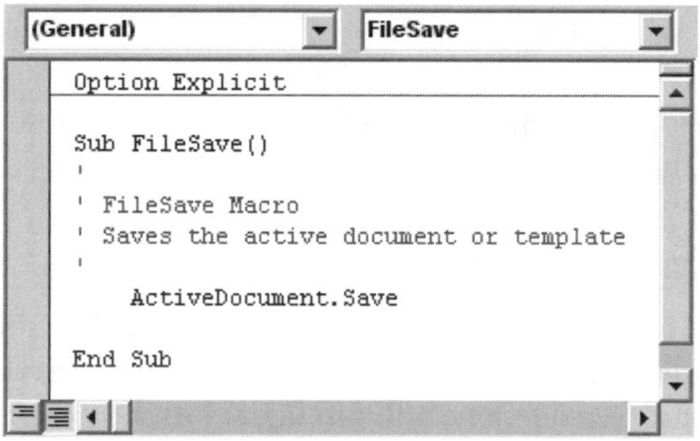

Figure 7-6. Word launches the Visual Basic Editor and fills in the VBA version of the command you selected

If you can find the command within the Word interface, press Ctrl-Alt and the "+" key on the number pad. Your cursor will turn into a cloverleaf (just like the Command symbol on a Macintosh). If you click any button or menu item, it will bring up the Customize Keyboard dialog shown in Figure 7-7, which will also tell you the name of the particular command.

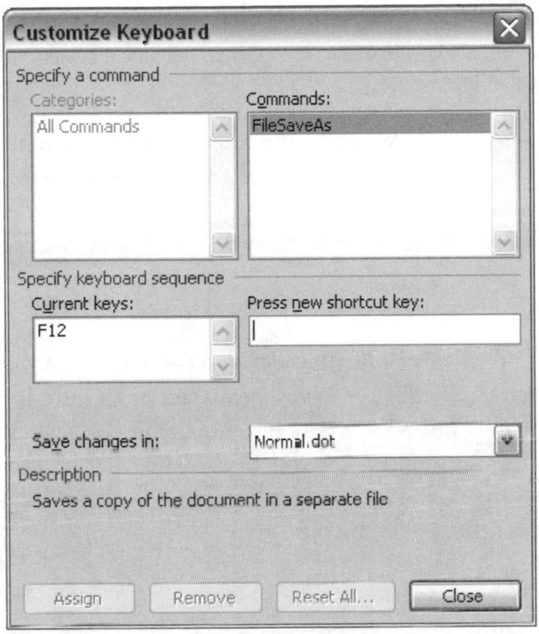

Figure 7-7. This dialog will tell you the name of a command

To get a list of all available commands, choose the ListCommands macro from the list of Word commands shown in Figure 7-5 and click the Run button to create a new document with a table listing each Word command. You can also find a more useful and detailed list of commands at *http://www.word. mvps.org/faqs/general/CommandsList.htm*.

Command Precedence

What happens if an intercept macro in a document shares the same name as one in the Normal template? When you execute a command, Word first searches the document for any macros with the same name as the command, then it searches the document template, then it searches the installed global templates. If it finds a macro with the same name as the command, Word runs the macro instead of the command, and then stops looking.

See Also

- "Disable Overtype Permanently" [Hack #35]
- "Apply Context-Sensitive Formatting" [Hack #39]
- "Corral Basic Bullets and Numbering" [Hack #42]

HACK #62 Keep Custom Menus Under Control

This hack reveals how to make sure macros that create custom menu items clean up after themselves.

This hack shows you how to automatically add a menu item for the RevertToSaved macro [Hack #5] in a global template named *MacrosTemplate. dot*. It adds the menu item underneath the Save As command on the File menu. The hack also shows how to use VBA to remove the menu item.

The Code

The code uses two procedures: AddMenuItem and RemoveMenuItem. The AddMenuItem macro first calls the RemoveMenuItem procedure to delete the custom menu item if it already exists. It then creates a new menu item just below the Save As command on the File menu. If, for some reason, the macro can't find the Save As command on the File menu, it places the custom item at the bottom of the menu.

```
Sub AddMenuItem( )

Dim lPos As Long
Dim oFileMenu As CommandBar
Dim oSaveAsMenuItem As CommandBarControl
Dim oCustomMenuItem As CommandBarControl
Dim sMenuItemTag As String

' Define a tag for the custom menu item
' so you can find it later to delete
sMenuItemTag = "Custom_RevertToSaved"
CustomizationContext = NormalTemplate

' Delete the custom menu item if it already exists
Call RemoveMenuItem

Set oFileMenu = Application.CommandBars("File")
Set oSaveAsMenuItem = oFileMenu.Controls("Save As...")
If oSaveAsMenuItem Is Nothing Then
    lPos = oFileMenu.Controls.Count
Else
    lPos = oSaveAsMenuItem.Index
End If
```

```
Set oCustomMenuItem = oFileMenu.Controls.Add(msoControlButton, _
    1, , lPos + 1, True)

oCustomMenuItem.Caption = "Revert To Saved"
oCustomMenuItem.Tag = sMenuItemTag
oCustomMenuItem.OnAction = "MacrosTemplate.RevertToSaved"

End Sub
```

As stated above, the RemoveMenuItem macro checks for the custom item on the File menu. If the macro finds the item, it deletes it. To make sure the custom menu item won't be left behind when the macro it runs isn't available, run this procedure when the global template exits:

```
Sub RemoveMenuItem( )

Dim lPos As Long
Dim oFileMenu As CommandBar
Dim oCustomMenuItem As CommandBarControl
Dim sMenuItemTag As String

' Define a tag for the custom menu item
' so you can find it later to delete
sMenuItemTag = "Custom_RevertToSaved"
CustomizationContext = NormalTemplate

Set oFileMenu = Application.CommandBars("File")
Set oCustomMenuItem = oFileMenu.FindControl(Tag:=sMenuItemTag)

If Not oCustomMenuItem Is Nothing Then
    oCustomMenuItem.Delete
End If
End Sub
```

To ensure that these procedures run when the global template is loaded and unloaded, you should call them from AutoMacros [Hack #60]. Put the following code in the same *MacrosTemplate.dot* template:

```
Sub AutoExec( )
Call AddMenuItem
End Sub

Sub AutoExit( )
Call RemoveMenuItem
End Sub
```

Use Word Dialogs in a Macro

HACK #63

Using Word's own dialogs in your macros allows the person using the macros to work with a familiar interface, which can make even complicated macros seem easy to use.

Macros that must interact with the person using them are generally harder to write than those that just run from start to finish without needing any user input. In many cases, however, Microsoft has already done the work of designing a useful interface for modifying the same sorts of things your macro probably does (i.e., parts of a Word document).

For example, if you've got a macro that inserts a particular kind of table into your document, you might want to let the user choose the number of rows and columns to put in the table each time the macro is run. Rather than create your own user form in the Visual Basic Editor, you can use Word's InsertTable dialog—just show the dialog and capture the row and column numbers selected, and your macro can insert the right-sized table.

This hack shows you two different ways of exploiting Word dialogs from within a macro.

Put the macros in this hack into the template of your choice **[Hack #50]** and run them from the Tools → Macro → Macros dialog.

Use Dialogs to Execute Commands Interactively

Say you've created a macro to open a new file and fill it with useful information, such as a table of available system fonts **[Hack #15]**. But before the macro finishes, you want it to prompt the user to save the new document. The following code creates a new, blank document, and then displays Word's own FileSaveAs dialog (the same one that appears whenever you save a new document for the first time):

```
Sub ShowFileSaveAsDialog( )
Dim dial As Dialog
Dim doc As Document
Set dial = dialogs(wdDialogFileSaveAs)
Set doc = Documents.Add
dial.Show
MsgBox "Thanks! You either saved the document or canceled the dialog."
End Sub
```

When the FileSave dialog appears, the user can click either the Save button or the Cancel button, but this version of the macro has no way of knowing which one the user clicked. If you want your macro to behave differently depending on which button the user clicks, you can evaluate the dialog's *return value*, which is like the answer to a question. As an example of using a return value, the following macro displays the number of currently open documents, which it finds by getting the return value from the Count property:

```
Sub HowManyDocumentsAreOpen( )
Dim iNumberOfDocuments As Integer
iNumberOfDocuments = Documents.Count ' Getting a return value
MsgBox iNumberOfDocuments ' Displaying that return value
End Sub
```

A dialog used in a macro returns a value that indicates which button in the dialog the user clicked to exit the dialog. If the user clicked the Cancel button, or the Close button in the top corner of the dialog, the return value is 0. You can use this information to modify the ShowFileSaveAsDialog macro so that it "knows" whether the user clicked the Save or Cancel button and reacts accordingly:

```
Sub ShowFileSaveAsDialog
Dim dial As Dialog
Dim doc As Document
Set dial = dialogs(wdDialogFileSaveAs)
Set doc = Documents.Add
If dial.Show <> 0 Then
    ' Didn't press Cancel
    MsgBox "Thanks for saving the document."
Else
    ' Pressed Cancel
    MsgBox "Afraid of commitment?"
End If
End Sub
```

In this version, if the user clicks the Save button, the macro displays its gratitude. If the user clicks the Cancel button, it displays a sarcastic message.

If you also want to suggest a specific name for the new document created by the macro, you can supply values for certain dialog components. For the FileSaveAs dialog, you can suggest a name by assigning a value to the Name property before showing the dialog:

```
Sub ShowFileSaveAsDialogAndSuggestName
Dim dial As Dialog
Dim doc As Document
Set dial = dialogs(wdDialogFileSaveAs)
Set doc = Documents.Add
dial.Name = "YourNewDocument.doc"
If dial.Show <> 0 Then
    MsgBox "Thanks for saving the document."
Else
    MsgBox "Still afraid of commitment?"
End If
End Sub
```

To find the names of the properties available in each dialog, do a search in the VBA help files for "built-in dialog arguments," as shown in Figure 7-8.

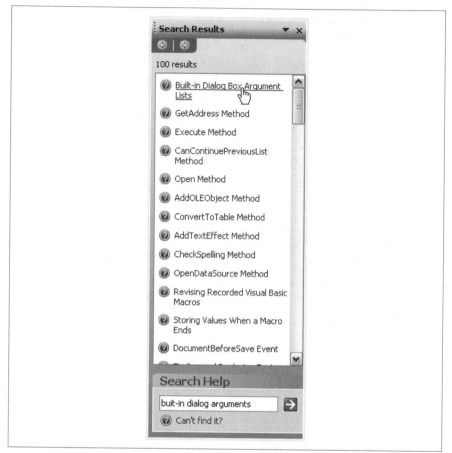

Figure 7-8. Getting a list of arguments for the built-in dialogs

Use Dialogs Just to Get Input

Sometimes a Word dialog is the best way to get certain types of information from the person running your macro, even if you don't want the dialog to "do" its usual duty.

For example, the following macro displays the FileSaveAs dialog from the previous section. But after you click the Save button, a message box appears showing the filename you chose instead of saving the document. The difference is that instead of using the Show method, as in the previous section, this macro uses the Display method, as indicated in bold.

```
Sub ShowFileSaveAsDialog( )
Dim dial As Dialog
Set dial = dialogs(wdDialogFileSaveAs)
dial.Display
MsgBox "You asked to save the file as: " & dial.Name & ". Too bad."
End Sub
```

With Show, the dialog does what you expect; in the case of FileSaveAs, clicking the Save button saves the current document with the name you provide. But with Display, the dialog captures the name you entered but doesn't actually do the save.

To return to the scenario of inserting a table described at the beginning of this hack, the following macro inserts a two-row, three-column table at the insertion point. The first row is styled as "Heading 1," and the rest of the table is styled as "Heading 2":

```
Sub TableWithSpecialHeadings( )
Dim tbl As Table
Set tbl = Selection.Tables.Add(Range:=Selection.Range, _
     NumRows:-2, NumColumns:- 3)
tbl.Range.Style = wdStyleHeading3
tbl.Rows(1).Range.Style = wdStyleHeading2
End Sub
```

This macro becomes more versatile if you can choose the number of rows and columns each time you run it. The following macro prompts the user with the InsertTable dialog, captures the column and row numbers chosen, and then inserts the special table:

```
Sub TableWithSpecialHeadings( )
Dim tbl As Table
Dim dial As Dialog
Set dial = Dialogs(wdDialogTableInsertTable)

If dial.Display = 0 Then
    ' User pressed Cancel, so quit now
    Exit Sub
End If

Set tbl = Selection.Tables.Add(Range:=Selection.Range, _
    NumRows:=dial.NumRows, _
    NumColumns:=dial.NumColumns)
tbl.Range.Style = wdStyleHeading3
tbl.Rows(1).Range.Style = wdStyleHeading2
End Sub
```

HACK
#64

Optimize Your VBA Code

As you create more complex macros, minor delays caused by poor coding can really add up. This hack will help your VBA code run faster.

This hack demonstrates six specific programmatic techniques you can apply to accelerate your code. The improvement can range from modest increases to increases of several orders of magnitude in performance.

Use Integer Division

Your application probably performs a majority of its division operations on integer values. Many developers use the slash (/) operator to divide two numbers, but this operator is optimized for floating-point division. If you divide integers, you should use the backslash (\) operator instead. With \, Word works at the integer level instead of the floating-point level, so computation happens faster. (Of course, this is useful only if you assign the results of the division operation to an integer. If you care about the fractional portion of the division, you need to use floating-point math and the / operator.) For example, instead of:

```
intX = intY / intZ
```

use:

```
intX = intY \ intZ
```

When Possible, Avoid Variants

Variants offer convenience at the expense of performance. When you use variants, Word often needs to perform type conversion to ensure the data is in the correct format. If you match the data type to your variable, you eliminate the need for type conversion, and your code runs faster. In addition, a variant variable is twice as large as an integer (on a 32-bit operating system), and thus takes longer to manipulate.

Test for Blank Strings with Len

You probably have code that tests for empty strings by comparing them to another empty string (""). However, because Word stores the length of the string as the first byte in the string, testing for a length of zero using the Len function is always faster. Instead of:

```
If strTemp = "" Then
    MsgBox "The string is blank"
End If
```

you can use this:

```
If Len(strTemp) = 0 Then
    MsgBox "The string is blank"
End If
```

Don't use a literal value ("") when you initialize a string. Instead, use the built-in vbNullString constant.

Assign Objects to Variables

If you refer to an object more than once in a section of code, assign it to an object variable. Every time you reference an object, Word has to perform some work to figure out which object you are referring to. This adds overhead to your code each time you reference the object. But if you assign the object to an object variable, Word "finds" the object once and caches the reference in memory. After the first reference, you can refer to the object through the object variable, and your code will run faster. For example, instead of this code:

```
Sub ReferencingTestSlowWay( )
Dim k As Long
Dim str As String
For k = 1 To 100000
    str = ActiveDocument.Paragraphs(1).Range.Characters(1).Text
Next k
End Sub
```

you can use this:

```
Sub ReferencingTestFastWay( )
Dim k As Long
Dim str As String
Dim rng As Range
Set rng = ActiveDocument.Paragraphs(1).Range.Characters(1)
For k = 1 To 100000
    str = rng.Text
Next k
End Sub
```

The difference between the two versions is dramatic: with a 2.6-GHz Celeron processor, the first macro took 62.16 seconds; the second took just 0.26 seconds.

Don't Skimp on Comments

Don't worry about comments. In VBA, the use of comments exacts no measurable performance penalty, but they will help you (and others who might use the code) understand how your code works.

Avoid IIf

Replace the IIf function with If... Then... Else to make your code run faster. For example, instead of:

```
MsgBox IIf(intX = 1, "One", "Not One")
```

you can use this:

```
If intX = 1 Then
    MsgBox "One"
Else
    MsgBox "Not One"
End If
```

—Adapted from Access Cookbook (O'Reilly)

HACK #65   Show Progress from VBA

When macros take a long time to run, people get nervous. Did it crash? How much longer will it take? Do I have time to run to the bathroom? Relax. This hack shows you two ways to create a macro progress bar using VBA.

Before adding a full-fledged progress bar to your macro, consider whether something more subtle might be effective enough to keep the macro user informed. Within a macro, you can use the StatusBar property to display text in Word's *status bar*—the little area at the bottom of the window that displays the current page, line count, and so forth.

The following macro displays a personalized message in the status bar. Put the macro in the template of your choice **[Hack #50]** and run it from Tools → Macro → Macros:

```
Sub SayHello()
StatusBar = "Hello, " & Application.UserName & _
    ". My that's a nice shirt you're wearing."
End Sub
```

You can take a tip from Word, which often displays messages in the status bar (e.g., when you save a document), and use the status bar as a means of communication from within a macro.

For example, the following macro uses a For Each loop **[Hack #66]** to highlight any paragraph set to outline Level 2 that contains more than 10 words. As it completes this task, it prints the text of the paragraph to the status bar:

```
Sub HighlightLongHeadings()
Dim para As Paragraph
For Each para In ActiveDocument.Paragraphs
    StatusBar = "Checking: " & para.Range.Text
    If para.OutlineLevel = wdOutlineLevel2 Then
        If para.Range.Words.Count > 10 Then
```

```
        para.Range.HighlightColorIndex = wdBrightGreen
      End If
    End If
  Next para
  StatusBar = ""
  End Sub
```

This solution usually provides enough visual feedback to keep users assured that the macro's still hard at work and that Word hasn't crashed.

If you want a more specific, or just less subtle, feedback method, you can create a custom progress bar that appears in its own dialog box while your macro runs. The following sections describe two ways to create your own progress bar using VBA. Both adapt the HighlightLongHeadings macro shown above.

Continuous Progress

The first technique combines the code for the progress bar with the code for the macro.

To keep the example simple, you should put this code in your Normal template. Select Tools → Macro → Visual Basic Editor, choose Normal in the Project Explorer (near the top left of the window), and then select Insert → UserForm. Next, choose View → Toolbox to display the Toolbox (it may already be showing). Select the Label control (the one with the "A" on it). Now move your cursor to the UserForm and drag the cursor to create a new label, like the one shown in Figure 7-9. Try to position the top-left corner of the label near the top left of the UserForm.

Next, select View → Code and insert the following code:

```
Private Sub UserForm_Activate( )
Dim lParaCount As Long
Dim i As Integer
Dim para As Paragraph
Dim lMaxProgressBarWidth As Long
Dim sIncrement As Single

' Resize the UserForm
Me.Width = 240
Me.Height = 120

' Resize the label
Me.Label1.Height = 50
Me.Label1.Caption = ""
Me.Label1.Width = 0
Me.Label1.BackColor = wdColorBlue
```

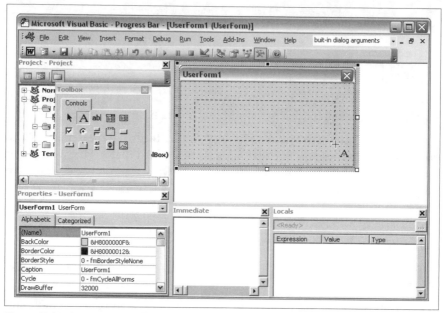

Figure 7-9. Creating a simple progress bar with a UserForm

```
lMaxProgressBarWidth = 200
lParaCount = ActiveDocument.Paragraphs.Count
sIncrement = lMaxProgressBarWidth / lParaCount
i = 1

For Each para In ActiveDocument.Paragraphs
    Me.Label1.Width = Format(Me.Label1.Width + sIncrement, "#.##")
    Me.Caption = "Checking " & CStr(i) & " of " & CStr(lParaCount)
    Me.Repaint
    If para.OutlineLevel = wdOutlineLevel2 Then
        If para.Range.Words.Count > 10 Then
            para.Range.HighlightColorIndex = wdBrightGreen
        End If
    End If
i = i + 1
Next para

Unload Me

End Sub
```

From the Project Explorer, select one of the code modules in Normal, as
shown in Figure 7-10. If you don't have any code modules in Normal, select
Insert → Module to create one.

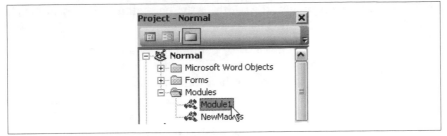

Figure 7-10. Select one of the code modules in your Normal template

In the code module you've selected, insert the following code:

```
Sub HighlightLongHeadings()
    UserForm1.Show
End Sub
```

Now select File → Close and Return to Microsoft Word. To run the macro, select Tools → Macro → Macros and choose HighlightLongHeadings. When you run the macro, you'll see a progress bar like the one shown in Figure 7-11.

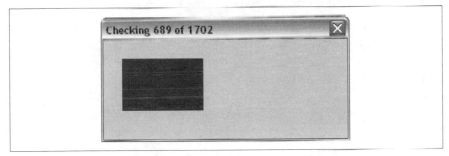

Figure 7-11. A simple progress bar in action

If the document is very short, you probably won't see the progress bar—it'll finish filling in too fast. Test this out on a long document to really see it in action.

One of the lines in the UserForm code deserves a closer look:

```
Format(Me.Label1.Width + sIncrement, "#.##")
```

The variable sIncrement is the final width of the progress bar divided by the total number of paragraphs in the document. As the macro visits each paragraph in the document, the width of the bar increases by the value of sIncrement. Since the maximum width of the bar in this example is 200 pixels (as defined in the variable lMaxProgressBarWidth), if there are 10 paragraphs in the document, the width of the bar will increase by 20 pixels as each paragraph is examined.

If there are hundreds or thousands of paragraphs in a document, the value of sIncrement can become quite small—smaller than the measurements UserForms are designed to handle. When that happens, VBA will round the number according to its own internal rounding rules, which can cause the width of the progress bar to eventually exceed the width of the UserForm. However, if you use the Format function, the increment amount will be rounded more precisely, keeping it confined to the boundaries of the UserForm.

Incremental Progress

One drawback to the technique described in the previous section is that the code for the progress bar is mixed with the code used to modify the document. To create another macro that displays a similar progress bar, you'd need to create another, similar UserForm. But by separating the code for the progress bar from the code that works on the document, you can reuse your progress bar in a variety of situations.

This section shows you how to create a dialog that reports the progress of a macro as a percentage, in increments of 10%, as shown in Figure 7-12. You can use this same progress bar from within any macro whose progress can be translated into a percentage.

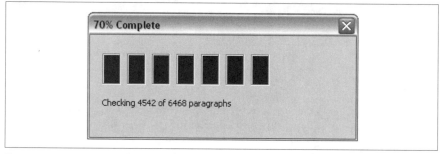

Figure 7-12. A progress bar that displays percentage increments

To keep the example simple, you should put this code in your Normal template. Select Tools → Macro → Visual Basic Editor, choose Normal in the Project Explorer (near the top left of the window), and then select Insert → UserForm. Next, choose View → Toolbox to display the Toolbox (it may already be showing).

On the Toolbox, select the Frame control (the box with "xyz" at the top), and then draw a single frame on your blank UserForm. With the frame selected, go to the Properties window. Change the frame's height to 30 and its width to 18 and set its Visible property to False. Then delete the frame's caption and change its background color to blue, as shown in Figure 7-13.

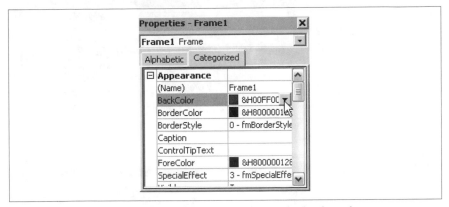

Figure 7-13. Change the frame's caption and background color from the Properties window

In the listbox at the top of the Properties window, select UserForm1 instead of Frame1, and then change the ShowModal property to False. While in the Properties window, change the name of the UserForm to IncrementalProgress.

Now go back to the UserForm itself and select the frame. Choose Edit → Copy, and then paste the frame nine times. Align the 10 frames as best you can in a single row. While holding down the Ctrl key, select all of the frames. Then select Format → Align and align the centers and tops of all the frames.

Next, select the Label control from the Toolbox (the one with the "A" on it) and draw a label underneath the frames, as shown in Figure 7-14. From the Properties window, delete the label's caption.

With this method, you display the dialog when your macro starts, then periodically increment its progress as a percentage. It involves more code, but it's more versatile than the first method.

Now select View → Code and insert the following:

```
Private Sub UserForm_Initialize( )
Me.Caption = "0% Complete"
End Sub

Public Function Increment(sPercentComplete As Single, _
    sDescription As String)
On Error Resume Next
Me.Label1.Caption = sDescription
Me.Repaint
```

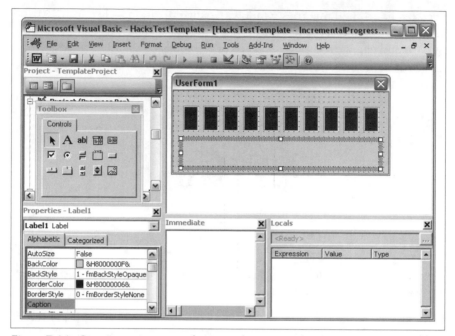

Figure 7-14. Creating an incremental progress bar

```
Dim iPercentIncrement As Integer
iPercentIncrement = Format(sPercentComplete, "#")

Select Case iPercentIncrement
    Case 10
        Me.Frame1.visible = True
        Me.Caption = "10% Complete"
        Me.Repaint
    Case 20
        Me.Frame2.visible = True
        Me.Caption = "20% Complete"
        Me.Repaint
    Case 30
        Me.Frame3.visible = True
        Me.Caption = "30% Complete"
        Me.Repaint
    Case 40
        Me.Frame4.visible = True
        Me.Caption = "40% Complete"
        Me.Repaint
    Case 50
        Me.Frame5.visible = True
        Me.Caption = "50% Complete"
        Me.Repaint
    Case 60
        Me.Frame6.visible = True
```

```
            Me.Caption = "60% Complete"
            Me.Repaint
        Case 70
            Me.Frame7.visible = True
            Me.Caption = "70% Complete"
            Me.Repaint
        Case 80
            Me.Frame8.visible = True
            Me.Caption = "80% Complete"
            Me.Repaint
        Case 90
            Me.Frame9.visible = True
            Me.Caption = "90% Complete"
            Me.Repaint
        Case 100
            Me.Frame10.visible = True
            Me.Caption = "100% Complete"
            Me.Repaint
    End Select
End Function
```

You can now use the progress bar from within your macros. All you need to do is provide the percentage and any text you'd like displayed underneath the progress bars.

The following is the `HighlightLongHeadings` macro, revised to use this progress bar. The lines shown in bold are the ones that interact with the progress bar.

```
Sub HighlightLongHeadings()
Dim lParaCount As Long
Dim sPercentage As Single
Dim i As Integer
Dim para As Paragraph
Dim sStatus As String

IncrementalProgress.Show

lParaCount = ActiveDocument.Paragraphs.Count
i = 1

For Each para In ActiveDocument.Paragraphs

    sPercentage = (i / lParaCount) * 100
    sStatus = "Checking " & i & " of " & lParaCount & " paragraphs"
    IncrementalProgress.Increment sPercentage, sStatus

    If para.OutlineLevel = wdOutlineLevel2 Then
        If para.Range.Words.Count > 10 Then
            para.Range.HighlightColorIndex = wdBrightGreen
        End If
    End If
```

```
i = i + 1
Next para
```

```
Unload IncrementalProgress
End Sub
```

Running this macro will display the progress bar shown in Figure 7-12.

Your macros will take longer to run, because the progress bar adds over-head. You should test versions of your macros with and without the progress bar to determine whether you find the performance hit acceptable.

> The above code assumes you will hit each percentage stop along the way. If you expect to skip increments, modify the code to make sure you "turn on" all the increment frames lower than the current one. For example:

```
...
Case 40
    With Me
        .Frame1.Visible = True
        .Frame2.Visible = True
        .Frame3.Visible = True
        .Frame4.Visible = True
        .Caption = "40% Complete"
        .Repaint
    End With
...
```

HACK #66 Hack Documents with For Each Loops

When you need a quick and dirty solution, you don't always have time to find the best tool for the job. This hack introduces you to the Swiss Army Knife of VBA programming.

In the Unix world, a handy utility program called *sed* has been doing the dirty work of editing text files for more than 30 years. Other programs and languages have come along that can do the same thing sed does (and more), but thousands of users still fire up sed every single day. Why? Because sed reads and edits text files the same way people do: line by line; so it's easy for people to "tell" sed what to do. It's not the fastest, and it's not the prettiest, but it's hard to beat for automating rote tasks. A technique for writing macros in VBA shares that same trait of "thinking" the way people do, but about Word documents. It's a For Each loop, and you should consider it your tool of first resort for quick and dirty solutions to everyday problems.

A lot of the simple but tedious tasks you do in Word come about when you need to modify something. For example, say you've got a document peppered with dozens of tables of varying size. Some of the tables have a heading row with bold applied to all the text in the row. Since some of those tables might span multiple pages, you want the heading row to repeat [Hack #20] on each page.

One option is to use Word's "Browse by Object" feature to scan the text for each table, as shown in Figure 7-15. To browse a document table by table, click the blue circle between the two double arrows, just below your vertical scrollbar. After you choose "Browse by Table," click one of the double arrows to jump to the next or previous table in the document. If the table has a bold heading row, select it, and then select Table → Heading Rows Repeat. This procedure is just complicated enough to require your full attention but simple and repetitive enough to make it a real chore.

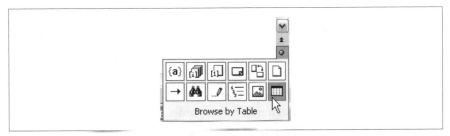

Figure 7-15. Browsing a document, one object at a time

When the instructions are simple—*look at each table in the document, and if the first row is in bold, then select the option to repeat that row across pages*—it's often easy to translate them into terms a macro can understand. A big hint that a For Each loop might be useful here is the presence of the word "each" in the instructions.

If you want to run the sample macros in this hack, place them in the template of your choice [Hack #50] and run them either from the Tools → Macro → Macros dialog or from within the Visual Basic Editor.

Excluding comments and the required Sub and End Sub parts, you can take care of the tables with just six lines of fairly understandable VBA code:

```
Sub CheckTableHeadings( )
' Declare a variable of type "Table"
Dim tbl As Table
' Look at each table in the document
For Each tbl In ActiveDocument.Tables
    ' If the first row is bold
    If tbl.Rows(1).Range.Font.Bold = True Then
        ' Select the option to repeat that row across pages
        tbl.Rows.HeadingFormat = True
    End If
Next tbl
End Sub
```

A generalized version of that macro would be the following:

```
Sub DoForEach( )
Dim variablename As Thing
For Each variablename in ActiveDocument.Things
    ' Do stuff to the current "Thing"
Next variablename
End Sub
```

The *Thing* in this code could be tables, comments, bookmarks, fields, paragraphs, revisions, and so forth. For example, the following macro changes the author of any comment written by Marlowe to Shakespeare:

```
Sub ChangeComments
Dim oComment as Comment
For Each oComment In ActiveDocument.Comments
    If oComment.Author = "Marlowe" Then
        oComment.Author = "Shakespeare"
    End If
Next oComment
End Sub
```

For Each loops are ideal for single-use macros because you can code them fast without investing a lot of development time.

> The Word object model does include Characters and Words collections, but there's no corresponding singular Character or Word object. If you want to visit each character or word in a document, as in "Find and Replace Without Find and Replace" [Hack #32], declare a Range variable for use in your loop:
>
> ```
> Sub BoldLongWords( )
> Dim oWord as Range
> For Each oWord In ActiveDocument.Words
>     If oWord.Characters.Count > 10 Then
>         oWord.Bold = True
>     End If
> Next oWord
> End Sub
> ```

When to Avoid For Each Loops

A For Each loop is a poor choice if your macro needs to delete any of the "things" mentioned in the previous section. In these cases, you'd want to use another, more traditional type of loop: a For... Next loop. For... Next loops use a *counter variable* to keep track of their place, as the following macro, which counts from 1 to 5, shows:

```
Sub CountUp( )
Dim i As Integer ' This is the counter variable
For i = 1 to 5
```

```
    MsgBox i & " Mississippi"
Next i
End Sub
```

For... Next loops can also count backward, when you use the optional Step statement, as the following macro shows:

```
Sub CountDown( )
Dim i As Integer ' This is the counter variable
For i = 3 to 1 Step -1 ' Going backward from 3 to 1
    MsgBox i
Next i
MsgBox "Contact!"
End Sub
```

So why are there two different kinds of loops? Well, the For Each loops described in the previous section are really just modified For... Next loops, designed to iterate through objects in a collection using a simpler syntax—and, more importantly, to execute *much* faster.

To show the difference in the syntax, here's the CheckTableHeadings macro from the previous section rewritten using a regular For... Next loop:

```
Sub SlowerCheckTableHeadings( )
Dim tbl As Table
Dim i as Integer
For i = 1 To ActiveDocument.Tables.Count
    Set tbl = ActiveDocument.Tables(i)
    If tbl.Rows(1).Range.Style = "TableHeading" Then
        tbl.Rows.HeadingFormat = True
    End If
    Set tbl = Nothing
Next i
End Sub
```

With the For Each version, that Set statement is implicit, and the loop automatically goes one at a time from the first to the last item. But that speed comes at a price: if you delete any of the "things" that a For Each loop is visiting, the loop can lose its place and may skip over items.

Instead, to delete some (or all) of the objects in a collection, as in "Unlink Every Hyperlink" [Hack #28], use a For... Next loop and run it backward from the end of the document:

```
Sub DeleteFootnotes
Dim i as Integer
For i = ActiveDocument.Footnotes.Count to 1 Step -1
    ActiveDocument.Footnotes(i).Delete
Next i
End Sub
```

Store Settings and Data in .ini Files

HACK
#67

VBA includes a way to store and retrieve information using plain-text files
that are easy to create, easy to edit, and easy to remove.

Before Windows 95 came along with the Windows registry for storing system information, Windows used *.ini* files—text files used to store program-
specific data. Many programs, and even Windows, still use these files to
store certain information. A search on your hard drive for **.ini* files will
likely turn up dozens or even hundreds of entries.

These files are very useful for storing data after a macro finishes running in
VBA, or for things like numbering documents sequentially **[Hack #77]** and creating an improved MRU **[Hack #13]** after Word closes.

The *.ini*, or *Config*, files have a simple structure. Each file is divided into one
or more sections, and each section contains sets of *key/value* pairs. The contents of a Config file look like the following:

```
[MRU_Files]
MRU01=C:\Dox\Doc 1.doc
MRU02=C:\Dox\Doc 2.doc
```

Each section name is on its own line and surrounded by brackets. Each line
within the section contains a key/value pair separated by an equals sign (=).

VBA includes a feature called the `PrivateProfileString` property, which you
can use from any macro, to read and write these files. When you read from
or write to a Config file, you need three values: the filename, the section
name, and the key name. If you're writing to the file, you also need the value
to assign to the key.

To store the name of the current document in a Config file under the key
CurrDoc in the section *WordInfo* in a file named *WordSettings.ini*, you'd use
the following syntax:

```
System.PrivateProfileString("WordSettings.ini", "WordInfo", "CurrDoc") = _
    ActiveDocument.Name
```

If no file named *WordSettings.ini* exists, the macro creates one. If the file
does exist, it replaces any value already associated with the key CurrDoc in
the section WordInfo.

To retrieve this same information from the Config file, use the following
syntax:

```
strSetting = System.PrivateProfileString("WordSettings.ini", _
    "WordInfo", "CurrDoc")
```

If the file, section, or key doesn't exist, it returns an empty string.

The following example shows you how to use a Config file from within a macro. These two AutoMacros [Hack #60], when placed in your Normal template, will record the name of the active document when you quit Word and then open that document the next time you start Word:

```
Sub AutoExec
Dim sDocName as String
sDocName = System.PrivateProfileString("WordSettings.ini", _
    "WordInfo", "CurrDoc")
If Len(sDocName) <> 0 Then
    Documents.Open(sDocName)
End If
End Sub

Sub AutoExit
System.PrivateProfileString("WordSettings.ini", "WordInfo", "CurrDoc") = _
    ActiveDocument.FullName
End Sub
```

Because Config files are just plain-text files, they can be viewed and edited using any standard text editor, such as Notepad.

HACK #68 Generate Random Numbers

Randomization is an esoteric area of most programming languages, and VBA's no exception. This hack gives you easy access to two of its most common forms.

Random numbers are a helpful way to ensure that a particular value, such as a bookmark name for a cross-reference [Hack #44], is unique. Word even uses random numbers in its own cross-reference bookmarks. But getting a random number from VBA in the form you need can be a challenge.

The first time you need a random number from VBA, you'll look up the syntax in the help files, and then you'll have to figure out a way to get the kind of number you need. The second time you need a random number—probably months later—chances are you'll have long since forgotten the syntax, and you'll spend needless time looking it up again and trying to figure out how to coax the kind of number you need from it. The functions in this hack can help you save yourself the aggravation.

VBA includes the Rnd function to generate a random number, but it always returns a value between 0 and 1. By putting Rnd to work alongside two other built-in functions, Int and Randomize, you can get back numbers more suitable for things like creating your own cross-references [Hack #44].

Bounded Random Numbers

This function generates a random number between two ranges:

```
Function GenerateBoundedRandomNumber( _
    lLowerBound As Long, _
    lUpperBound As Long) As Long
Randomize
GenerateBoundedRandomNumber = Int( _
    (lUpperBound - lLowerBound + 1) _
    * Rnd + lLowerBound)
End Function
```

The lLowerBound and lUpperBound values are inclusive and can be any signed numbers between –999,999,999 and 999,999,999. If lLowerBound is greater than lUpperBound, the function will still work, but the results will exclude both boundary numbers.

n-Digit Random Numbers

This function generates a random number of the specified length:

```
Function GenerateFixedLengthRandomNumber( _
    iLength As Integer) As Long
Randomize
GenerateFixedLengthRandomNumber = Int(((((10 ^ iLength) - 1) _
    - (10 ^ (iLength - 1)) + 1) _
    * Rnd + (10 ^ (iLength - 1)))
End Function
```

iLength can be any positive number between 1 and 9. A number greater than 9 will generate an "Overflow" error. However, you can get around the nine-digit limit by converting the return value to a string using the Cstr( ) function and concatenating it with another converted return value from the same function. So in the following statement, the variable sMyString would get a string containing a 15-digit number:

```
sMyString = CStr(GenerateFixedLengthRandomNumber(8)) & _
            CStr(GenerateFixedLengthRandomNumber(7))
```

Running the Hack

Put these functions in a code module in your Macros template [Hack #50]. The Public keyword before the function name means you can use these functions from other code modules in the same template.

#69 Hack with Application Events

Application events offer a powerful way to run VBA code when certain things happen within Word.

Windows is an events-based operating system. Most everything you do, from typing at the keyboard to scrolling within a window, triggers an *event*, which is then acted on by the program or the operating system.

Word exposes several events to you for use within your macros. For example, you can run a specific macro whenever the Word window is resized, or whenever the user right-clicks within a Word window.

If you have two Word documents open and you toggle between the two from the Window menu, three different events happen (in this order):

1. The WindowDeactivate event
2. The WindowActivate event
3. The DocumentChange event

At any of those stages (or all of them), you can specify VBA code to run every time that particular event "fires."

Application events fire when they occur anywhere within Word, not just within the document or template that contains the event-handling code. If your document (or the template on which your document is based) contains no macros, you can still work with events related to the document if you have defined event-handling code in your Normal template or in a currently loaded add-in.

A handy feature in Word 2002 and 2003 can help you remember to accept revisions or remove comments before you print or save a document. This hack will show you how to replicate this feature in earlier versions of Word.

Setting Up the Event Handler

For this hack, create a new template and name it *Event Handlers.dot*. Next, select Tools → Macro → Visual Basic Editor, choose the *Event Handlers.dot* template in the Project Explorer, and then select Insert → Class Module. The default name for a new class is Class1. Rename your class module EventHandler, as shown in Figure 7-16.

Double-click the new EventHandler class to open it and insert this code:

```
Public WithEvents oThisWordApp As Application

Private Sub oThisWordApp_DocumentBeforePrint(ByVal Doc As Document, _
        Cancel As Boolean)
    Dim lResponse As Long
```

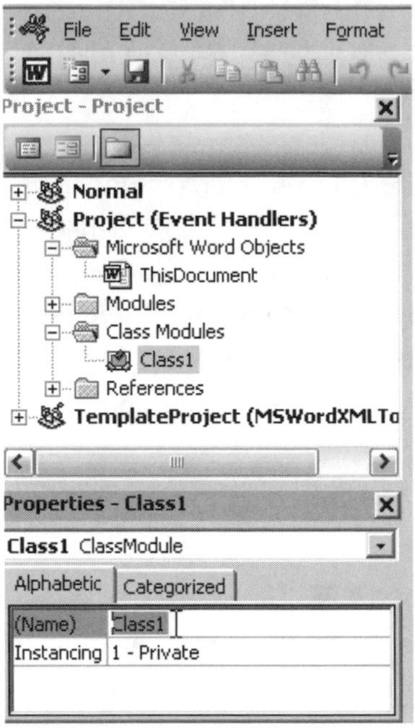

Figure 7-16. Renaming an inserted class module

```
        If Doc.Comments.Count <> 0 Or Doc.Revisions.Count <> 0 Then
            lResponse = MsgBox(Chr(34) & Doc.Name & Chr(34) _
                & " contains comments or tracked changes." & vbCr _
                & "Continue with printing?", vbYesNo)
            If lResponse = vbNo Then Cancel = True
        End If
    End Sub

    Private Sub oThisWordApp_DocumentBeforeSave(ByVal Doc As Document, _
                SaveAsUI As Boolean, Cancel As Boolean)
      Dim lResponse As Long
        If Doc.Comments.Count <> 0 Or Doc.Revisions.Count <> 0 Then
            lResponse = MsgBox(Chr(34) & Doc.Name & Chr(34) _
                & " contains comments or tracked changes." & vbCr _
                & "Continue with save?", vbYesNo)
            If lResponse = vbNo Then Cancel = True
        End If
    End Sub
```

Notice that the two events that are handled, `DocumentBeforePrint` and
`DocumentBeforeSave`, each take several arguments. Word will include these
arguments as needed when you select an event that requires them. In the
lefthand pull-down menu just above your code, select `oWordApp`. In the pull-
down menu on the right, you can choose among the available application

events. When you choose one, the appropriate shell code (sometimes called a "stub") is inserted, including any arguments, as shown in Figure 7-17.

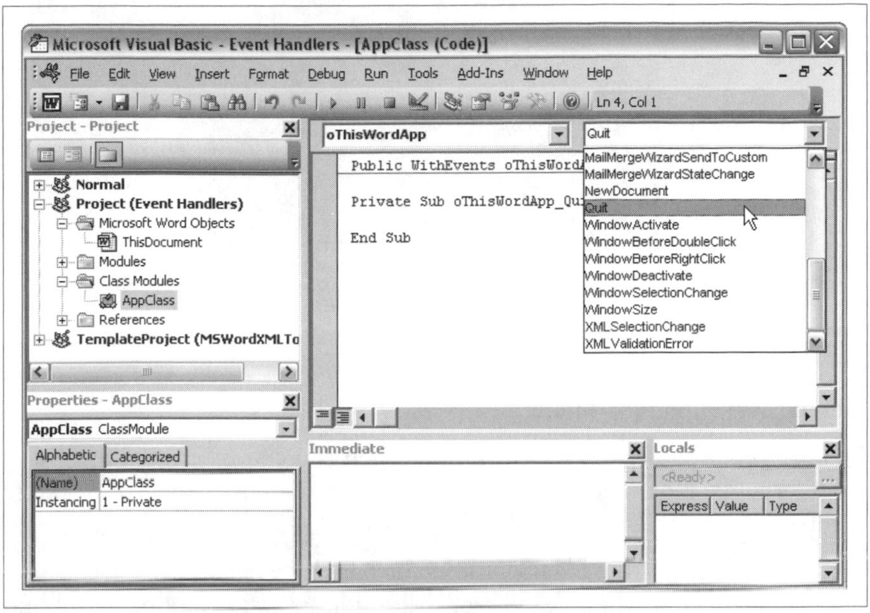

Figure 7-17. Choosing from available application events

Now that you've created the class module that will handle the Word events, you need to create an instance of the class within a standard code module. To ensure that the event handler is activated as soon as the Event Handlers template is loaded, place the necessary code in an AutoMacro [Hack #60].

Select the Event Handlers template in the Project Explorer and choose Insert → Code Module. Insert the following code in the new module's *declarations* section. The declarations section is at the top of the code module, before any procedures.

```
Dim oEventHandler As New EventHandler
```

Below that declaration, insert the following code, which creates an instance of the EventHandler:

```
Sub AutoExec()
Set oEventHandler.oThisWordApp = Word.Application
End Sub
```

Running the Hack

Save and close your *Event Handlers.dot* template. Next, select Tools → Templates and Add-Ins and click the Add button to load it as a global template.

As soon as *Event Handlers.dot* is loaded, whenever you save or print a document that contains comments or unaccepted revisions, you'll be prompted to confirm, as shown in Figure 7-18.

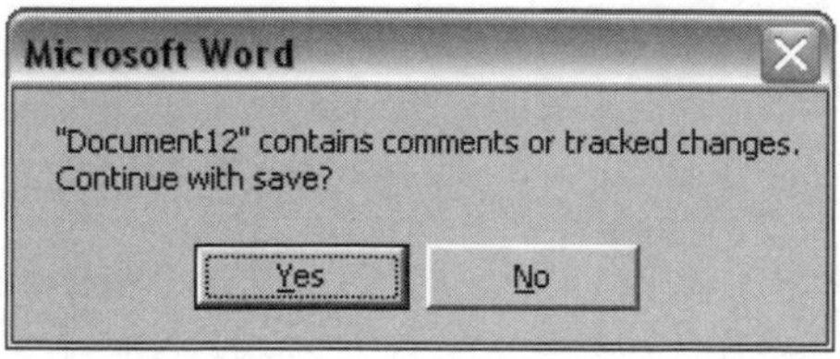

Microsoft Word ☒

"Document12" contains comments or tracked changes. Continue with save?

| Yes | No |

Figure 7-18. Using the DocumentBeforeSave event to warn if a document contains revisions or comments

Though similar to intercepting built-in commands [Hack #61], this event handler has two important differences.

First, the DocumentBeforeSave event fires when you choose either the Save or Save As commands. The other method forces you to intercept each separate command.

Second—and this is the biggie—the event handler will run even if you save the document from within a macro, making it an even more powerful and flexible technique than the command intercept.

> If a macro tries to save a document and your event handler cancels the save, VBA may return an error. If you use event handlers, you need to include extra error handling in your macros.

Forms and Fields
Hacks 70–79

Many of Word's most useful features, such as page numbering and cross-referencing, are implemented with *fields*. Most of Word's fields act as placeholders, gathering, updating, and displaying content that may change throughout a document's lifetime.

For example, when you insert a DATE field, rather than just inserting today's date as plain text, Word inserts a special code that says "Whenever this field is updated, go and find out what the current date is and display that." (Of course, Word says it a bit more tersely.) To see a DAIL field in action, press Ctrl-F9 to insert a pair of *field braces*—special characters that can't be typed in using the standard keys—and type the word **Date** in between the braces. Select the field you just created and press F9 to update its contents. Word will gladly report today's date.

The hacks in this chapter show a few ways to take fields beyond the basics—in some cases, *way* beyond the basics. Working with fields isn't for the easily frustrated, and the learning curve is on the steep side. But once you've seen what they can do, you'll find that fields are a very useful addition to your Word toolbox.

Many of the fields in this chapter are quite complex, and Word is unforgiving of incorrect syntax. Many of the fields in this chapter are also quite long. Optional line breaks have been inserted, as indicated with the "↵" character, so that the fields can fit the width of a printed page. A line break is inserted in Word by pressing Shift-Enter. To save yourself some trouble, download all the fields shown in this chapter from this book's web site, at *http://www.oreilly.com/catalog/wordhks*.

When working with fields, go to Tools → Options → View and make sure "Field shading" is set to Always. Don't worry, the shading won't appear when you print the document.

HACK #70   Fake (and Easy) Fill-in Forms

This hack shows you how to quickly create "click-to-replace" text in any document.

People use Word templates to store boilerplate text for letters and contracts. However, they often create novel approaches to mark the replaceable text in the template or document, as shown in Figure 8-1.

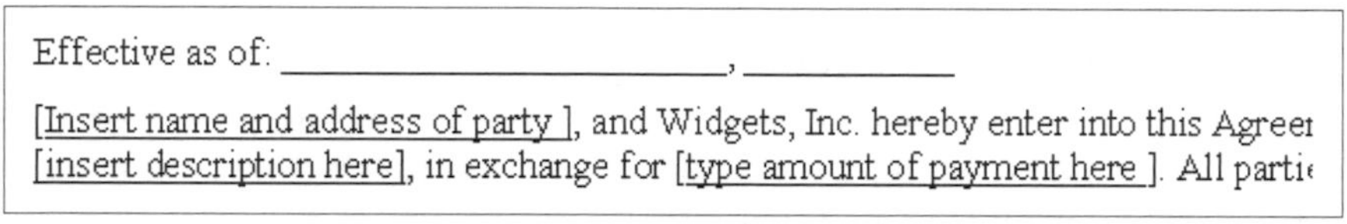

Effective as of: _____, _____

[Insert name and address of party], and Widgets, Inc. hereby enter into this Agreer [insert description here], in exchange for [type amount of payment here]. All parti

Figure 8-1. A document with text to be filled in

To remove all the brackets and keep the correct spacing in the sample agreement above requires some serious cursor gymnastics. It would be better if the person filling out the agreement could just click and type at each of the places that needed new text. You can do that with a MACROBUTTON field that runs a nonexistent macro.

Wherever you want to note an area in the text that should be filled in, do the following:

1. Press Ctrl-F9 to insert an empty pair of field braces.
2. In between the field braces, type the following:

   `MACROBUTTON FakeMacroName Text to Display`

   You can replace *Text to Display* with whatever text should appear on the page.
3. Press F9 to update the field.

To create field braces, you must press Ctrl-F9 or select Insert → Field.

Lather, rinse, and repeat for other parts of your document, which will now look more like the one shown in Figure 8-2. (Make sure you select Tools → Options, click the View tab, and turn on field shading.)

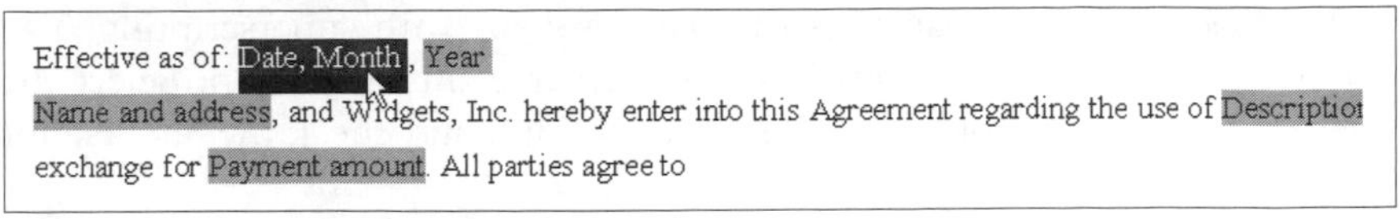

Effective as of: Date, Month , Year
Name and address, and Widgets, Inc. hereby enter into this Agreement regarding the use of Description
exchange for Payment amount. All parties agree to

Figure 8-2. The same document, reworked with replaceable fields

Since there is no macro called FakeMacroName, when you click the field, the entire field is selected, as shown in Figure 8-2. Just start typing to replace the field with your text.

If the text used in the field spans more than one line, Word will complain, as shown in Figure 8-3. You'll need to shorten the text in order for the field to work properly.

DisplayText cannot span more than one line!

Figure 8-3. Word complains when the display text in a MACROBUTTON field is too long

Hack DATE Fields
#71 Perform advanced date calculations with this grab bag of field hacks.

Dates are an important part of many Word documents, especially leases and contracts. When these dates involve calculations (such as "What date is 6 months from today?" or "How old is someone born on September 12, 1978?"), you can let Word do the grunt work for you.

When following the examples in this hack, press Ctrl-F9 or select Insert → Field for each set of braces in the field (most of the fields in this hack use several nested fields), taking care to put them in the correct order—some are nested, and some are adjacent—and then fill in the field codes as shown. In some cases, you'll need to format parts of the field code, which will be described in the text. Select the entire field and press F9 to display its results. Line breaks, indicated with the "↵" character, are included to aid in readability, but they are not required for the fields to work properly.

Display Long Forms of Dates

To include the day of week with today's date, use the following field:

```
{DATE \@ "dddd 'the {DATE \@ d \*Ordinal} of' MMMM, yyyy"}
```

The field displays today's date in the form below:

```
Monday the 5th of July, 2004
```

Word fields ordinarily can't display date ordinals with superscripting. The following example shows you how to overcome this limitation. Select the characters shown in bold, choose Format → Font, and check the Superscript box:

```
{DATE \@ "dddd 'the' d'{IF{=(mod({DATE \@ d},10)<4)*↵
(mod({DATE \@ d},10)<>0)*({DATE \@ d}<>11)*↵
({DATE \@ d}<>12)*({DATE \@ d}<>13)}= 1 ↵
{=mod({DATE \@ d},10)-2 \# rd;st;nd} th} of' MMMM, yyyy"}
```

The field displays the same result shown above, but with the ordinal superscripted:

```
Monday the 5th of July, 2004
```

Determine a Date's Place in the Year

The following field shows you what number day of the year today's date is. Again, you should superscript the characters shown in bold.

```
{QUOTE↵
"Today's date ({DATE \@ "MMMM d yyyy"}) falls on the "↵
{SET yd{={DATE \@ d}+INT((({DATE \@ M}-0.986)*30.575)-↵
IF({DATE \@ M}>2,2-(MOD({DATE \@ yy},4)=0)-↵
(MOD({DATE \@ yyyy},400)=0)+(MOD({DATE \@ yy},100)=0),0)}}↵
{=yd \# 0}↵
{IF{=(mod(yd,10)<4)*(mod(yd,10)<>0)*(mod(yd,100)<>11)*(mod(yd,100)<>12)*↵
(mod(yd,100)<>13)}= 1 {=mod(yd,10)-2 \# rd;st;nd} th}" day of the year."}
```

The field displays today's date in the form below:

```
Today's date (July 24 2004) falls on the 206th day of the year.
```

Automatically Insert a Past or Future Date

The following fields calculate any past or future date from today's date, based on the Gregorian calendar. Setting the Delay parameter in the fields allows for the required date to be many days, months, and/or years ahead or behind (to achieve the latter, express the Delay parameter as a negative number).

You can change the DATE parameters in the fields to CREATEDATE, SAVEDATE, or PRINTDATE to modify the date from which you calculate, if needed.

> If you change the DATE parameter to SAVEDATE or PRINTDATE, you must save or print the document to get a valid output.

Calculate a month using n months delay. The following will display the name of the month 10 months from today's date:

```
{QUOTE{Set Delay 10}{=MOD({DATE \@ M}+Delay-1,12)+1}/00 \@ MMMM}
```

Calculate a month and year using n months delay. The following displays the month and year 10 months from today's date:

```
{QUOTE{SET Delay 10}↵
{SET m"{=MOD({DATE \@ MM}+Delay-1,12)+1}/0"}↵
{SET y{={DATE \@ yyyy}+INT((Delay+{DATE \@ M}-1)/12)}}↵
{m \@ MMMM}160{y}}
```

The above field uses an undocumented switch, "{*FieldResult*}/0", to store the result of the month calculation in a form that Word recognizes as a month. Note also the use of ASCII character 160 to create a nonbreaking space.

Calculate a month and year using n years delay. The following field displays the month and year one year from today:

```
{QUOTE{SET Delay 1}{DATE \@ MMMM}160{={DATE \@ yyyy}+Delay}}
```

Calculate a day, date, month, and year using n years delay. The following field displays the full date exactly one year from today, and is considerably more complicated than the previous example, because it accounts for leap years:

```
{QUOTE↵
{SET Delay 1}↵
{SET yy{={DATE \@ yyyy}+Delay}}↵
{SET dd{={DATE \@ d}-({DATE \@ d}>28)*({DATE \@ M}=2)*↵
((MOD(yy,4)>0)+(MOD(yy,400)>0)-(MOD(yy,100)>0))}}↵
{=dd*10^6+{DATE \@ M}*10^4+yy \# "00'-'00'-'0000"} \@ "dddd, MMMM d yyyy"}
```

Calculate a day, date, month, and year using n months delay. This field displays the full date exactly 10 months from today, taking into account leap years and differences in the length of months:

```
{QUOTE↵
{SET Delay 10}↵
{SET mm{=MOD({DATE \@ M}+Delay-1,12)+1}}.↵
{SET yy{={DATE \@ yyyy}+INT((Delay+{DATE \@ M}-1)/12)}}↵
{SET dd{=IF((({DATF \@ d}>28)*(mm=2)*((MOD(yy,4)-0)+↵
(MOD(yy,400)=0)-(MOD(yy,100)=0))=1,28,IF((mm=4)+(mm=6)+(mm=9)+(mm=11)+↵
({DATE \@ d}>30)=1,30,{DATE \@ d}))}}↵
{=mm*10^6+dd*10^4+yy \# "00'-'00'-'0000"} \@ "dddd, MMMM d yyyy"}
```

Calculate a day, date, month, and year using n days delay. The following field displays the full date exactly 301 days from today. This field, and the next one, work by converting the date to a Julian day number, adding or subtracting the delay, then converting the new Julian day number back to a date.

```
{QUOTE↵
{SET Delay 301}↵
```

```
{SET a{=INT((14-{DATE \@ M})/12)}}↵
{SET b{={DATE \@ yyyy}+4800-a}}↵
{SET c{={DATE \@ M}+12*a-3}}↵
{SET d{DATE \@ d}}↵
{SET jd{=d+INT((153*c+2)/5)+365*b+INT(b/4)-↵
INT(b/100)+INT(b/400)-32045+Delay}}↵
{SET e{=INT((4*(jd+32044)+3)/146097)}}↵
{SET f{=jd+32044-INT(146097*e/4)}}↵
{SET g{=INT((4*f+3)/1461)}}↵
{SET h{=f-INT(1461*g/4)}}↵
{SET i{=INT((5*h+2)/153)}}↵
{SET dd{=h-INT((153*i+2)/5)+1}}↵
{SET mm{=i+3-12*INT(i/10)}}↵
{SET yy{=100*e+g-4800+INT(i/10)}}↵
{=mm*10^6+dd*10^4+yy \# "00'-'00'-'0000"} \@ "dddd, MMMM d yyyy"}
```

Calculate a day, date, month, and year using n weeks delay. The following field displays the full date exactly 43 weeks from today:

```
{QUOTE↵
{SET Delay 43}↵
{SET a{=INT((14-{DATE \@ M})/12)}}↵
{SET b{={DATE \@ yyyy}+4800-a}}↵
{SET c{={DATE \@ M}+12*a-3}}↵
{SET d{DATE \@ d}}↵
{SET jd{=d+INT((153*c+2)/5)+365*b+INT(b/4)-↵
INT(b/100)+INT(b/400)-32045+INT(Delay*7)}}↵
{SET e{=INT((4*(jd+32044)+3)/146097)}}↵
{SET f{=jd+32044-INT(146097*e/4)}}↵
{SET g{=INT((4*f+3)/1461)}}↵
{SET h{=f-INT(1461*g/4)}}↵
{SET i{=INT((5*h+2)/153)}}↵
{SET dd{=h-INT((153*i+2)/5)+1}}↵
{SET mm{=i+3-12*INT(i/10)}}↵
{SET yy{=100*e+g-4800+INT(i/10)}}↵
{=mm*10^6+dd*10^4+yy \# "00'-'00'-'0000"} \@ "dddd, MMMM d yyyy"}
```

Internationalizing dates. To use the above four examples with a "Day, Month, Year" format instead of the "Month Day, Year" format shown, you can change the date switches to suit your needs. For example, change each last line of the field codes in the previous four examples from:

```
{QUOTE{=mm*10^6+dd*10^4+yy \# "00'-'00'-'0000"} \@ "MMMM d yyyy"}."}
```

to this (changes are indicated in bold):

```
{QUOTE{=dd*10^6+mm*10^4+yy \# "00'-'00'-'0000"} \@ "d MMMM yyyy"}."}
```

Express a Date in Fiscal-Year Terms

The following field expresses today's date in fiscal-year terms, showing the year, month number, and week number within the month, assuming a July 1 to June 30 fiscal year:

```
{QUOTE↵
"Fiscal Year {date \@ yy}/{={DATE \@ yy}+1 \# 00}, Month: {=MOD(↵
{DATE \@ M}+5,12)+1}, Week: {=INT((({date \@ dd}-1)/7)+1}"}}
```

The field displays results like the following:

```
Fiscal Year 04/05, Month: 1, Week: 4
```

Calculate a Person's Age

The following field uses an ASK field for date of birth to perform an age calculation:

```
{QUOTE↵
{ASK BirthDate "What is the Birthdate?"}↵
{SET by {BirthDate \@ yyyy}}↵
{SET bm {BirthDate \@ M}}↵
{SET bd {BirthDate \@ d}}↵
{SET yy {DATE \@ yyyy}}↵
{SET mm {DATE \@ M}}↵
{SET dd {DATE \@ d}}↵
{SET md{=IF((mm=2),28+(mm=2)*((MOD(yy,4)=0)+(MOD↵
(yy,400)=0)-(MOD(yy,100)=0)),31-((mm=4)+(mm=6)+(mm=9)+(mm=11))))}}↵
{Set Years{=yy-by-(mm<bm)-(mm=bm)*(dd<bd)}}↵
{Set Months{=MOD(12+mm-bm-(dd<bd),12)}}↵
{Set Days{=MOD(md+dd-bd,md) \# 0}}.↵
"If your Date of Birth was {↵
Birthdate \@ "MMMM d yyyy"}, then your age is {↵
Years} Year{IF{Years}= 1 "" s}, {Months} Month{↵
IF{Months}= 1 "" s} and {Days} Day{IF{Days}= 1 "" s}."}
```

The field displays results like the following:

```
If your Date of Birth was September 12 1978, then your age is 25 Years, 10
Months and 12 Days.
```

Use Print and Save Information in a Field

The following field reports whether or not a document has been saved since it was last printed:

```
{IF{PRINTDATE \@ yyyyMMddHHmm}>{SAVEDATE \@ yyyyMMddHHmm}↵
" Not Saved Since Last Print" "Not Printed Since Last Save"}
```

If you haven't saved your document since you last printed it, the field displays the following:

```
Not Saved Since Last Print
```

—Paul Edstein

HACK #72   Perform Calculations with Formula Fields

You can do a surprising amount of number crunching without resorting to an Excel spreadsheet. This hack introduces you to Word's formula fields.

Formula fields let you calculate and compare numbers, but not text. This hack shows you one way around this limitation.

The syntax for a formula field follows:

```
{=Formula [Bookmark] [\# Numeric Picture]}
```

For example, the following set of fields asks you to enter a number, assigns the number to a bookmark named *MyNum*, and then uses a formula field to calculate the square of the number:

```
{ QUOTE { ASK "Enter a Number" MyNum } { =MyNum^2 } }
```

To get the square of a different number, select the field and press F9.

To create this field, or any of the fields shown in this hack, press Ctrl-F9 or select Insert → Field for each set of braces in the field (most of the fields in this hack use several nested fields), and then fill in the field codes as shown. Line breaks are included to aid in readability, but they are not required for the fields to work properly.

The *Numeric Picture* includes formatting instructions that tell Word how to display the results of a calculation. These are discussed in "Format Numeric Field Results" [Hack #73].

A formula can use any combination of numbers, bookmarked numbers, or fields that output numbers, along with any of Word's numeric operators and functions (shown in the following sections).

Formula Field Arithmetic Operators

To perform basic arithmetic operations such as addition, subtraction, or multiplication; combine numbers; and produce numeric results, you can use any combination of the arithmetic operators listed in Table 8-1 with numeric values.

Table 8-1. Arithmetic operators for formula fields

Operation	Operator
Addition	+
Subtraction	–
Multiplication	*
Division	/
Percentage	%
Powers and roots	^

For example, to add one value to another, use a field like the following:

```
{=2+2}
```

You can also combine operations. For example, to calculate a square root, use a field like the following:

```
{=3^(1/2)}
```

Formula Field Comparison Operators

You can compare two numeric values with any of the operators listed in Table 8-2. The result of such a comparison is a logical value, either TRUE (1) or FALSE (0)

Table 8-2. Comparison operators for formula fields

Operation	Operator
Equal to	=
Not equal to	<>
Less than	<
Less than or equal to	<=
Greater than	>
Greater than or equal to	>=

For example, to test whether two values are equal, use a field coded like the following:

```
{=3=2+1} or {=NOT(3<>2+1)}
```

Formula Field Functions

A formula field can use values returned by any of the functions listed in Table 8-3.

Table 8-3. Functions for formula fields

Function	Returns
ABS(*x*)	The positive value of a number or formula, regardless of its actual positive or negative value. For example, {=ABS(-5)} and {=ABS(5)} both return 5.
AVERAGE( )	The average of a list of values; e .g., {=AVERAGE(1,2,3)} returns 2.
COUNT( )	The number of items in a list. For example, {=COUNT(1,2,3)} returns 3.
DEFINED(*x*)	The value 1 (true) if the expression *x* is valid, or the value 0 (false) if the expression can't be computed; e.g., {=DEFINED(1/0)} returns 0.
FALSE	The value 0. For example, {=FALSE} returns 0.
INT(*x*)	The numbers to the left of the decimal place in the value or formula *x*. For example, {=INT(5.15)} returns 5.
MIN( )	The smallest value in a list. For example, {=MIN(1,2,3)} returns 1.
MAX( )	The largest value in a list. For example, {=MAX(1,2,3)} returns 3.
MOD(*x*,*y*)	The remainder that results from dividing the value *x* by the value *y* a whole number of times. For example, {=MOD(5.15,2)} returns 1.15.
PRODUCT( )	The result of multiplying a list of values. For example, {=PRODUCT(2,4,6,8)} returns 384.
ROUND(*x*,*y*)	The value of *x* rounded to the specified number of decimal places *x*,*y* can be either a number or the result of a formula. For example, {=ROUND(123.456,2)} returns 123.46, {=ROUND(123.456,1)} returns 123.5, {=ROUND(123.456,0)} returns 123, and {=ROUND(123.456,-1)} returns 120.
SIGN(*x*)	The value 1 if *x* is a positive value, or the value –1 if *x* is a negative value. For example, {=SIGN(-123)} returns –1, and {=SIGN(123)} returns 1.
SUM( )	The sum of a list of values or formulas. For example, {=SUM(1,2,3)} returns 6.
TRUE	The value 1. For example, {=TRUE} returns 1.

> Functions shown with empty parentheses can accept any number of arguments separated by commas (,) or semicolons (;). Arguments can be numbers, other formulas, or bookmark names.

Formula Field Logical Functions

The logical functions that formula fields can use are listed in Table 8-4.

Table 8-4. Logical functions for formula fields

Function	Returns
AND(*x*,*y*)	The value 1 (true) if the logical expressions *x* and *y* are both true, and the value 0 (zero, false) if either expression is false. For example, {=AND(5=2+3,3=5-2)} returns 1.
OR(*x*,*y*)	The value 1 (true) if either or both of the logical expressions *x* and *y* are true, and the value 0 (zero, false) if both expressions are false. For example, {=OR(5=2+3,3=5-2)} returns 1.

Table 8-4. Logical functions for formula fields (continued)

Function	Returns
NOT(x)	Reverses the logic of its argument. Returns the value 0 (false) if the logical expression x is true, or the value 1 (true) otherwise. For example, to test whether two values are equal, you could use {=NOT(3<>2+1)}, which is equivalent to {=(3=2+1)} and returns 1.
IF(x,y,z)	Specifies a logical test to perform, where x is any value or expression that can be evaluated to TRUE or FALSE, y is the value that is returned if x evaluates to TRUE, and z is the value that is returned if x evaluates to FALSE. For example, {IF(5=2+3,2*3,2/3)} returns 6 and {IF(5<>2+3,2*3,2/3)} returns 0.667.

AND and OR: Testing multiple logical numeric expressions. Word's AND and OR functions can test only two logical numeric expressions at a time, and they can't directly test text strings at all. For testing more than two logical numeric expressions, you can nest multiple AND or OR functions, but there is a better way:

- The logical function {=AND(AND(5=2+3,3=5-2),2=5-3)}, which returns 1, can just as readily be expressed as {=(5=2+3)*(3=5-2)*(2=5-3)}, which also returns 1 and avoids the AND function's limitations.
- The logical function {=OR(OR(5=2+3,3=5-2),2=5-3)}, which returns 1, can just as readily be expressed as {=((5=2+3)+(3=5-2)+(2=5-3)>0)}, which also returns 1 and likewise avoids the OR function's limitations. Alternatively, to test whether only one of a range of possibilities is true (an "exclusive OR"), you can use {=((5=2+3)+(3=5-2)+(2=5-3)=1)}, replacing the final 1 with the required number of true results. The formula returns 0 here, because more than one test condition is true.

Testing or returning text strings with logical functions in bookmarks. Though you can't use formula fields directly to compare text values, you can fake it with IF fields. For example, the following set of fields asks you to enter your name. If the name you enter is Bob, the field displays "Hello, Bob." If the name you enter isn't Bob, the field displays "What have you done with Bob?"

```
{ QUOTE { ASK  Name "What's your name?"}
{IF{ Name }= "Bob" "Hello, Bob"
"What have you done with Bob?"}}
```

To enter a different name, just select the field and press F9.

Referencing Data in a Table

As in Excel, in Word you can reference table cells for use in a formula.

Referencing cells containing numbers. When you use cell references in a table, you reference table cells using an alphanumeric column/row format (A1, A2, B1, B2, and so on).

For example, select Table → Insert → Table, choose two rows and two columns, click the OK button, and enter the values shown in Table 8-5. Remember, to create the field braces, press Ctrl-F9 (or select Insert → Field) and then enter the text.

Table 8-5. Put the following table in a document to see cell referencing in action

12	23
The value of the cell above is {=A1}.	The sum of the values in the first two cells in the first row is {=A1+B1}.

When you select the fields and press F9, the correct results will display in the bottom row. If you change the values in the first row, just update the fields again (select the fields and press F9) to see the new results.

> Cell references in Word, unlike those in Excel, are always absolute and are not shown with dollar signs. For example, referring to a cell as A1 in Word is the same as referring to a cell as A1 in Excel.

Reference operators. You can combine ranges of cells in a table or across tables for calculations with either one or both of the reference operators listed in Table 8-6.

Table 8-6. Table reference operators

Operator	Description	Example
: (colon)	Range operator. Returns all cells between and including the two reference cells.	=SUM(A1:A5)
, (comma)	Union operator. Combines multiple discontinuous cell ranges in one reference.	=SUM(A1:A5,A10:A15,A20)

Referencing an entire row or column. You can also reference an entire row or column in a calculation:

- Use a row or column range that includes only the row letter or column number. For example, use 1:1 to reference the first row in the table or A:A to reference the first column in the table. This form of referencing includes all the cells in the row or column, even if you add or delete rows or columns later.

If you use this form of referencing within the row or column being referenced, your formula will include a circular reference to itself in the evaluation, which will cause arithmetic errors that will increase every time the field updates.

- Use a range that identifies specific cells or ranges of cells. For example, for a four-row table, D1:D4 refers to the cells on rows one to four in column D. This form of referencing restricts the calculation to include only specific cells. If you add or delete cells later, you may need to edit the calculation.

Referencing table cells from outside the table. Only the following functions can accept references to table cells as arguments from outside that table:

- AVERAGE( )
- COUNT( )
- MAX( )
- MIN( )
- PRODUCT( )
- SUM( )

Before you can reference a cell value from outside a table, you need to create a bookmark in the table to identify it. With your cursor in the table, select Insert → Bookmark and give the table a name, such as *Table1*. You can now refer to the contents of this table in calculations elsewhere in your document.

To refer to the contents of a cell from outside a table, you always need to use one of the six functions shown above, even to get a single value. For example, if you put a bookmark named Table1 in the table you created earlier in this hack, you can reference the value in the first cell with the following field (remember, use Ctrl-F9 or Insert → Field to insert the field braces):

```
{=SUM {Table1 A1}}
```

This technique can be useful when you need to refer to one or more table values in the document's text, do math with them, or even refer to them in another table.

If you use a number as the last character in a bookmark's name, make sure the name includes at least three text characters before the number. Otherwise, Word might interpret the bookmark name as a cell reference.

Referencing row and column totals from outside a table. A common use for referencing cells outside their tables is to report totals from specific columns in a table, where the last row in the table contains the totals of each column. If the number of rows might change, but the last row always contains the total, you can reference that total without needing to know the row number. Since the last row contains the total of all previous rows, if you sum the entire contents of the column and divide by two, you'll get the desired sum. For example, if you had a table bookmarked as Table1, you could use the following field to reference the total of the fourth (D) column in the table:

```
{=SUM{Table1 D:D)/2}
```

—Paul Edstein

HACK #73   Format Numeric Field Results

How you display the result of a calculation can be almost as important as the result itself. This hack shows you how to get field results into the format you need.

If you use fields to calculate numbers, such as the sum of the values in a table column [Hack #72], you'll usually want some control over how those results are formatted. For example, you might want the number rounded to two decimal points with a currency symbol. To control how numbers appear in fields, you use *numeric picture switches*.

A numeric picture switch is indicated in a field's code with \# and can include a variety of instructions to Word on how to format the numeric results of a particular field.

For example, insert the following field in a document (to create field braces, you must press Ctrl-F9 or select Insert → Field):

```
{=2+2 \# 00.0000}
```

Select the field and press F9. The numeric picture switch tells Word to display the results of this sum in the form 04.0000.

If you use the switch \# 0, Word rounds the result to the nearest integer. The following field would display the value 3 in a document:

```
{=3.1415 \# 0}
```

If you omit the numeric picture switch, Word makes its own decisions as to whether to display a calculation's result as an integer or round the number to one or two decimal places.

You can also include a currency symbol in a numeric picture switch. The following field displays $82.37 in your document:

```
{=50 + 32.37 \# $00.00}
```

Compound Picture Switches

Numeric picture switches actually take three arguments, separated by semicolons: positive value format, negative value format, and zero value format. If you omit these arguments, as in the previous examples, the switch uses the positive value format to format the results. If you want to format negative values differently, you can add a second parameter to the switch. For example, the switch \# #;(#) used in a field would tell

If no value is given for one of the three arguments (positive, negative, and zero), Word won't display those results. For example, the switch \# #;; displays the results only if they're greater than zero.

You could also use a switch like \# #;-#;Ø to display Ø for zero values (hold down the Alt key and type 0216 on the number pad to get the Ø character). You can also display different text outputs for positive and negative values. For example, the following switch:

```
\# Profit\ $,0.00;Loss\ $,0.00;Break\ Even
```

prefaces positive values with the word Profit and negative values with the word Loss. If the value is zero, it displays only the term Break Even, with no number. Notice that a backslash is placed in front of a space to tell Word to display the space in the field results. A significant benefit of adding text and/or suppressing zeros this way (instead of using IF tests to output nulls or spaces) is that the field will continue to evaluate as a number in other formulas.

In addition, the field results reflect any font formatting applied to the numeric picture switch. For example, in the above switch, you could color the Profit portion of the switch blue, the Loss portion red, and the Break Even portion green.

—*Paul Edstein*

Use Fields for Heavy-Duty Calculations

HACK #74

By combining several types of Word fields, you can perform some surprisingly complex calculations.

The built-in formula fields [Hack #72] give you most of the math power needed for typical Word work. But what if you need something more sophisticated? With some old-fashioned algebra, you can use those formula fields as building blocks for more complicated calculations. This hack shows you two such field combinations for calculating logarithms and a few trigonometry functions.

Use Fields for Heavy-Duty Calculations

> To create field braces, you must press Ctrl-F9 or select Insert
> → Field.

The line breaks shown in the field codes for this hack have been added for readability. While not necessary, they make these mammoth fields much easier to read and modify.

Logarithms

When you update the following field, you're prompted to enter a number. The field then calculates the log of the number you entered. Because Word does not include a built-in log function, this hack uses a Taylor Series Approximation to calculate the results.

```
{QUOTE↵
{SET l2l 0.301029995663981}↵
{SET l3l 0.477121254719662}↵
{SET l5l 0.698970004336019}↵
{SET l7l 0.845098040014257}↵
{SET l11l 0.0413926851582251}↵
{SET l13l 0.113943352306837}↵
{SET l17l 0.230448921378274}↵
{SET l19l 0.278753600952829}↵
{ASK z "What positive number do you want the log of?"}↵
{SET a{=abs(z)}}↵
{SET b{=9-(a<10^9)-(a<10^8)-(a<10^7)-(a<10^6)-↵
(a<10^5)-(a<10^4)-(a<10^3)-(a<10^2)-(a<10^1)-↵
(a<10^0)-(a<10^-1)-(a<10^-2)-(a<10^-3)-(a<10^-4)-↵
(a<10^-5)-(a<10^-6)-(a<10^-7)-(a<10^-8)}}↵
{SET c{=int(a/10^b)+mod(a,10^b)/10^b}}↵
{SET d{=(c<1.05)*0+(c>=1.05)*(c<1.2)*l11l+(c>=1.2)*(c<1.5)*l13l+↵
(c>=1.5)*(c<1.8)*l17l+(c>=1.8)*(c<1.95)*l19l+(c>=1.95)*(c<2.5)↵
*l2l+(c>=2.5)*(c<3.5)*l3l+(c>=3.5)*(c<4.5)*l2l*2+(c>=4.5)↵
*(c<5.5)*l50l+(c>=5.5)*(c<6.5)*(l2l+l3l)+(c>=6.5)*(c<7.5)↵
*l7l+(c>=7.5)*(c<8.5)*l2l*3+(c>=8.5)*l3l*2}}↵
{SET e{=a-10^(b+d)}}↵
{SET f{=b+d+0.434294481903251*((e/10^(b+d))↵
-(e/10^(b+d))^2/2+(e/10^(b+d))^3/3-(e/10^(b+d)↵
)^4/4+(e/10^(b+d))^5/5-(e/10^(b+d))^6/6+(e/10^(b+d)↵
)^7/7-(e/10^(b+d))^8/8+(e/10^(b+d))^9/9-(e/10^(b+d)↵
)^10/10)}}↵
"The logarithm of {a} is {IF{=10^b}= a "" "approximately "}{f}."}
```

As coded, the field gives results to 13 decimal places, which should be enough for most purposes. If you need to calculate the logs of larger or smaller values, increase the values in parameter b (the exponent) accordingly.

References to constants in tables or bookmarks (as in the SET fields used here to define certain logarithmic values) need only be established once for the whole document.

Trigonometry

Word's formula fields also lack trigonometric functions, such as sine, cosine, and tangent. Again, you can use Taylor Series Approximations to generate quite accurate results (to 13 decimal places). Here's how to create a table that will give you the sine, cosine, and tangent values for a given angle, as shown in Figure 8-4.

Angle	Sine	Cosine	Tangent
35	0.573576	0.819152	0.700208

Figure 8-4. Viewing the trig values calculated for an angle

First, create a new table in a Word document with four columns and two rows. Title the first column *Angle*, the second *Sine*, the third *Cosine*, and the fourth *Tangent*. In the second row, enter the field codes for each value, shown in the next four sections.

To create the "Ø" character, hold down the Alt key and type 0216 on the numeric keypad [Hack #30].

Angle. Enter the following field code in the second row of the first column:

```
{QUOTE{ASK Ø "What angle do you want the trig values for?"}{Ø}}
```

Sine. Enter the following field code in the second row of the second column:

```
{QUOTE↵
{SET x{=0.0174532925199433*(1+MOD(Ø-1,90))}}↵
{SET SinØ{↵
=x-x^3/6+x^5/120-x^7/5040+x^9/362880-x^11/39916800+x^13/6227020800}}↵
{=SinØ*(1-MOD(INT(Ø/180),2)*2) \# 0.000000}}
```

Cosine. Enter the following field code in the second row of the third column:

```
{QUOTE↵
{SET x{=0.0174532925199433*(1+MOD(Ø-1,90))}}↵
{SET CosØ{=1-x^2/2+x^4/24-x^6/720+x^8/40320-x^10/3628800+↵
x^12/479001600-x^14/87178291200}}↵
{=CosØ*(1-MOD(INT((Ø+90)/180),2)*2) \# 0.000000}}
```

Tangent. Enter the following field code in the second row of the fourth column:

```
{QUOTE↵
{SET x{=0.0174532925199433*(1+MOD(Ø-1,90))}}↵
{SET TanØ{=(x-x^3/6+x^5/120-x^7/5040+x^9/362880-↵
x^11/39916800+x^13/6227020800)/(1-x^2/2+x^4/24-x^6/720↵
+x^8/40320-x^10/3628800+x^12/479001600-x^14/87178291200)}}↵
{IF{=(1+MOD(Ø-1,90))=90}= 1 "Infinite" {=TanØ*((1+MOD(Ø-1,90))↵
<>90)*(1-MOD(INT(Ø/180),2)*2)*(1-MOD(INT((Ø+90)/180),2)↵
*2) \# 0.000000}}}
```

To enter a new angle, select the entire table and press F9.

—Paul Edstein

HACK #75   Include an Interactive Calendar in Your Forms

This hack shows you how to implement an easy-to-use calendar for choosing dates from within a form or other document.

If you use Word's Forms feature, many of your forms probably include DATE fields. Word provides some dates for you, such as today's date and the date a document was created. However, if you want the form's user to fill in a date, you can prompt the user to select the date from an interactive calendar, such as the one shown in Figure 8-5.

The calendar used in Figure 8-5 is an ActiveX control included with Office. With some simple steps in the Visual Basic Editor, along with a few lines of code, you can easily add this calendar to any form. With your form template open, select Tools → Macro → Visual Basic Editor.

In the Project Explorer, select your template and choose Insert → UserForm. Next, select View → Toolbox to make the Toolbox visible. Right-click the Toolbox and choose Additional Controls to display the dialog shown in Figure 8-6. Scroll down and check the "Calendar Control 11.0" box (the version number may be slightly different on your system).

Click the OK button to add the Calendar control to your Toolbox. Click it and draw a new calendar on your blank UserForm, as shown in Figure 8-7. In the Properties window, change the UserForm's caption to "Calendar."

Next, select View → Code and insert the following code:

```
Private Sub UserForm_Activate()
    Me.Calendar1.Value = Date
End Sub

Private Sub Calendar1_Click()
    Selection.Text = Calendar1.Value
End Sub
```

Figure 8-5. An interactive calendar placed in a form

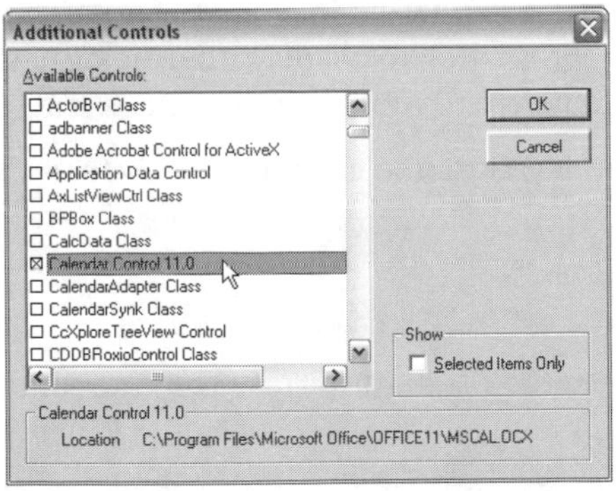

Figure 8-6. Activating the Calendar control

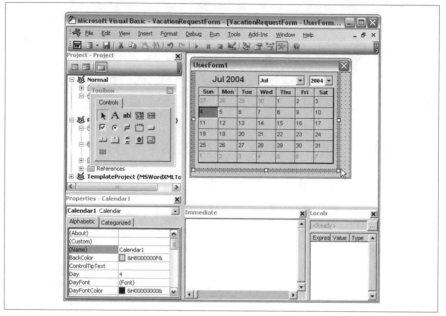

Figure 8-7. Add the Calendar control to a UserForm in the Visual Basic Editor

Now, in a code module in your template (if none exists, select Insert → Module), add the following code:

```
Sub ChooseDate( )
    UserForm1.Show
End Sub
```

Then select File → Close and Return to Microsoft Word.

Right-click the DATE field within the form in which you want the calendar to appear and choose Properties to display the dialog shown in Figure 8-8. Select the ChooseDate macro to run when the field is entered.

After choosing the date, close the calendar by clicking the Close button on its titlebar.

Hacking the Hack

Though it's ideally suited for fill-in forms, you may find the Calendar control useful in other documents too. To insert the Calendar control into any document, use a MACROBUTTON field, as shown in Figure 8-9. These fields assume you're using the same ChooseDate macro described above for activating the Calendar control. The field code is shown in the first field, and the field result is shown in the second field.

Figure 8-8. Select the macro to display the Calendar control

This lease begins on { Macrobutton ChooseDate Click Here to Select a Date }, and ends on Click Here to Select a Date .

Figure 8-9. The first field shows the field code; the second shows the field result

HACK #76 Use Custom Shortcut Menus to Make Frequent Selections

Use an AUTOTEXTLIST field to create a drop-down list you can right-click at any spot in a document.

If you regularly choose from a list of words, such as the names of staff members, you can use an AUTOTEXTLIST field to insert a drop-down list into your document, as shown in Figure 8-10.

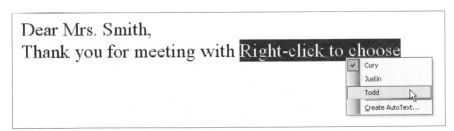

Figure 8-10. Choosing among entries in an AUTOTEXTLIST field

The following example shows you how to create the list shown in Figure 8-10.

First, create a new, blank document. You'll need a new paragraph style for grouping your entries. Select Format → Styles and Formatting (or Format → Style, depending on your version of Word), click the New Style button, and make a new style named *Staff*, as shown in Figure 8-11. To make this list available in all your documents, check the "Add to template" box.

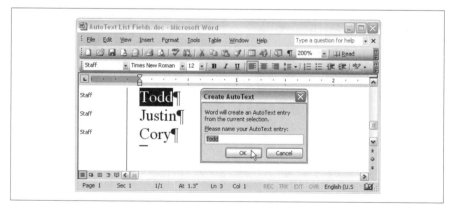

Figure 8-11. Creating a new style for your list

Next, create three blank paragraphs in your document (you should also select Tools → Options, click the View tab, and check the "Paragraph marks" box). Select all three paragraphs and apply the Staff style.

Now put one name in each paragraph. Select the first name (but *not* the paragraph mark just after the name) and press Alt-F3 to create a new Auto-Text entry for the selected text, as shown in Figure 8-12. Click the OK button and repeat for the other names in the list.

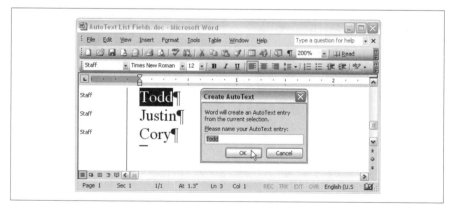

Figure 8-12. Creating the list of entries

Now delete the names from the document. Select a blank paragraph and apply the Normal style. Next, select Insert → Field, select AutoTextList from the list of fields, and click the Field Codes button. In the "Field codes" box in the Field dialog, enter the following text, as shown in Figure 8-13 (Word inserts the first word for you):

```
AUTOTEXTLIST "Right-click to choose" \s "Staff"
```

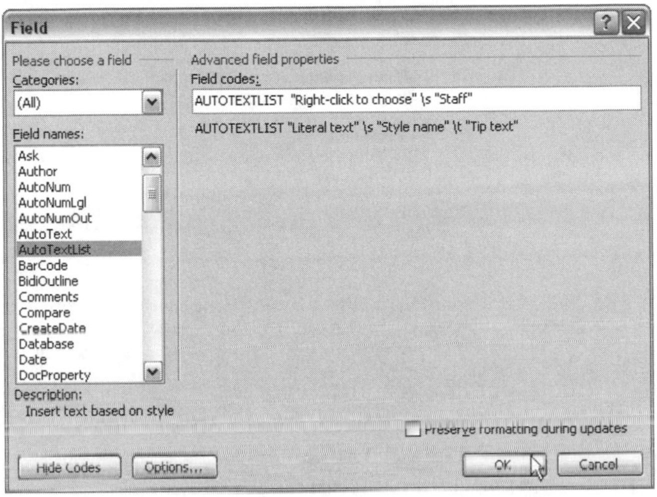

Figure 8-13. Creating an AUTOTEXTLIST field

Notice that "Staff" is the name of the custom paragraph style you created. Click the OK button to insert the field in your document.

Select the field (but *not* any paragraph mark that might come right after it) and press Alt-F3 again to create a new AutoText entry. Enter **staff** as the name of the entry and click the OK button. Now whenever you want the list in a document, type the word **staff**, and Word will prompt you with an offer to insert the AutoText entry. After inserting the AutoText entry, you can right-click the entry to choose a name, as shown in Figure 8-10.

HACK #77 Number Documents Sequentially

Many businesses use numbers to track forms such as invoices and purchase orders. Those numbers usually must go in order and can't repeat. This hack shows you how to use Word to keep track of the numbering for you.

If you need to generate invoices for a business, you might save time using a premade invoice template, such as the ones available from the Microsoft web site. One such template is pictured in Figure 8-14.

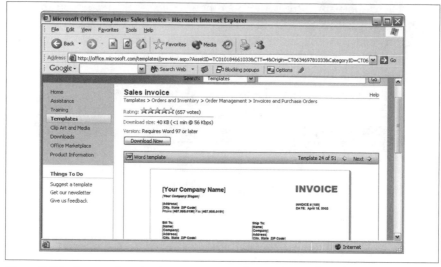

Figure 8-14. You can download an assortment of premade templates from Microsoft.com

The template uses MACROBUTTON fields [Hack #70] to mark the items you replace when filling out the template—for example, the invoice number field, which you replace with the correct number manually.

But how do you remember the last number you used? What if multiple users create invoices from the same template? A quick change to the invoice field and an AutoMacro [Hack #60] will give you a self-sequencing invoice template.

Create your own new template, either by downloading the Invoice template from Microsoft's web site (you can get there quickly in Word 2003 from the New Document Task Pane [Hack #9]) or by saving a new, blank document as a template.

Put your cursor at the spot in your template where you want the invoice number to appear. Select Insert → Field, choose DocVariable, and click the Field Codes button to display the dialog box shown in Figure 8-15. Enter **InvoiceNumber** in the "Field codes" box, as shown in Figure 8-15.

The next section describes the macro code used to increment the number.

The Code

Select Tools → Macro → Visual Basic Editor and insert the following macro in your template:

```
Sub AutoNew( )
Dim sINIFile As String
Dim sCurrentNumber As String
sINIFile = "C:\InvoiceTemplate.ini"
```

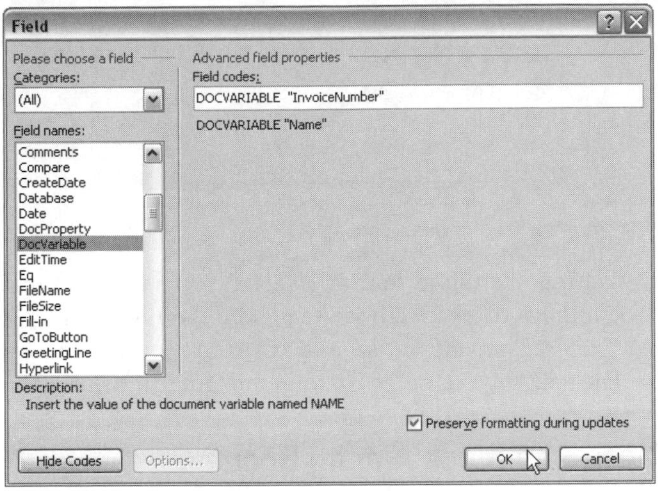

Figure 8-15. Inserting a DOCVARIABLE field

```
sCurrentNumber = System.PrivateProfileString(sINIFile, _
    "CurrentInvoice", "Number")
If Len(sCurrentNumber) = 0 Then
    sCurrentNumber = CStr(1)
End If

ActiveDocument.Variables("InvoiceNumber") = sCurrentNumber
ActiveDocument.Fields.Update

sCurrentNumber = CStr(CInt(sCurrentNumber) + 1)
System.PrivateProfileString(sINIFile, "CurrentInvoice", _
    "Number") = sCurrentNumber
End Sub
```

This macro uses a Config file **[Hack #67]** named *C:\InvoiceTemplate.ini* to track the invoice number. If the file doesn't exist yet, the macro creates one and starts the numbering at 1. The macro then puts the number from the file into a *document variable* named InvoiceNumber, which is referenced by the field you inserted in the template. Document variables are similar to document properties (which you view by choosing File → Properties), but document variables can be created, modified, and deleted only from a macro.

Save the changes and close your template. Now select File → New to create a new document based on the template. Each new document created from this template will have an invoice number one higher than the previous document.

If you need to modify the numbering, open the *InvoiceTemplate.ini* file with any text editor, as shown in Figure 8-16.

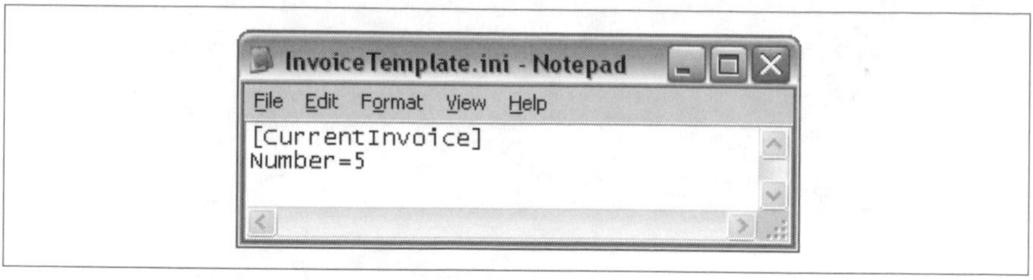

Figure 8-16. Editing the invoice number

If you want your numbering to start at 100, create a new document from the template to run the AutoNew macro and generate the *InvoiceTemplate.ini* file. Next, open *InvoiceTemplate.ini* in a text editor and change it to read Number=100. The next invoice based on the template will be numbered 100.

HACK #78   Cross-Reference Among Documents

This hack shows you how to create cross-references among different Word documents.

When you create a cross-reference in Word, no option exists for referencing content in another document. But sometimes you need to split your work into multiple files, like the chapters in a book. (Word once actually encouraged this practice; the Word 2.0 manual says, "If your document is longer than 20 pages, consider creating several smaller documents.") If you use fields and bookmarks, you can create your own dynamic cross-references among separate Word documents.

A cross-reference has two parts: the *reference* and the *target*. A target is sort of like an Internet URL, and a reference is like a link to that URL. Each target can have multiple references pointing to it, but each reference can point to only one target. Just like URLs, each target must have a unique identifier.

Understanding Word's Native Cross-Referencing

When you make a cross-reference in Word (Insert → References → Cross-reference or Insert → Cross-reference, depending on your version of Word), it displays the dialog shown in Figure 8-17. You can choose between several different reference types, but notice that there's no option for text in another document.

When you create a cross-reference this way, Word inserts a *bookmark* around the target text. Word hides the bookmark it creates to mark your reference target, but you can see its name if you look in the Insert → Bookmark dialog and check the "Hidden bookmarks" box, as shown in

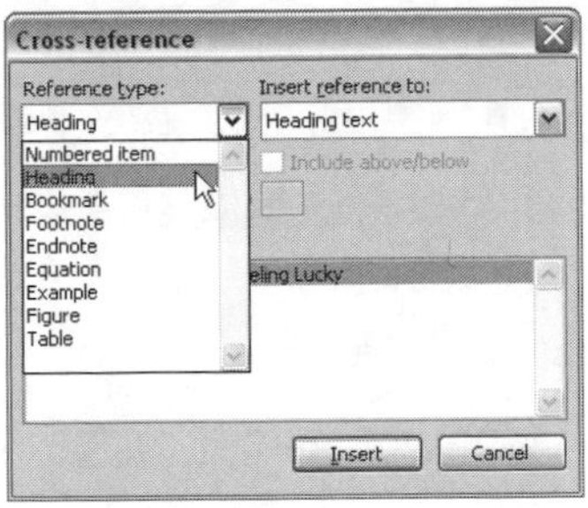

Figure 8-17. Word's Cross-reference dialog

Figure 8-18. If your hidden bookmarks don't show up in the dialog, uncheck and then recheck the box.

Figure 8-18. You can view your cross-reference bookmarks in the Bookmark dialog

Word assigns the bookmark's name, something like "_Ref46516798," to make the bookmark unique. The leading underscore denotes a hidden bookmark.

While the bookmark's name may be unique, it's not very useful. If you need to determine which bookmark belongs to which reference target, the list shown in Figure 8-19 offers little comfort.

Identifying specific bookmarks is an important part of troubleshooting cross-references, because bookmarks behave very, very strangely when you edit the text they enclose. For example, if you add text to the end of a heading that you cross-referenced and update the reference, the new text isn't included in the reference. Figure 8-20 shows this phenomenon using a manually created bookmark (so the ends are visible), but the same thing happens with Word's cross-reference bookmarks.

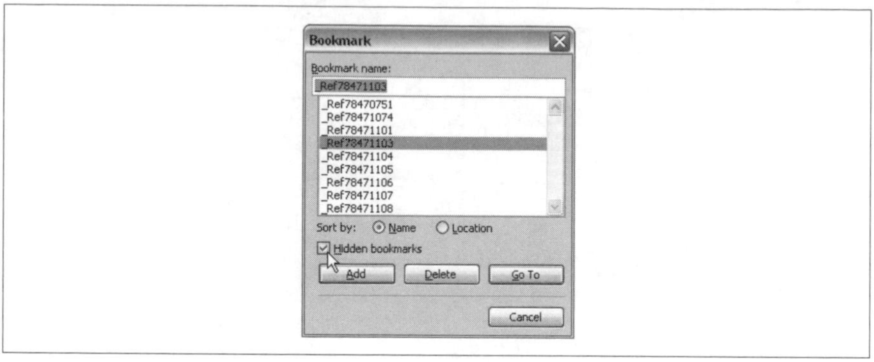

Figure 8-19. Word's decidedly unhelpful bookmark-naming convention for cross-references

[Just in Case] More Text¶

Some search engines are "case sens

Figure 8-20. When you add text at the end of a bookmarked paragraph, the bookmark doesn't expand

The solution? If you need to add text to a reference paragraph, you must put the new text before the last character and then delete the last character. But wait, it gets worse. Inserting text at the beginning of the paragraph works just fine, but if you hit Enter with your cursor at the beginning of the paragraph, the bookmark's beginning gets left behind, as shown in Figure 8-21.

[¶

Just in Case]¶

Some search engines are "case sens

Figure 8-21. A wayward bookmark

Now that you've gotten a peek into the way Word cross-references work, you're ready to create your own cross-references between two different documents.

Create Cross-References with INCLUDETEXT Fields

To reference text in a different document, you can use the same general method Word does: mark the target with a unique bookmark and then reference the contents of the bookmark with a field.

> When you use this technique, put all the related documents in the same folder so they can be moved around together without breaking any references.

For example, say you have a book with six chapters named "Chapter One," "Chapter Two," and so on. Chapter Two contains a section you want to reference in Chapter Three.

First, open the document containing the target (Chapter Two in this example) and go to the heading you want to reference. Select the entire heading, *except* for the trailing paragraph mark. Select Insert → Bookmark and give the bookmark a descriptive name, as shown in Figure 8-22. Word will warn you if you try to use any illegal characters, such as a space, in the name.

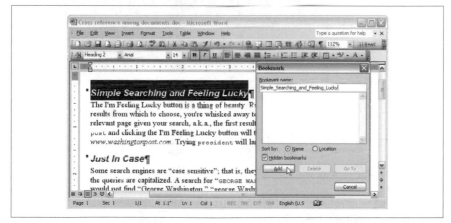

Figure 8-22. Choose a descriptive and unique name for your bookmark

Click the Add button to insert the bookmark. If you've chosen to show bookmarks (select Tools → Options and click the View tab), the bookmark's ends will appear as grey or black brackets, depending on your version of Word. Don't worry; the bookmarks will not appear when you print the document.

To avoid accidentally deleting or moving one end of a book-mark, you should work with bookmarks visible. You can always use Print Preview to see how your text will look without them.

Next, go to the document and find the location where you want the reference to appear. Press Ctrl-F9 (or select Insert → Field) to insert a blank set of field braces and type the following between them:

    INCLUDETEXT "Chapter Two.doc" *BookmarkName*

Note that you enclose the filename in quotes, but not the bookmark name.

Select the field and press F9. The reference will now display the book-marked text. With "Field shading" set to Always (select Tools → Options and click the View tab), you can easily spot your cross-references, as shown in Figure 8-23.

discussed in the section, Simple Searching and Feeling Lucky, there

Figure 8-23. A cross-reference to an external Word document

If Word displays a "Source File Not Found" error in your INCLUDETEXT field, go to File → Open, navigate to the folder containing the source document, and press Cancel. Then select the field and press F9.

With an INCLUDETEXT field, you insert more than just the bookmark's contents. The bookmark itself now appears in the reference document's list of bookmarks.

Any fields in the target text, such as a caption's SEQ field, also get mingled with the reference document's fields, which can throw off caption numbering.

For more hacks about cross-referencing in Word, check out "Cross-Reference Automatically" [Hack #43] and "Hack More Flexible Cross-Referencing" [Hack #44].

Convert Field Codes to Text and Back Again

When experimenting with fields, or using example fields culled from the Internet, it's often helpful to have an easy way to convert field codes to plain text, and vice versa.

As the other hacks in this chapter show, it can be difficult to represent field codes outside of Word (such as in a printed book) because of those special field braces unique to Word. For example, what if you want to post a particularly troublesome field to a newsgroup in the hopes of finding some help? (For a list of web sites with Word-related information and discussion groups, see the section "Where to Learn More" in the Preface.) While it's relatively simple to convert a field's result to plain text—just select the field and press Ctrl-Shift-F9—converting the field code to text is a trickier proposition.

A field's *result* is the text it displays after performing its work, such as the current page number or today's date. The field *code* is the special set of instructions a field uses to get that result. For example, one of the simplest field codes is simply DATE, which gets the current date. To see a field code in action, press Ctrl-F9 to insert a pair of empty field braces in a document. Then with your cursor between those braces, type the word DATE (you don't need to use all caps, but it's how field codes are typically shown). Select the field you just created and press F9 to update it, displaying today's date.

The macros in this hack use some heavy-duty VBA to quickly and accurately convert even a complex set of nested fields to plain text or convert some plain text (with the location of those special field braces indicated by regular braces) into fields.

Converting Field Codes into Plain Text

Conceptually, you need to replace each field with just its code, surrounded by a set of regular text braces ({}). This is trickier than it sounds, because if a field has any other fields nested inside it, you need to convert those to text first.

The code used in this hack to convert the fields to text is fairly simple, though it uses *recursion*—one of VBA's more advanced features. Recursion means that a function can call itself, and it's a common feature among programming languages (see the sidebar "A Recursion Primer" for more information).

The following macro converts the field codes of any selected fields to plain text, and surrounds the code for each field with standard brace characters, ({}). The code use the `FieldCodeToText` function to recursively examine all

A Recursion Primer

If you're not interested in how the guts of the macros in this hack work, or if you're already familiar with recursion, feel free to skip this sidebar. However, if you've never encountered recursion before or just aren't sure you understand it, read on.

Recursion lets you use very simple code to perform complicated tasks. This is accomplished by breaking the task down into bite-sized pieces and then writing code that tackles the task, one small bite at a time until it's all gone.

For example, say you need a macro to add all the digits from 1 to 4. At face value, it takes just one line:

```
Sub SumDigits()
    MsgBox 1+2+3+4
End Sub
```

But how do you write a macro that can sum all the digits from 1 to 1000 as easily as 1 to 10?

Let's say you want your program to add all the digits from 1 to k, where k is any whole number. Here's one possible algorithm for the problem:

1. If k is 1, then the answer is just k.
2. If k is greater than 1, the answer is k plus the sum of all the digits from 1 to k − 1.

So how do you calculate the sum of all the digits from 1 to k -1 in Step 2? Use your macro of course! Sound like a bit of circular logic? Well, in a way it is, which is the whole point of recursion. Here's that algorithm as a VBA procedure, followed by a macro to demonstrate it. Put both in the template of your choice [Hack #50], and step through the code as it runs in Visual Basic Editor [Hack #2]:

```
Function SumDigits(k As Long) As Long
    If k = 1 Then
        SumDigits = k
    Else
        SumDigits = k + SumDigits(k - 1)
    End If
End Function

Sub SumDigitsDemo()
    Dim sInput As String
    sInput = InputBox("Add all digits from 1 to ?")
    If Len(sInput) = 0 Then Exit Sub
    MsgBox SumDigits(CLng(sInput))
End Sub
```

the fields in a range (in this case the range of the current selection). Place both macros in the template of your choice [Hack #50].

```
Sub ConvertSelectedFieldsToText( )
Call FieldCodeToText(Selection.Range)
End Sub

Function FieldCodeToText(rngOrig As Range)
Dim rng As Range

Do
    If rngOrig.Fields.Count <= 1 Then
        ' Not more than one field in selection,
        ' so replace first field in selection
        ' with its code surrounded by braces
        rngOrig.Text = "{" & _
            rngOrig.Fields(1).Code.Text & "}"
    Else
        ' More than one field in selection,
        ' move to next field and check again,
        ' until there's only one field left
        Set rng = rngOrig.Duplicate
        rngOrig.Fields(2).Select
        Call FieldCodeToText(Selection.Range)
        rng.Select
    End If
Loop Until rngOrig.Fields.Count = 0

End Function
```

Converting Plain Text into Fields

For this conversion, the macro needs to do the reverse of what happened in the last section. This time around, any set of standard text braces ({}) and the text between them, should be replaced with a Word field. The field code is the text between the braces. The braces should be discarded.

The following macro converts any plain text surrounded with standard brace characters ({}) into "live" Word fields. The code uses the TextToFieldCode function to ensure that all fields are created in the correct order, which can be tricky business when there are several nested fields. Place both macros in the template of your choice [Hack #50].

```
Sub ConvertSelectedTextToFields( )
Call TextToFieldCodes(Selection.Range)
End Sub

Function TextToFieldCodes(rngOrig As Range)
Dim rng As Range
Dim fld As Field
Dim str As String
```

```
    Do
        Set rng = rngOrig.Duplicate
        str = rng.Text
            ' If there are any braces remaining in the range, except
            ' for the first and last characters, then there's still
            ' some pseuodo-fields to process, so collapse range to
            ' next set of braces and check again
        If InStr(Mid(str, 2, Len(str) - 2), "}") <> 0 Or _
            InStr(Mid(str, 2, Len(str) - 2), "{") <> 0 Then

                ' Move the beginning of the range forward
                ' until it's at a left brace

            Do While InStr(Right(str, Len(str) - 1), "{") > 0
                rng.MoveStart unit:=wdCharacter, Count:=1
                rng.MoveStartUntil cset:="{"
                str = rng.Text
            Loop

                ' Move the end of the range backward until it's at a right brace
            Do While InStr(Left(str, Len(str) - 1), "}") > 0
                rng.MoveEnd unit:=wdCharacter, Count:=-1
                rng.MoveEndUntil cset:="}", Count:=-Len(str)
                str = rng.Text
            Loop

                ' If either end of the range isn't a brace character,
                ' there's been an error.
            If Left(str, 1) <> "{" Or Right(str, 1) <> "}" Then
                GoTo ERR_HANDLER
            End If

                ' Continue searching for brace characters in this range
                ' with a recursive call to this function
            Call TextToFieldCodes(rng)
        Else
                ' No brace characters were found between
                ' the first and last characters

                ' If either end of the range isn't a brace character,
                ' there's been an error.
            If Left(str, 1) <> "{" Or Right(str, 1) <> "}" Then
                GoTo ERR_HANDLER
            End If

                ' Delete the braces on the ends of the range
            rng.Characters(1).Delete
            rng.Characters(rng.Characters.Count).Delete

                ' Cut the range and paste it in as the code
                ' of a new empty field, which preserves any
                ' codes in the range, as well as formatting
            rng.Cut
```

```
            Set fld = rng.Fields.Add(Range:=rng, _
                Type:=wdFieldEmpty, _
                Text:="", _
                PreserveFormatting:=False)
            fld.Code.Paste
        End If

    ' As long as there are braces left in the original range,
    ' keep trying to turn them into fields
    Loop While InStr(rngOrig.Text, "}") <> 0 Or _
        InStrRev(rngOrig.Text, "{") <> 0

    Exit Function
ERR_HANDLER:
    rng.Select
    If Left(rng.Text, 1) <> "{" Then
        MsgBox "Missing an expected left brace ( { )", vbCritical
    ElseIf Right(rng.Text, 1) <> "}" Then
        MsgBox "Missing an expected right brace ( } )", vbCritical
    Else
        MsgBox "An unknown error occurred", vbCritical
    End If
End Function
```

Running the Hack

To see these macros in action, first make sure the template you've stored them in is open. Then, in a blank document based on the template in which you've stored the macros, type Ctrl-F9 twice to insert two sets of field braces, one nested inside the other (you'll see actual field braces, not standard text braces):

{ { } }

Type the text QUOTE and DATE between the field braces as follows:

{ QUOTE { DATE } }

Next, select the fields and press F9. You should see today's date displayed. Select the fields again, then right-click and select Toggle Field Codes. Now you'll see the field codes again. With both fields selected, run the ConvertSelectedFieldsToText macro shown earlier, which replaces the fields with their field codes as plain text, surrounded by standard text braces.

Now select the text from the first brace to the last and run the ConvertSelectedTextToFields macro shown earlier, which replaces the plain text with actual fields, bringing you back to where you started.

Advanced Word Hacks
Hacks 80–89

Word is at its best as a word processor—creating, editing, and formatting documents. And with VBA, much of what Word does so well can be automated. But that easy programmability also makes Word capable of much more. The hacks in this chapter show several ways to go above and beyond vanilla VBA, hacking Word into an Emacs clone, a Windows backup utility, and even a fully scriptable tool for generating documents from HTML files.

HACK #80 Emulate Emacs with VBacs

You've already learned all those Emacs commands, so you might as well use them. This set of freeware macros replicates many common Emacs keyboard shortcuts within Word.

Emacs, a text editor usually associated with the Unix operating system (though it's available on most any platform), is in most ways the polar opposite of Word. No one just sits down with Emacs, expecting to hunt around a few menus to find the commands they need. While you can learn simple commands quickly, true Emacs mastery is a lifelong love affair for hackers around the world.

Emacs was born at a time when a window still meant something you opened to let in fresh air. You had to use the keyboard to issue every command, and often they required complex key combinations, such as Ctrl-X, Ctrl-S (the command to save the current file).

Though versions of Emacs have since been developed that include menus and even toolbars, most Emacs users rarely take their hands off the keyboard. So when someone who's mastered all those Emacs commands switches to Word, it can be a frustrating experience.

Fortunately, the free *VBacs* template, available for download at *http://rath. ca/Misc/VBacs*, modifies Word's key bindings to more closely match the native ones in Emacs and can make Word feel a little more like home.

 Word does support two-stage key bindings (such as Alt-L, S), but you can use the Ctrl key only in the *first* stage. This makes it impossible to recreate many Emacs commands, such as Ctrl-X, Ctrl-S. In these cases, VBacs gets as close as Word will permit; for example, Ctrl-X, S lets you save.

Installing VBacs

VBacs is offered as a standard *.dot* template file, released under the *GNU Lesser Public License*. Here's how to install the VBacs template as a global template that will automatically load every time you start Word.

First, download the VBacs template to your computer. Make sure you close Word and any other applications that may access Word, such as Outlook.

Next, locate your Word Startup folder, which is usually the following:

```
C:\Documents and Settings\username\Application Data\Microsoft\Word\STARTUP
```

If you're not sure where your *STARTUP* folder is located, you can open Word and select Tools → Options, click the File Locations tab, and make a note of the folder listed under *STARTUP*.

After you put *VBacs.dot* into your *STARTUP* folder, its key bindings will take effect the next time you start Word.

Using VBacs

Table 9-1 summarizes the VBacs commands and their key bindings. Some aren't actually Emacs commands or differ slightly from their Emacs counterparts.

Table 9-1. VBacs commands and key bindings

VBacs action	Key binding
Line up	Ctrl-P
Line down	Ctrl-N
End of line	Ctrl-E
Start of line	Ctrl-A
Start of buffer	Shift-Alt-<
End of buffer	Shift-Alt->
Character forward	Ctrl-F
Character backward	Ctrl-B

Table 9-1. VBacs commands and key bindings (continued)

VBacs action	Key binding
Word forward	Alt-F
Word backward	Alt-B
Page down	Ctrl-V
Page up	Alt-V
Go to previous page	Ctrl-X, [
Go to next page	Ctrl-X,]
Search	Ctrl-S, Ctrl-R
Replace	Alt-%
Cut selection	Ctrl-W
Paste selection	Ctrl-Y
Copy selection	Alt-W
Select whole buffer	Ctrl-X, H
Delete word	Alt-D
Word delete	Alt-Backspace
Delete	Ctrl-D
Delete to end of line	Ctrl-K
Edit undo	Shift-Ctrl--
Cancel	Ctrl-G
Tab	Ctrl-I
Save file	Ctrl-X, S
Close file	Ctrl-X, K
Exit MS Word	Ctrl-X, C
Open file	Ctrl-X, F
Undo	Ctrl-X, U
Open line above	Ctrl-O
Capitalize word	Alt-C
Upshift word	Alt-U
Downshift word	Alt-L
Delete window	Ctrl-X, 0
Close other windows	Ctrl-X, 1
Split window vertically	Ctrl-X, 2
Other window	Ctrl-X, O
Switch to buffer	Ctrl-X, B
Iconify MS Word	Ctrl-Z
Center paragraph	Alt-S
Transpose characters	Ctrl-T
Transpose words	Alt-T

Table 9-1. VBacs commands and key bindings (continued)

VBacs action	Key binding
Paste plain (unformatted text)	Ctrl-Shift-Y
Select all	Ctrl-Q, A
Bold	Ctrl-Q, B
Italic	Ctrl-Q, I
Print	Ctrl-Q, P
Hanging indent	Ctrl-Q, T
Tab (in a table)	Ctrl-Q, Tab

With VBacs installed, several editing and navigation tasks become immediately easier. For example, Ctrl-X, 2 splits the active window vertically, as shown in Figure 9-1.

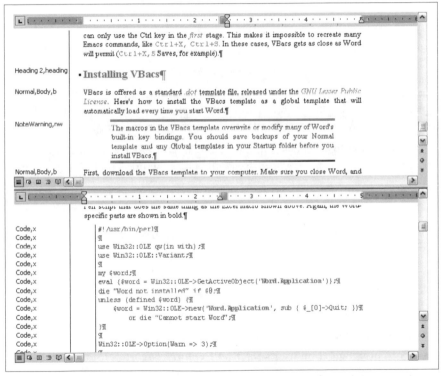

Figure 9-1. Quickly split a window with Ctrl-X, 2 in VBacs

The shortcut Ctrl-O (open line above) creates a new line above the cursor and then moves the cursor to the beginning of the new line. One more notable gem: Ctrl-K deletes from the cursor to the end of a line. In Word, navigating and editing by line—as opposed to by paragraph—can be tricky. With VBacs, it becomes a lot more manageable.

If you want to temporarily remove the VBacs key bindings, select Tools → Templates and Add-ins and uncheck *VBacs.dot* in the list of installed add-ins. When you click the OK button, Word will unload the template, and your key bindings will return to Word's default settings. VBacs will return the next time you start Word. To uninstall VBacs, just remove it from Word's *STARTUP* folder.

> For more information on Emacs, check out *http://www.gnu. org/software/emacs/emacs.html* and *Learning GNU Emacs* (O'Reilly).

—*Christopher Rath*

Use Word as a Windows Backup Utility

This hack introduces a freeware, hackable Word template for building system backups.

Backups usually end up on tomorrow's to-do list, but now you can create quick and easy backups with a freeware template, a great example of how you can hack Word into a serious system administration tool.

You can download the template used in this hack from *http://www. mousetrax.com/Downloads.html#backup*. The download includes two files:

- *WordBackup.dot*
- *ConfigWordBackup.cfg*

To test-drive the template, create a folder on your system called *C:\Backup*. Put both files in the new folder.

By default, the template creates a backup of each of the following system folders:

- Currently logged-on user's *My Documents* folder
- Currently logged-on user's *Templates* folder
- Currently logged-on user's *Internet Explorer Favorites* folder
- Windows *Fonts* folder
- Currently logged-on user's *Desktop* folder

The backups are created in the folder in which the *WordBackup.dot* template is located; here, it's *C:\Backup*.

Running the Hack

To begin the backup, just double-click the *WordBackup.dot* file icon. A new, blank Word document opens, and the backup begins.

The status bar notes the backup's progress. When the backup finishes, it launches Notepad and opens the *LogWordBackup.log* file created by the template, as shown in Figure 9-2.

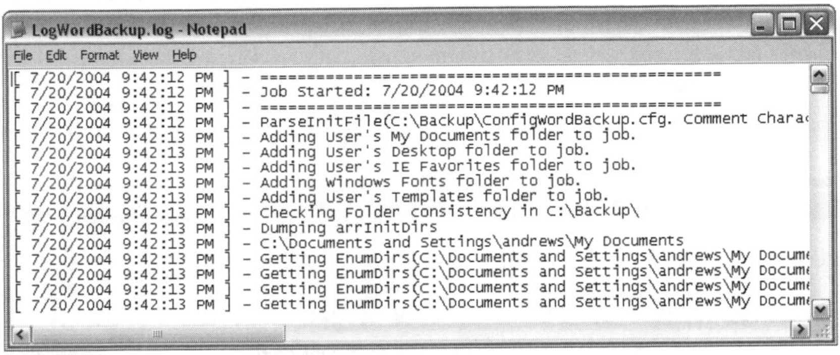

Figure 9-2. The log file created by the WordBackup.dot template

Depending on the size of your hard drive and the speed of your processor, the backup may take several minutes or more. Once it finishes, the *C:\Backup* folder will contain backup copies of all those important system folders.

The next time you need a backup, just double-click the template icon again. Subsequent backups are much faster, since the template backs up only files that have changed since the last backup (known as an *incremental backup*).

Hacking the Hack

If you've got important files in folders besides the standard system ones, or files on a network drive that should also be backed up, you can change how the WordBackup.dot template works by adjusting the settings in the *Config-WordBackup.cfg* file, which is just a plain-text configuration file [Hack #67].

To edit the *ConfigWordBackup.cfg* file, open it in a standard text editor, such as Notepad. The file contains two sections: *Parameters* and *Folders*.

The Parameters section. Here you can use the debug key to specify how verbose of a log file you're looking for. A value of 0 records only the start and stop time, and a value of 4 gives you full reporting. The *ConfigWordBackup.cfg* file includes details on each level.

If you want the backup in a different folder, use the altpath key. For example, to put the backup files in a folder named *C:\Foo\Backup*, change the altpath line to read as follows:

```
altpath=C:\Foo\Backup
```

The Folders section. In this section, you can have the template ignore one or more of the system folders that it backs up by default. The settings are already in the file but are commented out. To activate any of them, remove the semicolon at the start of the line. For example, if you want the template to ignore the *Fonts* folder, remove the semicolon from the ;NoFonts line, so it reads as follows:

```
NoFonts
```

Again, the *ConfigWordBackup.cfg* file includes further details.

If you want to back up folders besides the system folders, include each folder on its own line in the Folders section, as follows:

```
C:\Evil\Master Plans\World Domination
```

The template can also back up files on a network drive using standard Universal Naming Convention (UNC) notation, as in the following:

```
\\hal9000\flightplans\archive
```

> Make sure the folders you specify in the *ConfigWordBackup. cfg* file actually exist on your system, or you'll encounter errors during the backup.

—Greg Chapman

HACK #82 Perform Power Text Searches with Regular Expressions

When wildcards just aren't enough, tap VBScript for powerful string searching in Word.

Although Word's wildcard searching is much better than most users realize, if you've previously used a language like Perl, Python, or JavaScript, you might prefer sticking with the special characters you already know for your searches. Besides, sometimes wildcards just aren't up to the job.

To borrow an example from O'Reilly's *Learning Python*, suppose you need to replace any occurrence of "red pepper" or "green pepper" with "bell pepper" if and only if they occur together in a paragraph before the word "salad," but not if they are followed (with no space) by the string "corn." That's definitely way out of Word's wildcards' league. (The pattern is \b(red|green)(\s+pepper(?!corn)(?=.*salad)), for those of you too impatient to wait until the full example at the end of this hack.)

Though VBA doesn't have built-in support for regular expressions, Microsoft does include a RegExp object with VBScript. With a slight change to your settings in the Visual Basic Editor, you can use the RegExp object in your macros.

First, select Tools → Macro → Visual Basic Editor, and then choose Tools → References. In the next dialog, shown in Figure 9-3, check the "Microsoft VBScript Regular Expressions 5.5" box and click the OK button.

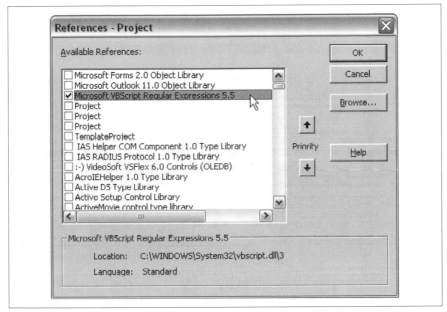

Figure 9-3. *Setting a reference to VBScript regular expressions from the Visual Basic Editor*

Now you can include instances of the RegExp object in your macros. The following section describes the RegExp object.

RegExp's Propeties and Methods

The RegExp object has four properties, described in the following list:

Pattern
    The pattern string to search for.

Global
> Whether search is for all occurrences that match Pattern, or just the first. This is a Boolean value, and the default is False.

IgnoreCase
> Whether search is case-sensitive. This is a Boolean value, and the default is False.

MultiLine
> Whether Pattern is matched across line breaks. This is a Boolean value, and the default is False.

The RegExp object has three methods, described in the following list:

Execute
> Returns a Matches collection containing the matched substrings and information about those substrings.

Replace
> Replaces all the substrings in a searched string that match a pattern with a replacement string. The syntax for this method is:

```
RegExpobject.Replace("string to search", "replacement pattern")
```

Test
> Whether a search has successfully matched a pattern. Returns a Boolean value. Since this method always returns True if there were one or more successful matches, there's no need to set the Global property when using this method.

The Matches collection returned by the Execute method contains one or more Match objects, which have three properties, shown in the following list:

FirstIndex
> The position of the Match's first character within the search string

Length
> The number of characters in the Match

Value
> The matched string

Using the RegExp Object in a Macro

The following macro interactively tests search patterns against the selected text.

Place this macro in the template of your choice [Hack #50] and either run it from the Tools → Macro → Macros dialog or put a button for it on a menu or toolbar [Hack #1].

```
Sub RegExpTest( )
Dim re As RegExp
Dim strToSearch As String
Dim strPattern As String
Dim strResults As String
Dim oMatches As MatchCollection
Dim oMatch As Match

strToSearch = Selection.Text

Set re = New RegExp
re.Global = True
re.IgnoreCase = True

Do While (1)
    strPattern = InputBox("Enter search pattern string:", _
                          "RegExp Search", "")
    If Len(strPattern) = 0 Then Exit Do

    re.Pattern = strPattern

    Set oMatches = re.Execute(strToSearch)
    If oMatches.Count <> 0 Then
        strResults = Chr(34) & strPattern & Chr(34) & _
                     " matched " & oMatches.Count & " times:" _
                     & vbCr & vbCr
        For Each oMatch In oMatches
            strResults = strResults & _
                         oMatch.Value & _
                         ": at position " & _
                         oMatch.FirstIndex & vbCr
        Next oMatch
    Else
        strResults = Chr(34) & strPattern & Chr(34) & _
                     " didn't match anything. Try again."
    End If

    MsgBox strResults
Loop

End Sub
```

When you run this macro, you'll be prompted with the dialog shown in Figure 9-4.

The dialog shown in Figure 9-5 displays the search results.

The RegExp object supports the same metacharacters you might have seen in Perl:

```
\ | ( ) [ { ^ $ * + ? .
```

You also get all the classic Perl character-class shortcuts:

```
\d \D \s \S \w \W
```

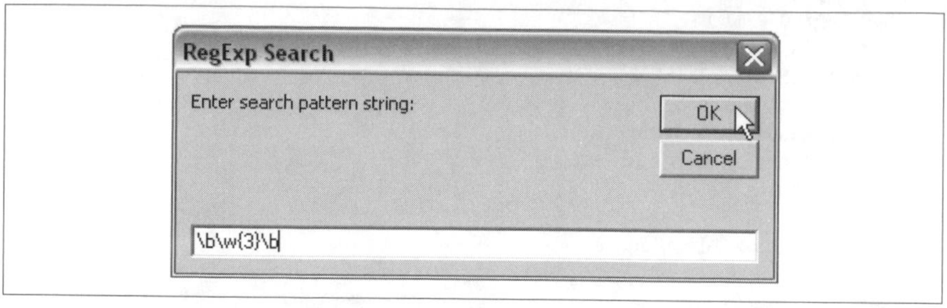

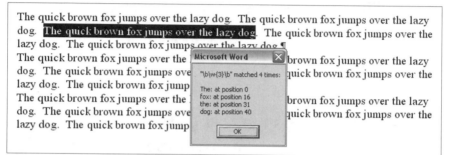

Figure 9-4. Enter your search pattern here, including any special characters

Figure 9-5. Fine-tune your search patterns interactively

For a full listing of special characters for using the RegExp object, see *http://msdn.microsoft.com/library/default.asp?url=/library/en-us/script56/html/vspropattern.asp*.

Performing Replacements

When using the Replace method, you can group and reuse parts of the matched pattern. Known as *backreferencing*, this is a powerful technique. The following code snippet demonstrates how to change the format of some dates in a string:

```
re.Replace("(September) (\d\d?), (\d{4})", "$2 $1, $3")
```

This code will change a date like "September 12, 1978" into "12 September, 1978." Modifying the code to replace September with a different month won't require making any change to the replacement string, thanks to backreferencing.

Bringing all of this together, the following macro shows you how to use the "bell pepper" pattern discussed at the beginning of this hack to get the results shown in Figure 9-6.

Before

This is a paragraph that mentions bell peppers multiple times. For one, here is a red pepper and dried tomato salad recipe. I don't like to use green peppers in my salads as much because they have a harsher flavor.

This second paragraph mentions red peppers and green peppers but not the "s" word (s-a-l-a-d), so no bells will show up.

The third paragraph mentions red peppercorns and green peppercorns, which aren't vegetables, but spices (by the way, bell peppers really aren't peppers, they're chilies, but would you rather have a good cook or a good botanist prepare your salad?

After

This is a paragraph that mentions bell peppers multiple times. For one, here is a bell pepper and dried tomato salad recipe. I don't like to use bell peppers in my salads as much because they have a harsher flavor.

This second paragraph mentions red peppers and green peppers but not the "s" word (s-a-l-a-d), so no bells will show up.

The third paragraph mentions red peppercorns and green peppercorns, which aren't vegetables, but spices (by the way, bell peppers really aren't peppers, they're chilies, but would you rather have a good cook or a good botanist prepare your salad?|

Figure 9-6. Performing complex replacements with regular expressions

Place this macro in the template of your choice [Hack #50] and either run it from the Tools → Macro → Macros dialog or put a button for it on a menu or toolbar [Hack #1]:

```
Sub FixPeppers( )
Dim re As RegExp
Dim para As Paragraph
Dim rng As Range
Set re = New RegExp
re.Pattern = "\b(red|green)(\s+pepper(?!corn)(?=.*salad))"
re.IgnoreCase = True
re.Global = True
For Each para In ActiveDocument.Paragraphs
    Set rng = para.Range
    rng.MoveEnd unit:=wdCharacter, Count:=-1
    rng.Text = re.Replace(rng.Text, "bell$2")
Next para
End Sub
```

 For more on regular expressions, check out "Hack Word from Python" [Hack #85], "Hack Word from Perl" [Hack #86], and *Mastering Regular Expressions* (O'Reilly).

H A C K
#83
Show a Directory Structure as a Word Outline

Use Outline view to quickly scan a directory for errant files or space hogs with this RTF hack.

When directory structures were small, you could figure out where all the space on your hard drive went by just using a bit of DOS at the command line:

```
> dir /os/n c:\somedir > summary.txt
```

But these days, a typical hard drive just has too many incidental subdirectories, and finding the large files (or a directory full of a million small files) in that *summary.txt* file would be like finding a needle in a haystack.

 This hack assumes that you have Perl installed on your system and that you can run Perl scripts from the DOS command line. To download a free version of Perl for Windows, go to the ActiveState web site at *http://www.activestate.com*.

But by massaging the data a bit and turning it into a Word outline, you can use the collapsible levels feature in Outline view to quickly sift through the data and find the unexpected space hogs.

The Code

This small Perl program surveys a directory that you specify and saves it to an RTF file, using a filename that you specify. Save this script as *directoryoutline.pl*.

```perl
use strict;
use File::Find;

my @items;
my $min_depth = 999;
my($dir, $out) = @ARGV;
die "Usage:\n $0 drive:/dir/to/scan output.rtf"
 unless @ARGV == 2 and -d $dir and $out =~ m/\.rtf$/is;
Scan_dirs( $dir );
open R, ">", $out or die "Can't write-open $out: $!";
RTF_tree( );
close R;
print "Surveyed $dir to $out\n";
exit;

sub Scan_dirs {
  my $count;
  my %dirsize;
```

```
  finddepth( { follow => 0, wanted => sub {
    if( -f $File::Find::name ) {
      $dirsize{ $File::Find::dir } += -s _;
    } elsif( -d _ ) {
      $dirsize{ $File::Find::dir } += $dirsize{ $File::Find::name };
      my $depth = $File::Find::name =~ tr{/\\}{};
      $min_depth = $depth if $depth < $min_depth;
      unshift @items, [ $depth, $dirsize{ $File::Find::name },
        ($_ eq '.') ? $File::Find::name : $_ ];
    }
  } }, $_[0] );
  return;
}

sub RTF_tree {
  die "Nothing to report?!" unless @items;

  print R q[{\rtf1\ansi\deff0
{\fonttbl {\f0 \froman Times New Roman;}}
\viewkind2 \fs24
];
  foreach my $item ( @items ) {
    my( $depth, $size, $name ) = @$item;
    $depth -= $min_depth;
    next if $depth > 8;
    printf R "\\outlinelevel%s {\\i %s \\scaps kb} : %s\\par\n",
      $depth, with_commas( int(.5 + $size/1024) ),
      rtf_escape_broadly( $name );
  }
  print R "}\n";
  return;
}

sub with_commas {
  my $x = $_[0];
  1 while $x =~ s/^(\d+)(\d{3})/$1,$2/;
  return $x;
}

sub rtf_escape_broadly {
  my $s = $_[0];
  $s =~ s/(\W)/"\\'".(unpack("H2",$1))/eg;
  return $s;
}
```

Running the Hack

To see the structure of the Perl directory on your system, open up a DOS prompt and navigate to your top-level C:\ directory. Enter the following at the DOS prompt:

```
> perl directoryoutline.pl "C:\Perl" "C:\PerlDirOutline.rtf"
```

Show a Directory Structure as a Word Outline

Figure 9-7 shows the output *PerlDirOutline.rtf* file in Word's Outline view. You can collapse and expand your view of each folder, as with any Word outline.

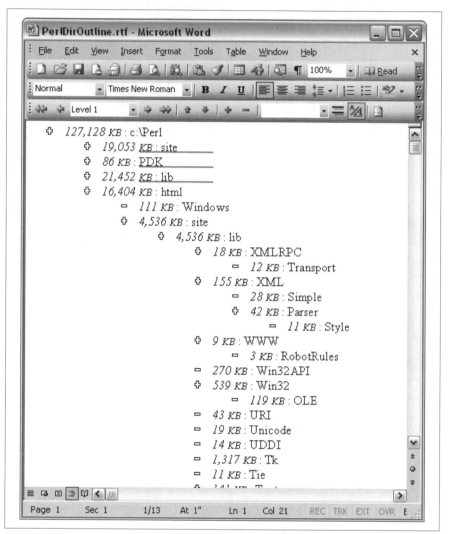

Figure 9-7. The Perl directory, shown in Word's Outline view

This view shows that roughly a quarter of the disk space used by the Perl directory is actually just (expendable) HTML versions of the standard Perl documentation (*html/lib* and *html/site*)—something that would have been much harder to discern using any other method.

—*Sean M. Burke*

Automate Word from Other Applications

Many of the same things VBA makes possible from within Word can be done from another application by using COM automation.

Word, like the rest of the Office suite, supports *COM automation*. COM (Component Object Model) is a technology developed by Microsoft that allows one application to control another without any regard to the differences in the programming languages used by either application. As long as both applications "speak" COM, they'll get along just fine.

Think about using an ATM. Each machine might be a different size, and sometimes the buttons are in different places, but you don't really care what the machine looks like, or how it works inside, as long as you can put in your card and get money. A COM *server* is like the ATM machine: as long as you (the application, or *client*) make a valid request for money (the *service*), the machine clicks and whirrs and spits out the cash. The client requesting the service cares only that the server respond in terms that it can use and understand.

Other applications that understand COM, such as Excel, or application development tools/languages such as C++, Visual Studio.NET, or even a scripting language like Perl, can use Word as a COM server and access its object model and control its behavior. And, conversely, if you create your own COM server application, you can use VBA to access it from within Word.

When controlling Word from another application, you can access familiar Word objects, such as paragraphs, comments, documents, and fields. These objects will, for the most part, behave the same way as they do in your Word macros. If you use another Office application to control Word, you will hardly notice a difference because the applications use the same objects *and* the same language (VBA) to control those objects. If you use a different language, you will need to determine how to best interact with Word's objects using that language. The following sections touch on each scenario.

Controlling Word from Another Office Application

The different parts of Microsoft Office play very well together. Controlling Word from within Excel, for example, isn't much different from working within Word. There's only one big difference: when you write a macro within Word, the parent Word.Application object is implicit. To display a dialog with the name of the active document from Word VBA, you can just use the following in your code (you can also type these statements directly into the Immediate window [Hack #2]):

```
MsgBox ActiveDocument.Name
```

You could also explicitly specify that you want Word's `ActiveDocument` object, as in the following:

```
MsgBox Word.Application.ActiveDocument.Name
```

But that's unnecessary; because you're working in VBA within Word, it's assumed that unless you say otherwise, you're talking about Word's objects. And as long as Word is open, the parent `Word` object exists and is implicitly used in all your macros.

When you want to control Word from another Office application, such as Excel, you need to explicitly refer to the `Word.Application` object used from your Excel macro.

To incorporate Word into an Excel macro, first set a reference to Word from the Visual Basic Editor in Excel. Select Tools → References and choose the Microsoft Word Object Library, as shown in Figure 9-8.

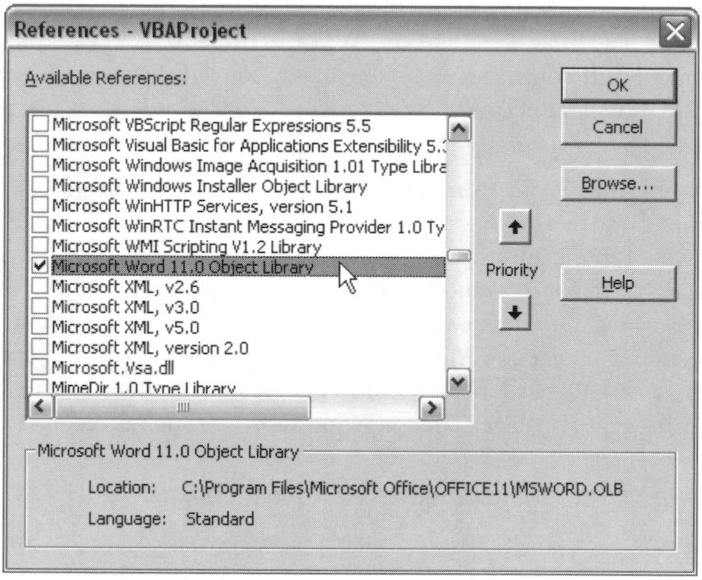

Figure 9-8. Setting a reference to the Word object model from Excel's Visual Basic Editor

By setting this reference, you provide Excel with access to all the parts of Word you'd get from within Word itself, including object names and built-in Word constants.

The following Excel macro starts a new instance of Word and then inserts a single line of text.

```
Sub HelloFromExcel()
Dim wd As Word.Application
Dim doc As Document

Set wd = New Word.Application
wd.Visible = True

Set doc = wd.Documents.Add
doc.Range.InsertAfter "Hello, Word"
doc.Range.Style = wdHeading1
End Sub
```

Since COM is designed as a means for two applications to communicate without an actual person involved, you need to use the Visible property to explicitly make Word visible on your screen. Otherwise, Word will still start and the macro will execute without your knowledge because it won't appear on your screen.

> While experimenting with and developing macros that use Word as a COM server, you should always set the Visible property to True. Otherwise, you may end up with multiple instances of Word running in the background, which can really slow down a system. If you do choose to run Word invisibly, make sure you use the Quit method to close it. In the previous example, the penultimate line of code would read:
>
> ```
> wd.Quit
> ```
>
> You should also set the object references to Nothing. Just before the End Sub, add the following line:
>
> ```
> Set wd = Nothing
> ```

The previous code created a new instance of Word, even if you already had the application open. To use the current instance of Word (or to open the application if no current instance is running), use the following version:

```
Sub HelloAlreadyOpenWordFromExcel()
Dim wd As Word.Application
Dim doc As Document
On Error Resume Next
Set wd = Word.Application

If Err.Number = 429 Then
    Set wd = New Word.Application
    Err.Clear
ElseIf Err.Number <> 0 Then
    MsgBox Err.Number & vbCr & Err.Description
```

```
        Exit Sub
    End If

    wd.Visible = True
    Set doc = wd.Documents.Add
    doc.Range.InsertAfter "Hello, Word"
    doc.Range.Style = wdStyleHeading1
    End Sub
```

This version uses the knowledge that error number 429 occurs when a COM (also known as ActiveX) component can't be created, as shown in Figure 9-9. To determine an error number, you often need to let the error occur and then make a note of its number.

Figure 9-9. The same error is generated when VBA can't create a COM object

Setting a reference from within the Visual Basic Editor provides the best performance possible for automating Word from another application, because it takes advantage of *early binding*. In other words, much of the work that needs to be done for the two applications to communicate is done long before the macro runs. This preparation is similar to a cooking show where the host premeasures all the ingredients in little bowls before he "starts" cooking. Early binding is always preferable if possible.

If your macro needs to run on systems that might not have that reference to Word already set, you'll need to use *late binding*. With late binding, you use the generic Object variable type.

The following version of the HelloFromExcel macro can run even if no reference to Word has been set:

```
    Sub HelloFromExcelLateBinding( )
    Dim wd As Object
    Dim doc As Object
    On Error Resume Next
    Set wd = GetObject(Class:="Word.Application")
    If Err.Number = 429 Then
        Set wd = CreateObject(Class:="Word.Application")
        Err.Clear
    ElseIf Err.Number <> 0 Then
```

```
        MsgBox Err.Number & vbCr & Err.Description
    End If

    wd.Visible = True
    Set doc = wd.Documents.Add
    doc.Range.InsertAfter "Hello, Word"
    doc.Range.Style = doc.Styles("Heading 1")
    End Sub
```

Notice that the code uses generic Object variables. Another important, but more subtle, difference is that without the reference set by early binding, you can't use Word's constants, like wdStyleHeading1, because those constants aren't defined in Excel. Instead, you must use the actual style names.

Without the reference set, you must do all of the prep work needed to get the two applications talking every time you run the macro. A macro that uses late binding will thus run more slowly than one using early binding.

Controlling Word from a Scripting Language

Upcoming hacks in this chapter cover the specifics for controlling Word from three popular scripting languages: Perl [Hack #86], Python [Hack #85], and Ruby [Hack #87]. This section covers the similarities between the three.

Translating what you already know about automating Word with VBA for use in another language can present some challenges. The biggest challenge is extricating your knowledge of the Word object model from that of the VBA language. A Word object is a Word object whether you control it from VBA or Perl, but the way you control it may be very different.

For example, here's the HelloFromExcelLateBinding macro from the previous section, but this time the parts that are just Word objects, and not part of the VBA language, are shown in bold:

```
    Sub HelloFromExcelLateBinding( )
    Dim wd As Object
    Dim doc As Object
    On Error Resume Next
    Set wd = GetObject(class:="Word.Application")
    If Err.Number = 429 Then
        Set wd = CreateObject(class:="Word.Application")
        Err.Clear
    ElseIf Err.Number <> 0 Then
        MsgBox Err.Number & vbCr & Err.Description
    End If

    wd.Visible = True
    Set doc = wd.Documents.Add
    doc.Range.InsertAfter "Hello, Word"
    End Sub
```

You will be reusing the parts in bold when controlling Word from a scripting language with COM. The rest is specific to VBA and may not be the same in another language. Even the "dot" syntax (where properties and methods of an object are noted with a ".", as in Documents.Add) can't be taken for granted. The following Perl script does the same thing as the Excel macro shown above. Again, the Word-specific parts are shown in bold.

```perl
#!/usr/bin/perl

use Win32::OLE qw(in with);
use Win32::OLE::Variant;

my $word;
eval {$word = Win32::OLE->GetActiveObject('Word.Application')};
die "Word not installed" if $@;
unless (defined $word) {
    $word = Win32::OLE->new('Word.Application', sub { $_[0]->Quit; })
        or die "Cannot start Word";
}

Win32::OLE->Option(Warn => 3);

$word->{'Visible'} = 1;
my $doc = $word->{'Documents'}->Add;
$doc->{'Range'}->InsertAfter('Hello, Word');
```

To run this script, save it as *HelloWord.pl* and run it from a DOS command line as follows:

```
> perl HelloWord.pl
```

While you may see some similarities, especially if you've worked with Perl before, these two scripts use very different syntax.

Using Perl is an admittedly extreme example. The other two scripting languages discussed in this chapter, Python and Ruby, share the "dot" syntax, and those scripts often more closely resemble their VBA counterparts.

Hack Word from Python

#85

Use Word from Python to create attractive printouts of HTML documents on the fly.

Python is a powerful scripting language, and its use on Windows systems as both a development and an administration tool has increased. This hack shows you how to use Python to import an HTML document into Word, tweak the formatting, save the document in native Word format, and print it to the default printer. This hack assumes you have a file named *C:\resume. html* on your system. It also assumes you have Python installed on your system and that you can run Python scripts from the DOS command line.

To download Python (for free), go to *http://www.python.org*. For detailed information on using Python on Windows systems, check out *Python Programming on Win32* (O'Reilly).

Because Python supports COM automation **[Hack #84]**, you can access Word from within a Python script. First, you'll need the `pywin32` module, which you can download from the SourceForge web site (*http://sourceforge.net/ project/showfiles.php?group_id=78018*).

Hello, Word

Once you've installed the `pywin32` module, you can use Word objects from within a Python script. The following script creates a new document, inserts some text, and applies the Heading 1 style to the text:

```
from win32com.client import Dispatch

def main( ):
    wrd = Dispatch('Word.Application')
    wrd.Visible = 1

    doc = wrd.Documents.Add( )
    rng = doc.Range(0,0)
    rng.InsertAfter('Hello, Word!')
    rng.Style - 'Heading 1'

if __name__==' __main__ ':
    main( )
```

Save this script as *C:\HelloFromPython.py* and run it from the DOS command line as follows:

```
> python HelloFromPython.py
```

As discussed in "Automate Word from Other Applications" **[Hack #84]**, Word objects created as COM servers aren't visible by default. You must explicitly set the `Visible` property to 1 if you want Word to appear onscreen.

Controlling Word Interactively

Python also includes an interactive command-line interpreter, which you launch by typing `python` at a DOS prompt:

```
> python
```

After some informational text is displayed, the prompt changes to indicate that you're in the Python interpreter.

```
Python 2.3.4 (#53, May 25 2004, 21:17:02) [MSC v.1200 32 bit (Intel)] on
win32
Type "help", "copyright", "credits" or "license" for more information.
>>>
```

You can now execute Python commands interactively, which is a useful way to experiment with controlling Word because you can see the results in real time. Enter the following sequence of commands after you launch the Python interpreter:

```
>>> from win32com.client import Dispatch
>>> w = Dispatch('Word.Application')
>>> w.Visible = 1
```

At this point, a new Word window opens, although Word doesn't create a new, blank document (considering that this instance of Word runs invisibly by default, that kind of makes sense). Though no blank document is created, all the global templates in the Startup folder [Hack #50] are loaded.

With the Python interpreter running and a Word window open, you can actually go back and forth between the two as you fiddle with Word. However, if you modify or remove objects currently referenced from Python within Word (for example, delete a paragraph or close a document), the Python objects may generate errors or become unstable and behave unexpectedly.

Now, create a new, blank Word document and insert a few lines of text with the following code:

```
>>> doc = w.Documents.Add( )
>>> rng = doc.Range( )
>>> rng.InsertAfter('To be or not to be - Shakespeare\n')
>>> rng.InsertAfter('Do be do be do be do - Sinatra')
```

By using the interactive interpreter, you can position the DOS window next to or on top of the Word window and watch your Python commands control Word, as shown in Figure 9-10.

To close the document and quit Word, enter the following:

```
>>> doc.Close( )
>>> wrd.Quit( )
```

Word won't close the document until you choose whether or not to save it. If you run Word invisibly and try the same thing, Word will stay hidden, but its Save As dialog will appear. If you write scripts that run Word invisibly, take care to avoid situations that might launch an unexpected dialog (and probably cause an error in your script). To avoid this particular one, you must either save the document or make Word think you've saved it. The following code shows both scenarios:

```
>>> doc.SaveAs('C:\Documents\Quotes.doc') # Save the file
>>> doc.Saved = 1 # Or fool Word into thinking it's been saved
```

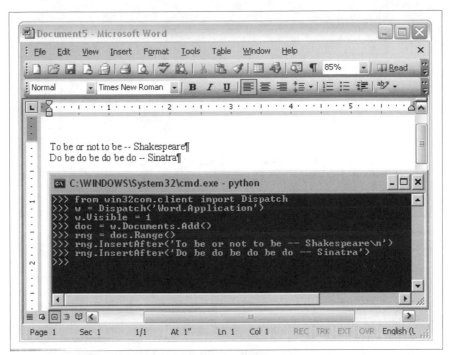

Figure 9-10. Controlling Word from the Python command line interpreter

Running the Hack

Word does an excellent job of importing HTML files—especially ones that use simple, standard HTML tags mapped to Word's built-in styles. You can easily translate existing HTML files into a useful printed format by importing them into Word. This process can be automated with Python and COM.

As an example, this hack will show you this process using an HTML file you might already have, and which is probably more up-to-date than any print version: your resume.

Again, this hack assumes you have a file named *C:\resume.html* on your system. The code presented below opens Word, opens the file, changes the appearance of the Heading 2 and Hyperlink styles, saves the document, and prints it out to your default printer:

```
from win32com.client import Dispatch

MYDIR = 'c:\\'

def main( ):
    wrd = Dispatch('Word.Application')
    confirm = wrd.Options.ConfirmConversions
    wrd.Options.ConfirmConversions = 0
```

```
wrd.Visible = 0
doc = wrd.Documents.Open(MYDIR + 'resume.html')
sty = doc.Styles('Heading 2')
sty.Font.Size = 18
sty.Font.Italic = 0

sty = doc.Styles('Hyperlink')
sty.Font.Underline = 0
sty.Font.Color = -16777216
sty.Font.Italic = 1

doc.SaveAs(FileName=MYDIR + 'resume.doc', FileFormat=0)
doc.PrintOut
doc.Close( )
wrd.Options.ConfirmConversions = confirm
wrd.Quit( )

if __name__=='__main__':
    main( )
```

Save this script as *resumeprinter.py* and run it from a DOS command line:

```
> python resumeprinter.py
```

A few parts of this script deserve closer attention.

Confirming conversions. Select Tools → Options, click the General tab, and check the "Confirm conversion at open" box. With this option checked, Word will prompt you before opening a file not in the *.doc* format. If this setting is enabled when the script opens the file, one of those unexpected dialogs will appear, even though the script runs Word invisibly. To make sure the *resume.html* file opens without confirming the conversion, this script explicitly sets the ConfirmConversions option to False. Before doing so, the script stores the current state in a variable named confirm; it then resets the option before it exits.

Word constants. This Python script doesn't have access to Word's constants (such as wdUnderlineNone and wdColorAutomatic) via COM. You must use their actual values, as this script does for the Underline and Color properties of the Hyperlink style. To get the value of a constant, query its value in the Immediate window [Hack #2] in the Visual Basic Editor, as shown in Figure 9-11.

Named arguments. When using Word from Python, as with VBA, you can use *named arguments*, which means you can specify the values for a function or method by keyword. When you don't use named arguments, each

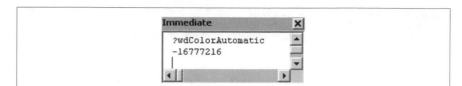

Figure 9-11. Getting a constant's value by using the Immediate window in the Visual Basic Editor

value passed as an argument must be in a particular order. For example, the syntax for the `MsgBox` function in VBA is:

```
MsgBox(prompt[, buttons] [, title] [, helpfile, context])
```

If you call this function in VBA without using named arguments, the function expects and interprets the values in the order specified by its syntax. To tell the function to display the prompt "Hello, World" with "Message in a Box" as the dialog's title, but without specifying a button type, insert the following:

```
Msgbox "Hello, World", ,"Message in a Box"
```

Notice the empty value in between the two commas. It tells Word to use its default value for the *buttons* argument. If you left out that empty value, Word would try to use "Message in a Box" as the *buttons* value, which would cause an error. When you use the named-argument syntax in VBA, you can do the same thing in a more readable way, and in any order you choose:

```
MsgBox Title:="Message in a Box", Prompt:="Hello, World"
```

Word uses its default settings for any of the arguments not specified. When using Word objects and methods from Python, you can use a similar syntax, as shown in the following line taken from the *resumeprinter.py* script shown above:

```
doc.SaveAs(FileName=MYDIR + 'resume.doc', FileFormat=0)
```

Note that in Python, you don't place a colon before the =, as you would in VBA.

 For information on creating Python objects that you can run from within Word using VBA, check out "Use Python from Word" **[Hack #88]**.

Hack Word from Perl

#86

Use Word from Perl to create attractive printouts of HTML documents on the fly.

This hack shows you how to use Perl to import an HTML document into Word, tweak the formatting, save the document in native Word format, and print it out to the default printer. This hack assumes you have a file named *C:\resume.html* on your system. It also assumes you have Perl installed on your system and can run Perl scripts from the DOS command line.

To download a free version of Perl for Windows, go to the ActiveState web site at *http://www.activestate.com*.

Because Perl supports COM automation [Hack #84], you can access Word from within a Perl script using the Win32::OLE module, which the ActiveState Perl distribution includes.

Hello, Word

The following Perl script creates a new document, inserts some text, and applies the Heading 1 style to the text:

```
use Win32::OLE qw(in with);
use Win32::OLE::Variant;

my $word;
eval {$word = Win32::OLE->GetActiveObject('Word.Application')};
die "Word not installed" if $@;
unless (defined $word) {
    $word = Win32::OLE->new('Word.Application', sub { $_[0]->Quit; })
        or die "Could not start Word";
}

$word->{'Visible'} = 1;
my $doc = $word->{'Documents'}->Add;
$doc->{'Range'}->InsertAfter('Hello, Word');
my $rng = $doc->{'Range'};
$rng->{'Style'} = 'Heading 1';
```

Save this script as *C:\HelloFromPerl.pl* and run it from the DOS command line as follows:

```
> perl HelloFromPerl.pl
```

As discussed in "Automate Word from Other Applications" **[Hack #84]**, Word objects created as COM servers aren't visible by default. You must explicitly set the Visible property to 1 if you want Word to appear onscreen.

Running the Hack

Word does an excellent job of importing HTML files—especially ones that use simple, standard HTML tags mapped to Word's built-in styles. You can easily translate existing HTML files into a useful printed format by importing them into Word. This process can be automated with Perl and COM.

As an example, this hack will show you this process using an HTML file you might already have, and which is probably more up-to-date than any print version: your resume.

Again, this hack assumes you have a file named *C:\resume.html* on your system. The code presented below starts Word, opens the file, changes the appearance of the Heading 2 and Hyperlink styles, saves the document, and prints it out to your default printer:

```
use Win32::OLE qw(in with);
use Win32::OLE::Variant;
use Win32::OLE::Const 'Microsoft Word';

my $word;
eval {$word = Win32::OLE->GetActiveObject('Word.Application')};
die "Word not installed" if $@;
unless (defined $word) {
    $word = Win32::OLE->new('Word.Application', sub { $_[0]->Quit; })
        or die "Could not start Word";
}

$word->{'Visible'} = 1;
my $confirm = $word->{'Options'}->{'ConfirmConversions'};
$word->{'Options'}->{'ConfirmConversions'} = 0;
my $doc = $word->{'Documents'}->Open("C:/resume.html");

my $style = $doc->Styles('Heading 2');
$style->{'Font'}->{'Size'} = 16;
$style->{'Font'}->{'Italic'} = 0;

$style = $doc->Styles('Hyperlink');
$style->{'Font'}->{'Color'} = wdColorAutomatic;
$style->{'Font'}->{'Underline'} = wdUnderlineNone;
undef $style;

$doc->SaveAs("C:/resume.doc", {
                'FileFormat' => wdFormatDocument
                    });
```

```
$doc->PrintOut( );
$doc->Close( );
$word->{'Options'}->{'ConfirmConversions'} = $confirm;
undef $doc;
undef $word;
```

Save this script as *resumeprinter.pl* and run it from a DOS command line:

```
> perl resumeprinter.pl
```

Note that Perl uses different and more cumbersome syntax for handling objects than VBA. For information on working with objects in Perl, check out O'Reilly's *Learning Perl Objects, References, and Modules*.

A few parts of this script deserve closer attention.

Confirming conversions. Select Tools → Options, click the General tab, and check the "Confirm conversion at open" box. With this option checked, Word will prompt you before opening a file not in the *.doc* format. If this setting is enabled when the script opens the file, a dialog will appear, even though the script runs Word invisibly. To make sure the *resume.html* file opens without confirming the conversion, this script explicitly sets the ConfirmConversions option to False. Before doing so, the script stores the current state in a variable named $confirm; it then resets the option before it exits.

Word constants. By using the Win32::OLE::Const module, as shown in this script, you can work with Word's constants (such as wdUnderlineNone and wdColorAutomatic) from within a Perl script.

Named arguments. When using Word from Perl, as with VBA, you can use *named arguments*, which means you can specify the values for a function or method by keyword. When you don't use named arguments, each value passed as an argument must be in a particular order. For example, the syntax for the MsgBox function in VBA is:

```
MsgBox(prompt[, buttons] [, title] [, helpfile, context])
```

If you call this function in VBA without using named arguments, the function expects and interprets the values in the order specified by its syntax. To tell the function to display the prompt "Hello, World" with "Message in a Box" as the dialog's title, but without specifying a button type, insert the following:

```
Msgbox "Hello, World", ,"Message in a Box"
```

Notice the empty value in between the two commas. It tells Word to use its default value for the *buttons* argument. If you leave out that empty value, Word tries to use "Message in a Box" as the *buttons* value, which causes an error. When you use the named-argument syntax in VBA, you can do the same thing in a more readable way, and in any order you choose:

```
MsgBox Title:="Message in a Box", Prompt:="Hello, World"
```

Word uses its default settings for any of the arguments not specified. When using Word objects and methods from Perl, you can use a similar syntax, as shown in the following lines taken from the *resumeprinter.pl* script shown earlier:

```
$doc->SaveAs("C:/resume.doc", {
              'FileFormat' => wdFormatDocument
                        });
```

For information on accessing Perl code from Word macros, check out "Use Perl from Word" [Hack #89].

—*Ian Burrell and Andrew Savikas*

Hack Word from Ruby

Use Word from Ruby to create attractive printouts of HTML documents on the fly.

Ruby is a newer language than Perl or Python, and it works very well as a tool to automate Word. This hack shows you how to use Ruby to import an HTML document into Word, tweak the formatting, save the document in native Word format, and print it out to the default printer. This hack assumes you have a file named *C:\resume.html* on your system. It also assumes that you have Ruby installed on your system and that you can run Ruby scripts from the DOS command line.

To download a free version of Ruby for Windows, go to *http://rubyforge.org*.

Because Ruby supports COM automation [Hack #84], you can access Word from within a Ruby script using the win32ole module, which the standard Windows Ruby distribution includes.

Hello, Word

The following Ruby script creates a new document, inserts some text, and applies the Heading 1 style to the text:

```
require 'win32ole'
wd = WIN32OLE.new('Word.Application')
```

```
wd.Visible = 1
doc = wd.Documents.Add( )
doc.Range.InsertAfter("Hello, Word")
doc.Range.Style = "Heading 1"
```

Save this script as *C:\HelloFromRuby.pl* and run it from the DOS command line as follows:

```
> Ruby HelloFromRuby.pl
```

As discussed in "Automate Word from Other Applications" [Hack #84], Word objects created as COM servers aren't visible by default. You must explicitly set the Visible property to 1 if you want Word to appear onscreen.

Controlling Word Interactively

Ruby includes an interactive command-line interpreter, which you launch by typing irb at a DOS prompt:

```
> irb
```

The interactive Ruby shell launches, and the prompt changes as follows:

```
irb(main):001:0>
```

You can now execute Ruby commands interactively, which is a useful way to experiment with Word because you can see the results in real time. Enter the following sequence of commands after you launch the Ruby shell (the commands you type are shown in bold, with the shell's response in plain text):

```
irb(main):001:0> require 'win32ole'
=> true
irb(main):002:0> w = WIN32OLE.new('Word.Application')
=> #<WIN32OLE:0x28cc070>
irb(main):003:0> w.Visible = 1
=> 1
```

At this point, a new Word window opens, although Word doesn't create a new, blank document (which makes sense considering that this instance of Word runs invisibly by default). Though no blank document is created, all the global templates in the *STARTUP* folder [Hack #50] are loaded.

With the Ruby shell running and a Word window open, you can actually go back and forth between the two as you fiddle with Word. However, if from within Word you modify or remove objects currently referenced from Ruby, those Ruby objects may become unstable and behave unexpectedly.

Now, create a new, blank document and insert a few lines of text (this time, only the commands you type are shown; the shell's response is omitted for the rest of this section):

```
irb(main):004:0> doc = w.Documents.Add( )
irb(main):005:0> rng = doc.Range( )
irb(main):006:0> rng.InsertAfter("To be or not to be - Shakespeare\n")
irb(main):007:0>rng.InsertAfter("Do be do be do be do - Sinatra")
```

Using the interactive interpreter, you can position the DOS window next to
or on top of the Word window and watch your Ruby commands control
Word, as shown in Figure 9-12.

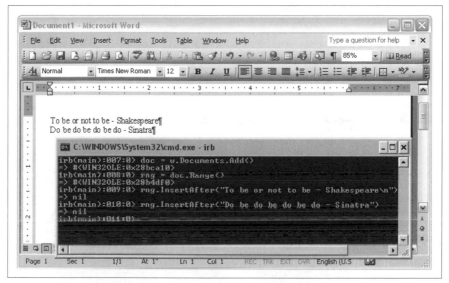

Figure 9-12. Controlling Word interactively from Ruby

To close the document and quit Word, enter the following:

```
irb(main):008:0> doc.Close( )
irb(main):009:0> wd.Quit( )
```

Word will not close the document until you choose whether or not to save
it. If you run Word invisibly and try the same thing, Word will stay hidden
but its Save As dialog will appear. If you write scripts that run Word invisibly, take care to avoid situations that might launch an unexpected dialog
(and probably cause an error in your script). To avoid this particular one,
you must either save the document or make Word think you've saved it.
The following code shows both scenarios:

```
irb(main):009:0>  doc.SaveAs('C:\Documents\Quotes.doc') # Save the file
irb(main):010:0>  doc.Saved = 1 # Or fool Word into thinking it's been saved
```

Running the Hack

Word does an excellent job of importing HTML files—especially ones that use simple, standard HTML tags mapped to Word's built-in styles. You can easily translate existing HTML files into a useful printed format by importing them into Word. This process can be automated with Ruby and COM.

As an example, this hack will show you this process using an HTML file you might already have, and which is probably more up-to-date than any print version: your resume.

Again, this hack assumes you have a file named *C:\resume.html* on your system. The code presented below starts Word, opens the file, changes the appearance of the Heading 2 and Hyperlink styles, saves the document, and prints it out to your default printer:

```ruby
require 'win32ole'
wrd = WIN32OLE.new('Word.Application')

confirm = wrd.Options.ConfirmConversions
wrd.Options.ConfirmConversions = 0
wrd.Visible = 1
doc = wrd.Documents.Open("C:/resume.html")

sty = doc.Styles("Heading 2")
sty.Font.Size = 18
sty.Font.Italic = 0

sty = doc.Styles('Hyperlink')
sty.Font.Underline = 0
sty.Font.Color = -16777216
sty.Font.Italic = 1

doc.SaveAs('FileName' => "C:/resume.doc", 'FileFormat' => 0)
doc.PrintOut
doc.Close()
wrd.Options.ConfirmConversions = confirm
wrd.Quit()
```

Save this script as *resumeprinter.rb* and run it from a DOS command line:

```
> ruby resumeprinter.rb
```

A few parts of this script deserve closer attention.

Confirming conversions. Select Tools → Options, click the General tab, and check the "Confirm conversion at open" box. With this option checked, Word will prompt you before opening a file not in the *.doc* format. If this setting is enabled when the script opens the file, a dialog will appear, even though the script runs Word invisibly. To make sure the *resume.html* file opens without confirming the conversion, this script explicitly sets the

`ConfirmConversions` option to `False`. Before doing so, the script stores the current state in a variable named `confirm`; it then resets the option before it exits.

Word constants. The Ruby script doesn't have access to Word's constants (such as `wdUnderlineNone` and `wdColorAutomatic`) via COM. You must use their actual values, as this script does for the `Underline` and `Color` properties of the Hyperlink style. To get the value of a constant, query its value in the Immediate window **[Hack #2]** of the Visual Basic Editor, as shown in Figure 9-11.

Named arguments. When using Word from Ruby, as with VBA, you can use *named arguments*, which means you can specify the values for a function or method by keyword. When you don't use named arguments, each value passed as an argument must be in a particular order. For example, the syntax for the `MsgBox` function in VBA is:

```
MsgBox(prompt[, buttons] [, title] [, helpfile, context])
```

If you call this function in VBA without using named arguments, the function expects and interprets the values in the order specified by its syntax. To tell the function to display the prompt "Hello, World" with "Message in a Box" as the dialog's title, but without specifying a button type, insert the following:

```
Msgbox "Hello, World", ,"Message in a Box"
```

Notice the empty value in between the two commas. It tells Word to use its default value for the *buttons* argument. If you left out that empty value, Word would try to use "Message in a Box" as the *buttons* value, which would cause an error. When you use the named argument syntax in VBA, you can do the same thing in a more readable way, and in any order you choose:

```
MsgBox Title:="Message in a Box", Prompt:="Hello, World"
```

Word uses its default settings for any of the arguments not specified. When using Word objects and methods from Ruby, you can use a similar syntax, as shown in the following line taken from the earlier *resumeprinter.rb* script:

```
doc.SaveAs('FileName' => "C:/resume.doc", 'FileFormat' => 0)
```

Use Python from Word

#88   This hack shows you how to create standalone Python objects that you can run from within Word using VBA.

"Hack Word from Python" **[Hack #85]** showed you how to control Word from Python using COM automation **[Hack #84]**. Python also includes a way to create your own COM objects, which you can then use from within a Word macro.

> This hack assumes that you have Python installed on your system and that you can run Python scripts from the DOS command line. To download Python (for free), go to *http://www.python.org*. For detailed information on using Python on Windows systems, see O'Reilly's *Python Programming on Win32*.

This sample shows you how to create a COM object with a single method, SplitString. This method has semantics identical to the standard Python function string.split: the first argument is the string to split, and the second (optional) argument is the delimiter string.

There are two steps to implement COM objects in Python:

1. Define a Python class with the methods and properties you wish to expose.
2. Annotate the Python class with special attributes required by the PythonCOM framework to expose the Python class as a COM object.

Both of these steps are accomplished by the code in the following section.

The Code

The following Python code shows a small COM server:

```
#SimpleCOMServer.py - A sample COM server - almost as small as they come!
#
# We expose a single method in a Python COM object
class PythonUtilities:
    _public_methods_ = [ 'SplitString' ]
    _reg_progid_ = "PythonDemo.Utilities"

    # NEVER copy the following ID!
    # Use "print pythoncom.CreateGuid()" to make a new one
    _reg_clsid_ = "{40CEA5F8-4D4C-4655-BD8B-0E7B6A26B556}"

    def SplitString(self, val, item=None):
        import string
        if item != None: item = str(item)
        return string.split(str(val), item)

# Add code so that when this script is run by
# Python.exe, it self-registers
if __name__=='__main__':
    print "Registering COM server..."
    import win32com.server.register
    win32com.server.register.UseCommandLine(PythonUtilities)
```

Save this code as *SimpleCOMServer.py*.

Note the following line from the script:

```
_reg_clsid_ = "{40CEA5F8-4D4C-4655-BD8B-0E7B6A26B556}"
```

In this line, you assign a unique identifier to your COM object. Windows uses these identifiers to keep track of the components installed on the system. Do *not* just copy the one from this sample into your own code. You need to create your own, which you can do easily with Python right from the DOS command line:

```
> python
>>> import pythoncom
>>> print pythoncom.CreateGuid( )
```

This prints a new, unique identifier to the command line. Use the number created on your system in place of the sample in the code above.

Running the Hack

Now you'll need to register the object with COM. You can do this by executing the code as a normal Python script. From the DOS command line, type:

```
> python SimpleCOMServer.py
```

After running the script, you'll see the following messages:

```
Registering COM server...
Registered: PythonDemo.Utilities
```

Now, to test the COM object from Word, put the following macro in the template of your choice [Hack #50] and run it from Tools → Macro → Macros:

```
Sub PythonObj( )
Dim py As Object
Dim vResponse As Variant
Dim v As Variant

Set py = CreateObject("PythonDemo.Utilities")

vResponse = py.SplitString("Hello from Python!")

For Each v In vResponse
    MsgBox v
Next v

End Sub
```

Running this code displays three message boxes, each showing one of the words in the phrase "Hello from Python!"

The default delimiter is a space, but you can also provide a delimiter string:

```
vResponse = py.SplitString("Hello, Word", ",")
```

To keep things tidy and help keep your registry clean, run your script again from the command line to unregister the sample COM server, but this time use the --unregister argument:

```
> python SimpleCOMServer.py --unregister
```

—*Mark Hammond*

Use Perl from Word

#89 This hack shows you two very different ways of getting at Perl from within a Word macro.

Perl's hard to beat for heavy-duty text processing, and if you've already got some Perl scripts lying around for performing certain tasks, you may want to use those from a Word macro rather than starting from scratch in VBA—a decidedly lighter-weight contender when it comes to text processing.

This hack assumes that you have Perl installed on your system and that you can run Perl scripts from the DOS command line. To download a free version of Perl for Windows, go to the ActiveState web site at *http://www.activestate.com*.

This hack demonstrates two ways to get at Perl code from a Word macro. The first is the more polished method and requires some special software from ActiveState, which lets you create standalone Windows *.dll* (dynamic link library) files. These files contain libraries of functions used to perform specific tasks. The second method is about as quick and dirty as they come and does not require any special software.

Creating COM Objects with the Perl Dev Kit

In addition to the free *ActivePerl* distribution, ActiveState sells software to help Perl developers create Windows applications. The *Perl Dev Kit* (PDK) lets you create standalone Windows executables, Microsoft installation files, and even .NET applications. You can try it free for 21 days, though any applications you build will expire at the same time as the evaluation period. You can, however, renew your trial period for an additional 21 days. The standard license costs $195. You can get the free trial version from *http://www.activestate.com/Products/Perl_Dev_Kit/*.

You need to download and install the PDK to do the rest of the stuff in this section. The method described in the next section, "Call Perl Directly with the VBA Shell Function," doesn't require the PDK.

One part of the PDK is `PerlCTRL`, which builds Windows *.dll* files from a Perl script. It involves a bit of setup work, but once you create the *.dll*, using it as a COM object **[Hack #84]** from VBA is a breeze.

This example is similar to "Use Python from Word" **[Hack #88]**; it shows you how to build a standalone interface to Perl's `split` function. A detailed explanation of `PerlCTRL` is beyond the scope of this hack, which demonstrates only a simple example.

Although VBA also includes a `split` function, with Perl's you can use a regular expression pattern as the delimiter rather than just a string, making it a much more powerful function.

The following is the base Perl code used to build the COM object. It's a simple wrapper around Perl's built-in `split` function:

```
package PerlSample;

sub Split {
    my $pattern = shift;
    my $string = shift;

    my @list = split(/$pattern/, $string);

    return \@list;
}
```

There are three main steps to turning this Perl code into a COM object:

1. Create a *template* file using the PDK. The template file contains boilerplate code and examples of the information that `PerlCTRL` needs to generate the *.dll*.

2. Modify the template file.

3. Generate the *.dll* from the template.

First, create a new folder on your system and name it *C:\PerlCOMSample*. Open a DOS command prompt and navigate to the folder you created. At the DOS prompt, type the following:

```
> PerlCtrl -t > template.pl
```

Now open the *template.pl* file in a text editor, such as Notepad. The file will look like the one shown in Figure 9-13.

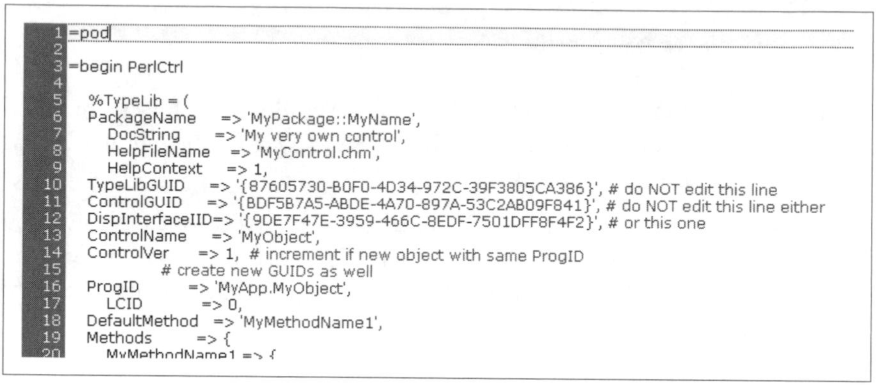

Figure 9-13. The template file generated by PerlCTRL

The template file also includes three unique identifiers that Windows will use to keep track of your *.dll*. PerlCtrl creates these identifiers when you generate the template file. As the comments in the template file indicate, *do not* edit those lines. Otherwise, modify the template file as follows:

```perl
package PerlSample;

sub Split {
    my $pattern = shift;
    my $string = shift;

    my @list = split(/$pattern/, $string);

    return \@list;
}

=pod

=begin PerlCtrl

%TypeLib = (
PackageName => 'PerlSample',
TypeLibGUID => '{26798342-6F54-4271-9668-B4C0D31EB5C8}', # do NOT edit this
line
ControlGUID => '{BD48D84F-C5C9-4E3B-8E36-24E019E4F48D}', # do NOT edit this
line
DispInterfaceIID=> '{FF546B71-4492-4E07-BD44-1EDE507CB5A4}', # or this one
ControlName    => 'PerlSample',
ControlVer     => 1,  # increment if new object with same ProgID
                      # create new GUIDs as well
ProgID         => 'PerlSample.Split',
DefaultMethod  => '',
```

```
Methods          => {
    'Split' => {
            RetType            => VT_ARRAY|VT_VARIANT,
            TotalParams        => 2,
            NumOptionalParams  => 0,
            ParamList          =>[ 'pattern' => VT_BSTR,
                                   'string' => VT_BSTR ]
        },
}, # end of 'Methods'
Properties       => {
}, # end of 'Properties'
); # end of %TypeLib

=end PerlCtrl

=cut
```

Again, use the three lines generated in your template file, *not* the ones shown in bold in this example.

Next, save this file as *PerlCOMObject.ctrl* in the same directory, and then run the following command at a DOS prompt:

```
> PerlCtrl PerlCOMObject.ctrl
```

You'll see the following output:

```
Created 'PerlCOMObject.dll'
```

Now you need to register the new *.dll* with Windows. At the DOS prompt, enter the following:

```
> regsvr32 PerlCOMObject.dll
```

In a few seconds, you'll see the dialog shown in Figure 9-14, indicating that the *.dll* file was successfully registered.

Figure 9-14. Windows notifies you when your .dll file is registered successfully

Now you can call the *.dll* as a COM object from within a Word macro. Open Word and create the following macro in the template of your choice [Hack #50]:

```
Sub TestPerlObject()
Dim p1 As Object
```

```
Set pl = CreateObject("PerlSample.Split")
Dim str As String
Dim var() As Variant
Dim v As Variant

str = "Hello from Perl!"
var = pl.Split(" ", str)
For Each v In var
    MsgBox v
Next v
End Sub
```

When you run the macro, you'll see three dialog boxes displayed in sequence, each showing one of the words in the string "Hello from Perl!"

If you'd like to remove the .dll from your system, enter the following at a DOS command prompt:

```
> regsvr32 /u PerlCOMObject.dll
```

Call Perl Directly with the VBA Shell Function

VBA includes a function you can use to launch other Windows applications. At its simplest, the Shell function is roughly equivalent to entering a command at a DOS prompt. For example, enter the following in the Visual Basic Editor's Immediate window [Hack #2] to launch the Notepad text editor:

```
Shell("notepad.exe")
```

Because Perl is an executable file, you can use Shell to run Perl scripts. For example, if you had a Perl script called C:\foo.pl, you could enter the following in the Immediate window to run the script:

```
Shell("C:\perl\bin\wperl.exe C:\foo.pl")
```

After the Shell function executes and the executable program starts, the VBA code continues.

wperl.exe is the "windowless" Perl. When run, it won't launch a new DOS window, unlike the regular perl.exe.

You can use the clipboard to pass and return values between VBA and Perl. For example, you can copy selected text to the clipboard and then call a Perl script that reads the clipboard, processes the text, and puts the result back on the clipboard to paste into your document.

However, the VBA macro might try to paste from the clipboard before the Perl script finishes. Thus, you also need a way to have VBA "wait" for the Perl script to finish. One solution is to use a *semaphore;* that is, have the macro create a temporary folder on your computer, and then have the Perl script delete it once it puts the script result on the clipboard. All you need is a few lines of VBA to check to see if the folder still exists and, if so, instruct the macro to wait a few seconds until the Perl script finishes.

 For a more thorough discussion of semaphores, see *http:// interglacial.com/~sburke/tpj/as_html/tpj23.html* and *http:// interglacial.com/~sburke/tpj/as_html/tpj24.html.*

Since it's likely you'd want to access a variety of Perl scripts from within a Word macro, it's worthwhile to create a reusable function to act as a wrapper around the Shell function call to Perl. The following function takes three arguments: the name of the Perl script to run, the name of the semaphore folder the Perl script should delete when it finishes, and finally the maximum time to wait for the Perl script to run before giving up. The function returns a value of True if the Perl script deleted the semaphore folder, or False if the folder still exists when the time limit is reached. Put this code into the template of your choice **[Hack #50]**:

```
Function RunPerl(sPerlScriptToRun As String, _
        sSemFolderName As String, _
        sngWaitMax As Single) As Boolean

Dim sPerlPath As String
Dim sFullShellCommand As String
Dim sSemDir As String
Dim sSemDirFullName As String
Dim sngStartTime As Single

' Full path of "Windowless" Perl executable
sPerlPath = "C:\perl\bin\wperl.exe"

' Get the full path from the environment variable
sSemDirFullName = Environ("TEMP") & "\" & sSemFolderName

' Put quotes around full script path.
' This allows for spaces in script path names, common on Windows systems.
sFullShellCommand = sPerlPath & " " & _
    Chr(34) & sPerlScriptToRun & Chr(34)

' Create semaphore directory, unless it already exists
If Not LCase(Dir(sSemDirFullName, vbDirectory)) = LCase(sSemFolderName) Then
    MkDir (sSemDirFullName)
End If

' Start the countdown to timeout
sngStartTime = Timer
```

```
' Run Perl script
Shell (sFullShellCommand)

' The script will stay in this loop until either
' the semaphore directory is deleted, or until the
' time limit set by sngMaxWaitTime has passed
Do While LCase$(Dir$(sSemDirFullName, vbDirectory)) = _
                sSemFolderName And _
        ((Timer - sngStartTime) < sngWaitMax)

    ' Display a countdown in status bar
    StatusBar = "Waiting " & _
        Int((sngWaitMax - (Timer - sngStartTime))) & _
        " more seconds for Perl ..."
Loop

If LCase$(Dir$(sSemDirFullName, vbDirectory)) = sSemFolderName Then
    ' Gave up waiting.
    RmDir (sSemDirFullName)
    StatusBar = "Gave up waiting for Perl"
    RunPerl = False
Else
    ' Perl script successfully deleted semaphore folder
    StatusBar = ""
    RunPerl = True
End If

End Function
```

To see an example of this function in action, and to borrow Tim Meadowcroft's example from *Computer Science and Perl Programming* (O'Reilly), the following code will demonstrate how to use Perl to standardize phone numbers that are in a variety of formats. (Note: This example uses U.K. phone numbers.)

For starters, the following Perl script called *FixPhoneNumbers.pl* pulls the text off the Windows clipboard, checks it using a series of regular expressions, then either puts the modified number on the clipboard, or the original, if it couldn't fix it. The standard ActiveState Windows Perl distribution includes the *Win32::Clipboard* module. Save this script as *C:\FixPhoneNumbers.pl*:

```perl
use Win32::Clipboard;

my $TEMP = $ENV{"TMP"};
my $clipcontents = Win32::Clipboard();
my $cliptext = $clipcontents->Get();
my $num = PerlFixPhone($cliptext);

if ($num != '') {
    $cliptext = $num
}
```

```
$clipcontents->Set($cliptext);
rmdir("$TEMP/vba_sem") || die "cannot rmdir $TEMP\\vba_sem: $!";

sub PerlFixPhone {
    # Tests:
    #   020 xxxx xxxx : fine as is
    #   xxx xxxx      : assume 020 7xxx xxxx
    #   2xxx          : Building 1 extension, assume 020 7457 2xxx
    #   8xxx          : Building 2 extension, assume 020 7220 8xxx
    #   0171 xxx xxxx : convert to 020 7xxx xxxx
    #   0181 xxx xxxx : convert to 020 8xxx xxxx
    #   Anything else is an error and should be ignored...
    #
    local $_ = shift;
    return $_ if /^020 \d{4} \d{4}$/;
    return $_ if s/^\s*(\d{3})[-\s]+(\d{4})\s*$/020 7$1 $2/;
    return $_ if s/^\s*(\d{3})[-\s]+(\d{4})[-\s]+(\d{4})\s*$/$1 $2 $3/;
    return $_ if s/^\s*(2\d{3})\s*$/020 7457 $1/;
    return $_ if s/^\s*(8\d{3})\s*$/020 7220 $1/;
    return $_ if s/^\s*0171[-\s]+(\d{3})[-\s]+(\d{4})\s*$/020 7$1 $2/;
    return $_ if s/^\s*0181[-\s]+(\d{3})[-\s]+(\d{4})\s*$/020 8$1 $2/;
    return '';
}
```

The following macro uses the RunPerl function shown above to run the
FixPhoneNumbers.pl script. Put this code in the same template as the
RunPerl function:

```
Sub UsePerlToFixSelectedPhoneNumber()
' Pass selected text to a Perl program
' to format/normalize phone numbers
Dim sel As Selection

Set sel = Selection
' Exit if selection doesn't include some text
If sel.Type - wdSelectionIP Then
    MsgBox "Please select some text first"
    Exit Sub
End If


' Copy selected text to clipboard for Perl
sel.Copy


' Run Perl script. If successful,
' paste in changed text from Perl
If (RunPerl(sPerlScriptToRun:="C:\FixPhoneNumbers.pl", _
            sSemFolderName:="vba_sem", _
            sngWaitMax:=5)) = True Then
    sel.Paste
Else
    MsgBox "Gave up waiting for Perl"
End If

End Sub
```

To see this macro in action, type the following four (U.K.) phone numbers into a Word document:

```
0171 123 6554
8000
220-8537
220 8537
```

Select each in turn and run the *UsePerlToFixSelectedPhoneNumber* macro from Tools → Macro → Macros. The macro will convert them to the following format, according to the rules laid out in the *FixPhoneNumbers.pl* script:

```
020 7123 6554
020 7220 8000
020 7220 8537
020 7220 8537
```

If your Perl program takes a long time to run, you may need to adjust the value passed in the sngWaitMax argument to the RunPerl function. This example sets it to five seconds, more than enough time for Perl to finish this little bit of text crunching.

—Sean M. Burke, Andy Bruno, and Andrew Savikas

CHAPTER TEN

Word 2003 XML Hacks

Hacks 90–100

Starting with Word 2003, you have a whole new way to access and process the information in Word documents. If you select File → Save As, you'll see a new entry under "Save as type" called "XML Document." XML (Extensible Markup Language) provides a standard way to encode information—data, documents, and everything in between—in a readable text format. It is an interoperable, OS-independent format, which means you can now process and generate Word documents using applications other than Microsoft Word.

All of the hacks in this chapter require either the standard or professional version of Word 2003 for Windows.

XML lets you define your own "document type" or "vocabulary" suited to your particular application or industry. For example, *DocBook* is an XML vocabulary used extensively for technical publishing. *WordprocessingML* is Microsoft's XML format for Word documents. It is a lossless format, which means it contains the same information that's stored in the *.doc* format, but in a plain-text XML format rather than a binary format that only a computer can understand. Most of the hacks in this chapter show you how you can use XML to gain powerful control over your Word documents.

Beyond some suggestive examples, this chapter will not spend a lot of time explaining WordprocessingML or how it works (or XML in general). Instead, it focuses on the kinds of things you can *do* with it, using XSLT (Extensible Stylesheet Language Transformations), a special programming language designed for processing XML. For more complete coverage of WordprocessingML and the other XML features of Office 2003, check out the following books, all published by O'Reilly Media:

- *Office 2003 XML*
- *Learning XSLT*
- *Learning XML*

Get a Command-Line XML Processor

Here's a rundown of the tools you'll need to work with the Word XML shown throughout this chapter.

When running these hacks, you'll need a *command-line processor*, an XSLT processor that runs from a DOS command prompt.

You can read about and download Microsoft's own command-line XSLT processor, *msxsl.exe*, at this URL:

> *http://www.microsoft.com/downloads/details.aspx?FamilyId=2FB55371-C94E-4373-B0E9-DB4816552E41&displaylang=en*

> After you download *msxsl.exe*, move it to the *C:\Windows* folder so you can run it from a DOS command prompt within any folder on your system.

The *libxml* project (hosted at *http://www.xmlsoft.org*) houses some quite useful command-line utilities for XML processing. Native Windows binaries for each of the libxml tools are available at *http://www.zlatkovic.com/libxml.en.html*. One particularly convenient tool in the libxml suite is the xmllint command. Its --format option, which inputs an XML document and outputs a printed version of it (adding line breaks and indentation), is an excellent tool for learning WordprocessingML and for helping to author stylesheets that create Word documents.

Figure 10-1 shows how a WordprocessingML document looks when opened in Notepad after just saving it from Word. The entire document is jammed onto four extremely long lines of text, making it a tad difficult to inspect.

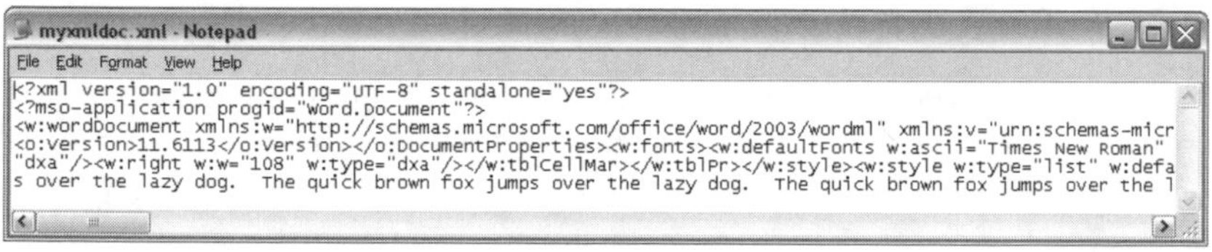

Figure 10-1. Word's "raw" XML output

Figure 10-2 shows a portion of the same document, after using the command xmllint --format. The indenting and line breaks make for a much more readable XML file.

```
myxmldoc_pretty.xml - Notepad                                              [_][□][X]
File  Edit  Format  View  Help
      </w:style>
    </w:styles>
    <w:docPr>
      <w:view w:val="normal"/>
      <w:zoom w:percent="120"/>
      <w:doNotEmbedSystemFonts/>
      <w:attachedTemplate w:val=""/>
      <w:defaultTabStop w:val="720"/>
      <w:punctuationKerning/>
      <w:characterSpacingControl w:val="DontCompress"/>
      <w:optimizeForBrowser/>
      <w:validateAgainstSchema/>
      <w:saveInvalidXML w:val="off"/>
      <w:ignoreMixedContent w:val="off"/>
      <w:alwaysShowPlaceholderText w:val="off"/>
      <w:compat>
        <w:breakWrappedTables/>
        <w:snapToGridInCell/>
        <w:wrapTextWithPunct/>
        <w:useAsianBreakRules/>
        <w:dontGrowAutofit/>
      </w:compat>
    </w:docPr>
    <w:body>
      <wx:sect>
        <w:p>
          <w:r>
            <w:t>The quick brown fox jumps over the lazy dog.  The quick brown fox jumps o
          </w:r>
```

Figure 10-2. An easier-to-read version, created with xmllint

The libxml project also contains its own XSLT processor, with a command-line tool called xsltproc. Other freely available XSLT processors you may want to try out include Saxon (*http://saxon.sourceforge.net*) and Xalan (*http://xml.apache.org/xalan-j/*), both of which are Java-based processors.

Create a Word Document in Notepad

HACK
#91

This hack demonstrates how you can use simple XML files to create Word documents.

If you save one of your Word documents—even a very simple one with just a line or two of text—in XML format, then open it in a standard text editor such as Notepad, you'll see that the file contains much more than just the text you typed.

Fortunately, Word can fill in most of that information if it's missing, so you don't need to be quite so verbose when creating XML documents meant to be opened in Word.

For example, open Notepad or another standard text editor and type the following:

```
<?xml version="1.0"?>
<?mso-application progid="Word.Document"?>
<w:wordDocument
  xmlns:w="http://schemas.microsoft.com/office/word/2003/wordml">
  <w:body>
    <w:p>
      <w:r>
        <w:t>Hello, World!</w:t>
      </w:r>
    </w:p>
  </w:body>
</w:wordDocument>
```

The w:body element contains the body of the document; the w:p element stands for "paragraph," the w:r element stands for "run," and the w:t element contains text in the document.

Now save the file as *Hello.xml*. If you look at the file in Windows Explorer (or from Notepad's Save As dialog box), you'll see that it has a special icon—a combination of the icon used for XML files and the icon used for Word documents, as shown in Figure 10-3.

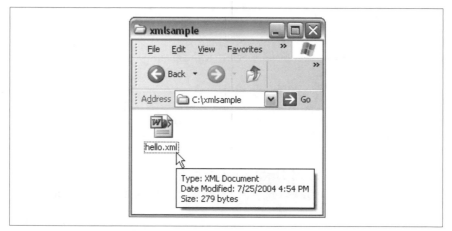

Figure 10-3. Windows recognizes the file as an XML file meant for Word

If you then double-click the file in Windows Explorer, Word launches rather than your default XML viewer (usually Internet Explorer). Figure 10-4 shows the *Hello.xml* document after Word has opened it. If you save the file from within Word, then open it in Notepad, you'll see that Word has added quite a bit of additional information (check out Figure 10-6 in [Hack #92] to see the information Word inserts).

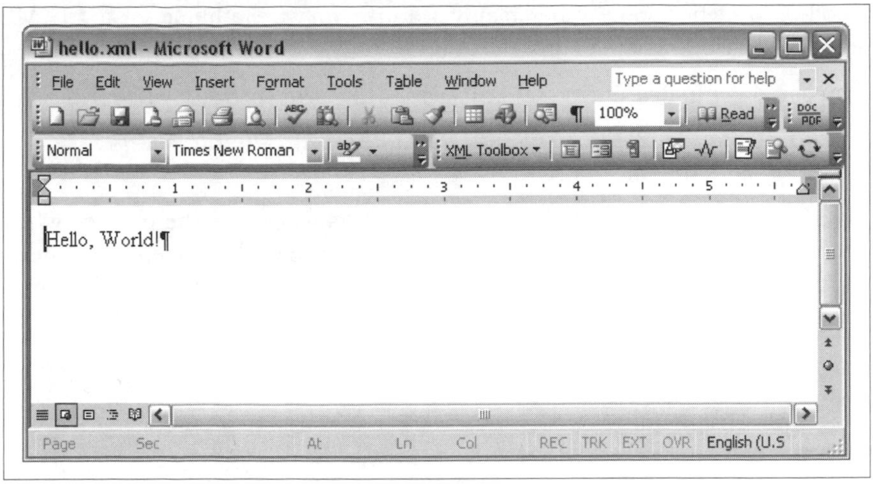

Figure 10-4. Your XML document opens in Word

The reason the file opened in Word, and not in Internet Explorer (or whatever program usually opens XML files on your system), is the following line included in the file:

```
<?mso-application progid="Word.Document"?>
```

This *processing instruction* (PI) associates the XML document with Word. It is also used for other applications in Microsoft Office: the progid pseudoattribute can have Excel.Sheet and InfoPath.Document as values, for example.

As you can see, there's nothing fancy here; Word used the Normal paragraph style to provide all the formatting information. However, this simple example shows how you can use plain text to create fully functional Word documents. See "Transforming XML into a Word Document" [Hack #94] for a more detailed example of using XML to create Word documents.

—*Evan Lenz*

HACK
#92

Get the XML Toolbox

This free add-in from Microsoft lets you inspect the XML in a Word document while the document remains open, making it an essential tool for working with XML in Word.

The XML Toolbox is a Word plug-in that acts much like a web browser's View Source function. You can view an entire document's WordprocessingML representation without having to save and close it first, or you can view the underlying WordprocessingML for only a partial selection of a document. The

Toolbox also has some other handy features for streamlining custom XML solution development in Word.

You can download and read an article about it from the following URL:

> http://msdn.microsoft.com/library/default.asp?url=/library/en-us/
> dnofftalk/html/odc_office01012004.asp

After you install the XML Toolbox, it appears as one of the choices when you select View → Toolbars. Figure 10-5 shows the toolbar open while viewing the *Hello.xml* file from "Create a Word Document in Notepad" **[Hack #91]**.

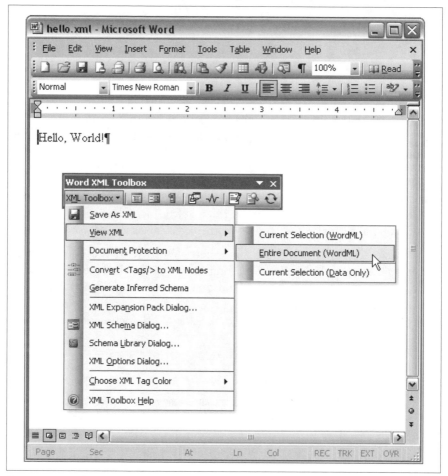

Figure 10-5. The XML Toolbox toolbar

Next, select XML Toolbox → View XML → Entire Document (WordML) to open a new XML Viewer window, as shown in Figure 10-6. You can then

save the XML as a separate file or copy it to the clipboard using the button
at the bottom of the Viewer window.

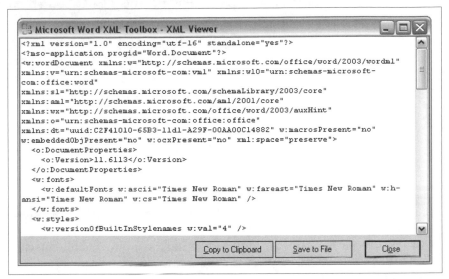

Figure 10-6. The XML Viewer window

Figure 10-6 shows the XML generated by Word from the
Hello.xml file in "Create a Word Document in Notepad"
[Hack #91]. When you open a simple XML document, Word
automatically inserts all the other information usually stored
in a Word file.

When you choose to view just the current selection, Word adds enough
additional XML to make the XML shown in the Viewer a standalone XML
document. For example, if you select just a single word in a Word document, choose XML Toolbox → View XML → Current Selection, and then
click the "Save to File" button in the XML Viewer, the file created will be its
own, fully functional Word document.

The XML Toolbox add-in requires .NET Programmability
support. If you did not install the .NET Framework 1.1 prior
to your Office 2003 installation, you may need to reinstall
Office. The Toolbox download page offers more information, including instructions on determining if .NET support
is installed on your system.

While the XML Toolbox is an indispensable learning aid, it leaves out some things from the XML, such as document metadata and spelling errors. When learning the ropes of WordprocessingML, you should also spend some time viewing Word documents saved as XML from other applications, such as a text editor or Internet Explorer.

—Evan Lenz

H A C K #93 Use IE to Inspect WordprocessingML Documents

Internet Explorer is a great tool for reading WordprocessingML files, but without a little hacking, it's hard to keep Word's hands off those files.

Internet Explorer's default tree-view stylesheet for XML documents provides a handy, readable way to investigate the structure of WordprocessingML documents, as shown in Figure 10-7. However, if you try opening a WordprocessingML document in Internet Explorer (i.e., right-click the file and select Open With → Internet Explorer), IE turns right around and launches Word. Why? IE recognizes WordprocessingML files as Word documents because of the single-line processing instruction [Hack #91]:

```
<?mso-application progid="Word.Document"?>
```

You can use two techniques to get around this little annoyance.

The first technique simply removes the `mso-application` line before it opens the WordprocessingML document in IE:

1. Save the Word document as XML and then close it.
2. Open the newly saved WordprocessingML document in Notepad.
3. Delete the line with the `mso-application` processing instruction and resave the file.

Internet Explorer will now display the document using its pretty XML tree view, even if Word subsequently updates the document to include the `mso-application` PI. Once it's been opened in IE, you can refresh IE to see how changes to the document from within Word affect the underlying WordprocessingML.

The second technique involves making a temporary change in your Windows registry, obviating the need to remove the `mso-application` line from each and every document you want to inspect:

1. Select Start → Run and type `regedit` to open the registry editor.
2. Find the subkey named `HKEY_LOCAL_MACHINE\SOFTWARE\Microsoft\Office\11.0\Common\Filter\text/xml`.

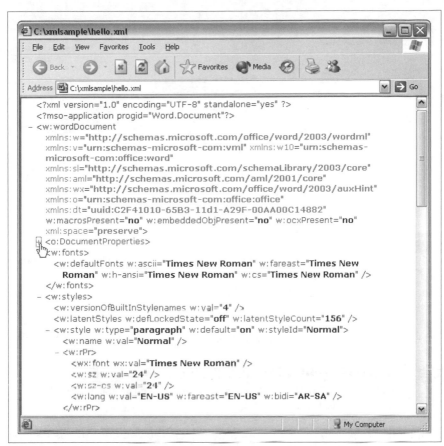

Figure 10-7. A WordprocessingML file viewed in Internet Explorer

3. Right-click the Word.Document string value entry and select Rename.

4. Change the name to something like Word.DocumentDISABLED.

 The Windows registry stores important system information. Before making any changes to the registry, set a system restore point by choosing Start → All Programs → Accessories → System Tools → System Restore (the exact location may be different on your system).

To restore the setting later, simply rename it again, removing the "DISABLED" part. Figure 10-8 shows the registry editor and the applicable entry being renamed.

With the WordprocessingML filter effectively disabled, IE will now open WordprocessingML documents using its default XML tree-view

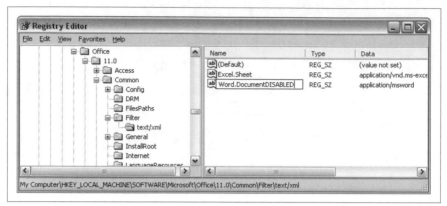

Figure 10-8. Getting around IE's refusal to render the XML source of WordprocessingML documents

stylesheet. Windows Explorer, however, will still continue to associate WordprocessingML documents with Word (if you double-click a Word-processingML file, you will always launch Word), which is probably what you want anyway.

—Evan Lenz

 ### HACK #94   Transforming XML into a Word Document

With the right XSLT stylesheet, you can quickly transform an XML document into a Word document.

A potential killer app for WordprocessingML is the ability to publish Word documents from dynamic XML content. In this hack, we'll look at a simple XML document that vaguely resembles HTML. The code for this hack will transform the document into a full-fledged WordprocessingML document you can open in Word. Type the following in a standard text editor such as Notepad and save it as *simpleDocument.xml*:

```
<doc>
    <h1>Hello, this is my document heading</h1>
    <para>This is <emphasis>italic</emphasis>.</para>
    <h2>This is a sub-heading</h2>
    <para>This text is <strong>bold</strong>.</para>
    <para>This text is <strong><emphasis>bold and italic</emphasis>
                </strong>.</para>
    <para><emphasis><strong>And so is this.</strong></emphasis>.</para>
    <para>And <emphasis>this is italic and <strong>this is both
                </strong></emphasis>.</para>
    <para>Finally, <strong>this is bold and <emphasis>this is both
                </emphasis> and back to just bold</strong>.</para>
</doc>
```

The file has a fairly flat structure, including a sequence of para, h1, and h2 elements inside the root doc element.

The code in this hack will show you how to transform the *simpleDocument.xml* file into a formatted Word document. Figure 10-9 shows the automatically generated WordprocessingML document after opening it in (any edition of) Word 2003. As you can see, the content of each of the different elements is formatted differently: the text from the h1 elements is rendered in a large font and is bold, the text from the emphasis elements is rendered in italic type, the text from the strong elements is rendered bold, and so on.

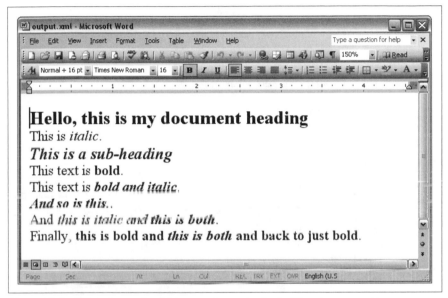

Figure 10-9. What the result of this transformation looks like when opened in any edition of Word 2003

The Code

The following code is the entire XSLT stylesheet used to render the document shown in Figure 10-9. Each xsl:template element represents a different *template rule*, which applies to particular kinds of nodes in the source document. The stylesheet matches the text of the document according to its context, then outputs the desired paragraphs (w:p elements), runs (w:r elements), and formatting properties.

Enter the following code in a standard text editor such as Notepad, save the file in the same folder as *simpleDoc.xml*, and name it *createWordDocument.xsl*:

```
<xsl:stylesheet version="1.0"
  xmlns:xsl="http://www.w3.org/1999/XSL/Transform"
  xmlns:w="http://schemas.microsoft.com/office/word/2003/wordml">

  <xsl:output indent="yes"/>

  <xsl:template match="/">
    <xsl:processing-instruction name="mso-application">
      <xsl:text>progid="Word.Document"</xsl:text>
    </xsl:processing-instruction>
    <w:wordDocument>
      <xsl:attribute name="xml:space">preserve</xsl:attribute>
      <w:body>
        <xsl:apply-templates select="/doc/*"/>
      </w:body>
    </w:wordDocument>
  </xsl:template>

  <xsl:template match="h1 | h2 | para">
    <w:p>
      <xsl:apply-templates/>
    </w:p>
  </xsl:template>

  <xsl:template match="h1/text()">
    <w:r>
      <w:rPr>
        <w:sz w:val="32"/>
        <w:b/>
      </w:rPr>
      <w:t>
        <xsl:copy/>
      </w:t>
    </w:r>
  </xsl:template>

  <xsl:template match="h2/text()">
    <w:r>
      <w:rPr>
        <w:sz w:val="28"/>
        <w:b/>
        <w:i/>
      </w:rPr>
      <w:t>
        <xsl:copy/>
      </w:t>
    </w:r>
  </xsl:template>

  <xsl:template match="para/text()">
    <w:r>
      <w:t>
        <xsl:copy/>
```

```
      </w:t>
     </w:r>
   </xsl:template>

   <xsl:template match="emphasis/text()">
     <w:r>
       <w:rPr>
         <w:i/>
       </w:rPr>
       <w:t>
         <xsl:copy/>
       </w:t>
     </w:r>
   </xsl:template>

   <xsl:template match="strong/text()">
     <w:r>
       <w:rPr>
         <w:b/>
       </w:rPr>
       <w:t>
         <xsl:copy/>
       </w:t>
     </w:r>
   </xsl:template>

   <xsl:template match="emphasis/strong/text() | strong/emphasis/text()"
                 priority="1">
     <W:r>
       <w:rPr>
         <w:i/>
         <w:b/>
       </w:rPr>
       <w:t>
         <xsl:copy/>
       </w:t>
     </w:r>
   </xsl:template>

 </xsl:stylesheet>
```

Let's pick out a couple of template rules, and I'll show what's going on in the code. The second template rule of the stylesheet matches three different kinds of elements: h1, h2, and para. When any of these elements are encountered (in the context of XSLT's automatic recursive descent), a w:p element is created, effectively turning each of these elements into a vanilla Word paragraph:

```
<xsl:template match="h1 | h2 | para">
  <w:p>
    <xsl:apply-templates/>
```

```
    </w:p>
  </xsl:template>
```

The `xsl:apply-templates` instruction causes the recursive descent of the source document to continue, allowing other template rules to fire when they match an input node. For example, this template rule matches text inside an emphasis element:

```
<xsl:template match="emphasis/text()">
  <w:r>
    <w:rPr>
      <w:i/>
    </w:rPr>
    <w:t>
      <xsl:copy/>
    </w:t>
  </w:r>
</xsl:template>
```

The most important element in this template rule is `w:i`. It causes this particular run of text to be rendered in italics. The `w:t` element, which stands for "text," functions as a container for the text in this run. The `xsl:copy` instruction copies the text node that's a child of the `emphasis` element in our source document straight to the result tree without modification.

Running the Hack

To run this hack, enter the following at a DOS command prompt within the folder that holds the *simpleDocument.xml* and *createWordDocument.xsl* files:

```
> msxsl simpleDocument.xml createWordDocument.xsl -o output.xml
```

A new file, *output.xml*, is created. Double-click the new file from Windows Explorer, and voila! You'll see the document shown in Figure 10-9.

Hacking the Hack

The stylesheet listed above creates a Word document with paragraphs that contain runs with direct formatting applied (bold and italic). The stylesheet listed below produces an identical-looking document to the one above, but it uses Word's styles instead. You must define the styles up front within your document, inside the `w:styles` element (naturally). The new parts of the stylesheet are shown in bold.

Enter the following into a standard text editor such as Notepad and save it in the same folder as the other files from this hack. Name it *createStyledWordDoc.xsl*.

```xsl
<xsl:stylesheet version="1.0"
  xmlns:xsl="http://www.w3.org/1999/XSL/Transform"
  xmlns:w="http://schemas.microsoft.com/office/word/2003/wordml">

  <xsl:output indent="yes"/>

  <xsl:template match="/">
    <xsl:processing-instruction name="mso-application">
      <xsl:text>progid="Word.Document"</xsl:text>
    </xsl:processing-instruction>
    <w:wordDocument>
      <xsl:attribute name="xml:space">preserve</xsl:attribute>
      <w:styles>
        <w:style w:styleId="h1" w:type="paragraph">
          <w:name w:val="Heading 1"/>
          <w:rPr>
            <w:sz w:val="32"/>
            <w:b/>
          </w:rPr>
        </w:style>
        <w:style w:styleId="h2" w:type="paragraph">
          <w:name w:val="Heading 2"/>
          <w:rPr>
            <w:sz w:val="28"/>
            <w:b/>
            <w:i/>
          </w:rPr>
        </w:style>
        <w:style w:styleId="emphasis" w:type="character">
          <w:name w:val="Italic"/>
          <w:rPr>
            <w:i/>
          </w:rPr>
        </w:style>
        <w:style w:styleId="strong" w:type="character">
          <w:name w:val="Bold"/>
          <w:rPr>
            <w:b/>
          </w:rPr>
        </w:style>
        <w:style w:styleId="emphasisAndStrong" w:type="character">
          <w:name w:val="Bold and Italic"/>
          <w:rPr>
            <w:b/>
            <w:i/>
          </w:rPr>
        </w:style>
      </w:styles>
      <w:body>
        <xsl:apply-templates select="/doc/*"/>
      </w:body>
    </w:wordDocument>
  </xsl:template>
```

```
<xsl:template match="h1">
  <w:p>
    <w:pPr>
      <w:pStyle w:val="h1"/>
    </w:pPr>
    <xsl:apply-templates/>
  </w:p>
</xsl:template>

<xsl:template match="h2">
  <w:p>
    <w:pPr>
      <w:pStyle w:val="h2"/>
    </w:pPr>
    <xsl:apply-templates/>
  </w:p>
</xsl:template>

<xsl:template match="para">
  <w:p>
    <xsl:apply-templates/>
  </w:p>
</xsl:template>

<xsl:template match="h1/text() | h2/text() | para/text()">
  <w:r>
    <w:t>
      <xsl:copy/>
    </w:t>
  </w:r>
</xsl:template>

<xsl:template match="emphasis/text()">
  <w:r>
    <w:rPr>
      <w:rStyle w:val="emphasis"/>
    </w:rPr>
    <w:t>
      <xsl:copy/>
    </w:t>
  </w:r>
</xsl:template>

<xsl:template match="strong/text()">
  <w:r>
    <w:rPr>
      <w:rStyle w:val="strong"/>
    </w:rPr>
    <w:t>
      <xsl:copy/>
    </w:t>
  </w:r>
</xsl:template>
```

```
<xsl:template match="emphasis/strong/text() | strong/emphasis/text( )"
              priority="1">
  <w:r>
    <w:rPr>
      <w:rStyle w:val="emphasisAndStrong"/>
    </w:rPr>
    <w:t>
      <xsl:copy/>
    </w:t>
  </w:r>
</xsl:template>

</xsl:stylesheet>
```

An explanation of the full details of this stylesheet is beyond the scope of this book, but in the context of this hack the important thing to know is that the w:rPr ("run properties") element now contains a *reference* to a style:

```
<xsl:template match="emphasis/text( )">
  <w:r>
    <w:rPr>
      <w:rStyle w:val="emphasis"/>
    </w:rPr>
    <w:t>
      <xsl:copy/>
    </w:t>
  </w:r>
</xsl:template>
```

In this case, the referenced style ID is "emphasis," which we declared earlier in the document:

```
<w:style w:styleId="emphasis" w:type="character">
  <w:name w:val="Italic"/>
  <w:rPr>
    <w:i/>
  </w:rPr>
</w:style>
```

The formatting effect is the same: text inside emphasis elements shows up as italic in the result. The difference is that now it is by way of a character style named *Italic*, rather than via direct formatting.

—Evan Lenz

HACK #95 Batch-Process Word Documents with XSLT

This hack shows you how to use XSLT to compile a report containing information from several different WordprocessingML documents.

Thanks to WordprocessingML and the powers of XSLT, it is now straight-forward to perform bulk processing on multiple Word documents. This particular hack is less about modifying the documents themselves (that's covered in "Standardize Documents with XSLT" [Hack #96]) than about generating a report that aggregates information from multiple Word documents. In this case, you want to extract and total all of the Word comments from a variable number of input documents. The resulting report format is just another Word document.

Say you have five Word documents in WordprocessingML format in a folder called *C:\Word Documents*. The files are named as follows:

- *word1.xml*
- *word2.xml*
- *word3.xml*
- *word4.xml*
- *word5.xml*

Each file contains multiple comments from multiple reviewers, and you'd like a list of all the comments from all the files (see Figure 10-10).

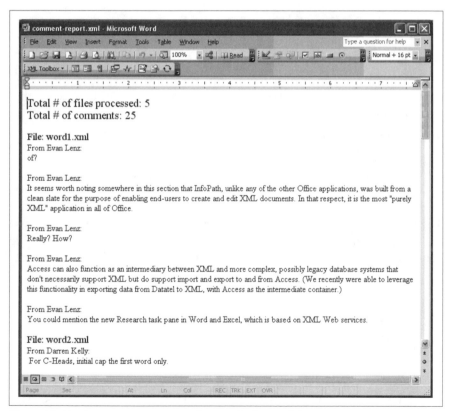

Figure 10-10. Aggregating comments from multiple Word documents via XSLT

To get started, enter the following code in a standard text editor such as Notepad, save it in the same folder as the files with the comments, and name it *file-list.xml*:

```
<input-files>
  <file>word1.xml</file>
  <file>word2.xml</file>
  <file>word3.xml</file>
  <file>word4.xml</file>
  <file>word5.xml</file>
</input-files>
```

To change the names of the files to be processed, just add to, modify, or delete the file elements.

The Code

To create the report, enter this code in a standard text editor such as Notepad, save it in the same folder as the other files, and name it *bulk-report.xsl*:

```
<xsl:stylesheet version="1.0"
  xmlns:xsl="http://www.w3.org/1999/XSL/Transform"
  xmlns:w="http://schemas.microsoft.com/office/word/2003/wordml"
  xmlns:aml="http://schemas.microsoft.com/aml/2001/core">

  <xsl:variable name="input-docs" select="document(/input-files/file)"/>

  <xsl:variable name="all-comments"
    select="$input-docs//aml:annotation[@w:type='Word.Comment']"/>

  <xsl:template match="/">
    <xsl:processing-instruction name="mso-application">
      <xsl:text>progid="Word.Document"</xsl:text>
    </xsl:processing-instruction>
    <w:wordDocument>
      <xsl:attribute name="xml:space">preserve</xsl:attribute>
      <w:body>
        <w:p>
          <w:r>
            <w:rPr>
              <w:sz w:val="32"/>
            </w:rPr>
            <w:t>Total # of files processed: </w:t>
            <w:t>
              <xsl:value-of select="count(input-files/file)"/>
            </w:t>
            <w:br/>
            <w:t>Total # of comments: </w:t>
            <w:t>
              <xsl:value-of select="count($all-comments)"/>
            </w:t>
```

```
          </w:r>
        </w:p>
        <w:p/>
        <xsl:for-each select="input-files/file">
          <w:p>
            <w:r>
              <w:rPr>
                <w:sz w:val="28"/>
              </w:rPr>
              <w:t>File: <xsl:value-of select="."/></w:t>
            </w:r>
          </w:p>
          <xsl:apply-templates select="document(.)//aml:annotation
                                  [@w:type='Word.Comment']"/>
        </xsl:for-each>
      </w:body>
    </w:wordDocument>
  </xsl:template>

  <xsl:template match="aml:annotation">
    <w:p>
      <w:r>
        <w:t>From <xsl:value-of select="@aml:author"/>:</w:t>
      </w:r>
    </w:p>
    <xsl:copy-of select="aml:content/*"/>
    <w:p/>
  </xsl:template>

</xsl:stylesheet>
```

First, you create a few lines that look like headers, containing the total number of files processed and the total number of comments found:

```
<w:t>Total # of files processed: </w:t>
<w:t>
  <xsl:value-of select="count(input-files/file)"/>
</w:t>
<w:br/>
<w:t>Total # of comments: </w:t>
<w:t>
  <xsl:value-of select="count($all-comments)"/>
</w:t>
```

Next, you iterate through each of the file elements in the source document, outputting a pseudoheading to group the results by filename:

```
<xsl:for-each select="input-files/file">
  <w:p>
    <w:r>
      <w:rPr>
        <w:sz w:val="28"/>
      </w:rPr>
      <w:t>File: <xsl:value-of select="."/></w:t>
```

```
      </w:r>
    </w:p>
    ...
</xsl:for-each>
```

 The w:sz (size) element and its w:val attribute measure font size in half points rather than full points—hence, <w:sz w:val="28"/> for a font size of 14 points.

With the help of XSLT's document function, you then grab all the aml: annotation elements of the type Word.Comment from each input document:

```
<xsl:apply-templates select="document(.)//aml:annotation
        [@w:type='Word.Comment']"/>
```

And for each comment, you display who authored the comment, followed by the text of the comment itself in a subsequent paragraph:

```
<xsl:template match="aml:annotation">
  <w:p>
    <w:r>
      <w:t>From <xsl:value-of select="@aml:author"/>:</w:t>
    </w:r>
  </w:p>
  xsl:copy-of select="aml:content/*"/>
  <w:p/>
</xsl:template>
```

Running the Hack

To run this hack, enter the following at a DOS command prompt within the same folder as the files:

```
> msxsl file-list.xml bulk-report.xsl -o comment-report.xml
```

If you double-click the newly created file, *comment-report.xml*, you'll see a document like the one shown in Figure 10-10

—Evan Lenz

HACK #96 Standardize Documents with XSLT

Before you print or distribute a document, you'll often want to put it into a consistent format without any extraneous items, such as comments left over from editing. This hack shows you how to use XSLT to scrub a document clean.

The previous examples showed you how to generate Word documents [Hack #94] and extract information from Word documents [Hack #95]. This hack shows you how to use XSLT to *modify* Word documents. Actually, in reality, XSLT never modifies anything; it only creates new documents. But if a new document varies only slightly from the original—and if you overwrite the original with the new one—then for all practical purposes, you've effectively modified the document, right? That is the approach taken here with XSLT.

The XSLT stylesheet in this hack strips out a number of different pieces of information: Author and Title document properties, custom document properties, comments, spelling and grammatical errors, deletions, formatting changes, and insertion marks. It even resets the document's view and zoom percentage (to Normal at 100%).

The Code

Enter the following code in a standard text editor such as Notepad and save it as *cleanup.xsl*:

```
<xsl:stylesheet version="1.0"
  xmlns:xsl="http://www.w3.org/1999/XSL/Transform"
  xmlns:w="http://schemas.microsoft.com/office/word/2003/wordml"
  xmlns:o="urn:schemas-microsoft-com:office:office"
  xmlns:aml="http://schemas.microsoft.com/aml/2001/core">

  <!-- By default, recursively copy everything through -->
  <xsl:template match="@*|node()">
    <xsl:copy>
      <xsl:apply-templates select="@*|node()"/>
    </xsl:copy>
  </xsl:template>

  <!-- Normalize document's view and zoom percentage (Normal at 100%) -->
  <xsl:template match="w:docPr">
    <xsl:copy>
      <w:view w:val="normal"/>
      <w:zoom w:percent="100"/>
      <xsl:apply-templates select="*[not(self::w:view or self::w:zoom)]"/>
    </xsl:copy>
  </xsl:template>

  <!-- Remove all but the Author and Title document properties -->
  <xsl:template match="o:DocumentProperties">
    <xsl:copy>
      <xsl:copy-of select="o:Author|o:Title"/>
    </xsl:copy>
  </xsl:template>

  <!-- Remove all custom document properties -->
  <xsl:template match="o:CustomDocumentProperties"/>
```

```
<!-- Remove all comments and comment references -->
<xsl:template match="aml:annotation[starts-with(@w:type,
    'Word.Comment')]"/>

<!-- Remove all spelling and grammatical errors -->
<xsl:template match="w:proofErr"/>

<!-- Remove all deletions -->
<xsl:template match="aml:annotation[@w:type='Word.Deletion']"/>

<!-- Remove all formatting changes -->
<xsl:template match="aml:annotation[@w:type='Word.Formatting']"/>

<!-- Remove all insertion marks -->
<xsl:template match="aml:annotation[@w:type='Word.Insertion']">
  <!-- Process content, but do not copy -->
  <xsl:apply-templates select="aml:content/*"/>
</xsl:template>

</xsl:stylesheet>
```

The stylesheet uses a process known as *identity transformation*. The very first template rule in the stylesheet is the most important one:

```
<xsl:template match="@*|node( )">
  <xsl:copy>
    <xsl:apply-templates select="@*|node( )"/>
  </xsl:copy>
</xsl:template>
```

It may seem cryptic, but it is powerful. An identity transformation recursively copies all nodes through to the output, unchanged. At least, that is the *default* behavior. If you didn't include any other template rules in the document, the resulting document would be identical to the source document. However, because they have higher *priority* (a technical term in XSLT), the other template rules override the default copying behavior for certain nodes in the source document. If such a template rule is empty, the node that triggers that template rule effectively gets stripped out from the result. (Technically, it is merely excluded from being copied to the result, but since everything else gets copied through, it has the appearance of being stripped.) For example, the following template rule matches an o:CustomDocumentProperties element:

```
<!-- Remove all custom document properties -->
<xsl:template match="o:CustomDocumentProperties"/>
```

Rather than copying the element to the result, this template rule *does nothing*, thereby effectively stripping the element from the document (if it was there in the first place).

Running the Hack

To run this hack, create a simple Word document that contains some comments and spelling or grammatical errors in Web Layout view (see Figure 10-11). Save the file as *dirty.xml* in the same folder as the *cleanup.xsl* file. Then type the following at a DOS command prompt in the same folder:

```
> msxsl dirty.xml cleanup.xsl -o clean.xml
```

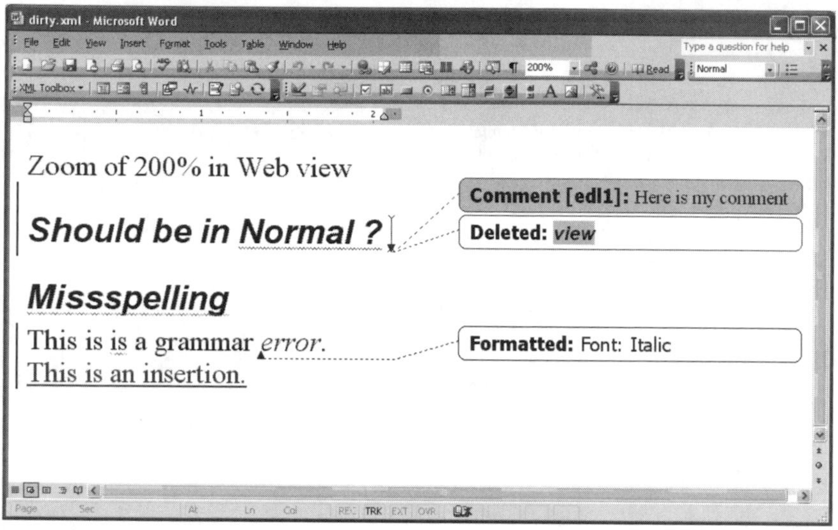

Figure 10-11. Document with lots of editing cruft (dirty.xml)

After you apply the stylesheet, you'll easily be able to see the changes in the new file, *clean.xml* (shown in Figure 10-12).

All of the tracked changes and comments have been removed, and the document view has been set to Normal view at 100% zoom. The file still contains a misspelled word, but it is no longer annotated as such. Likewise, the squiggly line for the grammar error has been stripped out.

Hacking the Hack

Using XSLT to modify Word documents is not just a hare-brained idea we thought up. If you have Office 2003 Professional or the standalone version of Word 2003, you can invoke this cleanup process right from within Word when you save your document.

Open *dirty.xml* in Word, select File → Save As, and choose XML Document from the "Save as type" drop-down menu. Next, check the "Apply transform" box, click the Transform button, and then select *cleanup.xsl* (see

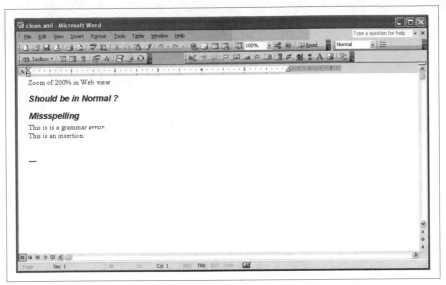

Figure 10-12. The same document with all the cruft removed (clean.xml)

Figure 10-13). Word applies the XSLT transformation, which always creates a new document, and then immediately overwrites the original file (*dirty.xml*, in this case) with the new document.

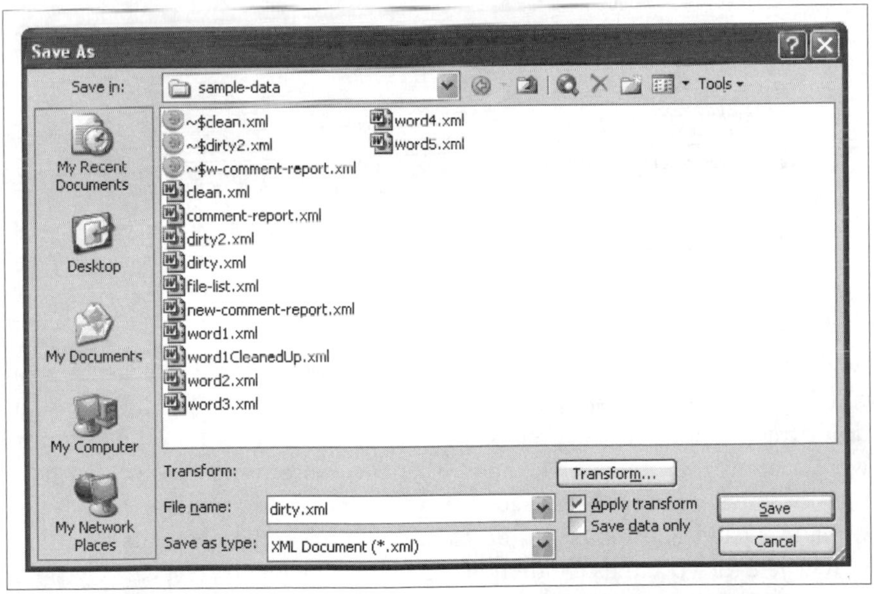

Figure 10-13. The "Apply transform" option for invoking an XSLT stylesheet on save

If you run a different edition of Word 2003, such as the version included with Office 2003 Basic, you won't see the extra checkbox options in the "Save As" dialog, as shown earlier.

—Evan Lenz

HACK #97   Remove Direct Formatting with XSLT
Strip out non-style-based formatting from Word documents.

A common "cleanup" task in Word is to remove any formatting from a document that hasn't been applied with a style. It's a bit of a chore within Word, but it turns out to be remarkably concise in XSLT.

The Code

Enter the following code in a standard text editor such as Notepad and save it as *removeDirectFormatting.xsl*:

```
<xsl:stylesheet version="1.0"
  xmlns:xsl="http://www.w3.org/1999/XSL/Transform"
  xmlns:w="http://schemas.microsoft.com/office/word/2003/wordml">

  <!-- By default, recursively copy everything through -->
  <xsl:template match="@*|node()">
    <xsl:copy>
      <xsl:apply-templates select="@*|node()"/>
    </xsl:copy>
  </xsl:template>

  <!-- Remove all direct paragraph formatting -->
  <xsl:template match="w:p/w:pPr/*[not(self::w:pStyle)]"/>

  <!-- Remove all direct run formatting -->
  <xsl:template match="w:r/w:rPr/*[not(self::w:rStyle)]"/>

</xsl:stylesheet>
```

As in "Standardize Documents with XSLT" [Hack #96], this hacks uses an XSLT *identity transformation*. The first template rule copies all nodes that don't trigger the other two template rules. The other two are both empty, which means that nodes that match them will effectively be stripped from the document. In this case, there are two particular contexts in which you want to exclude elements: inside the w:pPr and w:rPr elements—particularly where they occur as children of w:p and w:r elements, respectively.

Child elements of w:pPr and w:rPr set various formatting properties. There is one special child of each, however: the w:pStyle and w:rStyle elements are used not to apply direct formatting, but rather to associate the current paragraph or run with a paragraph or character style, respectively. Thus, these template rules are careful to avoid stripping out the w:pStyle and w:rStyle elements.

Running the Hack

To run this hack on a document named *formatted.xml* located in the same folder as the *removeDirectFormatting.xsl* stylesheet, type the following at a DOS command prompt in the same folder:

```
>msxsl formatted.xml removeDirectFormatting.xsl -o no-direct-formatting.xml
```

—Evan Lenz

Remove Linked "Char" Styles with XSLT
This hack shows you how to clean out the hidden, linked character styles Word likes to spontaneously create with a dose of XSLT.

"Clean Out Linked "Char" Styles" [Hack #55] showed how to use VBA to remove unwanted linked character styles from your Word documents. Word 2003 gives you another option: XSLT.

To see how this works, create a new document and deliberately create a linked style, as described in "Clean Out Linked "Char" Styles" [Hack #55]. Save the file as *linkedCharStyle.xml*.

The Code

Enter the following code in a standard text editor such as Notepad, save it as *removeLinkedCharStyles.xsl*, and then put it in the same folder as *linkedCharStyle.xml*:

```
<xsl:stylesheet version="1.0"
  xmlns:xsl="http://www.w3.org/1999/XSL/Transform"
  xmlns:w="http://schemas.microsoft.com/office/word/2003/wordml">

  <!-- By default, recursively copy everything through -->
  <xsl:template match="@*|node()">
    <xsl:copy>
      <xsl:apply-templates select="@*|node()"/>
    </xsl:copy>
  </xsl:template>

  <!-- Remove all linked character styles -->
  <xsl:template match="w:style[@w:type='character' and w:link]"/>

  <!-- Remove the w:link element from linked paragraph styles -->
  <xsl:template match="w:link"/>
```

```
<!-- Remove w:rStyle elements that refer to linked character styles -->
<xsl:template match="w:rStyle[@w:val = /w:wordDocument/w:styles/w:style
          [@w:type='character' and w:link]/@w:styleId]"/>
```

```
</xsl:stylesheet>
```

The first template rule is the *identity transformation*, discussed in "Remove Direct Formatting with XSLT" [Hack #97]. The rest of the template rules override the default copying behavior of the first template rule. The first of these rules strips out all linked character styles. A character-style definition is easily identified as a w:style element that has a w:type attribute whose value is character and that contains a w:link element:

```
<xsl:template match="w:style[@w:type='character' and w:link]"/>
```

In addition to stripping out all the linked character styles, you need to strip out otherwise dangling references to them. These occur in two places. First, you strip out the remaining w:link elements (inside linked paragraph-style definitions):

```
<xsl:template match="w:link"/>
```

Then, you strip out all the document's w:rStyle elements that refer to linked character styles:

```
<xsl:template match="w:rStyle[@w:val = /w:wordDocument/w:styles/w:style
          [@w:type='character' and w:link]/@w:styleId]"/>
```

This pattern is a little more complex, but it is pretty straightforward when you break it down into its respective parts. If you translated this pattern into English, it would read something like this:

> Match all w:rStyle elements whose w:val attribute is equal to the w:styleId attribute of any w:style element that has both a w:link element and a w:type attribute equal to character.

You could replace the last part of this translation (beginning with the word "any") with "any linked character style," thereby reducing the translation to:

> Match all w:rStyle elements whose w:val attribute is equal to the w:styleId attribute of any linked character style.

And since the w:styleId attribute is precisely what the w:rStyle element refers to in order to associate a run with a particular character style, you can further reduce the translation to our top-level intent: "Match all references to linked character styles." When a matching w:rStyle element triggers the rule, nothing happens, thereby excluding the linked character-style reference from the result.

Running the Hack

To run this hack, type the following at a DOS command prompt in the same folder as the files you created. Though shown as two lines, you should enter the following on a single line:

```
>msxsl linkedCharStyle.xml removeLinkedCharStyles.xsl
-o noLinkedCharStyle.xml
```

Figure 10-14 shows a Word document with a linked character style ("Heading 1 Char").

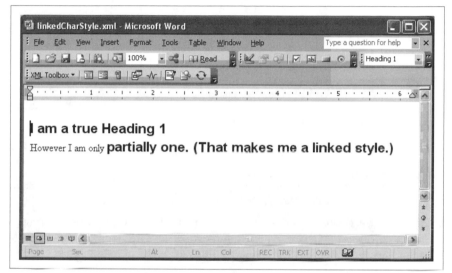

Figure 10-14. A document with a linked Char style

Figure 10-15 shows you what the document looks like after you apply the *removeLinkedCharStyles.xsl* stylesheet. It removes the Heading 1 Char style and associates the second paragraph of the document (including the heading) with the default paragraph font (i.e., no particular character style).

Hacking the Hack

The first example in this hack showed how to remove all linked character styles and style references. Now you'll supplement the stylesheet with a few more rules to delete the zombie "Char" styles that used to be linked styles.

This modification will also remove any character styles (and corresponding usages) whose names contain the string " Char" (including the leading space), much like the VBA shown in "Clean Out Linked "Char" Styles" [Hack #55]. Just a couple of extra template rules are necessary:

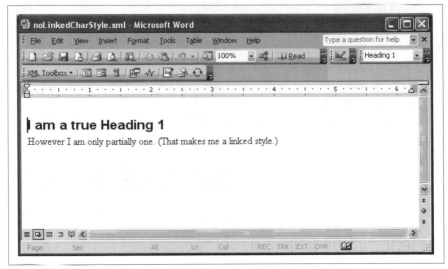

Figure 10-15. The same document, sans linked Char style

```
<xsl:template match="w:style[contains(w:name,' Char')]"/>

<xsl:template match="w:rStyle[@w:styleId =
    /w:wordDocument/w:styles/w:style[
    contains(w:name,' Char')]/@w:styleId"/>
```

Again, we effectively strip out the styles and their corresponding references by doing nothing when these template rules are invoked. This example removes any style that has the string " Char" in the style name.

—Evan Lenz

HACK #99   Use Google from Your Macros

This hack shows you how to access Google from your Word macros.

With a bit of hacking, you can use the ubiquitous Google search engine without ever leaving Word. This hack shows you a simple macro that lets you input a new search query, then displays the first 10 sites that Google says match your query.

Setting Up the Google Web Service

While Google's web site is a model of simplicity, it takes a bit of work to get to Google from your Word macros. Here are the steps you'll need to take.

1. First, install the free Microsoft Office 2003 Web Services Toolkit 2.01. Search for it on the Microsoft web site (*http://www.microsoft.com/downloads/*) or Google it.

2. Next, create a new template to hold your Google-related macros. The Web Services Toolkit will create some code so you can work with Google. A separate template will help you keep track of the code. Create a new, blank document and save it as a document template named *GoogleTools.dot*.

3. From your new *GoogleTools.dot* template, select Tools → Macro → Visual Basic Editor. The Web Services Toolkit will have added a new item called Web Service References on the Tools menu, as shown in Figure 10-16.

Figure 10-16. Creating a new reference for accessing Google

4. Select Tools → Web Service References to display the dialog shown in Figure 10-17. Enter "google" in the Keywords field and click the Search button. When the web service is found, check the box next to it and click the Add button.

When you click the Add button, you'll notice a flurry of activity on your screen as the Web Services Toolkit installs several new class modules into your template project, as shown in Figure 10-18.

> The Web Services Toolkit creates the code, but it actually comes from Google using WSDL (Web Services Description Language). The Toolkit interprets this information and generates the VBA code needed to access the web service (in this case, Google).

Getting a Google API Key

To access Google's Application Programming Interface (API) from within your macros (or from any program or script), you first need a *developer's*

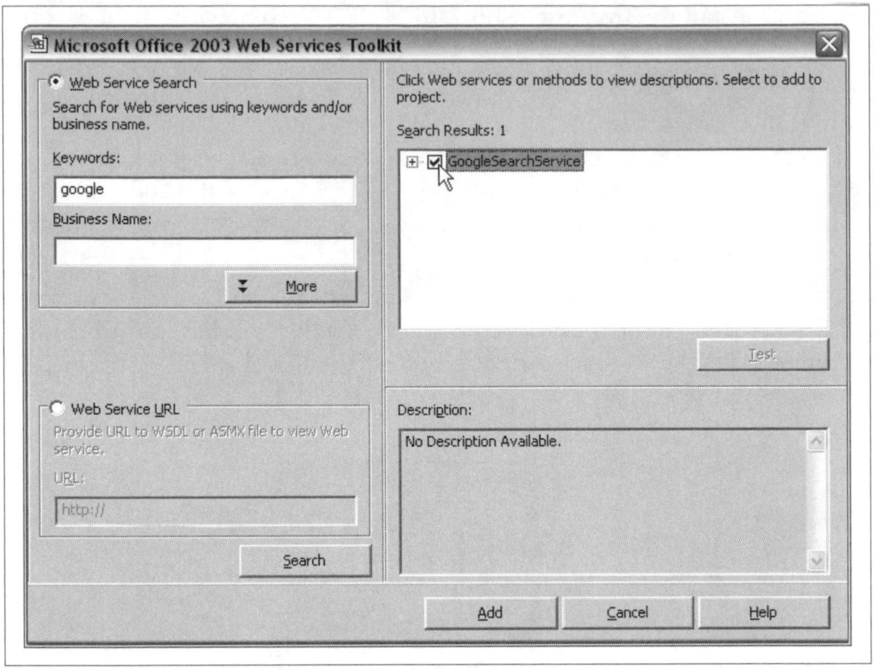

Figure 10-17. Locating the Google search web service

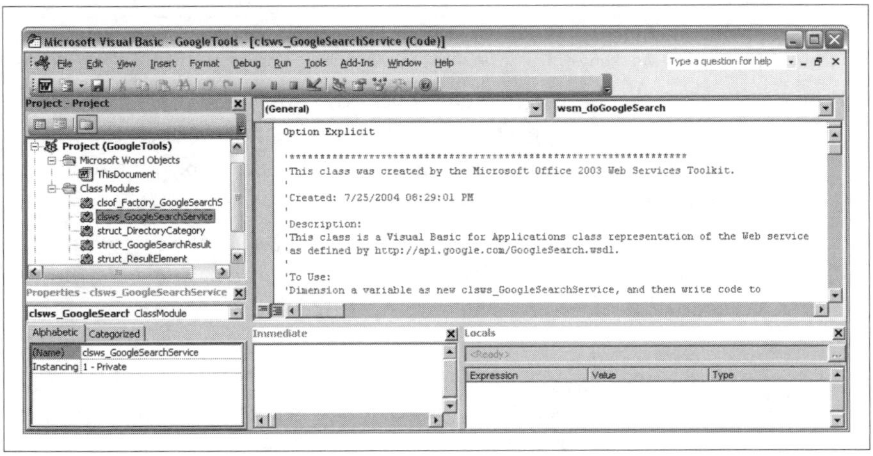

Figure 10-18. The code created by the Web Services Toolkit

key—a unique string assigned by Google to identify you when you make queries from within a program. You can get more information, along with a free developer's key, from *http://www.google.com/apis/*.

For full-on coverage of the Google API, check out *Google Hacks* (O'Reilly).

Once you've signed up for a developer's account, Google emails you a lengthy string of characters like the following:

```
12BuCK13mY5hOE/34KNOcK@ttH3DoOR
```

In the macro code shown in this hack, replace *your_key_here* with the actual key you got from Google.

The Code

With your *GoogleTools.dot* template open, go to the Visual Basic Editor, choose GoogleTools in the Project Explorer, and then select Insert → Module to create a new code module.

Insert the following code in the new module:

```
Sub SimpleGoogleSearch( )
Dim vSearchResults As Variant
Dim v As Variant
Dim sResults As String
Dim sGoogleAPIKey As String
Dim sSearchQuery As String
Dim lStart As Long
Dim lMaxResults As Long
Dim bFilter As Boolean
Dim sRestrict As String
Dim bSafeSearch As Boolean
Dim sLanguageRestrict As String
Dim sInputEncoding As String
Dim sOutputEncoding As String
Dim google_search As New clsws_GoogleSearchService

sGoogleAPIKey = "your_key_here"
lStart = 1
lMaxResults = 10
bFilter = True
sRestrict = ""
bSafeSearch = False
sLanguageRestrict = ""
sInputEncoding = "UTF-8"
sOutputEncoding = "UTF-8"

sSearchQuery = InputBox("Enter a Google query")
If Len(sSearchQuery) = 0 Then Exit Sub

vSearchResults = google_search.wsm_doGoogleSearch( _
        str_key:=sGoogleAPIKey, _
```

```
            str_q:=sSearchQuery, _
            lng_start:=lStart, _
            lng_maxResults:=lMaxResults, _
            bln_filter:=bFilter, _
            str_restrict:=sRestrict, _
            bln_safeSearch:=bSafeSearch, _
            str_lr:=sLanguageRestrict, _
            str_ie:=sInputEncoding, _
            str_oe:=sOutputEncoding).resultElements

    On Error Resume Next
    For Each v In vSearchResults
        sResults = sResults & v.URL & vbCr
    Next v
    If Len(sResults) <> 0 Then
        MsgBox "Found the following sites: " & vbCr & sResults
    Else
        MsgBox "Sorry, no results found"
    End If

    End Sub
```

Note the line:

```
Dim google_search As New clsws_GoogleSearchService
```

This line creates a new instance of one of the classes that the Web Services Toolkit installed in your template.

The call to the google_search object is a bit complex. Ten parameters are required for a Google API call. The following list, adapted from *Google Hacks*, describes the parameters:

str_key *(key)*
    This is where you put your Google API developer's key. Without a key, the query won't get very far.

str_q *(query)*
    This is your query, composed of keywords, phrases, and special syntaxes.

lng_start *(start)*
    Also known as the offset, this value specifies at what result to start counting when determining which 10 results to return. If this number were 16, the Google API would return results 16–25; if 300, it would return results 300–309 (assuming, of course, that your query found that many results). This is what's known as a "zero-based index"; counting starts at 0, not 1. The first result is result 0, and the 999th is 998. It's a little odd, admittedly, but you get used to it quickly—especially if you go on to do much programming. Acceptable values are 0 to 999 because Google returns only up to a thousand results for a query.

lng_maxResults *(maximum results)*

This integer specifies the number of results you'd like the API to return. The API returns results in batches of up to 10, so acceptable values are 1 through 10.

bln_filter *(filter)*

You might think this parameter concerns the SafeSearch filter for adult content. It doesn't. This Boolean value specifies whether your results go through automatic query filtering, removing near-duplicate content (i.e., where titles and snippets are very similar) and multiple (more than two) results from the same host or site. With filtering enabled, only the first two results from each host are included in the result set.

str_restrict *(restrict)*

No, this one doesn't have anything to do with SafeSearch either. It allows for restricting your search to one of Google's topical searches or to a specific country. Google has four topic restricts: U.S. Government (unclesam), Linux (linux), Macintosh (mac), and FreeBSD (bsd). You'll find the complete country list in the Google Web API documentation. To leave your search unrestricted, leave this option blank (usually signified by empty quotation marks, "").

bln_safeSearch *(safe search)*

Here's the SafeSearch filtering option. This Boolean specifies whether results returned will be filtered for questionable (read: adult) content.

str_lr *(language restrict)*

This one's a bit tricky. Google has a list of languages in its API documentation to which you can restrict search results, or you can simply leave this option blank and have no language restrictions.

There are several ways you can restrict to a language. First, you can simply include a language code. If you wanted to restrict results to English, for example, you'd use lang_en. But you can also restrict results to more than one language, separating each language code with a | (pipe), signifying OR. lang_en|lang_de, for example, constrains results to only those in English or German.

You can omit languages from results by prepending them with a minus sign (-). The phrase -lang_en returns all results but those in English.

str_ie *(input encoding)*

This stands for "input encoding," allowing you to specify the character encoding used in the query you're feeding the API. Google's documentation says, "Clients should encode all request data in UTF-8 and should expect results to be in UTF-8." In the first iteration of Google's API program, the Google API documentation offered a table of encoding options (latin1, cyrillic, etc.), but now everything is UTF-8. In fact, requests for anything other than UTF-8 are summarily ignored.

str_oe *(output encoding)*
This stands for "output encoding." As with input encoding, everything's UTF-8.

Running the Hack

To run the hack, close the Visual Basic Editor and return to Word. Select Tools → Macro → Macros, choose SimpleGoogleSearch, and click the Run button. You'll be prompted with the dialog box shown in Figure 10-19

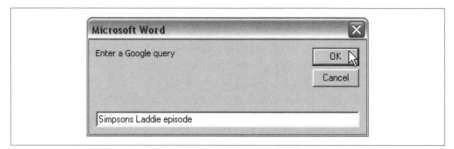

Figure 10-19. Doing a simple Google search from a macro

When you click the OK button, a new dialog appears, reporting the URLs Google found to match your query (Figure 10-20).

```
Microsoft Word                                        ⊠

  Found the following sites:
  http://www.tvtome.com/Simpsons/season8.html
  http://www.eeggs.com/items/5881.html
  http://www.able2know.com/forums/about11857-150.html
  http://www.doheth.co.uk/episodeguide.shtml
  http://www.snpp.com/episodes/4F16.html
  http://www.thesimpsons.com/episode_guide/0820.htm
  http://fox61.trb.com/entertainment/syn/stv-thesimpsons-syn-pkgseason8.special
  http://www.simpsoncrazy.com/episodeguide/season8.shtml
  http://www.erowid.org/psychoactives/humor/humor_simpsons1.shtml
  http://www.bbc.co.uk/cult/simpsons/episodeguide/season8/page20.shtml

                          [    OK    ]
```

Figure 10-20. The sites found by Google displayed in Word

This simple example will help you learn the Google API from Visual Basic and get you ready for your own hacking projects. For a more elaborate example, see "Google Without Leaving Word" [Hack #100].

Google Without Leaving Word

This hack shows you how to search Google from within Word and display the
results on the Task Pane.

You probably use Google a few dozen times a day. If you work in Word, this
means switching over to your web browser, checking the results, and then
going back to Word. Once you get Google working from a macro [Hack #99],
this hack will show how to display the search results in the New Document
Task Pane [Hack #9].

This hack uses a configuration file [Hack #67] to store data and some code that
uses VBScript regular expressions [Hack #82]. Before you dive in, check out
those hacks.

The Code

Open the *GoogleTools.dot* template you created when you installed the Web
Services Toolkit, as discussed in "Use Google from Your Macros" [Hack #99].
Select Tools → Macro → Macros and insert the following code, which consists of a procedure named GoogleToTaskPane and a supporting function
named StripHTML.

```
Sub GoogleToTaskPane( )
Dim vSearchResults As Variant
Dim v As Variant
Dim sResults As String
Dim sEntryName As String
Dim sEntryURL As String
Dim sLogFile As String
Dim sSearchDisplayTitle As String
Dim sSearchURL As String
Dim i As Integer

' Google API variables
Dim sGoogleAPIKey As String
Dim sSearchQuery As String
Dim lStart As Long
Dim lMaxResults As Long
Dim bFilter As Boolean
Dim sRestrict As String
Dim bSafeSearch As Boolean
Dim sLanguageRestrict As String
Dim sInputEncoding As String
Dim sOutputEncoding As String
Dim google_search As New clsws_GoogleSearchService

' Initialize variables
sLogFile = "C:\google_taskpane.ini"
sGoogleAPIKey = "your_key_here"
```

```
lStart = 1
lMaxResults = 10
bFilter = True
sRestrict = ""
bSafeSearch = False
sLanguageRestrict = ""
sInputEncoding = "UTF-8"
sOutputEncoding = "UTF-8"

' Hide the Task Pane
Application.CommandBars("Task Pane").Visible = False

' Remove existing items from New Document Task Pane
For i = 0 To 9
    sEntryURL = System.PrivateProfileString( _
            FileName:=sLogFile, _
            Section:="GoogleTaskPane", _
            Key:="URLName" & CStr(i))
    sEntryName = System.PrivateProfileString( _
            FileName:=sLogFile, _
            Section:="GoogleTaskPane", _
            Key:="EntryName" & CStr(i))
    If Len(sEntryURL) > 0 Then
        Application.NewDocument.Remove _
            FileName:=sEntryURL, _
            Section:=msoBottomSection, _
            DisplayName:=sEntryName, _
            Action:=msoOpenFile
    End If
Next i

' Get new search query
sSearchQuery = InputBox("Enter a Google query:")
If Len(sSearchQuery) = 0 Then Exit Sub

' Get search results
vSearchResults = google_search.wsm_doGoogleSearch( _
        str_key:=sGoogleAPIKey, _
        str_q:=sSearchQuery, _
        lng_start:=lStart, _
        lng_maxResults:=lMaxResults, _
        bln_filter:=bFilter, _
        str_restrict:=sRestrict, _
        bln_safeSearch:=bSafeSearch, _
        str_lr:=sLanguageRestrict, _
        str_ie:=sInputEncoding, _
        str_oe:=sOutputEncoding).resultElements

' Check for no results
On Error Resume Next
v = UBound(vSearchResults)
If Err.Number = 9 Then
    MsgBox "No results found"
```

```
      Exit Sub
ElseIf Err.Number <> 0 Then
    MsgBox "An error has occurred: " & _
        Err.Number & vbCr & _
        Err.Description
    Exit Sub
End If

' Add each result to the Task Pane
' and to the log file
i = 0
For Each v In vSearchResults
    sSearchURL = v.URL
    sSearchDisplayTitle = StripHTML(v.title)
    Application.NewDocument.Add _
        FileName:=sSearchURL, _
        Section:=msoBottomSection, _
        DisplayName:=sSearchDisplayTitle, _
        Action:=msoOpenFile

    System.PrivateProfileString( _
        FileName:=sLogFile, _
        Section:="GoogleTaskPane", _
        Key:="URLName" & CStr(i)) = sSearchURL
    System.PrivateProfileString( _
        FileName:=sLogFile, _
        Section:="GoogleTaskPane", _
        Key:="EntryName" & CStr(i)) = sSearchDisplayTitle
    i = i + 1
Next v

' Show the New Document Task Pane
CommandBars("Menu Bar").Controls("File").Controls("New...").Execute

End Sub

Function StripHTML(str As String) As String
Dim re As Object
Dim k As Long
On Error Resume Next
Set re = GetObject(Class:="VBScript.RegExp")
If Err.Number = 429 Then
    Set re = CreateObject(Class:="VBScript.RegExp")
    Err.Clear
ElseIf Err.Number <> 0 Then
    MsgBox Err.Number & vbCr & Err.Description
End If

' Check for common character entities by ASCII value
For k = 33 To 255
    re.Pattern = "&#" & k & ";"
    str = re.Replace(str, Chr$(k))
Next k
```

```
' Remove common HTML tags
re.Pattern = "<[^>]+?>|&[^;]+?;"
re.Global = True
str = re.Replace(str, vbNullString)
StripHTML = str
End Function
```

> Make sure you replace the value *your_key_here* with your Google developer's key.

This hack uses two parts of the Google search results: the URLs and titles. Google formats the search result title as HTML, but you can put only plain text in the Task Pane. The StripHTML function uses a few simple VBScript regular expressions to strip out common HTML tags (such as <b>) and replace character entities (such as @) with their ASCII character equivalents ("Use Character Codes to Find or Insert Special Characters" **[Hack #30]**).

> The StripHTML function uses *late binding*, as discussed in "Automate Word from Other Applications" **[Hack #84]**.

It can be tricky to remove files from the Task Pane using VBA unless you know their exact names, as discussed in "Tweak the New Document Task Pane" **[Hack #9]**. This macro, however, stores the search results in a *.ini* file. Thus, the next time you do a search, you can easily remove the previous results. The macro uses a file named *C:\google_taskpane.ini*, which is defined in the GoogleToTaskPane procedure.

Running the Hack

After you insert the code, switch back to Word. Next, select Tools → Macro → Macros, choose GoogleToTaskPane, and click the Run button to display the dialog shown in Figure 10-21.

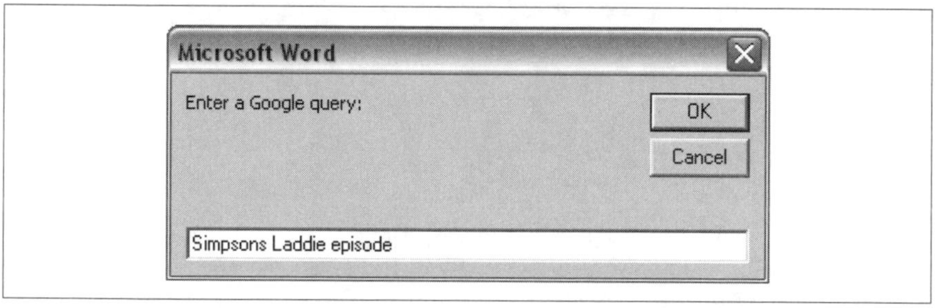

![Microsoft Word dialog box with "Enter a Google query:" label, OK and Cancel buttons, and a text field containing "Simpsons Laddie episode"]

Figure 10-21. Entering a Google search that will display in the Task Pane

Enter your search terms and click the OK button. The New Document Task
Pane will appear and display the search results, as shown in Figure 10-22.
Hover your mouse over any of the entries to display the URL. Click a URL
to open the site in your web browser.

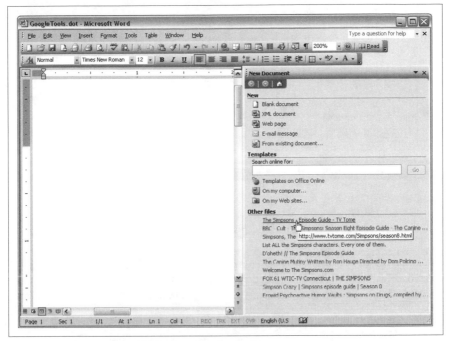

Figure 10-22. Google results displayed in the Task Pane

Every time you run a search, the macro removes the previous results from
the Task Pane. If you want to remove the previous results without displaying new ones, click the Cancel button in the dialog box shown in
Figure 10-21.

To make sure this handy macro loads automatically when Word starts [Hack
#50], put *GoogleTools.dot* into your *STARTUP* folder.

Hacking the Hack

To take this hack one step further, you can modify it to use the currently
selected text as the search text, rather than displaying an input box for you
to enter text in.

The following macro, named `GoogleSelectionToTaskPane`, does a Google
search of the currently selected text and displays the results in the Task
Pane. The modified code is shown in bold.

```
Sub GoogleSelectionToTaskPane( )
Dim vSearchResults As Variant
Dim v As Variant
Dim sResults As String
Dim sEntryName As String
Dim sEntryURL As String
Dim sLogFile As String
Dim sSearchDisplayTitle As String
Dim sSearchURL As String
Dim i As Integer

' Google API variables
Dim sGoogleAPIKey As String
Dim sSearchQuery As String
Dim lStart As Long
Dim lMaxResults As Long
Dim bFilter As Boolean
Dim sRestrict As String
Dim bSafeSearch As Boolean
Dim sLanguageRestrict As String
Dim sInputEncoding As String
Dim sOutputEncoding As String
Dim google_search As New clsws_GoogleSearchService

' Initialize variables
sLogFile = "C:\google_taskpane.ini"
sGoogleAPIKey = your_key_here
lStart = 1
lMaxResults = 10
bFilter = True
sRestrict = ""
bSafeSearch = False
sLanguageRestrict = ""
sInputEncoding = "UTF-8"
sOutputEncoding = "UTF-8"

' Hide the Task Pane
Application.CommandBars("Task Pane").Visible = False

' Remove existing items from New Document Task Pane
For i = 0 To 9
    sEntryURL = System.PrivateProfileString( _
            FileName:=sLogFile, _
            Section:="GoogleTaskPane", _
            Key:="URLName" & CStr(i))
    sEntryName = System.PrivateProfileString( _
            FileName:=sLogFile, _
            Section:="GoogleTaskPane", _
            Key:="EntryName" & CStr(i))
    If Len(sEntryURL) > 0 Then
        Application.NewDocument.Remove _
            FileName:=sEntryURL, _
            Section:=msoBottomSection, _
```

```
                DisplayName:=sEntryName, _
                Action:=msoOpenFile
        End If
Next i

' Move ends of selection to exclude spaces
' and paragraph marks
Selection.MoveStartWhile cset:=Chr (32) & Chr (19), _
    Count:=Selection.Characters.Count
Selection.MoveEndWhile cset:=Chr (32) & Chr (19), _
    Count:=-Selection.Characters.Count

' Get selection text for search
sSearchQuery = Selection.Text
If Len(sSearchQuery) = 0 Then Exit Sub

' Get search results
vSearchResults = google_search.wsm_doGoogleSearch( _
        str_key:=sGoogleAPIKey, _
        str_q:=sSearchQuery, _
        lng_start:=lStart, _
        lng_maxResults:=lMaxResults, _
        bln_filter:=bFilter, _
        str_restrict:=sRestrict, _
        bln_safeSearch:=bSafeSearch, _
        str_lr:=sLanguageRestrict, _
        str_ie:=sInputEncoding, _
        str_oe:=sOutputEncoding).resultElements

' Check for no results
On Error Resume Next
v = UBound(vSearchResults)
If Err.Number = 9 Then
    MsgBox "No results found"
    Exit Sub
ElseIf Err.Number <> 0 Then
    MsgBox "An error has occurred: " & _
        Err.Number & vbCr & _
        Err.Description
    Exit Sub
End If

' Add each result to the Task Pane
' and to the log file
i = 0
For Each v In vSearchResults
    sSearchURL = v.URL
    sSearchDisplayTitle = StripHTML(v.title)
    Application.NewDocument.Add _
        FileName:=sSearchURL, _
        Section:=msoBottomSection, _
        DisplayName:=sSearchDisplayTitle, _
        Action:=msoOpenFile
```

```
        System.PrivateProfileString( _
            FileName:=sLogFile, _
            Section:="GoogleTaskPane", _
            Key:="URLName" & CStr(i)) = sSearchURL
        System.PrivateProfileString( _
            FileName:=sLogFile, _
            Section:="GoogleTaskPane", _
            Key:="EntryName" & CStr(i)) = _
                sSearchDisplayTitle
        i = i + 1
    Next v

    ' Show the New Document Task Pane
    CommandBars("Menu Bar").Controls("File").Controls("New...").Execute

    End Sub
```

To help ensure a good Google search, the following two lines collapse two ends of the selection if they contain spaces or a paragraph mark:

```
    Selection.MoveStartWhile cset:=Chr (32) & Chr (19), _
        Count:=Selection.Characters.Count
    Selection.MoveEndWhile cset:=Chr (32) & Chr (19), _
        Count:=-Selection.Characters.Count
```

Add the GoogleSelectionToTaskPane macro to your Text shortcut menu [Hack #3], and Google results will be just a right-click away.

Index

A

Adaptive Menus, turn off, 2
add-ins, disabling, 175
age calculation, DATE field, 245
aliases
    styles, 69
    VBA, 71
AND logical operator, 249
angle operations, 255
animation, Office Assistant, 48
application events, VBA code and, 235
arguments, named arguments
    Perl, 302
    Python and, 298
    Ruby, 307
arithmetic operators in formula
    fields, 246
ASCII codes, 107, 108
    searches and, 109
author information, Track
    Changes, 133
AutoCorrect, placeholder text
    creation, 60
AutoMacros, 207
    disabling, 208
automation
    captions, 84
    COM automation, 289–294
    early binding and, 292
    late binding and, 292
    scripting languages and, 293
AUTOTEXTLIST field, 259

B

backreferencing, RegExp object
    and, 284
backups, Word as Windows utility, 278
bar graph creation, 72
BASIC, VBA and, 9
batch processes, 204
    XSLT and, 335
bookmarks
    cross-references and, 150, 264
    deleting all, 125
borders, imported images, 78–81
bounded random numbers, 234
built-in styles, renaming, 185
bullets and numbering, 137–145
    buttons, 138
        mapping styles to, 139
    paragraph styles, 138
buttons
    bullets and numbering, 138
        mapping styles to, 139
    images
        browsing all, 40
        custom, 44
    toolbar replacement, 3

C

Calculate command, 98
    macro, 101
    operators, 100
    reverse precedence order, 101

We'd like to hear your suggestions for improving our indexes. Send email to *index@oreilly.com*.

fonts
    constant-width, 67
    displaying
        Font menu, 61
        in names, 2
    recently used, 62
    system fonts, samples, 61
footnotes, tables, 75
    separators, 76
for each loops, 228
formatting
    context-sensitive, 128
    numeric field results, 252
    removing, XSLT and, 344
formatting restrictions, avoiding, 183
forms
    calendar, 256
    fill-in, fake, 240
formula fields, 246
    arithmetic operators, 246
    comparison operators, 247
    functions, 247
    logical functions, 248
functions, formula fields, 247

G

generating random numbers, 233
Ghostscript utility
    downloading, 86
    PDF creation, 85
GhostWord interface, 87
global templates, 168
    creating, 169
    disabling, 175
    macros, 169
globbing, 205
GNU Lesser Public License, VBacs
    and, 275
Google
    access from macros, 348
    from within Word, 355–362
    setup, 348
Google API, developer's key, 349
GoogleTools.dot template, 351
GoogleTools.dot template, Google
    access from within Word, 355
graphs, bar graphs, 72
GSview, downloading, 86

H

hackers, definition, xv
hacks, definition, xv
headers, repeating, 77
headings
    captions, styles, 82
    partial in TOC, 91
    styles, cross-references and, 145
Hello World program, 10
hexadecimal values, Unicode
    characters, 108
hiding/showing
    macros, Macros dialog, 203
    nonprinting characters, 6
HTML
    file import, Python and, 297
    printouts
        Perl and, 300
        Ruby and, 303
Hyperlink style, removing links
    and, 104
hyperlinks, unlinking, 102–106

I

identity transformation, XSLT and, 341,
    346
IIf function, VBA, 220
images
    borders, imported images, 78–81
    buttons
        browsing all, 40
        custom, 44
Immediate window, Visual Basic
    Editor, 16
importing images, borders on, 78–81
INCLUDETEXT fields, cross-references
    and, 267
incremental progress bar, macros, 224
.ini files, 232
input
    dialogs, 216
    users, macros, 200
integer division, VBA code and, 218
IntelliSense, Visual Basic Editor, 16
interactive calendars in forms, 256
interactive execution of commands,
    dialogs and, 214
intercept commands, 208

Visual Basic Explorer, Project
       Explorer, 12
vocabulary, XML, 319

W

watermark text, 87
    fields, 89
wildcards (see also regular
       expressions), 280
Woody's Watch web site, xviii
Word
    as backup, 278
    Excel macros and, 290
Word object model (see object model)
Word versions, xvii
Word.Application object, 289
WordBackup.dot file, 279
WordprocessingML, 320
    convert XML documents to
       Word, 328
    documents, 320
       batch processing and, 335
    Internet Explorer and, 326
Workgroup templates, 166

X

XML
    command-line tools, 320
    document conversion to Word, 328
    document types, 319
    libxml project, command-line
       utilities, 320
    PIs (processing instructions), 323
    vocabulary, 319
    Word document creation, in
       Notepad, 321
XML Toolbox, 323
XSLT
    batch processes and, 335
    document standardization and, 339
    formatting, removing, 344
    stylesheets
       identity transformation and, 341
       template rule and, 329
XSLT processor, 320

Y

year, DATE field, 242

Colophon

Our look is the result of reader comments, our own experimentation, and feedback from distribution channels. Distinctive covers complement our distinctive approach to technical topics, breathing personality and life into potentially dry subjects.

The tool on the cover of *Word Hacks* is a handheld mixer. The first patent for an electric mixer was issued in 1885. Many of the early mixers appeared very industrial, looking more suited for mixing paint than pound cake. By the 1930s, more modern glass-bottomed mixers were produced with a motor built into the lid. By World War II, mixers were mounted on a stand with a bowl underneath. Eventually mixers became smaller and contained entirely in a small plastic case with a handle: the modern handheld mixer. Today's consumer can choose from an assortment of manufacturers' handheld or the the more heavy-duty stand mixers.

Mary Anne Weeks Mayo was the production editor, Rachel Wheeler was the copyeditor, and Matt Hutchinson was the proofreader for *Word Hacks*. Sarah Sherman and Colleen Gorman provided quality control. Mary Agner provided production assistance. Johnna Dinse wrote the index.

Hanna Dyer designed the cover of this book, based on a series design by Edie Freedman. The cover image is an original photograph by Hanna Dyer. Clay Fernald produced the cover layout with QuarkXPress 4.1 using Adobe's Helvetica Neue and ITC Garamond fonts.

David Futato designed the interior layout. This book was converted Julie Hawks to FrameMaker 5.5.6 with a format conversion tool created by Erik Ray, Jason McIntosh, Neil Walls, and Mike Sierra that uses Perl and XML technologies. The text font is Linotype Birka; the heading font is Adobe Helvetica Neue Condensed; and the code font is LucasFont's TheSans Mono Condensed. The illustrations that appear in the book were produced by Robert Romano and Jessamyn Read using Macromedia FreeHand MX and Adobe Photoshop CS. This colophon was written by Mary Anne Weeks Mayo.

Better than e-books

Search
inside electronic versions of thousands of books

Browse
books by category. With Safari researching any topic is a snap

Find
answers in an instant

Read books from cover to cover. Or, simply click to the page you need.

Search Safari! The premier electronic reference library for programmers and IT professionals

Related Titles Available from O'Reilly

Hacks

Amazon Hacks

BSD Hacks

Digital Photography Hacks

eBay Hacks

Excel hacks

Flash Hacks

Gaming Hacks

Google Hacks

Harware Hacking Projects for Geeks

Home Theater Hacks

iPod & iTunes Hacks

Knoppix Hacks

Linux Desktop Hacks

Linux Server Hacks

Mac OS X Hacks

Mac OS X Panther Hacks

Network Security Hacks

PayPal Hacks

PDF Hacks

PC Hacks

Smart Home Hacks

Spidering Hacks

TiVo Hacks

Windows Server Hacks

Windows XP Hacks

Wireless Hacks

Word Hacks

Keep in touch with O'Reilly

1. Download examples from our books

To find example files for a book, go to:

www.oreilly.com/catalog

select the book, and follow the "Examples" link.

2. Register your O'Reilly books

Register your book at *register.oreilly.com*

Why register your books? Once you've registered your O'Reilly books you can:

- Win O'Reilly books, T-shirts or discount coupons in our monthly drawing.
- Get special offers available only to registered O'Reilly customers.
- Get catalogs announcing new books (US and UK only).
- Get email notification of new editions of the O'Reilly books you own.

3. Join our email lists

Sign up to get topic-specific email announcements of new books and conferences, special offers, and O'Reilly Network technology newsletters at:

elists.oreilly.com

It's easy to customize your free elists subscription so you'll get exactly the O'Reilly news you want.

4. Get the latest news, tips, and tools

http://www.oreilly.com

- "Top 100 Sites on the Web"—PC Magazine
- CIO Magazine's Web Business 50 Awards

Our web site contains a library of comprehensive product information (including book excerpts and tables of contents), downloadable software, background articles, interviews with technology leaders, links to relevant sites, book cover art, and more.

5. Work for O'Reilly

Check out our web site for current employment opportunities:

jobs.oreilly.com

6. Contact us

O'Reilly & Associates
1005 Gravenstein Hwy North
Sebastopol, CA 95472 USA

TEL: 707-827-7000 or 800-998-9938
         (6am to 5pm PST)

FAX: 707-829-0104

order@oreilly.com
For answers to problems regarding your order or our products.
To place a book order online, visit:

www.oreilly.com/order_new

catalog@oreilly.com
To request a copy of our latest catalog.

booktech@oreilly.com
For book content technical questions or corrections.

corporate@oreilly.com
For educational, library, government, and corporate sales.

proposals@oreilly.com
To submit new book proposals to our editors and product managers.

international@oreilly.com
For information about our international distributors or translation queries. For a list of our distributors outside of North America check out:

international.oreilly.com/distributors.html

adoption@oreilly.com
For information about academic use of O'Reilly books, visit:

academic.oreilly.com

O'REILLY®

Our books are available at most retail and online bookstores.
To order direct: 1-800-998-9938 • *order@oreilly.com* • *www.oreilly.com*
Online editions of most O'Reilly titles are available by subscription at *safari.oreilly.com*